The Cultural Politics of Food and Eating

Blackwell Readers in Anthropology

As anthropology moves beyond the limits of so-called area studies, there is an increasing need for texts that do the work of synthesizing the literature while challenging more traditional or subdisciplinary approaches to anthropology. This is the object of this exciting new series, *Blackwell Readers in Anthropology.*

Each volume in the series offers seminal readings on a chosen theme and provides the finest, most thought-provoking recent works in the given thematic area. Many of these volumes bring together for the first time a body of literature on a certain topic. The series thus both presents definitive collections and investigates the very ways in which anthropological inquiry has evolved and is evolving.

The Cultural Politics of Food and Eating

A Reader

Edited by

James L. Watson and
Melissa L. Caldwell

Blackwell
Publishing

Editorial material and organization © 2005 by Blackwell Publishing Ltd

BLACKWELL PUBLISHING
350 Main Street, Malden, MA 02148-5020, USA
9600 Garsington Road, Oxford OX4 2DQ, UK
550 Swanston Street, Carlton, Victoria 3053, Australia

First published 2005 by Blackwell Publishing Ltd

3   2005

Library of Congress Cataloging-in-Publication Data

The cultural politics of food and eating : a reader / edited by James L. Watson and Melissa L. Caldwell.
      p. cm. — (Blackwell readers in anthropology ; 8)
   Includes bibliographical references and index.
   ISBN 0-631-23092-0 (hardback : alk. paper) — ISBN 0-631-23093-9 (pbk. : alk. paper)
1. Food habits—Political aspects. 2. Food habits—Economic aspects. 3. Food preferences. 4. Food
industry and trade. 5. Politics and culture. 6. Consumption (Economics) 7. Globalization. I. Watson,
James L. II. Caldwell, Melissa L., 1969– III. Series.

GT2850.C853 2005
394.1'2—dc22   2004013999

ISBN-13: 978-0-631-23092-2 (hardback : alk. paper) — ISBN-13: 978-0-631-23093-9 (pbk. : alk. paper)

A catalogue record for this title is available from the British Library.

Set in 10/12pt Sabon
by Kolam Information Services Pvt. Ltd, Pondicherry, India.
Printed and bound in the United Kingdom
by TJ International, Padstow, Cornwall

The publisher's policy is to use permanent paper from mills that operate a sustainable forestry policy, and
which has been manufactured from pulp processed using acid-free and elementary chlorine-free practices.
Furthermore, the publisher ensures that the text paper and cover board used have met acceptable
environmental accreditation standards.

For further information on
Blackwell Publishing, visit our website:
www.blackwellpublishing.com

Contents

Notes on Contributors

Warren Belasco is Professor of American Studies at the University of Maryland Baltimore County.

Theodore C. Bestor is Professor of Anthropology and Japanese Studies at Harvard University.

Susan Brownell is Associate Professor of Anthropology at the University of Missouri–Saint Louis.

Hans Buechler is Professor of Anthropology at Syracuse University.

Judith-Maria Buechler is Professor of Anthropology at Hobart and William Smith College.

Melissa L. Caldwell is Assistant Professor of Anthropology at the University of California, Santa Cruz.

Susanne Freidberg is Associate Professor of Geography at Dartmouth College.

Maris Boyd Gillette is Associate Professor of Anthropology at Haverford College.

Walter L. Goldfrank is Professor of Sociology and of Latin American and Latino Studies at the University of California, Santa Cruz.

Eriberto P. Lozada, Jr. is Assistant Professor of Anthropology at Davidson College.

Purnima Mankekar is Associate Professor of Anthropology at Stanford University.

Daniel Miller is Professor of Material Culture in the Department of Anthropology at University College London.

Robert Paarlberg is Professor of Political Science at Wellesley College and Associate at the Weatherhead Center for International Affairs, Harvard University.

Sarah Drue Phillips is Assistant Professor of Anthropology at Indiana University.

Jeffrey M. Pilcher is Associate Professor of History at The Citadel.

Harriet Ritvo is the Arthur J. Conner Professor of History at the Massachusetts Institute of Technology.

William Roseberry was Professor of Anthropology at New York University.

Susan J. Terrio is Associate Professor of French and Anthropology with a joint appointment in the Department of French and the Edmund A. Walsh School of Foreign Service at Georgetown University.

James L. Watson is Fairbank Professor of Chinese Society and Professor of Anthropology at Harvard University.

Yunxiang Yan is Professor of Anthropology at the University of California, Los Angeles.

Editors' Acknowledgments

The idea for this reader originated from James Watson's class "Food and Culture" (Anthro. 105) at Harvard University. Melissa Caldwell was a Teaching Fellow for that course and has taught a similar course at Northeastern University. The editors would like to thank the Teaching Fellows and the two thousand (or more) undergraduate students who have participated in Anthro. 105 since its inception in 1990.

We would also like to thank Jane Huber, our editor at Blackwell, for her constant support and encouragement of this project, as well as her thoughtful suggestions for ways to improve the volume. The cheerful and conscientious work of Jane's former editorial assistants – Sarah Coleman, Annie Lenth, and Nathan Brown – at every stage of the process is also greatly appreciated. In particular, we want to thank her current assistant, Emily Martin, for seeing this project through to its completion. Finally, we would like to express our appreciation to our colleagues who have allowed us to include their work in this Reader.

Acknowledgments to Sources

The editor and publisher gratefully acknowledge the permission granted to reproduce the copyright material in this book:

1   Bestor, Theodore C. 2000. How Sushi Went Global. *Foreign Policy*, Dec. 2000:54–63. Reprinted with permission of *Foreign Policy*, www.foreignpolicy.com; permission conveyed through Copyright Clearance Center, Inc.

2   Freidberg, Susanne 2003. French Beans for the Masses: A Modern Historical Geography of Food in Burkina Faso. *Journal of Historical Geography* 29(3):445–63. Copyright © 2003 by Elsevier. Reprinted with permission from Elsevier.

3   Goldfrank, Walter L. 1994. Fresh Demand: The Consumption of Chilean Produce in the United States. In *Commodity Chains and Global Capitalism*, ed. Gary Gereffi and Miguel Korzeniewicz, pp. 267–79. Copyright © 1994 by Praeger. Reproduced with permission of Greenwood Publishing Group, Inc., Westport, CT.

4   Miller, Daniel 1998. Coca-Cola: A Black Sweet Drink from Trinidad. In *Material Cultures: Why Some Things Matter*, ed. Daniel Miller, pp. 169–87. Chicago: University of Chicago Press. Reprinted with permission of The University of Chicago Press and Taylor and Francis Books Ltd.

5   Watson, James L. 2000. China's Big Mac Attack. *Foreign Affairs* 79(3): 120–34. Copyright © 2000 by the Council on Foreign Relations, Inc. Reprinted by permission of Foreign Affairs.

6   Yan, Yunxiang 2000. Of Hamburger and Social Space: Consuming McDonald's in Beijing. In *The Consumer Revolution in Urban China*, ed. Deborah S. Davis, pp. 201–25. Berkeley: University of California Press. Copyright © 1999 The Regents of the University of California. Reprinted with permission of the Regents of the University of California and the University of California Press.

7   Gillette, Maris Boyd 2000. Children's Food and Islamic Dietary Restrictions in Xi'an. In *Feeding China's Little Emperors: Food, Children and Social Change*, ed. Jun Jing, pp. 71–93. Stanford, CA: Stanford University Press. Copyright © 2000 by the Board of Trustees of the Leland Stanford Junior University.

8   Roseberry, William 1996. The Rise of Yuppie Coffees and the Reimagination of Class in the United States. *American Anthropologist* 98(4): 762–75. Copyright © 1996 by the American Anthropological Association. Reprinted by permission of the University of California Press Journals.

9   Terrio, Susan J. 1996. Crafting *Grand Cru* Chocolates in Contemporary France. *American Anthropologist* 98(1):67–79. Copyright © 1996 by the American Anthropological Association. Reprinted by permission of the University of California Press Journals.

10   Lozada Jr., Eriberto P. 2000. Globalized Childhood? Kentucky Fried Chicken in Beijing. In *Feeding China's Little Emperors: Food, Children, and Social Change*, ed. Jun Jing, pp. 114–34. Stanford, CA: Stanford University Press. Copyright © 2000 by the Board of Trustees of the Leland Stanford Junior University.

11   Caldwell, Melissa L. 2004. Domesticating the French Fry: McDonald's and Consumerism in Moscow. *Journal of Consumer Culture* 4(1):5–26. Copyright © 2004 by Sage Publications, 2004. Reprinted by permission of Sage Publications Ltd

12   Mankekar, Purnima 2002. "India Shopping": Indian Grocery Stores and Transnational Configurations of Belonging. *Ethnos* 67(1): 75–98. Reprinted with permission of Taylor & Francis Ltd. http://www.tandf.co.uk/journals

13   Belasco, Warren 1999. Food and the Counterculture: A Story of Bread and Politics. In *Food in Global History*, ed. Raymond Grew, pp. 273–92. Westview Press. Reprinted with permission of Westview Press. Permission conveyed through Copyright Clearance Center.

14   Pilcher, Jeffrey M. 2002. Industrial Tortillas and Folkloric Pepsi: The Nutritional Consequences of Hybrid Cuisines in Mexico. In *Food Nations: Selling Taste in Consumer Societies*. Warren Belasco and Philip Scranton, eds. pp. 222–39. New York: Routledge. Copyright © 2002. Reproduced by permission of Routledge/Taylor & Francis Books, Inc.

15   Brownell, Susan 1995. Food, Hunger, and the State. In *Training the Body for China: Sports in the Moral Order of the People's Republic*, pp. 253–62. Chicago: University of Chicago Press. Reprinted with permission of The University of Chicago Press.

16   Buechler, Hans, and Judith-Maria Buechler 2000. The Bakers of Bernburg and the Logics of Communism and Capitalism. *American Ethnologist* 26(4):799–821. Copyright © 2000 by the American Anthropological Association. Reprinted by permission of the University of California Press Journals and the authors.

17   Paarlberg, Robert 2000. The Global Food Fight. *Foreign Affairs* 79(3):24–38. Copyright © 2000 by the Council on Foreign Relations, Inc. Reprinted by permission of Foreign Affairs.

18   Phillips, Sarah Drue 2002. Half-lives and Healthy Bodies: Discourses on "Contaminated" Food and Healing in Post-Chernobyl Ukraine. *Food and Foodways* 10:27–53. Copyright 2002 from *Food and Foodways* by Sarah Drue Phillips. Reproduced by permission of Taylor & Francis, Inc., http://taylor&francis.com.

19   Ritvo, Harriet 1998. Mad Cow Mysteries. *American Scholar* 67(2):113–22. © 1998 by Harrlet Ritvo Reprinted with permission of American Scholar.

Introduction

James L. Watson and Melissa L. Caldwell

Since the early 1990s, the study of food has moved from the margins to the center of intellectual discourse in the English-speaking world. Cooking shows are standard fare on television and books about food and foodways are displayed on the "hot topic" tables in major bookstores. Food studies now constitute recognized subdisciplines in the fields of anthropology, sociology, history, culture studies, medicine, and business. Undergraduate classes that focus explicitly on food are oversubscribed in many universities and graduate degrees in food studies open the door to many professions, not just nutrition counseling or advertising.

This recent surge in interest obscures the fact that food studies have a long and distinguished history. Within anthropology, the study of food parallels the development of the discipline itself, tracking methodological and theoretical trends from the late nineteenth century to the present. For anthropologists food is not just a topic worthy of inquiry in its own right; food is a universal medium that illuminates a wide range of other cultural practices. It is impossible to imagine studies of marriage, exchange, or religion that do not consider food.

The Cultural Politics of Food and Eating departs from earlier collections on this topic in several respects. First, rather than focusing on the anthropology of food as a general subject (surveying everything from health and nutrition to the interpretation of meal structures), we concentrate specifically on food as a window on the political. This reader begins with the premise that food practices are implicated in a complex field of relationships, expectations, and choices that are contested, negotiated, and often unequal. Food everywhere is not just about eating, and eating (at least among humans) is never simply a biological process.

Second, this reader presents articles that point to the future of food studies, not its past. The editors have selected provocative, methodologically diverse essays that pursue agendas that transcend the food practices under investigation. Some of the most enduring debates of twentieth-century anthropology reemerge in these essays, but with new points of departure and new theoretical frameworks. We have tried to present a vision of how continued attention to the most mundane and intimate aspects of people's ordinary lives – in this case, how they relate to food – can help us understand the big issues of twenty-first-century politics: State formation and collapse, global flows and anti-global reactions, and new notions of identity and the rebirth of nationalism (among other topics).

Although this volume appears in a series entitled *Blackwell Readers in Anthropology*, it is significant that some of our leading contributors are not, in fact, anthropologists (of the card-carrying, degree-holding type). The editors selected these essays with a transdisciplinary readership in mind. In our view, social science disciplines are artifacts of an outmoded early- to mid-twentieth-century (Anglo-American) intellectual tradition, a bureaucratic framework in which knowledge was conveniently compartmentalized to accommodate an undergraduate curriculum. Today's anthropologists operate in a disaggregated, continually reinvented intellectual world; one day we work closely with historians; the next we find ourselves in the company of epidemiologists and political scientists. What distinguishes anthropology today is its long-standing and defiant preoccupation with the mundane, the ordinary, and the intimate. Our primary methodology is talking – face-to-face, without intermediation. And our primary objective is to present the perspectives and experiences of our subjects on their terms, not ours. This reader is designed to help a new generation of food specialists (irrespective of disciplinary allegiance) who wish to pursue and develop these "anthropological" traditions.

Globalization and Food Politics

During the 1980s and 1990s many researchers were preoccupied with the rapid globalization of food-delivery systems, most notably those associated with the fast-food industry (Fantasia 1995; Leidner 1993; Reiter 1991; Ritzer 1993; Watson 1997). McDonald's became the icon of that era, as well as a universal symbol of American culture (the good, the bad, and the ugly). Beginning with an American franchise base in 1955, the corporation had spread to 117 countries by the end of the twentieth century. A new McDonald's restaurant opened somewhere in the world every eight hours during the mid-1990s. By 2003 the boom had subsided and the corporation had pulled out of three countries (Ecuador, Paraguay, and Trinidad), a retreat much reported in the international media. McDonald's also faced market saturation in Japan, Germany, and the United States – adding to its image problem. Today, if any American transnational represents the optimistic vision of globalization it is Starbucks, the new symbol of yuppified, wired American culture.

By the early 2000s McDonald's, Kentucky Fried Chicken (KFC), and Coca-Cola had become the favorite targets of anti-globalist demonstrators who use the technology of globalization (the internet) to coordinate worldwide protests. There is a good reason why food transnationals attract so much political attention: As food practices change, notions of national identity are threatened, especially when American corporate interests are involved.[1] It is no coincidence, for instance, that France, with its grand culinary traditions, has become the epicenter of the global anti-McDonald's movement. The fact that the corporation has flourished in France during recent years[2] points to a growing gap between the French intelligentsia and their working-class compatriots. Similar class divisions are evident in the United States and Britain. Have attitudes toward fast food become a global diagnostic of class? This is a topic that begs further research.[3]

It is clear that food and food politics have become a preoccupation (one is tempted to call it an obsession) among the educated elites in advanced capitalist societies. This correlates to a retreat from organized, party politics and involution into self – dwelling on the politics of the personal. The 1991 collapse of the Soviet Union marks this transition and made it possible by eliminating the fear of nuclear holocaust, a psychological pillar of late-twentieth-century politics.

The triumph of the personal is perhaps best illustrated by the movement to oppose genetically modified foods in post-Cold War Europe. The key to success is the ability to transform private worries about body and diet into an organized, worldwide movement – linked via the internet to allied groups that promote organic foods and/ or oppose fast foods. The mad cow fiasco that swept through Europe in the 1990s was a primary catalyst of this political sea change. Ordinary food (hamburger, roasts, steaks) suddenly became the convector of death; 139 Britons had died of variant Creutzfeldt-Jakob disease (the human version of mad cow disease) by the end of 2003.[4] At the outset of this catastrophe British government officials assured the public that local beef presented no dangers to human consumers. The early 2004 outbreaks of the avian flu seriously damaged poultry industries in Asia and North America. Government officials bent on eliminating all potential carriers of the disease have been pitted against farmers whose livelihoods depend on current and future sales of chickens and ducks. At the level of the nation-state, both the mad cow and avian flu scares have prompted politicians and safety inspectors to ban imports of meat from countries with documented cases of tainted food.

Largely as a consequence of the mad cow episode and subsequent outbreaks of food contamination, many Europeans and Asians no longer trust government officials or scientific experts when they comment on food safety. Precautions that once might have been treated as symptoms of behavioral neurosis (minute examination of labels, double-washing of produce, rejecting slightly bruised fruit) are now everyday practices in millions of middle-class homes. The essays in this reader provide a background for understanding these social developments. The authors remind us that food is everywhere political.

The Absence of Food

Anthropologists are only beginning to focus on the worldwide obesity epidemic and health problems associated with over-consumption (see concluding section). Meanwhile, more research needs to be done on the *absence* of food in everyday social life. Often depicted in policy studies as a consequence of economic or environmental factors, food deprivation is deeply embedded in the cultural, political, and religious processes that people take for granted. Furthermore, the actual experience of hunger differs dramatically in response to cultural circumstances. Political activists from Gandhi to Bobby Sands (an IRA prisoner in Northern Ireland) have used hunger strikes to publicize and gain legitimacy for their political beliefs. Politicians routinely link wartime food relief programs to foreign policy agendas, and will no doubt continue to do so – treating food as a weapon. Religious ascetics often demonstrate their spiritual powers through acts of extreme dietary abstinence. It is also notable that religious communities everywhere are keen to establish soup kitchens and food stations as a means of delivering ideological messages. The individuals who are classified as hungry, and therefore in need of food aid, often contest the values assigned to their circumstances by aid workers, donors, and policy-makers. In many cases food-aid recipients have resisted prevailing paradigms about hunger by appropriating food programs and reworking them to meet needs not previously envisioned by program coordinators (see e.g., Caldwell 2004).

Topics such as nutrition, dieting, fasting, and food relief offer informative means for understanding the power relationships, economic systems, and political interests in which deprivation is embedded. As Alexander de Waal (1989), Johan Pottier (1999), and Nancy Scheper-Hughes (1992), have demonstrated, food deprivation is a total social experience that intersects with the realms of the practical, experiential, symbolic, psychological, political, economic, religious, and environmental. Scheper-Hughes, for instance, carefully and compassionately describes what it is like for poverty-stricken Brazilians to manage their lives and create a sense of self in the face of uncertain food supplies.

Other anthropologists have focused on social relations that emerge in the aftermath of food deprivation (Aretxaga 1997; de Waal 1989; Hastrup 1993; Prindle 1979; Shack 1997). These connections have been addressed most successfully in ethnographies of the communities that are structured around food shortages. Excellent examples can be found in Rebecca Allahyari's ethnography of two church-based feeding programs in California (2000), Daniel Sack's ethnographically informed study of the role of American Protestant congregations in global hunger relief efforts (2000), Irene Glasser's description of a soup kitchen in Connecticut (1988), and Barbara Myerhoff's study of a Jewish senior citizens' center in California (1978). By treating feeding programs as communities and by focusing on the social dynamics within groups, these four researchers have poignantly demonstrated that hunger and poverty are intrinsically social.

Food, State Socialism, and Postsocialism

Perhaps the newest and most promising trajectory in the anthropology of food is that offered by the study of state socialism and postsocialism. Until recently, the bureaucratic and political obstacles to conducting fieldwork in socialist states such as the (former) Soviet Union and (still-at-this-writing Communist) Cuba meant that the ethnography of socialism was the missing elephant in late-twentieth-century anthropological discourse. There were efforts to fill this huge gap by drawing on the work of Soviet scholars who amassed data on the practices, beliefs, and daily lives of fellow citizens. Other Soviet studies of workplace canteens, nutritional manuals, and school feeding programs proved useful for understanding socialist society. In China during the heyday of Maoism (1958–76) few outsiders were allowed access to ordinary people and, hence, it was not until decades later that the full ramifications of the great famine of 1959–61 were widely known. Thirty to forty million people died as a consequence of bureaucratic mismanagement and political obfuscation during that policy-induced famine (see Sen 1981; Yang 1996). It was not until the 1990s, with the publication of ethnographies by Chinese anthropologists who were not constrained by ideology, that the study of socialist culture in China started in earnest (see, e.g., Huang 1989, Jing 1996, Yan 1996). Significantly, food and consumption patterns play leading roles in these recent ethnographic explorations.

Queuing, hoarding, and informal exchange activities emerged everywhere in the socialist world as citizens found ways to provision themselves and their families. The ideologies of communalism and egalitarianism were expressed most vividly in workplace canteens and public dining facilities that replaced private kitchens between the 1920s and 1940s in the Soviet Union (Borrero 1997, 2002; Rothstein and Rothstein 1997) and during the 1950s and 1960s in China (Yang 1996; Watson 1989; Yan 2003). Similarly, private garden plots supplemented state food supplies in many socialist countries – closing the gap between shortage and adequacy. So prominent was the place of food under state socialism that people throughout the world equated the Soviet Union with breadlines and Chinese Communism with the "iron rice bowl" (i.e., job security irrespective of effort or attendance).

In many ways, the postsocialist era (dating from the collapse of the Berlin Wall in 1989) has been equally noteworthy for the central role that food plays in national politics. Free-market rhetoric and consumer-oriented business practices challenged socialist visions of centralized production and state control. Fast-food chains were in the forefront of this movement: hamburgers, French fries, fried chicken, pizza, and espressos became the instruments of social revolution. In the early 1990s, after McDonald's opened its first restaurant near Red Square in Moscow, Tim Luke (1990) coined the phrase "McGulag Archipelago" to represent what he saw as the iron cage of capitalist rationality, descending to ensnare Soviet citizens. Similar accusations followed KFC and McDonald's when they first arrived in Beijing during the early 1990s, but China soon plunged headlong into the global economy, and "capitalism with Chinese characteristics" (i.e., state-managed market development) became the reigning ideology. McDonald's was promoted by Communist Party officials as a model for Chinese business administration (see Yan 1997). Elsewhere, soft drinks like Coca-Cola have been heralded as a symbol of personal and political sobriety, as is the case among religious evangelicals in Lithuania (Lankauskas 2002).

As state-owned industries and distribution systems are adapting to the investment requirements of global capitalism, food represents one of the best, and probably the most accessible, vehicles for understanding postsocialist cultures. When all else fails, people will always talk about food. The emergence of Western-style self-service and well-stocked grocery stores with computerized scanners, electronic cash registers, and shopping carts have changed the ways in which urban Russians, Chinese, and Poles shop. Prepared foods, packaged in glossy wrappers adorned with nutritional facts (typically written not in the local language but in English or German), challenge notions of what constitutes "cooking."[5] Does choice, as many neoliberal theorists claim, imply empowerment? Or is capitalism always accompanied by an "iron cage" that transforms comrade worker-producers into isolated, alienated consumers? In many parts of the postsocialist world even the architecture of family homes is changing as citizens assume new identities, reflected in American-style kitchens (Fehérváry 2002) and new approaches to food preparation and storage (Shevchenko 2002).

Careful attention to food practices in postsocialist and late socialist societies also sheds interesting new light on the age-old question of cultural change: What changes and what does not? What endures, irrespective of economic pressures? In her ethnographic study of a newly privatized fruit and vegetable processing plant in Poland, Elizabeth Dunn argues that the introduction of niche marketing – baby foods, for example – reveals striking continuities between the socialist past and the capitalist present (Dunn 1999). Similarly, Jennifer Patico's (2002) study of gift-giving in St. Petersburg shows how food items acquire multivalent significance, as commodities and as tokens of friendship (akin to comradeship ties under socialism). Although coffee and chocolates were once valued for their utility, particularly when such items were beyond the financial reach of ordinary Soviet citizens, today the gift of instant coffee carries significance as a verification of a recipient's social worth. The guiding principles of egalitarianism and classlessness may not have guided the conduct of everyday life during the collective era, but these ideas figure large in the nostalgia for socialism that is currently sweeping through Eastern Europe, Russia, and China. One ironic manifestation of this romanticization of the past has been the appearance of historically themed restaurants that allow diners to re-experience the highs (and lows) of communist-era food services at appropriately high capitalist prices.[6]

Frontiers of Food Research

Although there are many points of intersection among the articles in this reader, we have grouped them into three main sections that orient readers to several of the most significant and promising themes in contemporary food studies. By highlighting these themes in the articles collected here, our intent is not to reproduce studies that represent the best of previous anthropological research – for example, classic works by Mary Douglas (1966) and Claude Lévi-Strauss (1969). Instead we focus on recent studies that point to the future of anthropology as a transdisciplinary, methodologically diverse enterprise.

Upon close reading, it is apparent that the authors of these essays are engaging in conversations among themselves regarding the limits of globalization, the translatability of culture, and the nature of capitalism. Furthermore, the inclusion of interlocutors (our non-anthropologist contributors) challenges anthropologists to look to other disciplines, and other intellectual traditions, when they tackle food issues. It is our hope that these conversations will encourage anthropologists to find new ways to make ethnography meaningful to our colleagues in other fields.

We conclude this introduction by highlighting four areas of research that, in our opinion, command attention for the next phase of food research:

1   *The biotechnology revolution* World grain production is in the throes of a major revolution, as outlined by Robert Paarlberg in Chapter 17. American farmers shifted from 100 percent non-GMO[7] soybean production in 1994 to approximately 75–80 percent GMO by 2003. Genetically modified maize, canola oil, cassava,

papaya, cotton, and sugar beets (among other crops) are rapidly gaining market share – irrespective of the anti-GMO movements discussed above. Anthropologists have begun working on the social issues attendant to biotech food production (see, especially, Stone 2002a, 2002b). The next frontier of biotech is the production and marketing of genetically modified (and cloned) animals, redesigned for human consumption: pigs, cattle, sheep, poultry, and fish. Biotech food, and soon-to-emerge farmaceuticals (or nutriceuticals), are on the verge of transforming the human diet. Most of the published work on biotech foods has emphasized the scientific and corporate dimensions of development and marketing. Much more work, of an ethnographic nature, needs to be done on the producers of GMO foods, the distributors, and the end consumers – and not just those who reside in Europe and North America.

2 *The organic revolution* Partly as a consequence of the GMO revolution, a worldwide movement to embrace "natural" foods is growing rapidly. A search for websites dedicated to organic foods turns up thousands of hits, revealing a global network of interlinked companies, NGOs, government agencies, and amorphous interest groups. In the early 1990s the average American consumer was hard pressed to find attractive (let alone edible) organic produce; today supermarkets in every part of the United States are expanding into this area and food industries are responding with new product lines. The US Department of Agriculture recently adopted regulations for organic labeling, thereby removing much of the suspicion and confusion that held back production in the 1980s and early 1990s. Following the central theme of this reader, it is obvious that more is at issue here than food and diet. Organic movements are just taking form in China, Russia, Korea, and Mexico (among other countries), offering wide scope for comparative research.

3 *Food and ideology* One striking aspect of recent economic trends is that governments throughout the world have retreated from the centralized regulation of food production and ceded oversight authority to citizen groups and NGOs. This is a striking statement about the place of individuals and personal responsibility in the global market system. Furthermore, many states have reduced or eliminated programs that alleviate food shortages among citizens who have not benefited from globalization. To fill this gap private groups and individuals have stepped forward to provide – and increasingly control – these services. Religious groups, public service organizations, and fitness/dietary consultants alike have capitalized on these opportunities to spread their particular doctrines of morality and/or spirituality. Food has thus emerged as a new arena for ideological proselytism on a global scale. Although promising research has been done on these intersections in the context of organized religion, there is much more to be mined from this topic – notably in the realms of anti-organized, anti-authoritarian, anti-doctrinal religions (often categorized as New Age). The politics of the personal is central to these new, food-focused ideological movements.

4 *The politics of obesity* Obesity, and with it long-term health consequences of over-consumption, is fast becoming the hot-button issue of global health. News media are quick to report every new study that highlights the dangers of over-indulgence, often in societies that once suffered from periodic famine (e.g., China and India). The inevitable rise in health-care costs associated with obesity is certain to drain state funding that would otherwise underwrite education and social

security. Recent attempts by consumers and trial lawyers to sue McDonald's for promoting obesity in the United States are of special significance for the future of global food industries. At the time of writing (2004), legal actions of this type have failed but, to borrow a political slogan from the 1960s: The whole world is watching. The political battles associated with body image and consumption are just beginning. Watch this space.

NOTES

1   In the aftermath of the Iraq War, for instance, Coca-Cola faced competition from politically inspired brands, such as Mecca Cola and Arab Cola. In South Korea a brand called 815 Cola was marketed in opposition to Coca-Cola (815 commemorates Korea's liberation from Japanese occupation on August 15, 1945).
2   By the end of 2002 there were 973 McDonald's restaurants in France, a rise of 60 since 2001. A new outlet opens somewhere in France every six days (2003 figures).
3   Katherine Newman's ethnography of American fast-food workers in Harlem offers a striking example of where this research could lead in studies of class, race, and gender (1999).
4   "Mad Cow Toll in U.K. Is Less Than Feared," *Wall Street Journal*, January 12, 2004.
5   This is also true for many young people in the United States, where anything heated in a toaster oven or microwave qualifies as "cooked" food.
6   Perhaps the clearest examples are the many "Mao Restaurants" in China's major cities, where veteran Red Guards of the Cultural Revolution era (1966–76) meet to reminisce over corn fritters, ant soup, and roast locust – key dietary items from their revolutionary experiences in the Chinese countryside. Their poignant stories are frequently interrupted by cellphone calls from their secretaries or business partners.
7   Genetically modified organism.

REFERENCES

Allahyari, Rebecca Anne
    2000 Visions of Charity: Volunteer Workers and Moral Community. Berkeley: University of California Press.
Aretxaga, Begoña
    1997 Shattering Silence: Women, Nationalism, and Political Subjectivity in Northern Ireland. Princeton, NJ: Princeton University Press.
Borrero, Mauricio
    1997 Communal Dining and State Cafeterias in Moscow and Petrograd, 1917–1921. *In* Food in Russian History and Culture. Musya Glants and Joyce Toomre, eds. Pp.162–76. Bloomington: Indiana University Press.
——2002 Food and the Politics of Scarcity in Urban Soviet Russia, 1917–1941. *In* Food Nations: Selling Taste in Consumer Societies. Warren Belasco and Phillip Scranton, eds. Pp. 258–76. New York: Routledge.
Caldwell, Melissa L.
    2004 Not by Bread Alone: Social Support in the New Russia. Berkeley: University of California Press.

de Waal, Alexander
  1989 Famine that Kills: Darfu, Sudan, 1984–1985. Oxford: Clarendon Press.
Douglas, Mary
  1966 Purity and Danger: An Analysis of the Concepts of Pollution and Taboo. New York:
  Routledge (second edition, 2000).
Dunn, Elizabeth
  1999 Slick Salesmen and Simple People: Negotiated Capitalism in a Privatized Polish Firm. *In*
  Uncertain Transition: Ethnographies of Change in the Postsocialist World. Michael Burawoy
  and Katherine Verdery, eds. Pp. 125–50. Lanham, MD: Rowman & Littlefield.
Fantasia, Rick
  1995 Fast Food in France. Theory and Society 24:201–43.
Fehérváry, Krisztina E.
  2002 American Kitchens, Luxury Bathrooms, and the Search for a "Normal" Life in Postsocialist Hungary. Ethnos 67(3):369–400.
Glasser, Irene
  1988 More Than Bread: Ethnography of a Soup Kitchen. Tuscaloosa: University of
  Alabama Press.
Hastrup, Kirsten
  1993 Hunger and the Hardness of Facts. Man 28(4):727–39.
Huang, Shu-min
  1989 The Spiral Road: Change in a Chinese Village through the Eyes of a Communist Party
  Leader. Boulder, CO: Westview Press.
Jing, Jun
  1996 The Temple of Memories: History, Power, and Morality in a Chinese Village. Stan-
  ford, CA: Stanford University Press.
Lankauskas, Gediminas
  2002 On "Modern" Christians, Consumption, and the Value of National Identity in Post-
  Soviet Lithuania. Ethnos 67(3): 320–44.
Leidner, Robin
  1993 Fast Food, Fast Talk: Service Work and the Routinization of Everyday Life. Berkeley:
  University of California Press.
Lévi-Strauss, Claude
  1969 The Raw and the Cooked. New York: Octagon Press.
Luke, Tim
  1990 Postcommunism in the USSR: The McGulag Archipelago. Telos (84):33–42.
Myerhoff, Barbara
  1978 Number Our Days. New York: Simon & Schuster.
Newman, Katherine S.
  1999 No Shame in My Game: The Working Poor in the Inner City. New York: Vintage
  Books.
Patico, Jennifer
  2002 Chocolate and Cognac: Gifts and the Recognition of Social Worlds in Post-Soviet
  Russia. Ethnos 67(3):345–68.
Pottier, Johan
  1999 The Anthropology of Food: The Social Dynamics of Food Security. Cambridge: Polity
  Press.
Prindle, Peter H.
  1979 Peasant Society and Famine: A Nepalese Example. Ethnology 18(1):49–60.
Reiter, Esther
  1991 Making Fast Food: From the Frying Pan into the Fryer. Montreal: McGill-Queen's
  University Press.

Ritzer, George
1993 The McDonaldization of Society. Thousand Oaks, CA: Pine Forge Press.
Rothstein, Halina and Robert A. Rothstein
1997 The Beginnings of Soviet Culinary Arts. *In* Food in Russian History and Culture. Musya Glants and Joyce Toomre, eds. Pp. 177–94. Bloomington: Indiana University Press.
Sack, Daniel
2000 Whitebread Protestants: Food and Religion in American Culture. New York: St. Martin's Press.
Scheper-Hughes, Nancy
1992 Death without Weeping: The Violence of Everyday Life in Brazil. Berkeley: University of California Press.
Sen, Amartya K.
1981 Poverty and Famines: An Essay on Entitlement and Deprivation. Oxford: Oxford University Press.
Shack, William A.
1997 Hunger, Anxiety, and Ritual: Deprivation and Spirit Possession among the Gurage of Ethiopia. *In* Food and Culture: A Reader. Carole Counihan and Penny Van Esterik, eds. Pp. 125–37. New York: Routledge.
Shevchenko, Olga
2002 "In Case of Emergency": Consumption, Security, and the Meaning of Durables in a Transforming Society. Journal of Consumer Culture 2(2):147–70.
Stone, Glenn D.
2002a Biotechnology and Suicide in India. Anthropology News 43(5):5.
——2002b Both Sides Now: Fallacies in the Genetic-Modification Wars, Implications for Developing Countries, and Anthropological Perspectives. Current Anthropology 43(4):611–30.
Watson, James L.
1989 Feeding the Revolution: Public Canteens and Forced Commensality in Mao's China. Inaugural Lecture, Harvard University, Department of Anthropology.
——1997 Golden Arches East: McDonald's in East Asia. Stanford, CA: Stanford University Press.
Yan, Yunxiang, 1996 The Flow of Gifts: Reciprocity and Social Networks in a Chinese Village. Stanford, CA: Stanford University Press.
——1997 McDonald's in Beijing: The Localization of Americana. *In* Golden Arches East: McDonald's in East Asia. James L. Watson, ed. Pp. 39–76. Stanford, CA: Stanford University Press.
——2003. *Private* Life under Socialism: Love, Intimacy, and Family Change in a Chinese Village, 1949–1999. Stanford, CA: Stanford University Press.
Yang, Dali L.
1996 Calamity and Reform in China. Stanford, CA: Stanford University Press.

Part I

Food and Globalization

Introduction

This first part, "Food and Globalization," addresses problems and issues that arise from the global movement of commodities, fashions, and ideas. Articles by Theodore Bestor, Susanne Freidberg, and Walter Goldfrank address commodity chains as vehicles through which producers and consumers interact to create new relationships across economic, geographic, and political boundaries. By tracing the global paths of Atlantic sushi-grade tuna, African green beans, and Chilean grapes, the three authors provide vivid, down-to-earth visions of the global system. Bestor explains how Japanese consumers are linked in a symbiotic relationship of needs and expectations with New England fishermen. A secondary theme that emerges in this article is the creation of "value," as Japanese buyers judge fish by standards that mystify American producers. Freidberg investigates the ways in which producer–consumer relations have altered the nature of postcolonialism in Francophone Africa; her article also contributes to current debates regarding the theoretical and methodological significance of multi-sited ethnography. Goldfrank's article illustrates the impact that Chilean produce has had on American shoppers' dining practices, particularly ideas about seasonality and availability: Boston consumers now take it for granted that fresh blueberries will be available in January.

The articles by Daniel Miller, James Watson, and Yunxiang Yan take a different approach to the topics of globalization. Specifically, through analyses of food and beverage transnationals, these authors shed light on communities that emerge around and through global flows of ideas about eating and drinking. What is unusual about these three articles is the authors' analyses of the influence of food transnationals such as McDonald's and Coca-Cola. They depart from other scholars who have argued that food transnationals disrupt (at best) or destroy (at worst) local cultures and social relationships. Nor do these authors suggest that corporate America, as embodied in soft drinks or hamburgers, will lead other societies to the promised land of market socialism, as many journalists and business leaders have implied. Instead, through critical engagement and close ethnography, Miller, Watson, and Yan demonstrate that local consumers often use McDonald's and Coca-Cola for their own ends and create new versions of supposedly standardized food-delivery systems, through the process of localization. In his article on Coca-Cola in Trinidad, Miller analyzes how local actors redefine Coca-Cola as a symbol of both personal and national Trinidadian identity. Yan and Watson explore McDonald's "triumph" in China, where the corporation now has nearly 600 restaurants; careful examination shows that fast-food chains do not necessarily call the shots in emerging economies (see also the articles by Melissa Caldwell and Eriberto Lozada in Part II).

1

How Sushi Went Global

Theodore C. Bestor

A 40-minute drive from Bath, Maine, down a winding two-lane highway, the last mile on a dirt road, a ramshackle wooden fish pier stands beside an empty parking lot. At 6:00 p.m. nothing much is happening. Three bluefin tuna sit in a huge tub of ice on the loading dock.

Between 6:45 and 7:00, the parking lot fills up with cars and trucks with license plates from New Jersey, New York, Massachusetts, New Hampshire, and Maine. Twenty tuna buyers clamber out, half of them Japanese. The three bluefin, ranging from 270 to 610 pounds, are winched out of the tub, and buyers crowd around them, extracting tiny core samples to examine their color, fingering the flesh to assess the fat content, sizing up the curve of the body.

After about 20 minutes of eyeing the goods, many of the buyers return to their trucks to call Japan by cellphone and get the morning prices from Tokyo's Tsukiji market – the fishing industry's answer to Wall Street – where the daily tuna auctions have just concluded. The buyers look over the tuna one last time and give written bids to the dock manager, who passes the top bid for each fish to the crew that landed it.

The auction bids are secret. Each bid is examined anxiously by a cluster of young men, some with a father or uncle looking on to give advice, others with a young woman and a couple of toddlers trying to see Daddy's fish. Fragments of concerned conversation float above the parking lot: "That's all?" "Couldn't we do better if we shipped it ourselves?" "Yeah, but my pickup needs a new transmission now!" After a few minutes, deals are closed and the fish are quickly loaded onto the backs of trucks in crates of crushed ice, known in the trade as "tuna coffins." As rapidly as they arrived, the flotilla of buyers sails out of the parking lot – three bound for New York's John F. Kennedy Airport, where their tuna will be airfreighted to Tokyo for sale the day after next.

Bluefin tuna may seem at first an unlikely case study in globalization. But as the world rearranges itself – around silicon chips, Starbucks coffee, or sashimi-grade tuna – new channels for global flows of capital and commodities link far-flung individuals and communities in unexpected new relationships. The tuna trade is a prime example of the globalization of a regional industry, with intense international competition and thorny environmental regulations; centuries-old practices combined with high technology; realignments of labor and capital in response to international regulation; shifting markets; and the diffusion of culinary culture as tastes for sushi, and bluefin tuna, spread worldwide.

Growing Appetites

Tuna doesn't require much promotion among Japanese consumers. It is consistently Japan's most popular seafood, and demand is high throughout the year. When the Federation of Japan Tuna Fisheries Cooperative (known as Nikkatsuren) runs ad campaigns for tuna, they tend to be low-key and whimsical, rather like the "Got Milk?" advertising in the United States. Recently, the federation launched "Tuna Day" (Maguro no hi), providing retailers with posters and recipe cards for recipes more complicated than "slice and serve chilled." Tuna Day's mascot is Goro-kun, a colorful cartoon tuna swimming the Australian crawl.

Despite the playful contemporary tone of the mascot, the date selected for Tuna Day carries much heavier freight. October 10, it turns out, commemorates the date that tuna first appeared in Japanese literature, in the eighth-century collection of imperial court poetry known as the *Man'yoshu* – one of the towering classics of Japanese literature. The neat twist is that October 10 today is a national holiday, Sports Day. Goro-kun, the sporty tuna, scores a promotional hat trick, suggesting intimate connections among national culture, healthy food for active lives, and the family holiday meal.

Outside of Japan, tuna, especially raw tuna, hasn't always had it so good. Sushi isn't an easy concept to sell to the uninitiated. And besides, North Americans tend to think of cultural influence as flowing from West to East: James Dean, baseball, Coca-Cola, McDonald's, and Disneyland have all gone over big in Tokyo. Yet Japanese cultural motifs and material – from Kurosawa's *The Seven Samurai* to Yoda's Zen and Darth Vader's armor, from Issey Miyake's fashions to Nintendo, PlayStation, and Pokémon – have increasingly saturated North American and indeed the entire world's consumption and popular culture. Against all odds, so too has sushi.

In 1929, the *Ladies' Home Journal* introduced Japanese cooking to North American women, but discreetly skirted the subject of raw fish: "There have been purposely omitted . . . any recipes using the delicate and raw tuna fish which is sliced wafer thin and served iced with attractive garnishes. [These] . . . might not sound so entirely delicious as they are in reality." Little mention of any Japanese food appeared in US media until well after World War II. By the 1960s, articles on sushi began to show up in lifestyle magazines like *Holiday* and *Sunset*. But the recipes they suggested were canapés like cooked shrimp on caraway rye bread, rather than raw fish on rice.

A decade later, however, sushi was growing in popularity throughout North America, turning into a sign of class and educational standing. In 1972, the

New York Times covered the opening of a sushi bar in the elite sanctum of New York's Harvard Club. *Esquire* explained the fare in an article titled "Wake up Little Sushi!" Restaurant reviewers guided readers to Manhattan's sushi scene, including innovators like Shalom Sushi, a kosher sushi bar in SoHo.

Japan's emergence on the global economic scene in the 1970s as the business destination du jour, coupled with a rejection of hearty, red-meat American fare in favor of healthy cuisine like rice, fish, and vegetables, and the appeal of the high-concept aesthetics of Japanese design all prepared the world for a sushi fad. And so, from an exotic, almost unpalatable ethnic specialty, then to haute cuisine of the most rarefied sort, sushi has become not just cool, but popular. The painted window of a Cambridge, Massachusetts, coffee shop advertises "espresso, cappuccino, carrot juice, lasagna, and sushi." Mashed potatoes with wasabi (horseradish), sushi-ginger relish, and seared sashimi-grade tuna steaks show Japan's growing cultural influence on upscale nouvelle cuisine throughout North America, Europe, and Latin America. Sushi has even become the stuff of fashion, from "sushi" lip gloss, colored the deep red of raw tuna, to "wasabi" nail polish, a soft avocado green.

Angling for New Consumers

Japan remains the world's primary market for fresh tuna for sushi and sashimi; demand in other countries is a product of Japanese influence and the creation of new markets by domestic producers looking to expand their reach. Perhaps not surprisingly, sushi's global popularity as an emblem of a sophisticated, cosmopolitan consumer class more or less coincided with a profound transformation in the international role of the Japanese fishing industry. From the 1970s onward, the expansion of 200-mile fishing limits around the world excluded foreign fleets from the prime fishing grounds of many coastal nations. And international environmental campaigns forced many countries, Japan among them, to scale back their distant water fleets. With their fishing operations curtailed and their yen for sushi still growing, Japanese had to turn to foreign suppliers.

Jumbo jets brought New England's bluefin tuna into easy reach of Tokyo, just as Japan's consumer economy – a byproduct of the now disparaged "bubble" years – went into hyperdrive. The sushi business boomed. During the 1980s, total Japanese imports of fresh bluefin tuna worldwide increased from 957 metric tons (531 from the United States) in 1984 to 5,235 metric tons (857 from the United States) in 1993. The average wholesale price peaked in 1990 at 4,900 yen (US $34) per kilogram, bones and all, which trimmed out to approximately US $33 wholesale per edible pound.

Not surprisingly, Japanese demand for prime bluefin tuna – which yields a firm red meat, lightly marbled with veins of fat, highly prized (and priced) in Japanese cuisine – created a gold-rush mentality on fishing grounds across the globe wherever bluefin tuna could be found. But in the early 1990s, as the US bluefin industry was taking off, the Japanese economy went into a stall, then a slump, then a dive. US producers suffered as their high-end export market collapsed. Fortunately for them, the North American sushi craze took up the slack. US businesses may have written off Japan, but Americans' taste for sushi stuck. An industry founded exclusively on

Japanese demand survived because of Americans' newly trained palates and a booming US economy.

A Transatlantic Tussle

Atlantic bluefin tuna ("ABT" in the trade) are a highly migratory species that ranges from the equator to Newfoundland, from Turkey to the Gulf of Mexico. Bluefin can be huge fish; the record is 1,496 pounds. In more normal ranges, 600-pound tuna, 10 feet in length, are not extraordinary, and 250- to 300-pound bluefin, six feet long, are commercial mainstays.

Before bluefin became a commercial species in New England, before Japanese buyers discovered the stock, before the 747, bluefin were primarily sports fish, caught with fighting tackle by trophy hunters out of harbors like Montauk, Hyannis, and Kennebunkport. Commercial fishers, if they caught bluefin at all, sold them for cat food when they could and trucked them to town dumps when they couldn't. Japanese buyers changed all of that. Since the 1970s, commercial Atlantic bluefin tuna fisheries have been almost exclusively focused on Japanese markets like Tsukiji.

In New England waters, most bluefin are taken one fish at a time, by rod and reel, by hand line, or by harpoon – techniques of a small-scale fisher, not of a factory fleet. On the European side of the Atlantic, the industry operates under entirely different conditions. Rather than rod and reel or harpooning, the typical gear is industrial – the purse seiner (a fishing vessel closing a large net around a school of fish) or the long line (which catches fish on baited hooks strung along lines played out for many miles behind a swift vessel). The techniques may differ from boat to boat and from country to country, but these fishers are all angling for a share of the same Tsukiji yen – and in many cases, some biologists argue, a share of the same tuna stock. Fishing communities often think of themselves as close-knit and proudly parochial; but the sudden globalization of this industry has brought fishers into contact – and often into conflict – with customers, governments, regulators, and environmentalists around the world.

Two miles off the beach in Barbate, Spain, a huge maze of nets snakes several miles out into Spanish waters near the Strait of Gibraltar. A high-speed, Japanese-made workboat heads out to the nets. On board are five Spanish hands, a Japanese supervisor, 2,500 kilograms of frozen herring and mackerel imported from Norway and Holland, and two American researchers. The boat is making one of its twice-daily trips to Spanish nets, which contain captured Mediterranean tuna being raised under Japanese supervision for harvest and export to Tsukiji.

Behind the guard boats that stand watch over the nets 24 hours a day, the headlands of Morocco are a hazy purple in the distance. Just off Barbate's white cliffs to the northwest, the light at the Cape of Trafalgar blinks on and off. For 20 minutes, the men toss herring and mackerel over the gunwales of the workboat while tuna the size (and speed) of Harley-Davidsons dash under the boat, barely visible until, with a flash of silver and blue, they wheel around to snatch a drifting morsel.

The nets, lines, and buoys are part of an *almadraba*, a huge fish trap used in Spain as well as Sicily, Tunisia, and Morocco. The *almadraba* consists of miles of nets anchored to the channel floor suspended from thousands of buoys, all laid out to cut across the migration routes of bluefin tuna leaving the strait. This *almadraba* remains in place for about six weeks in June and July to intercept tuna leaving the Mediterranean after their spawning season is over. Those tuna that lose themselves in the maze end up in a huge pen, roughly the size of a football field. By the end of the tuna run through the strait, about 200 bluefin are in the pen.

Two hundred fish may not sound like a lot, but if the fish survive the next six months, if the fish hit their target weights, if the fish hit the market at the target price, these 200 bluefin may be worth $1.6 million dollars. In November and December, after the bluefin season in New England and Canada is well over, the tuna are harvested and shipped by air to Tokyo in time for the end-of-the-year holiday spike in seafood consumption.

The pens, huge feed lots for tuna, are relatively new, but *almadraba* are not. A couple of miles down the coast from Barbate is the evocatively named settlement of Zahara de los Atunes (Zahara of the Tunas) where Cervantes lived briefly in the late 16th century. The centerpiece of the village is a huge stone compound that housed the men and nets of Zahara's *almadraba* in Cervantes's day, when the port was only a seasonally occupied tuna outpost (occupied by scoundrels, according to Cervantes). Along the Costa de la Luz, the three or four *almadraba* that remain still operate under the control of local fishing bosses who hold the customary fishing rights, the nets, the workers, the boats, and the locally embedded cultural capital to make the *almadraba* work – albeit for distant markets and in collaboration with small-scale Japanese fishing firms.

Inside the Strait of Gibraltar, off the coast of Cartagena, another series of tuna farms operates under entirely different auspices, utilizing neither local skills nor traditional technology. The Cartagena farms rely on French purse seiners to tow captured tuna to their pens, where joint ventures between Japanese trading firms and large-scale Spanish fishing companies have set up farms using the latest in Japanese fishing technology. The waters and the workers are Spanish, but almost everything else is part of a global flow of techniques and capital: financing from major Japanese trading companies; Japanese vessels to tend the nets; aquacultural techniques developed in Australia; vitamin supplements from European pharmaceutical giants packed into frozen herring from Holland to be heaved over the gunwales for the tuna; plus computer models of feeding schedules, weight gains, and target market prices developed by Japanese technicians and fishery scientists.

These "Spanish" farms compete with operations throughout the Mediterranean that rely on similar high-tech, high-capital approaches to the fish business. In the Adriatic Sea, for example, Croatia is emerging as a formidable tuna producer. In Croatia's case, the technology and the capital were transplanted by émigré Croatians who returned to the country from Australia after Croatia achieved independence from Yugoslavia in 1991. Australia, for its part, has developed a major aquacultural industry for southern bluefin tuna, a species closely related to the Atlantic bluefin of the North Atlantic and Mediterranean and almost equally desired in Japanese markets.

Culture Splash

Just because sushi is available, in some form or another, in exclusive Fifth Avenue restaurants, in baseball stadiums in Los Angeles, at airport snack carts in

Amsterdam, at an apartment in Madrid (delivered by motorcycle), or in Buenos Aires, Tel Aviv, or Moscow, doesn't mean that sushi has lost its status as Japanese cultural property. Globalization doesn't necessarily homogenize cultural differences nor erase the salience of cultural labels. Quite the contrary, it grows the franchise. In the global economy of consumption, the brand equity of sushi as Japanese cultural property adds to the cachet of both the country and the cuisine. A Texan Chinese-American restauranteur told me, for example, that he had converted his chain of restaurants from Chinese to Japanese cuisine because the prestige factor of the latter meant he could charge a premium; his clients couldn't distinguish between Chinese and Japanese employees (and often failed to notice that some of the chefs behind his sushi bars were Latinos).

The brand equity is sustained by complicated flows of labor and ethnic biases. Outside of Japan, having Japanese hands (or a reasonable facsimile) is sufficient warrant for sushi competence. Guidebooks for the current generation of Japanese global *wandervogel* sometimes advise young Japanese looking for a job in a distant city to work as a sushi chef; US consular offices in Japan grant more than 1,000 visas a year to sushi chefs, tuna buyers, and other workers in the global sushi business. A trade school in Tokyo, operating under the name Sushi Daigaku (Sushi University) offers short courses in sushi preparation so "students" can impress prospective employers with an imposing certificate. Even without papers, however, sushi remains firmly linked in the minds of Japanese and foreigners alike with Japanese cultural identity. Throughout the world, sushi restaurants operated by Koreans, Chinese, or Vietnamese maintain Japanese identities. In sushi bars from Boston to Valencia, a customer's simple greeting in Japanese can throw chefs into a panic (or drive them to the far end of the counter).

On the docks, too, Japanese cultural control of sushi remains unquestioned. Japanese buyers and "tuna techs" sent from Tsukiji to work seasonally on the docks of New England laboriously instruct foreign fishers on the proper techniques for catching, handling, and packing tuna for export. A bluefin tuna must approximate the appropriate *kata*, or "ideal form," of color, texture, fat content, body shape, and so forth, all prescribed by Japanese specifications. Processing requires proper attention as well. Special paper is sent from Japan for wrapping the fish before burying them in crushed ice. Despite high shipping costs and the fact that 50 percent of the gross weight of a tuna is unusable, tuna is sent to Japan whole, not sliced into salable portions. Spoilage is one reason for this, but form is another. Everyone in the trade agrees that Japanese workers are much more skilled in cutting and trimming tuna than Americans, and no one would want to risk sending botched cuts to Japan.

Not to impugn the quality of the fish sold in the United States, but on the New England docks, the first determination of tuna buyers is whether they are looking at a "domestic" fish or an "export" fish. On that judgment hangs several dollars a pound for the fisher, and the supply of sashimi-grade tuna for fishmongers, sushi bars, and seafood restaurants up and down the Eastern seaboard. Some of the best tuna from New England may make it to New York or Los Angeles, but by way of Tokyo – validated as top quality (and top price) by the decision to ship it to Japan by air for sale at Tsukiji, where it may be purchased by one of the handful of Tsukiji sushi exporters who supply premier expatriate sushi chefs in the world's leading cities.

Playing the Market

The tuna auction at Yankee Co-op in Seabrook, New Hampshire, is about to begin on the second-to-last day of the 1999 season. The weather is stormy, few boats are out. Only three bluefin, none of them terribly good, are up for sale today, and the half-dozen buyers at the auction, three Americans and three Japanese, gloomily discuss the impending end of a lousy season.

In July, the bluefin market collapsed just as the US fishing season was starting. In a stunning miscalculation, Japanese purse seiners operating out of Kesennuma in northern Japan managed to land their entire year's quota from that fishery in only three days. The oversupply sent tuna prices at Tsukiji through the floor, and they never really recovered.

Today, the news from Spain is not good. The day before, faxes and e-mails from Tokyo brought word that a Spanish fish farm had suffered a disaster. Odd tidal conditions near Cartagena led to a sudden and unexpected depletion of oxygen in the inlet where one of the great tuna nets was anchored. Overnight, 800 fish suffocated. Divers hauled out the tuna. The fish were quickly processed, several months before their expected prime, and shipped off to Tokyo. For the Japanese corporation and its Spanish partners, a harvest potentially worth $6.5 million would yield only a tiny fraction of that. The buyers at the morning's auctions in New Hampshire know they will suffer as well. Whatever fish turn up today and tomorrow, they will arrive at Tsukiji in the wake of an enormous glut of hastily exported Spanish tuna.

Fishing is rooted in local communities and local economies – even for fishers dipping their lines (or nets) in the same body of water, a couple hundred miles can be worlds away. Now, a Massachusetts fisher's livelihood can be transformed in a matter of hours by a spike in market prices halfway around the globe or by a disaster at a fish farm across the Atlantic. Giant fishing conglomerates in one part of the world sell their catch alongside family outfits from another. Environmental organizations on one continent rail against distant industry regulations implemented an ocean away. Such instances of convergence are common in a globalizing world. What is surprising, and perhaps more profound, in the case of today's tuna fishers, is the complex interplay between industry and culture, as an esoteric cuisine from an insular part of the world has become a global fad in the span of a generation, driving, and driven by, a new kind of fishing business.

Many New England fishers, whose traditional livelihood now depends on unfamiliar tastes and distant markets, turn to a kind of armchair anthropology to explain Japan's ability to transform tuna from trash into treasure around the world. For some, the quick answer is simply national symbolism. The deep red of tuna served as sashimi or sushi contrasts with the stark white rice, evoking the red and white of the Japanese national flag. Others know that red and white is an auspicious color combination in Japanese ritual life (lobster tails are popular at Japanese weddings for just this reason). Still others think the cultural prize is a fighting spirit, pure machismo, both their own and the tuna's. Taken by rod and reel, a tuna may battle the fisher for four or five hours. Some tuna literally fight to the death. For some fishers, the meaning of tuna – the equation of tuna with Japanese identity – is simple: Tuna is nothing less than the samurai fish!

Of course, such mystification of a distant market's motivations for desiring a local commodity is not unique. For decades, anthropologists have written of "cargo cults" and "commodity fetishism" from New Guinea to Bolivia. But the ability of fishers today to visualize Japanese culture and the place of tuna within its demanding culinary tradition is constantly shaped and reshaped by the flow of cultural images that now travel around the globe in all directions simultaneously, bumping into each other in airports, fishing ports, bistros, bodegas, and markets everywhere. In the newly rewired circuitry of global cultural and economic affairs, Japan is the core, and the Atlantic seaboard, the Adriatic, and the Australian coast are all distant peripheries. Topsy-turvy as Gilbert and Sullivan never imagined it.

Japan is plugged into the popular North American imagination as the sometimes inscrutable superpower, precise and delicate in its culinary tastes, feudal in its cultural symbolism, and insatiable in its appetites. Were Japan not a prominent player in so much of the daily life of North Americans, the fishers outside of Bath or in Seabrook would have less to think about in constructing their Japan. As it is, they struggle with unfamiliar exchange rates for cultural capital that compounds in a foreign currency.

And they get ready for next season.

2

French Beans for the Masses: A Modern Historical Geography of Food in Burkina Faso

Susanne Freidberg

In southwestern Burkina Faso, one of the poorest and least-fed nations on earth, the regional cuisine includes recipes for French green beans as well as for fried caterpillars. Although neither food is part of the staple diet, caterpillars are the rarer delicacy, because they have to be collected in the bush and prepared by a knowledgeable cook. French beans are if anything too readily available at certain times of the year. Produced primarily for export to winter-time Europe, many green beans, rejected at the airport, end up in Burkina Faso's urban marketplaces, where they can be bought conveniently bagged, trimmed, and ready for the sauté pan.

Burkina Faso (formerly Upper Volta), like the Sahel region more generally, has hardly figured prominently in the chronicles of world culinary history.[1] In recent history, however, it has become one of several African countries supplying the counter-season and exotic fresh vegetables found in European upscale markets and restaurants. As an example of both Europe's increasingly globalized tastes and Africa's efforts to profit from them, the development of the "Afro-European" fresh vegetable trade has been well documented.[2] But few studies have considered how food consumption patterns in the export regions themselves have changed as a result of their incorporation into the global "non-traditional" food commodity marketplace.

On a general level, of course, the expansion of cash crop production in twentieth-century Africa has made small farmers and farm laborers more dependent on the market for their own food, while international trade and food aid programs have made the continent a bigger consumer of imports. These broad transformations in food supply, however, tell us little about changes in specifically how, or even *what* people eat, much less about changes in food consumption as a social and cultural practice. Yet this history is not necessarily any less rich and complex in poor countries than in North America and Europe, where most historical and sociological studies of food consumption have so far focused.

The twentieth-century history of food consumption in and around the city of Bobo-Dioulasso, in southwestern Burkina Faso, demonstrates this point quite well. Since the beginning of French colonial rule at the turn of the century, the region's diet and foodways have, indeed, been influenced by the "westernizing" forces of the marketplace, missionary education, and both colonial and postcolonial agricultural development strategies. Yet these influences have differed over time and place, and especially during the colonial era they need to be assessed in light of specific European powers' ideological, scientific and strategic objectives in Africa. In addition, food-ways in southwestern Burkina Faso have been affected by regional climatic and land use changes, shifts in the rhythms and places of work, and both regional and transnational flows of people, goods and ideas. The dearth of written records makes it difficult to quantify or even generalize about the effects of these forces on household consumption patterns over time. But this paper shows how qualitative research, attentive to different spaces and scales of change, can illuminate relation-ships between the changing geographies and meanings of food. It also suggests how geography might contribute to the historical study of consumption more generally, especially in places where many day-to-day consumption practices have taken place outside the formal market economy, and off the written historical record.

The first section briefly contrasts and critiques the dominant narratives of modern European and African food histories, and suggests how the latter could benefit from closer attention to the changing geographies of food provisioning at different scales. I then examine the scientific, ideological and practical rationales behind the food and agricultural policies that brought French beans (and other "European" garden vegetables) to West Africa. The rest of the paper then traces the modern historical geography of food in Burkina Faso, in the two senses identified by Graham and Nash:[3] it not only covers the modern era, including the present, but also pays explicit attention to the multiple identities and social-spatial relationships that have "emerged from and made modernity".[4] The first section considers how diet and meal patterns in the Bobo-Dioulasso region have changed during and since colonial rule (1897–1960), due partly to French cultural influences but also to urbanization and related changes in land use and daily work habits. The second section expands the scope of analysis to the national level, and examines some of the more ironic consequences of food and agricultural policies implemented during the era of "high development" (roughly the first 25 years after independence in 1960). The final section looks at how particular forces and manifestations of "globaliza-tion" – namely, regional trade liberalization, and the expanding reach of Western popular media – have raised popular concerns about the affordability and safety of certain foods and social customs.

This paper draws on two broader research projects conducted in Burkina Faso and France in 1993–4 and 2000–1. Due to the paucity and questionable reliability of colonial and even postcolonial documentation of regional food consumption pat-terns in Burkina Faso, the historical account of Bobo-Dioulasso foodways draws primarily on oral histories (which obviously have their own gaps and limits) and archival sources on the town's commercial history.[5] It does not attempt to list or quantify the foods consumed during any particular period, but focuses instead on the different geographic sources and scales of changing dietary norms and practices, including those in the quite recent past.

Food Narratives: Getting Worse All the Time?

On the table, the modern histories of African and European diet and foodways have long been closely linked, by crop and technology transfer as well as trade.[6] As narratives, however, these histories appear to diverge nearly from the moment of contact.[7] Between the fifteenth and early nineteenth centuries, the transatlantic slave trade brought labor and African knowledge to the plantation colonies of the New World, but left African agricultural societies depopulated and strife-ridden.[8] By the late nineteenth century, Africa itself had become an important supplier of Europe's cocoa, coffee, tea and sugar. Though not nutritional staples, the tropical stimulants became central to certain European dietary habits and social customs.[9] Along with African citrus and bananas, they were originally considered luxuries, but became goods that the working classes bought through good times and bad. The popularization of Europe's "fruits of empire" is one chapter in a larger narrative about rising consumer expectations, and about governments, markets and industries increasingly capable of meeting them. In a word, it is a narrative of progress.[10]

The dominant narrative of modern African food supply, by contrast, is one of nearly chronic material crisis and cultural loss. Colonial era taxation and conscription took labor and land away from food production in many agro-export regions, leading in some places (among them the Sahel) to environmental damage and repeated bouts of famine.[11] European traders and colonizers also introduced foreign crops, some of which the locals were forced to grow, and foreign dishes and processed foods, some of which became associated with elite status. Wheat bread, for instance, became a popular if not universally affordable food in cities throughout much of tropical Africa, where agroclimatic conditions for growing wheat are hardly ideal.[12]

Postcolonial food aid programs only deepened Africa's "wheat trap" – that is, the dilemma faced by African governments whose politically influential urban populations had become hooked on imported foodstuffs.[13] Corporate marketing of processed commodities (tomato paste, condensed milk, margarine) further encouraged rural as well as urban households to abandon locally produced alternatives.[14]

Import dependency, combined with famine and drought in the 1970 and 80s, provided abundant material for an Africanist "food crisis" literature.[15] In much of this literature, the very indicators of European progress were portrayed as evidence of a deeply African problem: namely, big governments that intervened in food marketing, big merchants that put the squeeze on small farmers, and urban consumers who wanted to breakfast on baguettes and Nescafe, even though millet gruel would have been much more prudent. This narrative of blame in turn provided justification for the initially quite draconian economic reform policies imposed by the International Monetary Fund and World Bank from the mid-1980s onwards.[16] The policies aimed, among other things, to correct artificially cheap urban food prices, and to force cutbacks in food imports. They provoked food riots and the fall of fragile regimes,[17] and over a somewhat longer term they made life harder for the urban poor.[18] Although the 1990s proved a better decade for overall food security than the 1980s in a number of countries (among them Burkina Faso), the continent's grain shortfalls continued to fuel calls for urgent measures, especially on the part of biotechnology proponents.

My objective here is not to assess either the accuracy of the crisis literature analyses or the effectiveness of the policy response.[19] Nor do I want to minimize the severity of the hunger and shortages facing certain regions. Rather I want to suggest that the overwhelmingly negative portrayal of modern African foodways – in terms of deprivation, resource deterioration, and undeserved urban appetites – obscures, albeit unintentionally, a much more complex alimentary history. Especially as historians and sociologists look increasingly to European cuisine and food customs for insights into broader political and social developments, the absence of any comparable appreciation of African foodways contributes, I believe, to the perception of the continent as a place *still* without history.[20]

Part of the problem lies in the scarcity of written records. While some nineteenth-century explorers and traders in Africa noted what they saw in markets, or what they were served by their hosts, careful documentation of different groups' diets and culinary habits are almost nonexistent prior to the twentieth century.[21] Even colonial era ethnographies, with a few exceptions, tended to give food and cooking short shrift. Audrey Richards' study of the Bemba of Northern Rhodesia (now Zambia) was extraordinary for its time because she not only recorded the prosaic details of what people ate when, where and with whom; she also linked Bemba malnutrition to changing rhythms and spaces of work, on both a daily and seasonal scale.[22] In particular, she argued that male seasonal migration to mining jobs in the Copperbelt had undermined the traditional *chitemene* farming system (a form of shifting agriculture), without spurring the development of local food markets. Richard's detailed records (many of which were never published) enabled Henrietta Moore and Meghan Vaughn to conduct a feminist restudy of the same area, helping to make the twentieth-century food history of Northern Zambia one of the most thoroughly documented on the continent.[23] This history makes clear, moreover, how both food consumption patterns and people's understanding of them have been affected by multiple levels of geographic change. These include changes in daily journeys-to-work, in regional demography and land-use, and in the broader ideological and political economic influences under European colonial rule.

Within geography, of course, this kind of multi-scalar historical analysis is nothing new; indeed it is one of the core methodological frameworks of political ecology.[24] Africanist political ecology, however, has traditionally focused on how the social and material dynamics of *production* (of food and other goods) transform localities and relations across space; its perspective treats changes in consumption – dietary and otherwise – as results of these processes.[25] Yet an abundant literature on commodity culture and consumerism (in which Africa, again, makes only rare appearances) shows how the meanings of consumption act as history-making forces in their own right.[26]

The French Bean Connection: Acclimatizing to Empire

In the history of French colonialism in Africa, the meanings that French consumers attached to particular foods mattered from an early date. They figured importantly into French colonial efforts to promote European vegetable production in the tropics, as well as into the closely linked efforts of French scientists exploring the possibilities of plant, animal and human acclimatization. The activities of the *Société Zoologique d'Acclimatisation*, founded in 1854, initially focused on enriching French agriculture and food supply through the import of exotic species, both plant and animal. But French naturalists such as Isidore Geoffroy Saint-Hilaire (the society's founder) also emphasized how much acclimatization research could contribute to the project of empire-building.[27] The successful colonization of tropical climes required knowledge of how to adapt crop and livestock species to new environmental conditions. Settlers needed a reliable and palatable food supply, and colonial economies needed crops suitable for export.

The Society's earliest and most ambitious colonial acclimatization activities took place in Algeria, where they sought to replace a centuries-old tradition of wheat, wine and olive production with tropical crops, such as coffee and spices, which would complement rather than compete with French farm goods.[28] Although the colony's French settlers did not share the botanists' and hydrological engineers' vision of a "tropicalized" Algerian agriculture, they did begin producing counter-season crops for the Parisian market, among them green beans.[29]

By the turn of the century, more modest experimental gardens (*jardins d'essai*) were multiplying across France's expanding colonial empire in West and Central Africa.[30] Although modeled after *jardins d'essai* in France, the African sites typically doubled as *potagers* (kitchen gardens) for local colonial officials, and their diverse crop mix included vegetables that the officials themselves habitually ate in France, such as *haricot vert*. These were not considered luxuries, but rather dietary necessities in places where local vegetation seemed strange and savage.[31] As one Madagascar colonial journal reported:

> The cultivation of vegetables in hot countries is indispensable for the hygiene of Europeans who are called to live in them. If, in certain intertropical regions, the native is content to use the plants that he finds at his door... one of our biggest preoccupations when we move to the colonies is to introduce and grow at least some of the many and excellent vegetables that we possess in our temperate country. This responds to a true need. It is necessary, from the point of view of health in the hot countries, to give great priority to vegetables in the diet...[32]

The idea that vegetables in the diet were necessary to "health in hot countries" – and thus to the larger project of acclimatizing Europeans to life in the tropics – was based on early twentieth-century theories of nutrition and "moral hygiene". It marked a significant departure from nutritional theories of a half-century earlier, when the influential German chemist Liebig briefly convinced doctors and army rations-planners that meat was the ideal human food, especially in trying climates and physical conditions.[33] The colonial hygiene propounded in turn-of-the-century popular manuals and medical texts drew on Pasteurian bacteriology, revised theories (contra Liebig) of human metabolism, and the testimonies of colonial administrators and military men who had lived to tell about their postings in the disease-ridden zones of equatorial Africa and Asia.[34]

The general tone of advice was overtly moralistic: good health in the tropics required moderated passions and "very careful living".[35] But this included careful nutrition; the texts counseled Europeans to eat lightly, and consume less meat, fat and alcohol than they would at home. One British army medical journal suggested following the French example:

> ...in the Tropics, where it is desirable to restrict the amount of meat consumed, English folk might with great advantage take lessons from our neighbors across the channel, by introducing to their tables "plats" of vegetables served up alone, and flavoured with some tasty stock, or simply a little butter. Well cooked, and served piping hot, such dishes are most tempting and wholesome...[36]

Hygienists generally recommended fresh vegetables over dried, provided they were carefully washed and, as suggested above, "well cooked". Indeed, once germ theory made clear that fresh fruits and vegetables did not themselves cause typhoid or cholera, hygienists' warnings shifted to the need for vigilance in the garden and kitchen, where native workers' presumably dirty habits might contaminate the food.[37] This advice nourished a whole new set of fears.[38] But it also indicated to colonial officials and settlers that, with careful control of tropical nature and tropical labor, it was both possible and desirable to bring the European garden to the colonies.

The Growth of a Garden City

Colonial officials as well as missionaries planted gardens around their settlements all across French West Africa.[39] The local agroclimatologies, however, were varied and not always ideal for gardening and eating à la français. In the Sahelian region, the main limiting factor was (and remains) year-round water supply, as rain falls only three months of the year. By this measure, the region around Bobo-Dioulasso offered relatively good conditions for dry-season horticulture, due to a network of small rivers.[40] But the region's earliest known inhabitants, the Bobo, traditionally produced most of their food during the June–August rainy season.

From the sixteenth until the late nineteenth century, the town of Bobo-Dioulasso itself served as an important market for itinerant Dioula and Hausa merchants, who transported gold and kola nuts from the southern forest zones and salt from the northern desert. The Bobo, however, had little to do with this long-distance commerce. They prided themselves on their skills as millet farmers (they called themselves "the cultivating people", or san-san) and also hunted, gathered wild foods, and in some places fished (the Houet river, which runs through Bobo-Dioulasso itself, was once a reliable source). Although the mid-nineteenth century explorer Binger observed Bobo village women selling shea nut butter and other prepared foods to passers-by, their own diet relied on the market for little besides salt.[41]

Like the diets of most African agrarian societies, the Bobo's fits into the "core-fringe" structure described by Mintz.[42] As in much of the Sahel, this diet has historically centered on millet, typically prepared as a stiff porridge (to). Unlike societies in more arid Sahelian regions, the Bobo have also traditionally cultivated alternative starches such as yams, sorghum and fonio (Digitaria exilis), and maize especially (also made into to) has become increasingly commonplace since the mid-twentieth century. Rice and potatoes (both sweet and Irish) are well-liked albeit more expensive core foods, cultivated in only a few localities near Bobo-Dioulasso. Of all the starch crops, however, millet alone figures centrally in Bobo mythology and seasonal ceremonies.[43]

In principle, responsibility for produced or purchased staple grains belongs to men. In practice it often falls to women, who are also expected to grow, gather or buy the ingredients for the daily sauce or soup. Like other "fringe" foods, the sauce makes a bland and (in the case of *to*) grainy starch dish more nutritious and palatable. Even though it provides relatively few calories, the sauce is a critical part of a "proper meal" – in Bobo society as in other parts of Africa – and a woman's sauce-making ability is highly valued.[44] But the definition of a good sauce has changed greatly over the last century.

Although the Portuguese had brought tomatoes and other New World vegetables to coastal West Africa centuries before, these foods had not, by the late nineteenth century, made their way into the culinary repertoire of Sahelian peoples like the Bobo.[45] According to the accounts of elderly Bobo women, sauces in their mothers' time were relatively simple. Except for salt and greens or peppers that some women cultivated in small kitchen gardens, everything came from the bush. A typical sauce might contain baobab leaves or a local spinach-like vegetable (fresh or dried, depending on the season), plus shea butter (made from the nut of the *shea* tree), *soumbala* (a pungent spice made from the seeds of the *nere* tree), salt, and occasionally fish or game meat.

The French first occupied the Volta region in 1897, mainly in order to secure a labor supply for plantations elsewhere in French West Africa.[46] The early years of colonial rule intruded relatively little on Bobo food provisioning practices. Although the central and northern provinces of Upper Volta appeared too arid for export crops besides cotton, the French considered the Bobo-Dioulasso region the colony's future *panier* (food basket). Soon after establishing a provincial administrative base in the town itself, French officials began planting imported seeds near their settlement. Agricultural ministry records from as early as 1903 reported success with a wide range of crops, from green beans and potatoes to sweet peas and strawberries.[47]

After the outbreak of World War I, the need to feed the thousands of African and French soldiers stationed at Bobo-Dioulasso's military camp, as well as expatriates in the region's other administrative outposts, led to more systematic efforts to increase local horticultural production. Alongside the river Houet, the provincial agricultural ministry built small dams and irrigation canals, and forced nearby villagers to cultivate, among other things, potatoes and green beans. The ministry provided seeds, but forbid villagers to sell their harvests. Instead they were requisitioned by the colonial authorities.[48]

Villagers learned a taste for potatoes and other new garden crops by eating whatever they were not required to deliver to the authorities nor able to sell on the local vegetable "black market".[49] Colonial officials admitted in their records that the combination of forced labor and crop requisitions (which included millet) took a heavy total on the local population. In all likelihood, then, the potato entered their diet under conditions of penury not terribly different from those prevailing when the potato won acceptance among wheat-eating Western Europeans in the eighteenth century.[50] Some children also learned new tastes as part of their formal education; by the 1930s European-style vegetable gardening was a required subject at all the local schools, intended not only to teach the local peasantry "improved" farming and nutrition, but also to provision the school canteens at minimal cost.

After the completion of a rail line to Abidjan (the capital of Côte d'Ivoire) in 1934, several trade firms opened shop in Bobo-Dioulasso. The expatriate European and Lebanese population increased, as did the availability of imported foodstuffs, such as sugar, coffee, tea, and wheat flour. Until the end of World War II, expatriates were the main consumers of these goods, as relatively few African households had much disposable income. After the war, however, forced labor and local trade restrictions were abolished, and the city entered an economic and demographic boom period.

A burst of French investment brought new schools, expanded government services, and a few light industries. Bobo-Dioulasso's population grew rapidly, fed by a combination of natural population growth, rural–urban migration, and the settlement of Voltaic war veterans.[51] Many of the veterans invested their pensions in trade, transport companies, and commercial farming.[52] Like the town's mission-schooled African civil servants, they had been exposed to Western (and particularly French) dietary habits, and had the means to adopt at least some of them.

To what extent these new African urban consumers did, in fact, start eating French-style meals is impossible to trace in any quantitative fashion. But as in other Francophone African cities, foods such as baguettes, omelettes and café au lait have since become standard menu items at Bobo-Dioulasso's open-air cafes, many of which consist of little more than a table, a bench, and a charcoal stove. These cafes cater mostly to working class men and students; wealthier families may also have coffee and bread for breakfast at home. But in both elite and poorer households, the "starch and sauce" structure of the midday and evening meals has remained the same, as it has elsewhere in West Africa.[53] Elite meals simply tend to be more abundant, and to include richer sauces.

This is hardly surprising, but also not the whole story. On one hand, the "core-fringe" structure of meals has been the norm for most agrarian societies for most of human history. Post-war urbanization and rural commercialization in Burkina Faso was not accompanied by the industrialization and massive economic growth associated with the North American/Western European shift to a meat-centered diet.[54] On the other hand, the postwar decades did see significant change at the "fringe" of daily foodways, as garden vegetables came to feature more prominently in both the mealtime sauce and between-meal snacks. This change must be understood in light of three distinct but interrelated social-spatial shifts in men's and women's seasonal and daily work patterns.

First, the supply and variety of fresh vegetables increased as Bobo men in hinterland villages converted more and more riverbank and floodplain land into dry-season vegetable gardens. Previously much of this land, which was controlled by the region's founding Bobo lineages, had either lain fallow or been parceled out to individual men for traditional crops such as tobacco and sorghum (for beer brewing). But the provincial administration, faced with a rapidly growing and increasingly politicized urban population, encouraged peri-urban villagers to use their riverine land for dry-season commercial food production. Colonial officials wanted not only more food from the hinterlands; they also hoped to cultivate there a prosperous, politically stable peasantry. The administration offered villagers loans, seeds, and gardening instruction, and beginning in the 1950s it sponsored annual fairs, awarding prizes to gardeners with the biggest cabbages and choicest tomatoes. The city built a covered central market as well as several neighborhood markets, while hotels, restaurants and Lebanese groceries purchased top-end crops such as strawberries, leeks and *petits pois*.

Commercial gardening thus became a well-respected and potentially lucrative livelihood, at least until the region's economic downturn in the 1980s. Garden revenue paid for relatively new needs and wants, such as bicycles, tin roofed-houses, and education for their children; it also went increasingly towards staple grain purchases. As this revenue became essential to household and individual economic security (or, at the least, sense of well-being) in hinterland villages, so did dry-season gardening become central to the daily and annual rhythms of work in those villages.

Second, the expansion of Bobo-Dioulasso's "garden belt" (by the 1980s it included villages 40 km away) not only reflected but also contributed to women's growing participation in the regional food market, as both traders and consumers. Even during the wartime years, women from the town's Dioula merchant families had purchased village vegetables to sell (often covertly) to resident Europeans; in the postwar era, they used their experience and capital to become powerful wholesalers and creditors.

Around the same time, Bobo women began to move out of their role as "helpers" in their husbands' gardens and into vegetable marketing. This negotiated shift in the gender division of labor – indicative of broader changes in Bobo identity and gender ideologies – gave women greater control over their time and their personal income.[55] Women who sold their husbands' produce could use a portion of the revenue to buy daily sauce ingredients; they could also use their time in town to sell firewood, home-prepared snacks and millet beer, and vegetables purchased from other gardeners. Urban expansion fueled demand for these goods not so much because the local population was becoming entirely proletarianized (the majority of Bobo-Dioualasso's residents still have access to land, albeit not always nearby) but rather because it transformed the "time-geographies" of both men's and women's daily lives. More people were eating, drinking and working away from home.

Third, urban expansion increased demand for garden produce because it transformed the ecology of the hinterlands where women had traditionally gathered both food and fuel. Although the Bobo-Dioulasso region appears relatively well-forested and lightly populated compared to the hinterlands of Ouagadougou (Burkina Faso's capital city), older Bobo women remember when thick brush surrounded their villages, and they foraged in groups to scare off wild animals. Now they live amongst orchards, fields, and new residential zones, and certain useful shrub and trees species, such as the *shea*, have become much scarcer. So women either have to spend more time and energy walking and gathering, or they have to rely more on the market for their fuel, food and trade supplies. One dietary consequence is that women do not often prepare foods that require extensive cooking, such as dry beans. The other is an expanded market for cultivated garden vegetables, in place of gathered varieties.

This spatial shift in the source of vegetables has in turn contributed to changing local standards of a *good* sauce. Baobab leaves and other wild greens are no longer everyday ingredients, and many women among the younger generation no longer know how to prepare them. For these women, the preferred sauce is made with cultivated vegetables. Tomatoes, onions and hot peppers are standard ingredients; other vegetables added depend in part on the starch base. Okra, sorrel leaves and eggplant go well on *to*, while cabbage and green peppers are commonly served on rice. The sauce known in Dioula as *Diaba-dji* for example, contains cabbage, onion, eggplant, tomatoes, peppers, garlic, spices, parsley, oil, meat or fish, and other vegetables as taste and availability dictate, such as carrots, turnips, or courgette.

Some of the variation in sauce preparation reflects the culinary influences of immigrants from other parts of Burkina Faso and West Africa. The Gouin of southern Burkina Faso, for instance, are known for a sesame-based sauce (made with tomatoes and fish, and served on rice) while Wolof women from Senegal prepare peanut-based vegetable sauces, or sauces containing mustard-marinated meat.[56]

Variation in the sauce composition is also highly seasonal. During the rainy season, most garden vegetables are scarce and costly, and poorer households especially may rely on dried leaves. But when the markets are glutted with garden produce during the high season (January–February), all kinds of non-traditional vegetables (i.e. carrots, courgettes, and the aforementioned French bean) become more affordable. Women vegetable traders, in particular, often end up adding perishable unsold produce to the evening meal, sometimes in unlikely combinations.[57] Women describe a sauce rich in vegetables (as well as oil or peanut sauce, spices and ideally meat or fish) as preferable to a "clear" or watery sauce, but both women and men say that a good cook, by definition, should be able to make a perfectly satisfactory meal with few ingredients, simply by artfully preparing them. They also say that a good cook does not need manufactured flavorings like Maggi bouillon cubes, but in fact this has become a very widely used alternative to locally produced flavorings, such as *soumbala*.[58]

Although most traditional vegetable preparations are thoroughly cooked, at least three villages on the outskirts of Bobo-Dioulasso have become specialized in the production of salad greens. Lettuce is not considered a very profitable garden crop, but because it grows quickly (30 days) and the seeds can be saved from year to year, it appeals to cash-poor gardeners. During January and February, therefore, lettuce pours into the city. Originally eaten only by expatriates, tossed green salad has become a popular high-season dish both in the villages and in town, where it can be bought ready-to-eat at the central marketplace. For most households, the limiting cost factor is not the lettuce itself but rather all the other ingredients needed to make a decent salad. Oil, for example, is a prerequisite, and lettuce growers in the 1990s remarked how rising cottonseed oil prices hurt their own sales. For young women interviewed in Bobo-Dioulasso, however, a good salad also includes ingredients such as tomato, cucumber, onion, boiled eggs, garlic, parsley, and vinegar or lemon.

Garden vegetables have also been incorporated into all kinds of street foods, from rice-and-sauce dishes to baguette sandwiches to Lebanese kebabs. Even peeled raw carrots, sold by young girls who carry them on head-pans, have become a common urban snack. As in many other parts of West Africa, street foods more generally are an important part of the diet of students, market traders, and the many workers who do not return home for the midday meal, either because it is too far or because no one is at home to cook. Studies of street foods testify to their nutritional and economic significance, but the role of street food vendors not just in preserving but also modifying local culinary traditions (perhaps partly to take advantage of changes in local supplies) deserves more attention.[59]

In sum, a number of regional historical processes have contributed to changing foodways in and around Bobo-Dioulasso. Some of these resulted quite directly from French colonialism. The early French colonials' determination to continue eating at least some familiar foods, for example, led to the introduction of crops and cultivation methods more familiar to the countryside of Provence than to the Sahel. The French also introduced a number of manufactured foods, such as wheat flour and instant coffee, and French ways of preparing them – in baguettes rather than the square bread loaves found in neighboring British colonies.

The resulting changes were significant, but they could hardly be described as simple "westernization". The expansion of commercial vegetable gardening transformed the landscape and economy of the Bobo-Dioulasso region, and thus certain patterns of daily food provisioning. But not all: most households, for example, still shop for food several times a week, if not daily, and mostly at outdoor markets. The town's *supermarchés* are small, as is their customer base. And while "French" vegetables and other foreign foods have become additional or alternative elements in the local diet, they have undermined neither its overall structure nor the central role of domestically produced millet and maize. In fact urban consumption of these staple grains, relative to imported rice and wheat, increased after a currency devaluation drove up the latter's prices in the mid-1990s.[60]

Moreover, certain traditional dishes are valued for reasons beyond affordability. Meals at festive occasions, such as weddings, still feature *to* and sauce, and at "Bobo-Fête" (Bobo-Dioulasso's biennial national cultural fair) recent winning recipes in the culinary contest have included a Bobo sauce made from caterpillars and *soumbala*. In cases where certain local ingredients have been replaced by introduced or imported ones, I would argue it is due at least as much to availability and other practical concerns as to a preference for things "Western". These concerns have arisen as urban growth has transformed the spatial and ecological conditions of daily work, particularly women's.

These geographic changes are not synonymous with the sociological understanding of dietary "urbanization", which in Africa describes the dietary trends (more rice, processed foods and animal products) associated with educated salary-earners, who happen to live disproportionately in cities.[61] Longitudinal quantitative dietary research in Bobo-Dioulasso would likely reveal some of these trends. My point here, though, is that an analysis of urban dietary changes is incomplete if it does not consider the geography of provisioning, which necessarily requires looking at changes in the urban hinterland. It also requires looking at food production and distribution on a national scale – the subject of the next section.

The Great Green Bean Schemes

The first two decades after independence in the early 1960s brought drought, crop failures and hunger to much of Sahelian West Africa. None of these problems were new to the region, but in the context of the Cold War and a general optimism about the possibilities of "techno-fix" development, they provoked an unprecedented aid response from both East and West.[62] In Burkina Faso (then still Upper Volta) much of this aid funded the construction of irrigation projects: reservoirs, dams and irrigation canals in the country's main floodplain areas.[63]

Although some of the irrigation schemes were intended primarily to produce rice for domestic consumption most also included some technical aid to promote dry season horticulture, and in particular green beans for export.[64] Why green beans? First, because the target market was France, which has not only the most regular air freight connections with its former colony but also one of the highest rates of per capita green bean consumption in Europe, if not the world.[65] The *haricot vert*, or French bean, is not a staple food *per se*, but it is a nearly ubiquitous side dish, served at neighborhood bistros, government functions, and holiday meals. Second, the French particularly like to serve the slender beans over the winter holidays, when it is too cold to grow them in France, but nearly ideal weather in Burkina Faso. Third, the labor intensive green bean production cycle generates more jobs than most commercial crops, but does not conflict with rainy-season staple food production. And finally, peasant farmers in certain parts of Burkina Faso already had considerable experience growing vegetables to French standards.

All these considerations influenced governmental and foreign donor efforts to promote green bean production even in irrigated areas more than five hours away (over rough roads) from the Ouagadougou airport. Peasant cooperatives produced the beans on small plots (typically 0·25 to one ha) worked by individuals or households, and the government controlled marketing. French import firms provided inputs and pre-season financing. Up through the mid-1980s, green beans brought modestly better living to villages that had few other sources of cash. Beans also brought the country foreign exchange (though not nearly as much as cotton, the main export crop) and recognition. Until the mid-1980s, Burkina Faso was the second largest African green bean exporter (after Kenya) and its country's label was a familiar sight in Parisian wintertime markets.

But logistical problems plagued the green bean sector from the beginning, especially in the realm of air transport. Frequent flight delays and cancellations resulted in tons of beans arriving in Paris in poor condition, or never even leaving Ouagadougou. The chronic unreliability of Air Afrique was initially tolerated by the French import market, but it generated frustration on all sides. In one now-legendary flight cancellation incident in the mid-'80s, the country's late president Thomas Sankara refused to let the stranded beans go to waste. Instead, he ordered government employees to take bagfuls of them, in place of part of their salaries.

The export sector has since been privatized and liberalized. But transportation problems persist, and some private exporters are notorious for abandoning contracted growers mid-season, leaving them with tons of beans to sell on the open market. Meanwhile production costs have increased, and the competition has intensified. Burkina Faso now competes for the French market not just with Kenya but also Morocco, Senegal, Mali, Zimbabwe and even Madagascar. Prices have dropped, and French importers have become increasingly unwilling to provide advance financing. Although some farmers have entirely given up on export green beans, on the grounds that the prices no longer justify the hard work and risk, others see few other means of earning cash.

During the December-high season, then, thousands of tons of green beans are harvested (an estimated 3,500 tons in 1997), but many never leave the country. Some are simply thrown out or fed to animals, but significant (though unrecorded) quantities end up on the domestic market. Market women buy abandoned and rejected beans at the farmgate and at the airport, then sell them for little more than the price of an equivalent volume of cabbage leaves.

Export horticultural crops do not always become incorporated into the local diet. In Kenya, Zimbabwe and Zambia, for example, there is very little domestic demand (beyond that of the white expatriate population) for green beans or other "white man's" vegetables. In Burkina Faso, however, green bean cuisine is now sophisticated and varied, albeit limited by the cost of accompanying ingredients. In Bobo-Dioulasso, Senegalese immigrants prepare green beans sautéed in butter; in Ouagadougou, they are fried with meat, and near Lac du Bam, one of the country's biggest green bean production zones, reject beans are commonly served mixed into millet meal – a sort of Sahelian risotto.

It is worth emphasizing that green beans are not the only fresh vegetables flooding Burkina Faso's urban marketplaces during the horticultural high season. National economic austerity policies in the late 1980s and early 1990s not only depressed urban consumer buying power; they also pushed more and more people into commercial gardening for the domestic market. In the mid-1990s, market women complained that "these days there are more producers than consumers". This is not the case everywhere in Burkina Faso; in the most arid and inaccessible regions, fresh produce is scarce and costly. But in the cities, an annual glut of edible greenery has become more predictable (and less welcome) than the annual rains. Green beans intended for the plates of Parisians end up amidst the piles of lettuce and tomatoes, accidental delicacies for anyone who buys them before they spoil.

Toxins Near and Far

Lastly, Burkina Faso's modern historical geography of food must be understood in light of the country's position in regional and global markets and media networks. As in Africa more generally, the formation of the World Trade Organization in 1994 raised concerns that the phasing out of preferential trade ties with Europe would leave the country unable to compete against Latin American agro-exporters.[66] In fact, this aspect of liberalization has not significantly affected trade in minor products like green beans. But the EU's more recent efforts to protect its consumers against the potential health risks of an increasingly globalized fresh produce trade (in particular, risks posed by pesticides) has, by contrast, placed low-income agro-exporters like Burkina Faso in an extremely perilous position. The EU has declared "zero tolerance" for certain older, cheaper pesticides commonly used in Africa.[67] So entire export sectors must either switch to new means of pest control or risk an EU-wide ban on their produce (the potential sanction if inspectors in Europe detect illegal residues on a single product).

In response to the new EU pesticide regulations, African horticultural exporters and growers (not just in Burkina Faso) have noted, rightly, that it was the European market's aesthetic and phytosanitary standards – combined with the marketing of multinational agrochemical companies – that got them using pesticides in the first place.[68] Yet as consumers themselves, Burkinabé men and women had no trouble understanding Europeans' growing anxiety about invisible food-related toxins more generally.

Most of the recent food safety literature assumes that such anxieties exist only in societies no longer threatened by food scarcity.[69] In societies where hunger is chronic and famine a not-too-distant memory, the population is presumed to be too poor and poorly educated to care much about carcinogens or other food-borne risks.

But is this assumption valid? It is certainly not based on much empirical evidence from Africa or other hunger-prone regions. It is true that market demand for certified "safe" food such as organic produce is concentrated in the wealthiest strata of the wealthiest countries. Yet it is important to distinguish between people's *awareness* of food-borne risks, their *anxieties*, and their *ability* to act upon them as consumers or, for that matter, as citizens. With this in mind, it is worth comparing the articulation of food safety concerns in contemporary Burkina Faso to other situations where consumer buying power was limited, and where the market had not provided an immediate alternative to an unsatisfactory food supply. This was precisely the situation in mid-nineteenth century Great Britain.[70]

To start, African journalistic accounts[71] as well as my own interviews with women from a variety of backgrounds in Bobo-Dioulasso suggest that poverty and illiteracy do not, in fact preclude concerns about food safety. Although most Burkinabé women do not attend more than a few years of school, their sources of information about food safety are diverse and far ranging. Radio and television news stations (which include Radio France International) report foreign food scares; in early 2000, everyone knew about Europe's mad cows, dioxin chickens, and contaminated Coca Cola, and each story led to musings about what toxic European foods Burkina Faso might be importing. Closer to home, women typically learn certain food safety rules from their mothers as well as from maternity nurses or other health care workers.[72]

Unlike some kinds of women's knowledge related to health and healing, these rules do not have a long history. Rather, they have been developed to deal with the relatively new food risks posed by urbanization, as well as international trade in both foodstuffs and agricultural inputs. Most women know, for example, that they should wash lettuce and other raw vegetables with a bleach solution, because they come from gardens irrigated with polluted river water. In addition, a number of women said that they tried to buy vegetables only from gardens upstream from the city, because the Bobo-Dioulasso hospital dumps waste in the river. Such vegetables are sold on one well-known downtown street corner at slightly higher prices than vegetables elsewhere. According to the women selling them, the premium reflects the fact that their regular clients are willing to pay extra. Buying upstream produce, unfortunately, provides no guaranteed protection against pesticides. Some women expressed concern about the occasional chemical odor on the produce they bought at market. It is common knowledge that the cheapest and most readily available pesticides are those intended for use on cotton and other non-food crops.

Carelessly applied pesticides are just one kind of risk posed by an increasingly commercialized food supply. Burkinabé consumers must also contend with unscrupulous or at least corner-cutting merchants. As in mid-nineteenth century England, an intensely competitive and minimally regulated food market has made adulteration attractive and easy, especially for artisanally processed sauce ingredients such as peanut butter and *soumbala*. Women interviewed in Bobo-Dioulasso said that rather than risk getting peanut butter made from rotten nuts or impure *soumbala*, they preferred either to make their own, or buy only from trusted suppliers. Some women even had their *soumbala* sent from villages in Mali, where they say the quality is generally much higher.

The industrial alternative to these local products is the ubiquitous "cube Maggi". Especially in cities, the bouillon cube has become a common sauce base, and one of the few food products widely promoted through company advertising as well as contests and free handouts (Maggi is a Nestlé subsidiary). But it is also the subject of suspicion and speculation; the ingredients are not listed on the packaging (monosodium glutamate is one of the main ones), and at least some consumers are wary of any products made by a European company primarily for a Third World market. Such goods are the stuff of postcolonial urban legends, rumored to contain substandard ingredients, worms, or worse.[73] At the least, the women I interviewed in Bobo-Dioulasso said that the cube Maggi, like any food full of *produits chimiques*, was simply not good for the health.

Dangerous chemical additives set off Burkina Faso's first twenty-first century food scare, when the national media reported in January 2000 that many *boulangeries* were using carcinogenic leavening agents that neighboring countries had banned two years earlier. Known as Magimix and Excel, these agents produced the kind of fat, fluffy baguettes that many consumers in francophone Africa preferred, even though they hardly resembled "authentic" French baguettes. In the wake of the media report, the Burkinabé government responded with its own ban, and then burned a mountain of Magimix and Excel boxes on national TV. In Ouagadougou, some boulangeries posted large signs stating: "Pas de Magimix!"

In mid-to-late 19th century England, exposés documenting widespread food and drink adulteration and fraud fueled demands for legislative reforms as well as alternative circuits of provisioning. The "pure food" activism of scientists, women's groups and other social reformers led to the passage of foundational national food safety laws and the proliferation of consumer cooperatives.[74] The pure food movement also helped create a new market for large manufacturers and retail chains, one where guarantees of hygiene and standardized quality came to matter as much as cheap prices.[75]

In Burkina Faso, the League of Burkinabé Consumers (LCB) has taken up the cause of food safety, along with related problems such as fraud and scale-fixing. The League seeks not only tougher regulation of the domestic market (where there is very little consumer protection legislation of any kind) but also tighter border controls. Regional trade liberalization in the 1990s, the League argues, opened up the Burkinabé market to the shoddy and potentially dangerous products of its neighbors.

As in the nineteenth century pure food movements, scientists and other intellectuals figure prominently in the LCB's 1500-person membership. But the League faces political and economic conditions much different than those of its European and American counterparts, either past or present. In the mid-to-late nineteenth century, the cleaning up of national food supplies coincided with significant improvements in consumer buying power, and the emergence of well-capitalized companies that could afford to invest in improved raw materials and production processes. Equally important, the popular and trade presses not only publicized and commented on the reform process (thus keeping pressure on legislators) they also provided venues for the companies to advertise their guaranteed-pure products.[76]

Burkina Faso's economy, by contrast, has grown slowly and haltingly for the past quarter-century (1.2 per cent annually on average), and remains dependent on primary commodity exports. Urban consumer buying power, in particular, deteriorated in the mid-1990s, as a World Bank-mandated structural adjustment program and a 1994 currency devaluation led to higher unemployment and inflation. Unlike in countries with large European expatriate populations (such as Côte d'Ivoire), Burkina Faso has not attracted investment by any large supermarket chains. So while resident Europeans and other wealthy urbanites can find reassuringly hygienic foodstuffs in a few expensive butcheries and grocery stores in their neighborhoods, most consumers cannot easily signal their concerns about food safety by, for example, choosing "natural" brands. These alternatives largely do not exist in Burkina Faso, except for a small number of products (yogurt, honey, cheese, solar-dried mangoes) that are made by religious communities or donor-sponsored projects, and are not part of most Burkinabés' daily diet.

In addition, cronyism amongst the country's political and economic elite has made government officials reluctant to crack down on well-connected traders and manufacturers. The LCB president claimed that not even the independent newspapers would cover stories implicating large companies, for fear of losing their advertising revenue. In other words, economic liberalization and globalization have brought Burkinabé consumers more foreign foods and more foreign media reports about food dangers. But these processes have so far done little to foster the kind of democratic institutions that consumers would need to articulate and defend their rights to safe food in their own country – namely, a free press and an accountable government.

Under these conditions the search for safe food has taken two different paths around the market. At the level of day-to-day provisioning, concerned consumers look to domestic and moral economies for trustworthy supplies. Food safety thus means extra work, especially for women. Household capacity to obtain safe food thus depends not only on income, but also on the availability of knowledgeable labor (typically that of an older kinswoman). At the level of the larger (albeit still small) consumer rights movement, the demand for a cleaner food supply has become foremost a demand for cleaner government. Put somewhat differently, the struggle for "consumer" rights has become a thinly disguised struggle for basic democratic rights.

Conclusion

The modern historical geography I have constructed here clearly does not depict the totality of foodways in Burkina Faso. The country's population remains, after all, predominantly rural, and many people never eat French beans or baguettes. A more comprehensive account would discuss, among other things, the diversity of the country's regional cuisines and indigenous plant foods, and the provisioning practices of the country's nomadic pastoralists. This article has instead sought to situate certain kinds of foodways in broader experiences of modernity at the local, regional and national scales. These experiences have been shaped by urban growth and landscape change, the partial commodification of food provisioning, colonial and postcolonial food security and rural development programs, and by both regional and transnational flows of people, goods and ideas. The French bean figures into the resulting modern historical geography not as a major crop, food, or foreign exchange earner, but rather as one example of the complex and ironic reasons for, and consequences of, changing food production and consumption patterns.

More broadly, this selective account has sought to show that beyond the dominant narratives of food in Africa – the narratives of imperiled custom and chronic crisis – there remains much to learn about the continent's diverse modern foodways. More broadly still, there remains much to understand about the spatial and historical dynamics of consumption even (and perhaps especially) in societies where most people, by Western standards, consume relatively little.

NOTES

1 For example, R. Tannahill, *Food in History* (New York 1989), and J.-L. Flandrin and M. Montanari (eds.) *Food: A Culinary History* (New York 1999).
2 H. Barrett, B. Ilbery, A. Browne and T. Binns, Globalization and the changing networks of food supply: the importation of fresh horticultural produce from Kenya into the UK, *Transactions of the Institute of British Geographers* 24 (1999) 159–74, I. Cook, New fruits and vanity: symbolic production in the global food economy, in A. Bonanno et al. (eds.) *From Columbus to ConAgra: The Globalization of Agriculture and Food.* (Lawrence, KS 1994) 232–48, W. Friedland, The new globalization: the case of fresh produce, in A. Bonanno et al., *op. cit.*, 210–31.
3 B. Graham and C. Nash (eds.), *Modern Historical Geographies* (Harlow 2000) 1.
4 C. Nash, Historical geographies of modernity, in Graham and Nash, *op. cit.*, 13.
5 The archives of colonial French West Africa in Dakar, Senegal, the archives of the Bobo-Dioulasso Catholic mission, and the Bobo-Dioulasso town hall archives were all consulted. The first project, conducted in 1993–4, aimed to trace the social history of market-gardening in Bobo-Dioulasso and its immediate hinterlands, and to understand how changing meanings of work in both the gardening villages and the marketplaces were related to broader political economic, social and environmental changes. For this project I interviewed a total of 135 individuals, both women and men, in two gardening villages, and 83 urban-based market women. I also collected several oral histories from village elders. The second project focused on the trade in French beans and other vegetables between Africa and Europe, with particular attention to how particular norms, practices and relationships within this trade have been shaped by both colonial and culinary history.
6 J. Walvin, *Fruits of Empire: Exotic Produce and British Taste, 1660–1800* (Houndmills, Basingstoke 1997) A. W. Crosby, *The Columbian Exchange: Biological and Cultural Consequences of 1492* (Westport, CT 1976).
7 Emory Roe uses the term "development narrative" to describe the "received wisdom" within the development community about the nature and severity of particular problems (i.e., environmental degradation, hunger) and what must be done about them. He suggests, moreover, that in Africa especially, "crises narratives" have long substituted for genuine understanding, helping perpetuate the notion that Africa is exceptionally

crisis-ridden. E. Roe, Except-Africa: postscript to a special section on development narratives, *World Development* 23 (1995) 1065–70.

8 J. Carney, The African origins of Carolina rice culture, *Ecumene* 7 (2000) 125–49. P. Manning, *Slavery and Africa Life: Occidental, Oriental, and African Slave Trades* (Cambridge 1990).

9 S. Mintz, *Sweetness and Power: the Place of Sugar in Modern History* (New York 1986). J. Walvin, *op. cit.*

10 Among the most articulate versions of this narrative is J. Burnett, *Plenty and Want: A Social History of Diet in England from 1815 to the Present Day* (London 1979). Also J. C. Drummond and A. Wilbraham, *The Englishman's Food; A History of Five Centuries of English Diet* (London 1958); Flandrin and Montanari, *op. cit.*

11 M. Watts, *Silent Violence: Food, Famine, and peasantry in Northern Nigeria*. (Berkeley, CA 1983), L. Timberlake and J. Timberlake, *Africa in Crisis: The Causes, the Cures of Environmental Bankruptcy* (London 1985).

12 H. Friedmann, The political economy of food: the rise and fall of the postwar international food order, in M. Burawoy and T. Skocpol (eds.) *Marxist Inquiries: Studies of Labor, Class and States* (Chicago 1982).

13 G. Andræ and B. Beckman, *The Wheat Trap: Bread and Underdevelopment in Nigeria* (London 1985).

14 J. Goody, *Cooking, Cuisine and Class: A Study in Comparative Sociology* (Cambridge 1982).

15 N. Chazan and T. Shaw (eds.) *Coping with Africa's Food Crisis* (Boulder, CO 1988). P. Lawrence (ed.) *World Recession and the Food Crisis in Africa* (Birmingham 1988). B. Rau, *From Feast to Famine: Official Cures and Grassroots Remedies to Africa's Food Crisis* (London 1991).

16 World Bank, *Sub-Saharan Africa: From Crisis to Sustainable Growth—A Long Term Perspective Study*. (Washington DC 1989). For critiques, see J. B. Riddell, Things fall apart again: structural adjustment programmes in Sub-Saharan Africa, *The Journal of Modern African Studies* 30 (1992) 53–68. G. Geiseler, Who is losing out? Structural adjustment, gender, and the agricultural sector in Zambia, *The Journal of Modern African Studies* 30 (1992) 113–39.

17 J. Walton and D. Seddon, *Free Markets and Food Riots: The Politics of Global Adjustment* (Oxford 1994).

18 P. Pinstrup-Andersen, M. D. Bale and H. DeHaen, Food prices and the poor in developing countries, *European Review of Agricultural Economics* 12 (1985) 69–81.

19 Though for critiques of the crisis literature, see M. Watts, The agrarian question in Africa: debating the crisis, *Progress in Human Geography* 13 (1989) 1–41, S. Berry, Food crisis and agrarian change in Africa: a review essay, *African Studies Review* 27 (1984) 57–112.

20 Scholars have looked at European foodways high and low to understand, for example, nineteenth-century bourgeois culture, the emergence of the working class consumer, and Europe's growing cosmopolitanism. R. L. Spang, *The Invention of the Restaurant: Paris and Modern Gastronomic Culture* (Cambridge, MA 2000), P. P. Ferguson, A cultural field in the making: gastronomy in 19th century France, *American Journal of Sociology* 104 (1998) 597–641, A. B. Trubek, *Haute Cuisine: How the French Invented the Culinary Profession* (Philadelphia 2000), S. Mennell, *All Manners of Food: Eating and Taste in England and France from the Middle Ages to the Present* (Oxford 1985), E. Wolf, *Europe and the People without History* (Berkeley, CA 1982).

21 L.-G. Binger, *Du Niger au Golfe de Guinée, par le Pays de Kong et le Mossi* (Paris 1982).

22 A. I. Richards, *Land, Labour and Diet in Northern Rhodesia: An Economic Study of the Bemba Tribe* (Oxford 1939). The only comparable study of food and cooking in West

Africa was conducted in Chad, in great detail, by the French colonial pharmacist, Paul Créach. P. Créach, *Nourrir au Sahel: l'Alimentation au Tchad* (Paris 1993). See also E. B. Ikpe, *Food and Society in Nigeria: A History of Food Customs, Food Economy and Cultural Change 1900–1989* (Stuttgart 1994).

23 H. L. Moore and M. Vaughan, *Cutting Down Trees: Gender, Nutrition, and Agricultural Change in the Northern Province of Zambia*, 1890–1990 (Portsmouth, NH 1994).

24 R. Bryant and S. Bailey, *Third World Political Ecology* (New York 1997) 33. For case studies see R. Peet and M. Watts (eds.) *Liberation Ecologies: Environment, Development and Social Movements* (London 1996), L. S. Grossman, *The Political Ecology of Bananas: Contract Farming, Peasants, and Agrarian Change in the Eastern Caribbean*, (Chapel Hill, NC 1998).

25 For example, D. Moore, Marxism, culture and political ecology: environmental struggles in Zimbabwe's Eastern Highlands, in Peet and Watts *op. cit.* 125–47. R. A. Schroeder, *Shady Practices: Agroforestry and Gender Politics in the Gambia* (Berkeley, CA 1999).

26 M. Weismantel, Tasty meals and bitter gifts: consumption and production in the Ecuadorian Andes, *Food and Foodways* 5 (1991) 79–94. J. Brewer and R. Porter (eds) *Consumption and the World of Goods* (New York 1993). D. Miller (ed.) *Acknowledging Consumption: A Review of New Studies* (Cambridge 1995). For an example of the all-too-rare works on consumer culture in Africa, see T. Burke, *Lifebuoy Men, Lux Women: Commodification, Consumption and Cleanliness in Modern Zimbabwe* (Durham, NC 1996).

27 M. A. Osborne, *Nature, the Exotic, and the Science of French Colonialism* (Bloomington, IN 1994).

28 Osborne, *op. cit.*, chapter six.

29 In order to create a suitably tropical climate, engineers proposed building an inland "Saharan Sea". See Osborne, *op. cit.* and Premier Congrès National de Culture Maraichère Commerciale, 24–25 Mai 1924, Nantes, Mémoires et Comptes Rendus (Orléans 1925) 22.

30 C. Bonneuil, *Des savants pour l'empire: la structuration des recherches coloniales au temps de la mise en valeur des colonies françaises 1917–1945* (Paris 1991) 105.

31 G. Reynaud, Hygiène des Colons (Paris 1903) 118.

32 M. D. Bois, La Culture des Plantes Potagères dans les Pays Chauds. *Journal officiel de Madagascar et Dépendances* (1924).

33 M. Finlay, Early marketing of the theory of nutrition: the science and culture of Leibig's extract of meat, in H. Kamminga and A. Cunningham (eds.) *The Science and Culture of Nutrition, 1840–1940* (Atlanta 1995) 48–76, 51–3.

34 For example, G. M. Giles, *Climate and Health in Hot Countries* (London 1904).

35 D. Livingstone, Tropical climate and moral hygiene: the anatomy of a Victorian debate, *British Journal of the History of Science* 32 (1999) 93–110.

36 Giles, *op. cit.*, 57.

37 W. Anderson, Immunities of empire: race, disease, and the new tropical medicine, 1900–1920, *Bulletin of the History of Medicine* 70 (1996) 94–118.

38 D. Kallman, Projected moralities, engaged anxieties: Northern Rhodesia's reading publics, 1953–1964, *International Journal of African Historical Studies* 32 (1999) 71–117.

39 P. Vennetier, *La Péri-urbanisation dans les pays tropicaux* (Bordeaux 1989), C. Schilter, *L'Agriculture Urbaine à Lomé: Approches Agronomique et Socioéconomique* (Paris 1991).

40 M. V. K. Sivakumar and F. Gnoumou, *Agroclimatology of West Africa: Burkina Faso* (Andhra Pradesh, India 1987).

41   H. Diallo, Introduction à l'étude de l'histoire de l'Islam dans l'ouest du Burkina Faso, *Islam et Sociétés au Sud du Sahara* 4 (1990) 33–45.

42   S. Mintz, *op. cit.*, 9–12.

43   G. Le Moal, *Les Bobo: Nature et Fonction des Masques* (Tervuren, Belgium 1999) 40.

44   Audrey Richards (*op. cit.*) described the nutritional and gustatory significance of the sauce (or relish, as she called it) in some detail; Gracia Clark has also written about the symbolic (and more specifically sexual) import of sauce preparation among the Ga of Ghana. G. Clark, Money, sex and cooking: manipulations of the paid/unpaid boundary by Asante market women, in H. Rutz and B. Orlove (eds.) *The Social Economy of Consumption* (Lanham, MD 1989) 323–48.

45   On the medieval history of West African trade between eco-zones, see G. E. Brooks, *Landlords and Strangers: Ecology, Society, and Trade in Western Africa, 1000–1630* (Boulder, CO 1993).

46   P. Englebert, *Burkina Faso: Unsteady Statehood in West Africa* (Boulder, CO 1996).

47   Archives Nationales de Senegal R5, Rapport sur les cultures indigens maraichéres; les essais de culture, la culture intensive, les industries agricoles, 1903.

48   Archives of Bobo-Dioulasso, *Journal de Cercle*, 1919–22.

49   According to elders in the gardening villages, this market arose in response to expatriate demand for "European" vegetables. Some Europeans came directly to the gardens to buy, but villagers also sold their produce to Dioula market women, who then delivered well-wrapped bundles of produce to their customers in town.

50   F. Braudel, *The Structures of Everyday Life* (Berkeley, CA 1992) 170.

51   Between 1945 and 1965, the population increased from 22,000 to 65,000. *Schema de développement et d'aménagement urbain de Bobo-Dioulasso* (Bobo-Dioulasso, Burkina Faso: 1992).

52   M. Saul, Development of the grain market and merchants in Burkina Faso, *Journal of Modern African Studies* 24 (1986) 127–53.

53   J. Goody, *Cooking, cuisine and class: a study in comparative sociology.* (Cambridge 1982). M.-J. Menozzi, Le bouillion cube, un goût de modernité? (Unpublished MA thesis, Université de Paris, René Descartes, Sorbonne: 1993).

54   S. Mintz, *op. cit.*, 9, 12.

55   S. Freidberg, To garden, to market: gendered meanings of work on an African urban periphery, *Gender, Place and Culture* 8 (2001) 5–24.

56   These recipes were collected with women from various ethnic groups, interviewed in Bobo-Dioulasso in January–February 2000.

57   For example, I sometimes saw women vegetable traders making sauces from wilted lettuce, cucumbers, or cauliflower (an uncommon vegetable there, typically sold only to Europeans).

58   Menozzi, *op. cit.*

59   I. Tinker, *Street Foods: Urban Food and Employment in Developing Countries* (Oxford 1997).

60   K. Savadogo and H. Kazianga, Substitution between domestic and imported food in urban consumption in Burkina Faso: assessing the impact of devaluation, *Food Policy* 24 (1999) 535–51.

61   D. Requier-Desjardins, *L'Alimentation en Afrique* (Paris: 1989).

62   R. Franke and B. Chasin, *Seeds of Famine: Ecological Destruction and the Development Dilemma in the West African Sahel* (Montclair, NJ 1980).

63   V. Compaore et al., *Burkina Faso: développement des cultures irriguées.* (Ouagadougou 1987).

64   The emphasis on rice farming came at a time of rapidly growing domestic demand; per capita rice consumption increased from 4·5 kg in 1960 to 8·2 kg in 1980. But as of the

mid-1990s, Burkina Faso was still importing more than 90 per cent of its total supply of rice. N. Bony, Comment inverser les tendances d'approvisionnement en riz? *Le Journal du Soir* [Ouagadougou], 28–9 May 1994, 6–7.

65 Per capita consumption in 1995 was estimated at 0.52 kg in France. It is actually higher in both the Netherlands and Germany, but the preferred variety in those countries is considerably thicker than the fine and extra fine varieties eaten in France.

66 C. Cosgrove, Has the Lomé Convention failed ACP trade?, *Journal of International Affairs* 48 (1994) 223–49.

67 M.-K. Chan and B. King, *Review of the Implications of Changes in EU Pesticide Legislation on the Production and Export of Fruits and Vegetables from Developing Country Suppliers* (Chatham, MD 2000).

68 This came up often in conversations with growers in both Zambia and Burkina Faso.

69 D. Miller and J. Reilly, Making an issue of food safety: the media, pressure groups, and the public sphere, in D. Maurer and J. Sobal (eds.) *Eating Agendas: Food and Nutrition as Social Problems* (New York 1995). This assumption also underlies Ulrich Beck's model of "risk society". See U. Beck, *Risk Society: Towards a New Modernity* (London 1992).

70 Burnett, *op. cit.*, chapter five.

71 Syfia Press Agency, *L'Afrique, côté cuisines: regards Africains sur l'alimentation* (Paris 1994).

72 Menozzi, *op. cit.*

73 Menozzi, *op. cit.*, 36.

74 M. French and J. Phillips, *Cheated Not Poisoned? Food Regulation in the United Kingdom, 1875–1938* (Manchester 2000), I. Paulus, *The Search for Pure Food* (London 1974), P. Gurney, *Co-operative Culture and the Politics of Consumption in England, 1870–1930* (Manchester 1996).

75 J. Burnett, *op. cit.*, chapter ten.

76 *Ibid.*, French and Phillips, *op. cit.*

3

Fresh Demand: The Consumption of Chilean Produce in the United States

Walter L. Goldfrank

When J. Alfred Prufrock, T. S. Eliot's bewildered and alienated modern Everyman, wondered if he dared to eat a peach as he walked along the beach, surely he focused neither on pesticide residues, nor vitamins and minerals, nor his middle-age spread, nor his food budget, nor the political morality of supporting dictators, nor yet the proprieties or status meanings of consuming relatively expensive counterseasonal produce. Presumably we have come a long way from the confused indecisiveness of poor Prufrock, because we spend millions of dollars to eat peaches year round, and not only peaches but grapes, nectarines, plums, cherries, raspberries, kiwis, and many more. A growing number of social scientists has in fact turned increasing attention to the internationalization of the fresh produce business, not long ago limited to local, regional, and national channels with the exception of a few items like bananas and coconuts.

For understandable reasons – above all, the economic importance of this business to the producing zones in the periphery and semiperiphery – virtually all of this attention has gone to the growing, packing, and transportation end of these commodity chains, and virtually none to their distribution, marketing, and consumption. It is this imbalance I mean to help correct in the following exploration of the consumption of Chilean produce in the United States.

Background

Cultural changes in the core are the driving force of this commodity chain, namely, the changing diet of affluent and middle-income consumers, abetted by the produce wholesalers and distributors who otherwise would have sharply reduced sales volumes in the winter months. But before exploring this process, two background conditions need mentioning: (1) the rise in produce exports as part of Chile's neoliberal economic reorientation, and (2) the aforementioned internationalization of the fresh produce business itself.

Starting with the latter, we can refer to Friedland's (1991) provisional summary of what researchers studying produce internationalization have learned to date. First, with the exception of one product (bananas) and one very small market segment (the "carriage trade," i.e., the ultra-rich, those who once rode in carriages), internationalization is a phenomenon of the last twenty years. The tables presented by Friedland reveal a worldwide quadrupling of fresh fruit and vegetable exports between the early 1970s and the mid-1980s, and growth of at least another 50 percent from that point to the end of the decade. (These tables do not, unfortunately, separate out the intracore and core-periphery dimensions; we know that intra-European commerce comprises an important proportion, much of it intracore rather than involving semiperipheral Portugal or Greece.)

Second, the social usage of the term "fresh" has come to mean "not ostensibly processed," or made into something visibly different, although many human hands have touched the commodities themselves before they reach the consumer. "Sell it or smell it" is the industry watchword, and governmental regulatory agencies police the use of the term "fresh," recently banning its use, for example, to describe reconstituted frozen orange juice. So the cachet of "fresh" may be claimed for produce picked weeks or even months in advance, cooled, stored, and/or shipped with the aid of spoilage-retardant chemicals, handled by workers at multiple job sites. Freshness, then, inheres in the pristine appearance of the foodstuff, not in its space-time proximity to the consumer.

Third, four innovations are driving expansion in this sector: the availability of counterseasonal produce thanks to the development of long-distance cool chains; the growth of a mass clientele for fresh as opposed to canned or frozen produce; further differentiation of the produce market with niches for new varieties as well as new products (so-called exotics); and the possibilities for value-adding at the retail level, increasing ease of preparation as with prewashed and cut salads, precored and peeled pineapples, and microwaveable trays of mushrooms. These last are now available, thanks to a Santa Cruz firm, with a choice of four sauces including an "Oriental" and a "Mexican" option that supermarkets are encouraged to feature in their Chinese New Year and 5 de Mayo promotions.

Taking a step beyond Friedland, one could assert that the internationalization of the fresh produce business implies a large-scale move toward the wholesalers' and retailers' dream of supplying affluent consumers everywhere with a complete line of temperate and tropical commodities throughout the calendar year, yet another triumph of capitalism over nature. As Dole has recently advertised in *The Packer* (November 7, 1992, p. C3), weekly newspaper of the US produce business, "Dole delivers variety... all year long" (ellipsis in the original).

The second necessary context for my subject is the neoliberal reorientation of the Chilean economy, in which fresh opposite-season produce exports have come to account for a significant proportion of both foreign exchange (about 10 percent in 1989) and waged employment (perhaps as much as 15 percent). In Goldfrank's previous papers (1990, 1991) and in collaborative work with Gomez (1991) – not to mention his and others' publications (e.g., Gomez and Echenique 1988) – many aspects of the Chilean produce boom have been analyzed. In terms of commodity chains (see Figure 3.1),

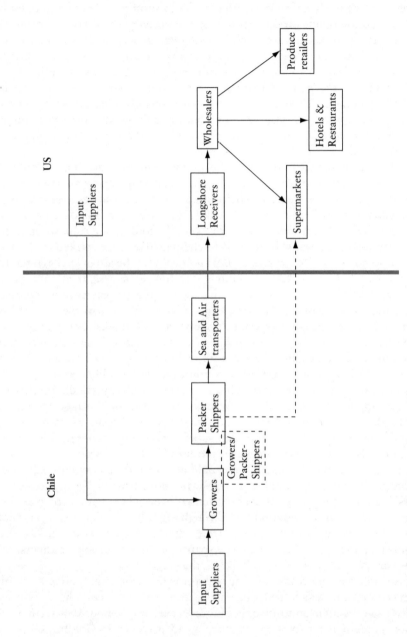

Figure 3.1 The Commodity Chain in Chilean Fruit

these include such upstream activities as research and development, technological transfer, input sourcing, infrastructural investments, and labor supply. They also include the organization of production itself among large, sometimes multinational corporations as well as medium and small growers, and their relations with packers and shippers. We have discussed as well some downstream activities, especially pertaining to transportation. Finally, we have analyzed the changes in Chile's rural class structure that facilitated the emergence of both a dynamic market in land and a desperate low-wage labor force. But the marketing and consumption of Chilean fruit, which supplies the northern hemisphere during its winter months, have received only passing mention, enumeration of some aspects, no more.

Diet for a Small Segment

In the prior work cited above, we have insisted, as has Friedland in his appraisal of internationalization, that a major factor causing the produce boom is dietary change among the core countries' upper and middle strata. Gomez (1991: 10) went so far as to call this change "*the* essential new fact" accounting for the Chilean agroexport boom, as if to remind his Chilean audience of their dependence on the possibly capricious preferences of distant strangers. There are many ways to characterize this shift in the upper third or so of the income hierarchy. As Mintz (1985: ch. 5) pointed out in his pioneering study of the promotion and consumption of sugar, the meat-and-potatoes habit of the wealthier Euro-Americans in the modern era represented an historical and cross-civilizational departure from the standard dietary pattern of "grain-plus," in which a core carbohydrate such as wheat or rice is "fringed" by other foods such as vegetables or fish, with (presumably scarce) meat reserved for festive occasions. The current shift, however, encompasses more than a departure from a carnicentric diet, and differs from a return to the cross-civilizational norm that preceded that diet: it includes variations on an entire complex of such value themes as nutrition, health, fitness, convenience, and cosmopolitanism. And this shift is happening very fast: the Harvard health letter reported last year that whereas, in 1982, 56 percent of faculty at the Medical School ate red meat four or more times a week, in 1991 that proportion had dropped to 11 percent (*Nutrition Action* 19, April 3, 1992, p. 2).

The following is another example, this one from the mass media: advice columnist Abigail Van Buren, "Dear Abby," recently printed a letter from a Minnesota woman (*San Francisco Chronicle*, March 27, 1992) outlining a contemporary version of the Jack Sprat problem. She and her fiancé are compatible in all but their eating habits. She loves fruits and vegetables and ethnic foods, while he is a meat-and-potatoes man who won't try anything new or different. She worries that after marriage, this incompatibility will cause serious problems.

In response, Ms Van Buren recommends seeing a dietician or the prospective family physician, tells her huge readership that the traditional US diet is worse than unhealthy, and predicts that unless the man wises up, the couple "will disagree three times a day for as long as [the] marriage (or [the] husband) lasts." Are we witnessing the emergence of a "produce-stand" ethic?

One measure of how important fresh produce has become is the volume of market research and economic analysis it has generated. Relying on much of this research, Roberta L. Cook (1990: 67–70) tells us the following about contemporary trends in the demand for produce. New product development in food accelerated in the 1980s, with 12,055 innovations in 1989 alone; the average supermarket produce department sold 65 items in 1975 but 210 in 1988. The changing age structure of the US population augurs well for produce sellers: those 55–64 years old buy 39 percent more fresh fruit and 34 percent more fresh vegetables than the national average. Aging baby boomers will want higher quality as well as larger quantities as they move into their peak earning years. Cook documents the increasingly clear division into "upscale and downscale markets," citing a Food Institute finding that households above the $40,000 income mark spend over 25 percent more on fresh produce than those earning between $20,000 and $30,000. She cites data showing an inverse correlation between household size and produce expenditure and indicating the preference of working women for convenience foods. She documents the trend toward fresh ("1988 was the first year that fresh vegetable consumption equalled processed" [p. 69]) and suggests that sometimes increasing health and nutrition awareness conflicts with the desire for convenience. What she fails to say, however, is that this is precisely where fresh fruit comes in, as it requires virtually no preparation beyond washing (apples or stone fruit, such as peaches) or peeling (bananas) or cutting (melon). In this sense fresh fruit is no less inconvenient than canned or frozen, unlike most vegetables, which require cooking and often seasoning. Table grapes, by far the single most important Chilean agricultural product shipped to the United States, have yet another advantage: they lend themselves to perfectly calibrated portion control.

Ports of Entry

Looking again at Figure 3.1, one sees first off that this is a particular type of buyer-driven commodity chain, in which the importer/wholesalers, some of whom are vertically integrated into exporting transnationals like Dole, are the key enterprises. Second, one notes that a considerable portion of the inputs to the primary production process in Chile comes from sources in the United States (research and development, chemicals) and Europe (chemicals). Third, it is clear that the wholesale and retail end of the chain has importance as a locus of profits, as Gereffi and Korzeniewicz (1990) show for semiperipheral footwear exports.

Selected inputs aside, the first US link in the commodity chain is at harborside, principally greater Philadelphia for markets east of the Rockies, and Los Angeles/ Long Beach for the west coast. Although both Chile and California face the Pacific Ocean, shipping from Valparaiso is about a day shorter and ten cents a box cheaper to the *eastern* United States – due north via the Panama Canal. Consumption of Chilean fruit is greater in both the East and West than in the Midwest and South by 40–50 percent, partly because of differences in class composition, partly because of lags in cultural trends, and partly ease of transportation from these ports of entry, which have major advantages in cooled warehousing capacity and refrigerated trucking services. The port of Houston has failed to make much of a mark in the receiving business, and with the Chapter 11 reorganization of International Cargo Network, its major importer, it appears that for 1992 and 1993 at least, Philadelphia and Los Angeles/Long Beach will handle virtually all of the deal. But Gulfport, Mississippi, and Tampa, Florida, are bidding to compete in the southern sector of the eastern market; the former already handles large volumes of Central American fruit and offers two fewer days and hence $40,000 to $50,000 lower costs per ship than Philadelphia. And other cities are bidding to compete with the established centers: Seattle, Tacoma, San Francisco, and San Diego on the Pacific; New Bedford, Wilmington, Baltimore, Norfolk, and Miami on the Atlantic.

Initial inquiry into the port activities of unloading, inspecting, warehousing, and trucking Chilean fruit led me to a paper presented by LaRue and Heinzelmann (1990) at the 2nd International Fruit Congress held in Santiago in late November 1990. Its authors are Executive Director of the Philadelphia Regional Port Authority and Director of Port Operations of the Delaware River Port Authority (DRPA); the DRPA has an office in Santiago to facilitate its dealings with Chilean shippers and growers. The major impression derived from this paper is the strength of the transnational sectoral alliance between Chileans and North Americans. The paper describes how over the previous three years the latter used the ideology of free trade to lobby Congress and the federal bureaucracy to remove the restrictions of US marketing orders limiting imports that might compete with California produce. It recounts multimillion-dollar public investments on both banks of the Delaware, investments in warehouse modernization and refurbishing, cooling, and heating facilities. It boasts of Philadelphia's having dispatched 25,000 truckloads of Chilean fruit during the previous (1989–90) season, 1,500 a week at the peak, via its excellent freeway system and its enormous fleet of "reefer" (i.e., refrigerated) trucks. It mentions that within a 300-mile radius of Philadelphia live 60 million consumers, or 25 percent of the US market; within 500 miles, 36 percent; within 1,000 miles, sixty-four percent. It describes an industry-wide conference at which (1) the ILA assured that not even a strike would interfere with the unloading operations, (2) the federal government assured that inspection would be routine and speedy, and (3) the port assured that it could manage increasing volumes of fumigation. In addition, stevedores were to receive increased training in how to handle delicate produce so as to minimize damage, and newspapers' food editors were to attend another round of workshops to further publicize the commodity. Then comes perhaps their most revealing datum: Chilean fruit represents about 700,000 man-hours of dockwork alone, more than one-third of the port's annual total. No wonder, then, that the DRPA and the Philadelphians are eager to please their commercial allies in Chile.

Wholesaling Produce

To the observer first encountering the wholesale produce business, it appears as a motley array of firms, in terms of both size and degree of specialization. Local, regional, national, and international markets are variously serviced by everything from transnational integrated packer-shippers with brand-name goods to single-commodity specialists. Some firms operate in spatially concrete terminal markets in large metropolitan areas; others bypass this step by delivering directly to supermarket chains' central warehouses (for a detailed description, see How, 1991). In terms of handling Chilean produce, the giant multinationals Dole and Chiquita-Frupac deal directly with giant retail merchants, including their Chilean imports along with all the other fresh commodities they sell. Before its acquisition by Chiquita, Frupac had worked through independent jobbers in California, but in 1991 achieved vertical integration. David Del Curto, the largest of all the Chilean grower-shippers and the only one of the largest firms wholly owned by Chileans, sells to retailers and local wholesalers through Jac Vandenberg on the east coast and David Oppenheimer on the west coast. Another large Chilean firm, with significant participation by Dutch capital, is Frutas Naturales, which markets its fruit under the brand name "Clee." Before the 1991–2 season began, it linked up with Florida-based DNE World Fruit Sales, the largest independent shipper of Florida citrus. This kind of integration appears to be growing in produce distribution, and independents such as Sbrocco International find themselves wholesaling internationalized lines that include along with Chilean grapes and stone fruits such items as Italian chestnuts, Spanish clementines, and Caribbean melons.

Yet another type of player in this market is Pandol, the Delano, California, firm specializing in table grapes, a firm that early on became involved in importing Chilean grapes. In the past few years, in partnership with the Chilean firm Andina, Pandol has started growing grapes in Chile's northernmost producing zone near Copiapo, which yields a harvest in November before the principal zones to the south begin theirs. This privileged temporal niche is similar to that enjoyed by California's Coachella Valley, where the grape harvest begins in early April; the overlap with the end of the Chilean season has caused friction regulated by the marketing orders.

Promotion

Advertising and promotion are essential to the commercial success of new products, and the Chileans have been quick to understand their value. To be sure, nothing in the produce business approaches the megabucks spent by Nike or Reebok to sell athletic shoes. For years the Chileans have concentrated on inexpensive radio spots and in-store displays, but recently the advertising agency representing the Winter Fruit Association and the public relations firm working with the Chilean Exporters Association have been branching out in new directions. For example, video recordings depicting growing, harvesting, and packing are now available for in-store viewing. For the 1991–2 season a Chilean tour was organized for food writers and editors from six major "women's" magazines (e.g., *Ladies' Home Journal*), four major newspapers, and two television food shows. According to the public relations executive, the editors will, among other things, visit Chilean families "so they can learn first-hand that Chilean society is a current counterpart to that in the United States" (*The Packer*, January 11, 1992, p. 4D). In 1992–3, one-third of the $3-million advertising budget will go to radio spots in sixteen major metropolitan markets and another one-fourth to store displays.

Newspaper advertising by supermarket chains and independent grocers is another vehicle of promotion. In the course of the 1991–2 season, Chilean fruit was featured or mentioned almost weekly, sometimes as simply available, sometimes as one of several special bargains of the week, occasionally even as a "loss leader," that is, an item sold at or below cost to attract customers to the store generally or to its produce department specifically. Having followed this sort of promotion for the last few years, my distinct impression is that the newspaper treatment has helped to normalize Chilean fruit, to make it a routinely expectable and affordable item among others. Sometimes the advertisements label it as "Chilean," sometimes as "South American," sometimes as merely "imported." But its treatment is no different from Washington apples, or Texas onions, or other featured products, although it is different from Mexican produce, whose country of origin rarely receives mention in advertisements.

Retailing

Supermarket chains, independents, and greengrocers account for most produce retailing, although restaurants and hotels provide an alternate route to the final consumer. In the latter connection several aspects deserve mention, among them the boundary between the upscale mass market and the carriage trade, and the competitive struggle for preference as a garnish among grapes, parsley, strawberries, and pickles. The presentation of entrees, as shown in photographed spreads in glossy magazines, may include small bunches of grape varieties such as Perlette or Flame or Thompson seedless, for color and for a suggestion of Roman luxury. Restaurant and hotel purveyors tend to be more interested in such air-shipped luxury items as raspberries and asparagus than in table grapes and stone fruit: the whole point of "dining out" (as opposed to fast food or "middle mass" convenience eating outside the home) is to escape from the quotidian and to assert – if only for one evening – one's difference from and superiority to the hoi polloi.

But direct retailing to the public accounts for by far the largest proportion of produce sales, and within this category, chain supermarkets have the largest market share – and it is growing. In Great Britain, nine chains now do 70 percent of the produce retailing, and as Ian Cook (1991) describes, the leaders among them have made significant efforts to increase consumer knowledge and purchases of imports, including exotics he calls "vanity" foods. In the United States, supermarkets have in the last decade increased the size and attractiveness of their produce departments. These are now estimated to account for 15 percent of profits on only 9 percent of sales, and with the exception of milk, shoppers are more likely to make a produce purchase than any other single acquisition, whether they have come to the supermarket on "stock-up," "routine," or "fill-in" trips.

The Produce-Stand Ethic

Here I present fragmentary data from two sources, a professional national sample survey[1] and home-grown semi-structured interviews. Nineteen-ninety-two was the first year in which the national produce survey included questions on fresh fruit imports, a fact that itself is a significant indicator of their rising importance. Consumers were asked if they saw or purchased (% saw/% purchased) New Zealand kiwis (59%/43%), Chilean table grapes (37%/29%), Chilean tree fruit

(30%/21%), and Central American melons (26%/16%). Males were significantly more likely to report having seen and bought Chilean fruit than females (49% to 35% seeing grapes, 40% to 28% seeing tree fruit; 36% to 27% buying grapes, 28% to 19% buying tree fruit).

The data on age are more intriguing, with noticing and buying both more likely in the older generation, but a significantly greater proportion of those who notice also purchasing among the younger age groups. Thus 26% of the 18–29-year-olds saw Chilean grapes in the market, compared to 47% of those over 60; but 20% of the 18–29 group bought them as compared to 33% of the older group. For tree fruit the difference is more pronounced: 22% of the young noticed and 18% bought, whereas among the older consumers 40% saw but only 22% bought. These findings strongly suggest that younger consumers, if sufficiently attuned to currently fashionable theories about the importance of eating fresh produce, are more likely than older ones to buy it from whatever suppliers make it available.

Not surprisingly, residents of the Northeast and West were more likely to see and to buy Chilean fruit than those of the North Central United States or the South. But there were no differences among the regions in the purchasing behavior of those who recall seeing Chilean fruit in their markets. As for income, households with more than $50,000 led the lower brackets in likelihood of seeing and purchasing, although the relationship between income and consumer behavior is not monotonic – the $35K–50K group trails both the $12.5K–22.5K and $22.5K–35K groups. Unfortunately, the data do not say anything about the volume or frequency of these purchases. But they do reveal judgements about quality. Chilean grapes were rated as excellent by 15%, good by 62%, fair by 18%, poor by 1%, and inconsistent by 3%. For tree fruit, the proportions are: excellent, 11%; good, 54%; fair, 23%; poor, 5%; and inconsistent, 6%.

These quantitative data reinforce the hope among Chilean producers that US sales have considerable potential for augmentation in the future. United States winter grape consumption is less than half that of summer, when California supplies the fruit; there clearly exist produce consumers who eat grapes in the summer but have not yet discovered or who cannot afford the Chilean product during the northern hemisphere winter.

As for more qualitative data, in the winter of 1992, I tried to go behind the numbers to discern some of the cultural meanings and attitudes surrounding Chilean winter fruit in the US market. I conducted twenty-eight focused interviews with a nonrandom sample of shoppers and consumers, eleven chosen from my own national circle of acquaintances, the rest accosted in and around local supermarkets. Some excerpts from my respondents' answers deserve quotation (my questions are in brackets).

Norma T. buys Chilean grapes from her New York neighborhood greengrocer and also from a street vendor's cart near her midtown office. At twenty-five, she is a college graduate who scuba dives, jogs, and bicycles; she describes herself as "addicted" to sushi and to highly spiced Asian and Mexican foods. She reports: "I love Chilean grapes, especially the red ones. They're so crunchy, they taste so fresh. [Does price matter?] Not at all, unless it's out of sight. I usually pay a dollar and a half for a nice bunch from the cart on the corner. I used to eat pretzels or bagels or even sometimes a hot dog. No more. No way."

Sarah S. described her discovery of Chilean nectarines as a revelation. Approaching fifty, she works as a middle manager in a Bay Area county's statistical service. With her attorney husband (they are so-called DINKs, double income, no kids), she enjoys a comfortable six-figure household income that allows for frequent dining out, strenuous world travel to eco-tourist hot spots, and more scuba diving. Since she often jogs at lunch hour, she prefers to eat at her desk, typically a meal of nonfat cottage cheese and sliced nectarines.

> The flavor's as good or better than the summer ones from California. I have them almost every day.... They don't cost too much, especially compared to eating out. They make me feel healthy. [Do you worry about pesticide residues or other chemicals?] Not really. Not from Chile. I just associate that country with cleanliness, high standards. Not like Mexico, I'm a little afraid of Mexican cantaloupes and veggies. [You seem to know a lot about produce.] Oh yeah, I have my own vegetable garden and some fruit trees. Some weeks that's all I eat, well, with grains or something. [Do you want to live forever?] Not really. But I can't stand the idea of being inactive or feeble or chronically ill. I mean, when it happens I just want to drop or die in my sleep as healthy as I am right now.

Polly M. gives the appearance of middle-class prosperity as she watches the checker total her grocery bill one February morning. I notice a sizable number of Chilean plums in her cart. [Do you like those Chilean plums?] "Oh. They're from Chile? I didn't know that. Yeah, this time of year you can't get a decent tomato. I buy these for my salads."

Andrea M. is a middle-aged staff worker in a university office. Armed with Chilean grapes, she battles her tendency to gain weight. "It's a treat, you know, something a little special that's better for me than cookies or pastry. I need treats, sometimes more than once a day. Coming from the far North [she is a native of Saskatchewan], I can't believe I'm eating grapes in January. They just help keep me going."

William and Laura H. are Californian political progressives and professional educators with adult children and a substantial income. They admit to obsessing about their food consumption and their budget; they buy Chilean fruit throughout the winter. They explain this seeming extravagance with reference to their overall shopping basket:

> We used to buy a lot of meat, good meat, expensive lean cuts. Now we don't see meat unless it shows up in something Thai or Chinese. Even over a dollar a pound it's [fruit] a lot cheaper than beef or lamb. And there's no cholesterol, zero. [Ever boycott grapes?] Oh, sure, even picketed at the Safeway. For years I would never buy grapes except at a farmers' market. But I got into the Chilean stuff a couple of winters ago, right around when they got rid of the dictator, you know, what's his name, Pinochet. Now I'm hooked. [How's the quality?] Great, really good, except, um, sometimes the peaches. Well, the California peaches can be pretty mediocre too, you know, they're not like in France or Italy.

What are these respondents telling us about themselves and this commodity? Foremost seems to be a concern with health, part narcissism, part dread. To be overweight, or to show "symptoms" of aging, frightens them. It perhaps defies analysis to disentangle the status-marking and social-acceptability aspects of so-called healthy eating from the rational effort to avoid illness, but for this middle to upper-middle end of the stratification hierarchy, red meat approaches tobacco as a taboo. Strong moral overtones accompany the emphasis on healthy eating, as if the working class and the poor deserve to be sicker because they do not take good enough care of themselves. A privatized form of prayerful communion with produce – combined with the ardent pursuit of exercise – has replaced reading the Bible as the individual's path to salvation. But this new "produce-stand" ethic is simultaneously a hedonistic one: both the food consumption and the physical exercise bring sensual pleasure even as they represent self-discipline and self-denial.

Conclusion

It is perhaps worth recalling the original meaning that Karl Marx gave to the concept of the fetishism of commodities, that is, the way the appearance of things conceals relationships of social and economic power. This chapter has attempted to convey the final steps in a long chain of such relationships, which are routinely hidden from the consciousness of health- and status-seeking consumers. In our contemporary conquest of nature, we have come to take for granted the availability of many goods that were once produced by our own or our neighbors' quite visible hands, in plain view, displayed and sold at local produce stands, farmers' markets, or greengrocers. Now the livelihoods of thousands of workers and commercial inter-mediaries depend on the changing and partially manipulated consumer preferences of a global upper stratum disproportionately located in North America, Western Europe, and Japan. Too much knowledge of the exploitation of human beings and/ or the spoliation of nature required to satisfy those preferences could leave a bad taste in their mouths.

NOTE

1   Market research on imported fresh fruit was kindly made available to me by Vance Research Services, which conducts the national sample survey reported annually in *Fresh Trends*, a glossy publication of *The Packer*, the weekly newspaper of the produce business.

REFERENCES

Cook, Ian. 1991. "New Fruits and Vanity: Highlighting the Role of Symbolic Production in the Global Food Economy." Paper presented at the International Multidisciplinary Confer-ence on the Globalization of the Agricultural and Food Order, June 2–6, Columbia. MO.

Cook, Roberta L. 1990. "Challenges and Opportunities in the U.S. Fresh Produce Industry." *Journal of Food Distribution Research*, February, pp. 67–74.

Friedland, William H. 1991. "The New Globalization: The Case of Fresh Produce." Paper presented at the International Multidisciplinary Conference on the Globalization of the Agricultural and Food Order, June 2–6, Columbia, MO.

Gereffi, Gary, and Korzeniewicz, Miguel. 1990. "Commodity Chains and Footwear Exports in the Semiperiphery." In *Semiperipheral States in the World-Economy*, edited by William G. Martin, pp. 45–68. Westport, CT: Greenwood Press.

Goldfrank, W. L. 1990. "Harvesting Counterrevolution: Agricultural Exports in Pinochet's Chile." In *Revolution in the World-System*, edited by T. Boswell, pp. 189–98. Westport, CT: Greenwood Press.

———. 1991. "State, Market, and Agriculture in Pinochet's Chile." In *Semiperipheral States in the World-Economy*, edited by William G. Martin, pp. 69–77. Westport, CT: Greenwood Press.

Gomez, Sergio. 1991. "La Uva Chilena en el Mercado de los Estados Unidos." Paper delivered to the Workshop on The Globalization of the Fresh Fruit and Vegetable System, December 6–9, Santa Cruz, CA.

Gomez, Sergio, and Echenique, Jorge. 1988. *La Agricultura Chilena*. Santiago: FLACSO.

Gomez, Sergio, and Goldfrank, W. L. 1991. "Evolución del mercado agrario mundial: el caso del Chile neoliberal." *Agricultura y Sociedad* 60 (July–Sept.): 13–28.

How, R. Brian. 1991. *Marketing Fresh Fruits and Vegetables*. New York: Van Nostrand, Reinhardt.

LaRue, John, and Heinzelmann, Ray. 1990. "En Preparación para la Temporada 1990/1991 en Estados Unidos." Paper presented at the 2nd International Fruit Congress, November 26–29, Santiago.

Mintz, Sidney. 1985. *Sweetness and Power*. New York: Viking.

4

Coca-Cola: A Black Sweet Drink from Trinidad

Daniel Miller

The context for much of the current interest in material culture is a fear. It is a fear of objects supplanting people. That this is currently happening is the explicit contention of much of the debate over postmodernism which is one of the most fashionable approaches within contemporary social science. It provides the continuity between recent discussions and earlier critical debates within Marxism over issues of fetishism and reification, where objects were held to stand as congealed and unrecognized human labour. This is often an exaggerated and unsubstantiated fear, based upon the reification not of objects but of persons. It often implies and assumes a humanity that arises in some kind of pure pre-cultural state in opposition to the material world, although there is no evidence to support such a construction from either studies of the past or from comparative ethnography, where societies are usually understood as even more enmeshed within cultural media than ourselves. Rather our stance is one that takes society to be always a cultural project in which we come to be ourselves in our humanity through the medium of things.

This fear, at least in its earlier Marxist form, was not, however, a fear of material objects *per se* but of the commodity as vehicle for capitalist dominance, and this raises a key issue as to whether and when societies might be able to resist this particular form of object domination. Although this is a general issue, there are certain objects which have come to stand with particular clarity for this fear, and to in some sense encapsulate it. A few key commodities have come to signify the whole problematic status of commodities. Recently a new theory has been developed to consider this kind of "meta-" status in the form of a book on the history of the swastika by Malcolm Quinn (1994). Quinn provides what he calls a theory of the meta-symbol. The swastika is unusual in that instead of standing as the icon for a specific reference it has tended to stand more generally for a meta-symbolic level that evokes the idea that there exists a higher, more mystical level of symbolization. At first after discoveries at Troy and elsewhere this was the power of symbolism in the ancient past or mystic East, but later this kind of empty but latent status allowed the Nazis to appropriate it as a generalized sign that their higher level and cultic beliefs stemmed from some deep historicity of the swastika itself. Quinn argues that the reason the swastika could achieve such importance is that whatever its particular evocation at a given time, it had come to stand above all for the general sense that there exists a symbolic quality of things above and beyond the ordinary world. This allowed people to attach a variety of mystical beliefs with particular ease to the swastika.

There may well be a parallel here to a few commodities that also occupy the position of meta-symbol. Coca-Cola is one of three or four commodities that have obtained this status. In much political, academic and conversational rhetoric the term Coca-Cola comes to stand, not just for a particular soft drink, but also for the problematic nature of commodities in general. It is a meta-commodity. On analogy with the swastika this may make it a rather dangerous symbol. It allows it to be filled with almost anything those who wish to either embody or critique a form of symbolic domination might ascribe to it. It may stand for commodities or capitalism, but equally Imperialism or Americanization. Such meta-symbols are among the most difficult objects of analytical enquiry since they operate through a powerful expressive and emotive foundation such that it becomes very difficult to contradict their claimed status. So Coca-Cola is not merely material culture, it is a symbol that stands for a debate about the materiality of culture.

The title of this chapter has therefore a specific intention. It is a joke, designed to plunge us down from a level where Coke is a dangerous icon that encourages rhetoric of the type West versus Islam, or Art versus Commodity, and encourages instead the slower building up of a stance towards capitalism which is informed and complex, so that any new critique has firm foundations resting on the comparative ethnogaphy of practice within commodity worlds.

The literature on Coke that is most readily available is that which best supports the expectations raised by the meta-symbolic status of this drink. These are the many books and articles about the Coca-Cola company and its attempts to market the product. Almost all are concerned with seeing the drink as essentially the embodiment of the corporate plans of the Coca-Cola company. A good example of this is an interview published in *Public Culture* (O'Barr 1989). This is held with the head of the advertising team of the transnational agency McCann Erickson, the firm used by Coke. It focuses upon the specific question of local–global articulation. The interview traces the gradual centralization of advertising as a means to control the manner in which its image became localized regionally. In fact the advertiser notes, "it wasn't until the late '70s that the need for advertising specifically designed for the international markets was identified". In a sense this meant more centralization since "the benchmark comes from the centre and anybody that needs to produce locally, for a cultural reason, a legal reason, a religious reason, or a marketing reason, has to beat it". Many examples are given in the interview as to re-takes around a core advertisement, e.g. re-shot with more clothed models for Muslim countries. The interview also included discussions about the phrase "I feel Coke" which represents a kind of Japanesed English for that market and about what attitude worked for Black Africa. Although the advertiser claims, "I don't think Coca-Cola projects. I think that Coca-Cola reflects", the interview satisfies our desire to know what this product is by having exposed the underlying corporate strategies for global localization.

Most of the literature on the company, irrespective of whether it is enthusiastically in favour or constructed as a diatribe against the drink, acts to affirm the assumption that the significance of the drink is best approached through knowledge of company strategy. The literature is extensive and probably few companies and their advertising campaigns are as well documented today as Coca-Cola.

There are, however, many reasons for questioning this focus and questioning the theory of commodity power that is involved in assuming that the company controls its own effects. Indeed Coca-Cola could be argued to be a remarkably unsuitable candidate for this role as the key globalized corporation. Two reasons for this emerge through the recent comprehensive history of the company, Pendergrast's book *For God, Country and Coca-Cola* (1993). The first piece of evidence was that which Pendergrast (1993: 354–71; see also Oliver 1986) calls the greatest marketing blunder of the century. His account (and there are many others) shows clearly that the company had absolutely no idea of what the response might be to their decision to change the composition of the drink in the 1980s in response to the increasing popularity of Pepsi. The enforced restitution of Classic Coke was surely one of the most explicit examples of consumer resistance to the will of a giant corporation we have on record. After all, the company had behaved impeccably with respect to the goal of profitability. The new taste scored well in blind tests, it responded to a change in the market shown in the increasing market share of Pepsi and seemed to be a sensitive response that acknowledged the authority of the consumer. Despite this, when Coke tried to change the formula, in marketing terms all hell broke loose, and the company was publicly humiliated.

The second reason why Coca-Cola is not typical of globalization is that from its inception it was based upon a system of franchising. The company developed through the strategy of agreeing with local bottling plants that they would have exclusivity for a particular region and then simply selling the concentrate to that bottler. It is only in the last few years that Coke and Pepsi have begun centralizing the bottling system and then only within the USA. There are of course obligations by the bottlers to the company. The most important are the quality control which is common to most franchising operations and the second is control over the use of the company logo. Indeed this was one of the major early sources of contention resolved in a US Supreme Court decision. In other respects the franchise system allows for a considerable degree of local flexibility, as will be shown in this chapter. Felstead (1993) documents the relationship between the specific case of Coke and more general trends in business franchising.

Coca-Cola in Trinidad

In some ways Coca-Cola is perhaps less directly associated with the States within the USA, where its presence is taken for granted, than in an island such as Trinidad, where its arrival coincided with that of an actual US presence. Coke came to Trinidad in 1939. In 1941 the British government agreed to lease certain bases in Trinidad for 99 years. As a result US troops arrived in some force. This had a profound effect upon Trinidad, no less traumatic because of core contradictions in the way in which Trinidadians perceived these events. Trinidad was already relatively affluent compared to other West Indian islands, thanks to its oil industry, but the wage levels available on the US bases were of quite a different order, leading to a mini-boom. Furthermore the US soldiers were seen as highly egalitarian and informal compared with the aloof and hierarchical British colonial authorities. In addition there was the presence of Black American soldiers and particularly a few well-remembered Black soldiers who took a sympathetic and active role in assisting the development of local Trinidadian institutions such as education.

The Americans reflected back upon themselves this benign side of the relationship in extracting the Trinidadian calypso "Rum and Coca-Cola", which was a tremendous hit within the USA. There was, however, another side to "Rum and Coca-Cola" that was evident within the lyrics of the calypso itself, as in the lines "mother and daughter working for the Yankee dollar", but are found in more detail in the resentment echoed in the book with the same title written by the Trinidadian novelist Ralph de Boissiere (1984). There were many US soldiers who looked upon Trinidadians merely as a resource and were remembered as brutal and exploitative. At the time many Trinidadians felt that it was the commoditization of local sexuality and labour that was objectified through the mix of rum and Coke.

In general, however, given the ideological needs of the independence movement from Britain that followed, it was the benign side of the American presence that is remembered today. Another legacy is the drink rum and Coke which has remained ever after as the primary drink for most Trinidadians. This not only secures the market for Coke but also makes it, in this combination, an intensely local nationalist drink, whose only rival might be the beer Carib. Before reflecting on the meaning of the drink in consumption, however, we need to examine the commercial localization of Coke.

The Trinidadian Soft Drink Industry

Since Coke always works by franchise, its localization as a business comes through the selection of a local bottling plant. In Trinidad Coke is bottled by the firm of Cannings. This is one of the oldest grocery firms in the island. Established in 1912, it was described in 1922 as follows:

> His establishment became the leading place in Port of Spain for groceries, provisions, wines and spirits. It gives employment to about one hundred and ten persons.... It would be difficult to find anywhere a stock more representative of the world's preserved food products.... An example of the firm's progressive policy in all they undertake is also found in the electrical machinery equipment of their contiguous aerated water factory, where all kinds of delicious non-alcoholic beverages are made from carefully purified waters. (Macmillan 1922: 188)

The franchise for Coca-Cola was obtained in 1939 and was later expanded with the bottling of Diet Coke and Sprite. Coke by no means dominated Cannings, which continued to expand in its own right and developed with Hi-Lo what remains the largest chain of grocery stores on the island. An interesting vicarious insight into this relationship is provided by the Trinidadian novelist V. S. Naipaul (1967). The protagonist of his book *The Mimic Men* is a member of the family that own the Bella Bella bottling works which holds the Coca-Cola franchise for the semi-fictional island of Isabella. In the book a child of the owner is shown taking immense pride and personal prestige from the relationship, viewing the presence of Pepsi as a discourtesy to his family, and showing school groups around the Coke bottling works. The novel thereby provides a glimpse into the earlier localization of Coca-Cola manufacture into local circuits of status (1967: 83–6).

In 1975, Cannings was taken over, as were many of the older colonial firms, by one of the two local corporations that were becoming dominant in Trinidadian business. Unlike many developing countries which are clearly controlled by foreign transnationals, the firm of Neil & Massey along with ANSA McAl together represent the result of decades of mergers of Trinidadian firms (for details see Miller 1997: ch. 3). Both are locally owned and managed and are more than a match for the power of foreign transnationals. Indeed Neil & Massey, which took over Cannings, is clearly itself a transnational although retaining its Trinidadian base. Begun in 1958 and becoming a public company in 1975, it is now the largest firm in the Caribbean. The 1992 annual report noted assets of over TT$1.5 billion, 7,000 employees and subsidiary companies in 16 countries including the USA.[1]

Although ownership lies with Neil & Massey, the bottling section is still, in the public mind, largely identified with Cannings. This relationship is long standing and it cannot be assumed that the local company is dominated by Coke. Cannings represents reliability and quality of a kind that Coke needs from its bottlers. So while Coke would like to push Fanta as its product, and thus increase its own profits, Cannings, which makes good money on its own orange flavour, has simply refused to allow the product into Trinidad. At times it has also bottled for other companies with complementary products such as Schweppes and Canada Dry.

In effect the services offered by Coke Atlanta are largely paid for in the cost of the concentrate which is the most tax-efficient way of representing their financial relationship. In marketing, pricing, etc. the bottler has considerable autonomy to pursue its own strategies. But Cannings has little incentive to do other than follow Atlanta which will often put up 50 per cent of the costs for any particular marketing venture, and can provide materials of much higher quality than the local company could produce. As it happens McCann Erikson, which is Coca-Cola's global advertiser, is present as the sole transnational advertising agency at present operating in Trinidad.

Cannings and in turn Neil & Massey do not, however, represent localization in any simple sense, since both derive from old colonial firms. While they may therefore be seen as representing national interests as against foreign interests they may also be seen as representing white elite interests as against those of the dominant populations in the country which is split between a 40 per cent ex-African, originally mainly though by no means entirely ex-slave, and a 40 per cent ex-South Asian, almost entirely originally ex-indentured labourers (for further details on Trinidad see Miller 1994).

The importance of this identification is clarified when its competitors are brought into the picture. There are six main bottlers of soft drinks in Trinidad. Each has a specific reputation which bears on the drinks they produce. Solo is owned by an Indian family, which started in the 1930s with the wife boiling up the syrup and the husband bottling by hand. It then become one of the earlier larger firms to be outside of the control of whites and it has been either the market leader or at least a key player in the soft drink market ever since. Its main product is a flavour range called Solo and it has one franchise called RC Cola. In a sense while Solo is seen as a local "as opposed to white", the firm of S. M. Jaleel is generally regarded as more specifically "Indian". This is because it has the only factory in the South which is the area most dominated by the Indian population, and historically it grew from roots in a red drink that was sold mainly to Indians. Today its own flavour range is called Cole Cold but it has tried out various franchises such as for Schweppes, Seven Up and Dixi Cola.

The firm of L. J. Williams is regarded locally as the "Chinese" bottlers. As traders and importers they are not associated with their own label but with the brand of White Rock, together with franchises for drinks including Peardrax and Ribena from Britain. The final major company is called Bottlers, though it was recently taken over by a larger firm called Amar. Bottlers have the contract for Pepsi Cola, which at times has had a significant presence in Trinidad but has been languishing with a smaller market share mainly through its inability to find ties with a reliable distributor. Its presence is mainly felt through its links with Kentucky Fried Chicken and the large amount of advertising that has continued despite its lack of market share. It also has a flavour range called USA Pop.

Marketing materials suggest that brand share would be around 35 per cent Coke, 20 per cent Solo, 10 per cent each for Cannings and Cole Cold, with the rest divided between both the other brands mentioned and various minor brands. The industry was probably worth around TT$200 million with a bottle costing 1 dollar to the consumer. The industry sees itself as an earner of foreign currency for Trinidad. This is because the only major imported element is the concentrate. Trinidad is a sugar producer; it also has a highly efficient local producer of glass bottles which manufactures for companies around the Caribbean and sometimes even for Florida. The gas is also produced as a by-product of a local factory. Soft drinks are in turn exported to a number of Caribbean islands, for example nearby Grenada is largely dominated by Trinidadian products and there is some exporting to expatriate populations in, for example, Toronto, New York and London. All the main companies involved are Trinidadian. Indeed even the local Coca-Cola representative is a Trinidadian who is responsible for the company's operations not only in Trinidad but also in five other countries including Guyana in South America. There is also a representative from Atlanta based in Puerto Rico.

When sitting in the offices of the companies concerned, the overwhelming impression is of an obsession with the competition between these firms. Indeed I argue elsewhere (Miller 1997) that it is the actions of rival companies rather than the actions of the consumers that is the key to understanding what companies choose to do. Money spent on advertising, for example, is justified in terms of one's rival's advertising budget rather than the needs of the product in the market. The competition is intense, so that the price in Trinidad is significantly lower than in Barbados where there are only three soft drink companies.

In studying the industry in detail a number of generalizations emerge that seem to command the logic of operations almost irrespective of the desires of particular companies. The first is the cola-flavours structure. Virtually all the companies involved consist of a range of flavours usually made by the companies and a franchised Coke such as Coca-Cola, Dixi Cola, RC Cola or Pepsi. The cola product has become essential to the self-respect of the company as a serious operator, but being a franchise the profits to be made are somewhat less than the flavour ranges where the concentrate is much cheaper.

The second feature seems to be the law of range expansion. Since the 1970s each year has tended to see the entry of a new flavour such as grape, pear, banana, etc., but also a more gradual increase in choice of containers, from bottles to cans to plastic, from 10 oz to 1 litre and 2 litre to 16 oz. In general the company that starts the innovation makes either a significant profit as Solo did with canning or Jaleel did with the litre bottle, or the innovation flops and a loss is incurred. Where there is success all the other companies follow behind so that the final range for the major companies is now very similar. Taking all combinations together they may produce around 60 different products.

This logic is actually counterproductive in relation to the third law, which seems to be that the key bottleneck in company success is distribution. Some of the major advances made by companies have been in finding better ways to distribute their products to the countless small retailers, known as parlours, which are often located as part of someone's house in rural areas. Jaleel, which was a pioneer here through using smaller 3-ton trucks, developed the slogan "zero in on a Cole Cold" precisely to draw attention to its greater availability. This need to streamline delivery is, however, undermined by the increasing diversity of product, since the latter means that a greater number of crates are required to restock the needs of any particular location. This is only one example of the way in which the imperatives within the industry may act in contradiction to each other rather than as a streamlined set of strategic possibilities.

What is Trinidadian about these business operations? Well, if, as in some anthropology, local particularity is always something that derives from some prior original diversity that somehow resists the effects of recent homogenized tendencies, then the answer is "very little". If, however, one regards the new differentiation of global institutions such as bureaucracy and education as they are manifested in regions, as just as an authentic and important form of what might be called a posteriori diversity, then the case is not without interest. Although the various details of how business operates may not be tremendously surprising, it is actually quite distinct from any generalized models that business management with its reliance of universalized models from economics and psychology would like to promote.

In almost any area of business, such as for example, the conditions that control entry of new companies to the market, the situation in the Trinidadian soft drink industry would be quite different from the situation described in the business literature in, for example, the USA (e.g. Tollison et al. 1986). Partly for that reason I found that executives with business training abroad often pontificated in a manner that clearly showed little understanding of their own local conditions.

Some of the particularities, for example the degree to which the public retains knowledge about the ownership of companies or as another example the fluctuating between competition and price fixing, may have to do with the relatively small size of the market and indeed the country. Others, such as the constant link between franchised colas and local flavour groups, have to do with more fortuitous aspects of the way this industry has been developing locally. Overall this industry, as so much of Trinidadian capitalism, no more follows from general models of business and capitalism than would the particular operation of kinship in the region follow from knowing general models and theories of kinship. Profitability, like biology in kinship, may be a factor but only as manifested through politics, personal prestige, affiliation, particular historical trajectories and so forth.

To give one last example, ethnicity alone might seem an important consideration, but Solo, although Indian, is not seen as ethnic in the same way as Jaleel, which is Indian and operates in the South. Yet in terms of politics the positions are reversed. The family that owns Solo has been associated with opposition to a government that has largely been dominated by African elements and severe difficulties have been put in its way from time to time as a result, as for example preventing it from introducing diet drinks; while Jaleel, being Muslim and thus a minority within a minority, has historically been associated politically with the government against the dominant Hindu group of the dominated Indian party.

To conclude – to understand the details of marketing Coke in Trinidad demands knowledge of these local, contingent and often contradictory concerns that make up the way capitalism operates locally, together with the way these affect the relationship between local imperatives and the demands emanating from the global strategists based in Atlanta. Often the net result was that Coke representatives in Trinidad were often extremely uncertain as to the best marketing strategies to pursue even when it came to choosing between entirely opposing possibilities such as emphasized its American or its Trinidadian identity.

The Consumption of Sweet Drinks

The companies produce soft drinks. The public consume sweet drinks. This semantic distinction is symptomatic of the surprising gulf between the two localized contexts. The meaning of these drinks in consumption can easily be overgeneralized and the following points may not apply well to local elites whose categories are closer to those of the manufacturers. But to understand how the mass middle-class and working-class population perceive these drinks, one needs a different starting point. For example, sweet drinks are never viewed as imported luxuries that the country or people cannot afford. On the contrary they are viewed as Trinidadian, as basic necessities and as the common person's drink.

Apart from this being evident ethnographically, it is also consistent with the policy of the state. For many years the industry was under price control. This meant that prices could be raised only by government agreement and, since this severely restricted profitability, price control was thoroughly opposed by the industry. The grounds given were that this was a basic necessity for the common person and as such needed to be controlled. The reality was that to the extent that this was true (and still today consumption is around 170 bottles per person per annum), the government saw this as a politically astute and popular move. Furthermore until the IMF (International Monetary Fund) recently ended all protectionism, Coke was protected as a locally made drink through a ban on importing all foreign-made soft drinks.

As a non-alcoholic beverage, sweet drinks compete largely with fruit juices and milk drinks such as peanut punch. All are available as commodities but also have home equivalents as in diluted squeezed fruit, home-made milk drinks, and sweet drinks made from water and packet crystals. Water competes inside the home, but no one but the most destitute would request water *per se* while ordering a meal or snack. Unlike their rivals sweet drinks are also important as mixers for alcohol.

The importance of understanding the local context of consumption as opposed to production is also evident when we turn to more specific qualities of the drinks. From the point of view of consumers, the key conceptual categories are not the flavours and colas constantly referred to by the producers. In ordinary discourse much more important are the "black" sweet drink and the "red" sweet drink.

The "red" sweet drink is a traditional category and in most Trinidadian historical accounts or novels that make mention of sweet drinks it is the red drink that is referred to. The attraction of this drink to novelists is probably not only the sense of nostalgia generally but the feeling that the red drink stands in some sense for a transformation of the East Indian. While the African has become the non-marked population, the Indian has been seen as an ethnic group with its own material culture. The red sweet drink was a relatively early example of the community being objectified in relation to a commodity as opposed to a self-produced object. The red drink is the quintessential sweet drink inasmuch as it is considered by consumers to be in fact the drink highest in sugar content. The Indian population is also generally supposed to be particularly fond of sugar and sweet products and this in turn is supposed to relate to their entry into Trinidad largely as indentured labourers in the sugar cane fields. They are also supposed to have a high rate of diabetes which folk wisdom claims to be a result of their overindulgence of these preferences.

The present connotation of the red drink contains this element of nostalgia. Partly there is the reference to older red drinks such as the Jaleel's original "red spot". There is also the presence of the common flavour "Kola Champagne" which is itself merely a red sweet drink.[2] Adverts that provide consumption shots will most often refer to a "red and a roti" as the proper combination; the implication being that non-Indians also would most appropriately take a red drink with their roti when eating out, since the roti[3] has become a general "fast food" item that appeals to all communities within Trinidad.

The centrality of the black sweet drink to Trinidadian drinking is above all summed up in the notion of a "rum and Coke" as the core alcoholic drink for most people of the island. This is important as rum is never drunk neat or simply on the rocks but always with some mixer. Coke does not stand on this relationship alone, however. The concept of the "black" sweet drink as something to be drunk in itself is nearly as common as the "red" sweet drink. Coke is probably the most common drink to be conceptualized as the embodiment of the "black" sweet drink, but any black drink will do. This is most evident at the cheapest end of the market. In a squatting community where I worked, a local product from a nearby industrial estate called "bubble up" was the main drink. This company simply produced two drinks: a black (which it did not even bother calling a cola) and a red. People would go to the parlour and say "gimme a black" or "gimme a red". At this level Coke becomes merely a high status example of the black sweet drink of my title.

This distinction between drinks relates in part to the general discourse of ethnicity that pervades Trinidadian conversation and social interaction (see Yelvington 1993). Thus an Indian talked of seeing Coke as a more white and "white oriented people" drink. The term "white oriented" is here a synonym for Black African Trinidadians. Many Indians assume that Africans have a much greater aptitude for simply emulating white taste and customs to become what is locally termed "Afro-Saxons". Africans in turn would refute this and claim that while they lay claim to white culture Indians are much more deferential to white persons.

Similarly an African informant suggested that "[a certain] Cola is poor quality stuff. It would only sell in the South, but would not sell in the North". The implication here is that sophisticated Africans would not drink this substitute for "the real thing", while Indians generally accept lower quality goods. In many respects there is a sense that Black culture has replaced colonial culture as mainstream while it is Indians that represent cultural difference. Thus a white executive noted that in terms of advertising spots on the radio "we want an Indian programme, since marketing soft drinks has become very ethnic".

The semiotic may or may not become explicit. One of the most successful local advertising campaigns in the sweet drink industry to occur during the period of fieldwork was for Canada Dry, which was marketed not as a ginger ale but as the "tough soft drink". The advert was produced in two versions. One had a black cowboy shooting at several bottles, as on a range, and finding that Canada Dry deflected his bullets. The other had an American Indian having his tomahawk blunted by this brand, having smashed the others. As the company told me, the idea was to cover the diversity of communities and the (as it were) "red" Indian was adopted only after marketing tests had shown that there would be empathy and not offence from the South Asian Indian community of Trinidad.

I do not want to give the impression that there is some simple semiotic relationship between ethnicity and drinks. What has been described here is merely the dominant association of these drinks, red with Indian, black with African. This does not, however, reflect consumption. Indeed marketing research shows that if anything a higher proportion of Indians drink Colas, while Kola champagne as a red drink is more commonly drunk by Africans. Many Indians explicitly identify with Coke and its modern image. This must be taken into account when comprehending the associated advertising. In many respects the "Indian" connoted by the red drink today is in some ways the African's more nostalgic image of how Indians either used to be or perhaps still should be. It may well be therefore that the appeal of the phrase "a red and a roti" is actually more to African Trinidadians, who are today avid consumers of roti. Meanwhile segments of the Indian population have used foreign education and local commercial success to sometimes overtrump the African population in their search for images of modernity and thus readily claim an affinity with Coke.

In examining the connotations of such drinks we are not therefore exploring some coded version of actual populations. Rather, as I argued in more detail elsewhere (Miller 1994: 257–90), both ethnic groups and commodities are better regarded as objectifications that are used to create and explore projects of value for the population. These often relate more to aspects or potential images of the person than actual persons. What must be rejected is the argument of those debating about "postmodernism" that somehow there is an authentic discourse of persons and this is reduced through the inauthentic field of commodities. Indeed such academics tend to pick on Coca-Cola as their favourite image of the superficial globality that has replaced these local arguments.

Nothing could be further from the Trinidadian case. Here Coca-Cola both as brand and in its generic form as "black" sweet drink becomes an image that develops as much through the local contradictions of popular culture as part of an implicit debate about how people should be. If one grants that the red sweet drink stands for an image of Indianness then its mythic potential (as in Lévi-Strauss 1966) emerges. This is an image of Indianness with which some Indians will identify, some will not, and more commonly some will identify with only on certain occasions. But equally for Africans and others the identity of being Trinidadian includes this presence of Indian as a kind of "otherness" which at one level they define themselves against, but at a superordinate level they incorporate as an essential part of their Trinidadianness. The importance of the ethnicity ascribed to drinks is that individual non-Indians cannot literally apply a piece of Indianness to themselves to resolve this contradiction of alterity. Instead they can consume mythic forms which in their ingestion in a sense provide for an identification with an otherness which therefore "completes" this aspect of the drinker's identity. To summarize the attraction of such adverts is that Africans drinking a red sweet drink consume what for them is a highly acceptable image of Indianness that is an essential part of their sense of being Trinidadian.

Ethnicity is only one such dimension, where Coca-Cola as myth resolves a contradiction in value. Drinks also carry temporal connotations. Coke retains a notion of modernness fostered by its advertising. But it has actually been a presence in Trinidad for several generations. It has therefore become an almost nostalgic, traditional image of being modern. For the Indians or indeed for any group where the desire not to lose a sense of tradition is complemented by a desire to feel modern, this is then an objectification of the modern that is literally very easily ingested. Solo retains its high market share precisely because it provides the opposite polarity. Although as a mass product it is less old than Coke, it is perceived as nostalgic. The Solo returnable is the old squat variety of glass bottle, and I cannot count the number of times I was regaled with the anecdote about how this was the bottle used a generation before to give babies their milk in. The desire for particular commodities are often like myth (following Lévi-Strauss 1966, rather than Roland Barthes 1973) an attempt to resolve contradictions in society and identity. This is nothing new; it is exactly the conclusion Marchand (1985) comes to with regard to his excellent study of advertising in the USA in the 1930s.

Consumption v. Production

These are just examples from the complex context of consumption which often frustrate the producers who are looking for a consistency in the population that they can commoditize. The problem was evident in a conversation with a Coke executive. He started by noting with pleasure a survey suggesting that the highly sophisticated advertising campaign currently being run by Coke was actually the most popular campaign at that time. But he then noted that what came second was a very amateur-looking ad for Det insecticide which had a particularly ugly calypso-nian frightening the insects to death. His problem was in drawing conclusions from this survey that he could use for marketing.

In discussing this issue of production's articulation with consumption, it is hard to escape the constant question of "active" or "passive" consumers, i.e. how far consumers themselves determined the success of particular commodities. For example, I do not believe that the idea that sweet drinks are considered a basic necessity to be the result of a successful company promotion that results in people "wasting" their money on what "ought" to be a superfluous luxury. Nor was it an invention by government that became accepted. This assertion as to the past autonomy of the consumer derives partly from historical evidence in this case but also on the basis of what can be observed of the response to current campaigns.

Perhaps the primary target of soft drink advertising in 1988–9 was the return of the returnable bottle. Here what was at issue was precisely the industry attempting to second-guess the consumer's concern, in this case for thrift and price. The industry reasoned that its own profitability would be best served by trying to save the consumer money. But it was the executives who felt that the public "ought" to respond to the depths of recession by favouring the returnable bottle. The problem was that despite heavy advertising by more than one company, the consumers seemed unwilling to respond to what all the agencies were loudly announcing to be the inevitable move-ment in the market. The campaigns were generally a failure, especially given that they were intended to collude with a trend rather than "distort" public demand.

Companies can, of course, often respond well to complexity. They also compen-sate for those attributes that have become taken for granted. Thus Jaleel as a highly localized company used the most global style high-quality advertising, while Coke often tried to compensate for its given globality by emphasizing its links to Trinidad through sponsorship of a multitude of small regional events or organizations.

That, however, a gulf can exist between producer and consumer context is most evident when each rests upon different conceptualizations of the drinks. A prime example is the distinction between the sweet drink and the soft drink. Localisms such as sweet drink are not necessarily fostered by company executives who come from a different social milieu, and whose social prejudices often outweigh some abstract notion of profitability. The producers are part of an international cosmo-politanism within which high sugar content is increasingly looked upon as un-healthy. In connection with this, sweetness increasingly stands for vulgarity and in some sense older outdated traditions. The executives would wish to see themselves, by contrast, as trying to be in the vanguard of current trends.

There were, therefore, several cases of companies trying to reduce the sugar content of their drinks, and finding this resulted in complaints and loss of market share. As a result the sugar content remains in some cases extremely high. A good proportion of the cases of failure in the market that were recorded during fieldwork seemed to be of drinks with relatively high juice content and low sugar content. As one executive noted, "we can do 10 per cent fruit as in Caribbean Cool. We are following the international trend here to higher juice, but this is not a particularly popular move within Trinidad. Maybe because it not sweet enough".

Indeed while the executives consider the drinks in relation to the international beverages market, this may not be entirely correct for Trinidad. The term "sweet" as opposed to "soft" drink may have further connotations. The food category of "sweets" and its associated category of chocolates is here a much smaller domain in the market than is found in many other areas such as Europe or the USA. Although sweets are sold in supermarkets and parlours they do not seem to be quite as ubiquitous as in many other countries and there are virtually no sweet shops *per se*. Given that the most important milk drink is actually chocolate milk, there is good reason to see drinks as constituting as much the local equivalent of the sweets and chocolates domain of other countries as of their soft drinks. But once again this emerges only out of the consumption context and one would have a hard time trying to convince local Trinidadian executives that they might actually be selling in liquid form that which other countries sell as solids.

It is this that justifies the point made earlier that to endeavour to investigate a commodity in its local context, there are actually two such contexts, one of production and distribution and the other of consumption. These are not the same and they may actually contradict each other to a surprising extent. There is an important general point here in that Fine and Leopold (1993) have argued with considerable force that consumption studies have suffered by failing to appreciate the importance of the link to production which may be specific to each of what they call "systems of provision", i.e. domains such as clothing, food and utilities. What this case study shows is that while production and consumption should be linked, they may be wrong to assume that this is because each domain evolves its own local consistency as an economic process. Quite often they do not.

The reason that this is possible is that, although the formal goal of company practice is profitability, there are simply too many factors that can easily be blamed for the failures of campaigns. At best companies have marketing information such as blind tests on particular brands, and point-of-sale statistics. But even this information is little used except as *post-hoc* justification for decisions that are most often based on the personal opinions and generalized "gut" feelings of the key executives. Given peer pressure based on often irrelevant knowledge of the international beverage market, producers often manage to fail to capitalize on developments in popular culture that are available for commoditization.

Similarly consumers do not regard companies as merely functional providers. In a small island such as Trinidad consumers often have decided views, prejudices, and experiences with regard to each particular company as well as their products. As such the reaction of consumers to a particular new flavour may be determined in large measure by those factors that make the consumer feel that it is or is not the "appropriate" firm with which to associate this flavour. So there are cases of several firms trying out a new flavour until one succeeds. What the ethnography suggests is that there are often underlying reasons that one particular company's flavour tasted right.

Conclusion

This case study has attempted to localize production and consumption separately and in relation to each other. The effect has been one of relativism, using ethnography to insist upon the local contextualization of a global form. It follows that

Coke consumption might be very different elsewhere. Gillespie (1995: 191–7) has analyzed the response to Coke among a group of West London youths from families with South Asian origins. The attraction to Coke is if anything greater in London than in Trinidad, but the grounds are quite different. In London, where immigration from South Asia is a much more recent experience, the focus was on the portrayal of the relative freedom enjoyed by youth in the USA as a state to be envied and emulated. There is no local contextualization to the consumption of the drink comparable to Trinidad. Furthermore the primary emphasis in London was on the advertisements rather than the drink itself.

The point of engaging in these demonstrations of relativism was declared at the beginning of this chapter to be an attempt to confront the dangers of Coke as meta-symbol. I confess I wanted to localize Coke partly because I was disenchanted with tedious anecdotes, often from academics, about Coke and global homogenization and sensed that the kind of glib academia that employed such anecdotes was possibly serving a rather more sinister end.

Anthropology seemed a useful tool in asserting the importance of a posteriori diversity in the specificity of particular capitalisms. A critical appraisal of capitalism requires something beyond the lazy term that ascribes it a purity of instrumentality in relation to profitability as goal seeking which does not usually bear closer inspection, any more than kinship can be reduced to biology. I therefore felt that prior to embarking upon a reformulated critique of capitalism it was important first to encounter capitalism as a comparative practice, not just a formal economistic logic (see Miller 1997).

But such a point could be made with many commodities. Coke is special because of its particular ability to objectify globality. This chapter has not questioned this ability, it has argued only that globality is itself a localized image, held within a larger frame of spatialized identity. As has been shown within media studies (Morley 1992: 270–89), an image of the global is not thereby a universal image. The particular place of globality and its associated modernity must be determined by local setting. Indeed Caribbean peoples with their extraordinarily transnational families and connections juxtaposed with often passionate local attachments well exemplify such contradictions in the terms "local" and "global". Trinidadians do not and will not choose between being American and being Trinidadian. Most reject parochial nationalism or neo-Africanized roots that threaten to diminish their sense of rights of access to global goods, such as computers or blue jeans. But they will fiercely maintain those localisms they wish to retain, not because they are hypocritical but because inconsistency is an appropriate response to contradiction.

So Coke and McDonald's are not trends, or symbolic of trends. Rather like whisky before them, they are particular images of globality that are held as a polarity against highly localized drinks such as sorrel and punch a creme, which unless you are West Indian you will probably not have heard of. Mattelart's (1991) *Advertising International* showed the commercially disastrous result when Saatchi & Saatchi believed its own hype about everything becoming global. The company nearly collapsed. In an English pub we would also find an extension of the range of potential spatial identifications from international or European lagers to ever more parochial "real ales". No doubt many aspiring anthropologists would choose one of the new "designer" beers which typically derive from some exotic location, such as

Mexico or Malaysia where anthropologists have a distinct advantage in boring other people with claimed knowledge of the original homeland of the beer in question. The point this brings home is that semiotics without structuralism was never much use, as Coca-Cola found when it tried to change its formula and was humiliated by the consumer.

Finally we can turn back to the meta-context of this chapter, which asserts the scholarship of such contextualization against the common academic use of Coca-Cola as glib generality. There are many grounds for favouring theoretical and comparative approaches in anthropology against a tradition of ethnography as mere parochialism, which is hard to justify in and of itself. In this case, however, there are specific grounds for an ethnography of localism because here localism makes a particular point. Vanguard academics seem to view Coca-Cola as totalized, themselves as contextualized. This chapter shows, by example, how ordinary vulgar mass consumption is proficient in sublating the general form back into specificity. By contrast, in much of the academic discussion of postmodernism as also in political rhetoric we find the totalizing of Coca-Cola as a meta-symbol. This discourse when detached from its historical and localized context comes to stand for the kind of anti-enlightenment irrationalism and aestheticism that was once the main instrument used by fascism against the rationalist tradition of the enlightenment. The point is not dissimilar to Habermas's (1987) argument in *The Philosophical Discourse of Modernity* against these same trends in modern academic thought.

The concept of meta-symbol certainly fits postmodern assertions about nothing referring to anything in particular any more. I do not accept at all that this is true for commodities such as Coke when investigated in production or consumption contexts, although this is what the academic asserts. But it might just be true of the way academics themselves use the image of Coke. First accepting its globality in a simple sense, Coke then becomes a general Capitalism, Imperialism, Americanization, etc. Then in discussions of postmodernism it may emerge as a kind of generalized symbol standing for the existence in commodities of a level of irrationalized meta-symbolic life (Featherstone 1991 provides a summary of these kinds of academic discussions). This parallels what Quinn (1994) sees happening to the swastika:

> Returning to the definition of the swastika as the "sign of nonsignability", we can see that here the image comes to represent the symbolic realm or the symbolic process per se, as a meta-symbol or "symbol of symbolism", a status that Aryanism reflected by naming the image as the "symbol of symbols" set apart from all others and representable only by itself (Quinn 1994: 57).

Both the Coca-Cola Corporation but even more a trend in academics and politics would wish to push Coca-Cola onto this kind of plateau. In collusion with the drinkers that consume it and often the local companies that bottle it, this chapter is intended to form part of a counter movement that would push Coca-Cola downwards back into the muddy dispersed regions of black sweet drinks.

NOTES

The material for this chapter is taken in part from a larger study of business in Trinidad called *Capitalism: An Ethnographic Approach* (Miller 1997), which contains a wider discussion of the industry, while this chapter draws out the specific implications of Coca-Cola. A full acknowledgement of those who assisted in this project is contained in that volume. A version of this chapter has also been published in Danish in the journal *Tendens*.

1 At the time the exchange rate was approximately TT$4.25 to US$1.
2 This particular marketing ploy of calling fizzy drinks champagne is found in Britain in the nineteenth century, when drinks were made from a syrup called twaddle. This may well be the origin of the expression "a load of twaddle", a fact entirely unrelated to the rest of this chapter!
3 Roti is the traditional Indian unleavened bread, sold in Trinidad wrapped around some other food to make a meal.

REFERENCES

Barthes, R. 1973. *Mythologies*. London: Paladin.
de Boissiere, R. 1984. *Rum and Coca-Cola*. London: Allison & Busby.
Featherstone, M. 1991. *Consumer Culture and Postmodernism*. London: Sage.
Felstead, A. 1993. *The Corporate Paradox*. London: Routledge.
Fine, B. & E. Leopold 1993. *The World of Consumption*. London: Routledge.
Gillespie, M. 1995. *Television, Ethnicity and Cultural Change*. London: Routledge.
Habermas, J. 1987. *The Philosophical Discourse of Modernity*. Cambridge, MA: MIT Press.
Lévi-Strauss, C. 1966. *The Savage Mind*. London: Weidenfeld & Nicolson.
Macmillan, A. 1922. *The Red Book of the West Indies*. London: Collingridge.
Marchand, R. 1985. *Advertising the American Dream*. Berkeley: University of California Press.
Mattelart, A. 1991. *Advertising International*. London: Routledge.
Miller, D. 1994. *Modernity: An Ethnographic Approach*. Oxford: Berg.
Miller, D. 1997. *Capitalism: An Ethnographic Approach*. Oxford: Berg.
Morley, D. 1992. *Television Audiences and Cultural Studies*. London: Routledge.
Naipaul, V. S. 1967. *The Mimic Men*. Harmondsworth: Penguin.
O'Barr, W. 1989. The airbrushing of culture. *Public Culture* 2(1), 1–19.
Oliver, T. 1986. *The Real Coke: The Real Story*. London: Elm Tree.
Pendergrast, M. 1993. *For God, Country and Coca-Cola*. London: Weidenfeld & Nicolson.
Quinn, M. 1994. *The Swastika*. London: Routledge.
Tollison, R., D. Kaplan, R. Higgins (eds.) 1986. *Competition and Concentration: The Economics of the Carbonated Soft Drink Industry*. Lexington, MA: Lexington Books.
Yelvington, K. (ed.) 1993. *Trinidad Ethnicity*. London: Macmillan.

5

China's Big Mac Attack

James L. Watson

Ronald McDonald Goes to China

Looming over Beijing's choking, bumper-to-bumper traffic, every tenth building seems to sport a giant neon sign advertising American wares: Xerox, Mobil, Kinko's, Northwest Airlines, IBM, Jeep, Gerber, even the Jolly Green Giant. American food chains and beverages are everywhere in central Beijing: Coca-Cola, Starbucks, Kentucky Fried Chicken, Häagen-Dazs, Dunkin' Donuts, Baskin-Robbins, Pepsi, TCBY, Pizza Hut, and of course McDonald's. As of June 1999, McDonald's had opened 235 restaurants in China. Hong Kong alone now boasts 158 McDonald's franchises, one for every 42,000 residents (compared to one for every 30,000 Americans).

Fast food can even trump hard politics. After NATO accidentally bombed the Chinese embassy in Belgrade during the war in Kosovo, Beijing students tried to organize a boycott of American companies in protest. Coca-Cola and McDonald's were at the top of their hit list, but the message seemed not to have reached Beijing's busy consumers: the three McDonald's I visited last July were packed with Chinese tourists, local yuppies, and grandparents treating their "little emperors and empresses" to Happy Meals. The only departure from the familiar American setting was the menu board (which was in Chinese, with English in smaller print) and the jarring sound of Mandarin shouted over cellular phones. People were downing burgers, fries, and Cokes. It was, as Yogi Berra said, déjà-vu all over again; I had seen this scene a hundred times before in a dozen countries. Is globalism – and its cultural variant, McDonaldization – the face of the future?

Imperialism and a Side of Fries

American academe is teeming with theorists who argue that transnational corporations like McDonald's provide the shock troops for a new form of imperialism that is far more successful, and therefore more insidious, than its militarist antecedents. Young people everywhere, the argument goes, are avid consumers of soap operas, music videos, cartoons, electronic games, martial-arts books, celebrity posters, trendy clothing, and faddish hairstyles. To cater to them, shopping malls, supermarkets, amusement parks, and fast-food restaurants are popping up everywhere. Younger consumers are forging transnational bonds of empathy and shared interests that will, it is claimed, transform political alignments in ways that most world leaders – old men who do not read *Wired* – cannot begin to comprehend, let alone control. Government efforts to stop the march of American (and Japanese) pop culture are futile; censorship and trade barriers succeed only in making forbidden films, music, and Web sites irresistible to local youth.

One of the clearest expressions of the "cultural imperialism" hypothesis appeared in a 1996 *New York Times* op-ed by Ronald Steel: "It was never the Soviet Union, but the United States itself that is the true revolutionary power. ... We purvey a culture based on mass entertainment and mass gratification. ... The cultural message we transmit through Hollywood and McDonald's goes out across the world to capture, and also to undermine, other societies. ... Unlike traditional conquerors, we are not content merely to subdue others: We insist that they be like us." In his recent book, *The Lexus and the Olive Tree*, Thomas Friedman presents a more benign view of the global influence of McDonald's. Friedman has long argued in his *New York Times* column that McDonald's and other manifestations of global culture serve the interests of middle classes that are emerging in autocratic, undemocratic societies. Furthermore, he notes, countries that have a McDonald's within their borders have never gone to war against each other. (The NATO war against Serbia would seem to shatter Friedman's Big Mac Law, but he does not give up easily. In his July 2, 1999, column, he argued that the shutdown and rapid reopening of Belgrade's six McDonald's actually prove his point.)

If Steel and his ideological allies are correct, McDonald's should be the poster child of cultural imperialism. McDonald's today has more than 25,000 outlets in 119 countries. Most of the corporation's revenues now come from operations outside the United States, and a new restaurant opens somewhere in the world every 17 hours.

McDonald's makes heroic efforts to ensure that its food looks, feels, and tastes the same everywhere. A Big Mac in Beijing tastes virtually identical to a Big Mac in Boston. Menus vary only when the local market is deemed mature enough to expand beyond burgers and fries. Consumers can enjoy Spicy Wings (red-pepper-laced chicken) in Beijing, kosher Big Macs (minus the cheese) in Jerusalem, vegetable McNuggets in New Delhi, or a McHuevo (a burger with fried egg) in Montevideo. Nonetheless, wherever McDonald's takes root, the core product – at least during the initial phase of operation – is not really the food but the experience of eating in a cheerful, air-conditioned, child-friendly restaurant that offers the revolutionary innovation of clean toilets.

Critics claim that the rapid spread of McDonald's and its fast-food rivals undermines indigenous cuisines and helps create a homogeneous, global culture. Beijing and Hong Kong thus make excellent test cases since they are the dual epicenters of China's haute cuisine (with apologies to Hunan, Sichuan, and Shanghai loyalists). If McDonald's can make inroads in these two markets, it must surely be an unstoppable force that levels cultures. But the truth of this parable of globalization is subtler than that.

The Secret of My Success

How did McDonald's do it? How did a hamburger chain become so prominent in a cultural zone dominated by rice, noodles, fish, and pork? In China, adult consumers often report that they find the taste of fried beef patties strange and unappealing. Why, then, do they come back to McDonald's? And more to the point, why do they encourage their children to eat there?

The history of McDonald's in Hong Kong offers good clues about the mystery of the company's worldwide appeal. When Daniel Ng, an American-trained engineer, opened Hong Kong's first McDonald's in 1975, his local food-industry competitors dismissed the venture as a nonstarter: "Selling hamburgers to Cantonese? You must be joking!" Ng credits his boldness to the fact that he did not have an M.B.A. and had never taken a course in business theory.

During the early years of his franchise, Ng promoted McDonald's as an outpost of American culture, offering authentic hamburgers to "with-it" young people eager to forget that they lived in a tiny colony on the rim of Maoist China. Those who experienced what passed for hamburgers in British Hong Kong during the 1960s and 1970s will appreciate the innovation. Ng made the fateful decision not to compete with Chinese-style fast-food chains that had started a few years earlier (the largest of which, Café de Coral, was established in 1969). The signs outside his first restaurants were in English; the Chinese characters for McDonald's (Cantonese *Mak-dong-lou*, Mandarin *Mai-dang-lao*) did not appear until the business was safely established. Over a period of 20 years, McDonald's gradually became a mainstay of Hong Kong's middle-class culture. Today the restaurants are packed wall-to-wall with busy commuters, students, and retirees who treat them as homes away from home. A 1997 survey I conducted among Hong Kong university students revealed that few were even aware of the company's American origins. For Hong Kong youth, McDonald's is a familiar institution that offers comfort foods that they have eaten since early childhood.

Yunxiang Yan, a UCLA anthropologist, hints that a similar localization process may be underway in Beijing. McDonald's there is still a pricey venue that most Chinese treat as a tourist stop: you haven't really "done" Beijing unless you have visited the Forbidden City, walked around Tiananmen Square, and eaten at the "Golden Arches." Many visitors from the countryside take Big Mac boxes, Coke cups, and napkins home with them as proof that they did it right. Yan also discovered that working-class Beijing residents save up to take their kids to McDonald's and hover over them as they munch. (Later the adults eat in a cheaper, Chinese-style restaurant.) Parents told Yan that they wanted their children to "connect" with the world outside China. To them, McDonald's was an important stop on the way to Harvard Business School or the MIT labs. Yan has since discovered that local yuppies are beginning to eat Big Macs regularly. In 20 years, he predicts, young people in Beijing (like their counterparts in Hong Kong today) will not even care about the foreign origin of McDonald's, which will be serving ordinary food to people more interested in getting a quick meal than in having a cultural experience. The key to this process of localization is China's changing family system and the emergence of a "singleton" (only-child) subculture.

The Little Emperors

In China, as in other parts of East Asia, the startup date for McDonald's corresponds to the emergence of a new class of consumers with money to spend on family entertainment. Rising incomes are dramatically changing lifestyles, especially among younger couples in China's major cities. Decisions about jobs and purchases no longer require consultations with an extended network of parents, grandparents, adult siblings, and other kin. More married women in Hong Kong, Beijing, and Shanghai work outside the home, which in turn affects child-rearing practices, residence patterns, and gender relations. At least in the larger cities, men no longer rule the roost. One of China's most popular television shows features a search for the "ideal husband," a man who does the shopping, washes the dishes, and changes the baby's diapers – behavior inconceivable in Mao's heyday.

Most Chinese newlyweds are choosing to create their own homes, thereby separating themselves from parents and in-laws. The traditional system of living with the groom's parents is dying out fast, even in the Chinese countryside. Recent research in Shanghai and Dalian (and Taipei) shows that professional couples prefer to live near the wife's mother, often in the same apartment complex. The crucial consideration is household labor – child care, cooking, shopping, washing, and cleaning. With both husband and wife working full time, someone has to do it, and the wife's mother is considered more reliable (and less trouble) than the husband's mother, who would expect her daughter-in-law to be subservient.

In response to these social and economic changes, a new Chinese family system is emerging that focuses on the needs and aspirations of the married couple – the conjugal unit. Conjugality brings with it a package of attitudes and practices that undermine traditional Chinese views regarding filial piety and Confucianism. Should younger couples strive, irrespective of personal cost, to promote the welfare of the larger kin group and support their aging parents? Or should they concentrate on building a comfortable life for themselves and their offspring? Increasingly, the balance is shifting toward conjugality and away from the Confucian norms that guided earlier generations.

The shift also coincides with a dramatic decline in China's birth rate and a rise in the amount of money and attention lavished on children. The Communist Party's single-child family policy has helped produce a generation of "little emperors and empresses," each commanding the undivided affection and economic support of two parents and (if lucky) four grandparents. The Chinese press is awash with articles bemoaning the rise of singletons who are selfish, maladjusted, and spoiled beyond repair – although psychologists working on China's singletons find them little different from their American or European counterparts.

McDonald's opened in Beijing in 1992, a time when changes in family values were matched by a sustained economic boom. The startup date also coincided with a public "fever" for all things American – sports, clothing, films, food, and so on.

American-style birthday parties became key to the company's expansion strategy. Prior to the arrival of McDonald's, festivities marking youngsters' specific birth dates were unknown in most of East Asia. In Hong Kong, for instance, lunar-calendar dates of birth were recorded for use in later life – to help match prospective marriage partners' horoscopes or choose an auspicious burial date. Until the late 1970s and early 1980s, most people paid little attention to their calendar birth date if they remembered it at all. McDonald's and its rivals now promote the birthday party – complete with cake, candles, and silly hats – in television advertising aimed directly at kids.

McDonald's also introduced other localized innovations that appeal to younger customers. In Beijing, Ronald McDonald (a.k.a. Uncle McDonald) is paired with an Aunt McDonald whose job is to entertain children and help flustered parents. All over East Asia, McDonald's offers a party package that includes food, cake, gifts, toys, and the exclusive use of a children's enclosure sometimes known as the Ronald Room. Birthday parties are all the rage for upwardly mobile youngsters in Hong Kong, Beijing, and Shanghai. Given that most people in these cities live in tiny, overcrowded flats, the local Kentucky Fried Chicken or McDonald's is a convenient and welcoming place for family celebrations.

For the first time in Chinese history, children matter not simply as future providers but as full-scale consumers who command respect in today's economy. Until the 1980s, kids rarely ate outside the home. When they did, they were expected to eat what was put in front of them. The idea that children might actually order their own food would have shocked most adults; only foreign youngsters were permitted to make their opinions known in public, which scandalized everyone within earshot. Today children have money in their pockets, most of which they spend on snacks. New industries and a specialized service sector have emerged to feed this category of consumers, as the anthropologist Jun Jing has noted in his new book, *Feeding China's Little Emperors*. In effect, the fast-food industry helped start a consumer revolution by encouraging children as young as three or four to march up to the counter, slap down their money, and choose their own food.

In Hong Kong, McDonald's has become so popular that parents use visits to their neighborhood outlet as a reward for good behavior or academic achievement. An old friend told me that withholding McDonald's visits was the only threat that registered with his wayward son. "It is my nuclear deterrent," he said.

McDonald's could not have succeeded in East Asia without appealing to new generations of consumers – children from 3 to 13 and their harried, stressed-out parents. No amount of stealth advertising or brilliant promotions could have done the trick alone. The fast-food industry did not create a market where none existed; it responded to an opportunity presented by the collapse of an outdated Confucian family system. In effect, McDonald's tailgated the family revolution as it swept through East Asia, first in Japan and Hong Kong (1970s), then in Taiwan and South Korea (1980s), and finally in China (1990s). There is no great mystery here, unless one is predisposed to seeing imperialist plots behind every successful business.

Grimace

In 1994 students protesting against California's Proposition 187, which restricted state services to immigrants, ransacked a McDonald's in Mexico City, scrawling "Yankee go home" on the windows. In August 1999 French farmers dumped tons of manure and rotting apricots in front of their local McDonald's to protest US sanctions on European food imports. During the past five years, McDonald's restaurants have been the targets of violent protests – including bombings – in over 50 countries, in cities including Rome, Macao, Rio de Janeiro, Prague, London, and Jakarta.

Why McDonald's? Other transnationals – notably Coca-Cola, Disney, and Pepsi – also draw the ire of anti-American demonstrators, but no other company can compete with the "Golden Arches." McDonald's is often the preferred site for anti-American demonstrations even in places where the local embassies are easy to get at. McDonald's is more than a purveyor of food; it is a saturated symbol for everything that environmentalists, protectionists, and anticapitalist activists find objectionable about American culture. McDonald's even stands out in the physical landscape, marked by its distinctive double-arched logo and characteristic design. Like the Stars and Stripes, the Big Mac stands for America.

Despite the symbolic load it carries, McDonald's can hardly be held responsible for the wholesale subversion of local cuisines, as its many critics claim. In China's larger cities, traditional specialties are supported by middle-class connoisseurs who treat eating out as a hobby and a diversion. Beijing's food scene today is a gourmet's paradise compared to the grim days of Maoist egalitarianism, when China's public canteens gave real meaning to the term "industrialized food." Party leaders may have enjoyed haute cuisine on the sly, but for most people, eating extravagantly was a counterrevolutionary crime. During the 1960s, refugee chefs kept microregional specialties alive in the back streets of Hong Kong and Taipei, where Panyu-style seafood, Shandong noodles, and Shunde vegetarian delights could be had at less than a dollar a head. Today, many Cantonese and Taiwanese lament the old refugees' retirement and complain that no one has carried on their culinary traditions; the chefs' own children, of course, have become brokers, lawyers, and professors.

Meanwhile, there has been an explosion of exotic new cuisines in China's cities: Thai, Malaysian, Indonesian, French, Spanish, Nepali, Mexican, and Hong Kong's latest hit, Louisiana creole. Chinese-style restaurants must now compete with these "ethnic" newcomers in a vast smorgasbord. The arrival of fast food is only one dimension of a much larger Chinese trend toward the culinary adventurism associated with rising affluence.

McDonald's has not been entirely passive, as demonstrated by its successful promotion of American-style birthday parties. Some try to tag McDonald's as a polluter and exploiter, but most Chinese consumers see the company as a force for the improvement of urban life. Clean toilets were a welcome development in cities where, until recently, a visit to a public restroom could be harrowing. The chain's preoccupation with cleanliness has raised consumer expectations and forced competitors to provide equally clean facilities. Ray Kroc, the legendary founder of McDonald's, was once asked if he had actually scrubbed out toilets during the early years of his franchise: "You're damn right I did," he shot back, "and I'd clean one today if it needed it." In a 1993 interview, Daniel Ng described his early efforts to import the Kroc ethos to his Hong Kong franchise. After an ineffectual first try, one new employee was ordered to clean the restrooms again. The startled worker replied that the toilets were already cleaner than the collective facilities he used at home. Ng told him that standards at McDonald's were higher and ordered him to do it again.

Another innovation is the line, a social institution that is seldom appreciated until it collapses. When McDonald's opened in Hong Kong, customers clumped around the cash registers, pushing their money over the heads of the people ahead of them – standard procedure in local train stations, banks, and cinemas. McDonald's management appointed an employee (usually a young woman) to act as queue monitor, and within a few months, regular consumers began to enforce the system themselves by glaring at newcomers who had the effrontery to jump ahead. Today the line is an accepted feature of Hong Kong's middle-class culture, and it is making headway in Beijing and Shanghai. Whether or not McDonald's deserves the credit for this particular innovation, many East Asian consumers associate the "Golden Arches" with public civility.

Have It Your Way

At first glance, McDonald's appears to be the quintessential transnational, with its own corporate culture nurtured at Hamburger University in Oak Brook, Illinois. But James Cantalupo, the president of McDonald's Corporation, maintains that his strategy is to become as much a part of local culture as possible and protests when people call McDonald's a multinational or a transnational. "I like to call us multi-local," he told *The Christian Science Monitor* in 1991. McDonald's goes out of its way to find local suppliers whenever it enters a new market. In China, for instance, the company nurtures its own network of russet-potato growers to provide french fries of the requisite length. McDonald's has also learned to rely on self-starters like Daniel Ng to run its foreign franchises – with minimal interference from Oak Brook. Another winning strategy, evident everywhere in East Asia, is promoting promising young "crew" (behind-the-counter) workers into management's ranks. Surprisingly few managers are dispatched from the Illinois headquarters. Yan found only one American, a Chinese-speaker, on McDonald's Beijing management team.

Critics of the fast-food industry assume that corporations always call the shots and that consumers have little choice but to accept what is presented to them. In fact, the process of localization is a two-way street, involving changes in the local culture as well as modifications of the company's standard mode of operation.

The hallmark of the American fast-food business is the displacement of labor costs from the corporation to consumers. For the system to work, consumers must be educated – or "disciplined" – so that they voluntarily fulfill their side of an implicit bargain: we (the corporation) will provide cheap, fast service if you (the customer) carry your own tray, seat yourself, eat quickly, help clean up afterward, and depart promptly to make room for others. Try breaking this contract in Boston or Pittsburgh by spreading out your newspaper and starting to work on a crossword puzzle in McDonald's. You will soon be ousted – politely in Pittsburgh, less so in Boston.

Key elements of McDonald's pan-national system – notably lining up and self-seating – have been readily accepted by consumers throughout East Asia. Other aspects of the Oak Brook model have been rejected, especially those relating to time and space. In Hong Kong, Taipei, and Beijing, consumers have turned their neighborhood restaurants into leisure centers for seniors and after-school clubs for students. Here, "fast" refers to the delivery of food, not its consumption.

Between 3:00 and 5:30 p.m. on Hong Kong weekdays, McDonald's restaurants are invaded by armies of young people in school uniforms. They buy a few fries, pour them out on a tray for communal snacking, and sit for at least an hour – gossiping, studying, and flirting. During the midmorning hours, the restaurants are packed with white-haired retirees who stay even longer, drinking tea or coffee (free refills for senior citizens) and lingering over pancake breakfasts. Many sit alone, reading newspapers provided by the management. Both retirees and students are attracted by the roomy tables, good light, and air- conditioning – a combination not easily found in Hong Kong, Beijing, or Shanghai. In effect, local citizens have appropriated private property and converted it into public space.

The process of localization correlates closely to the maturation of a generation of local people who grew up eating fast food. By the time the children of these pioneer consumers entered the scene, McDonald's was an unremarkable feature of the local landscape. Parents see the restaurants as havens for their school-age children: smoking is banned and (in China and Hong Kong) no alcohol is served, effectively eliminating drugs and gangs. McDonald's has become so local that Hong Kong's youth cannot imagine life without it.

Everyone has heard the story: Japanese little leaguers tour California and spot a McDonald's, whereupon they marvel that America also has Japanese food. Such anecdotes are not apocryphal. The children of visiting colleagues from Taiwan and South Korea were overjoyed when they saw a McDonald's near their temporary homes in the Boston suburbs: "Look! They have our kind of food here," one eight-year-old Korean exclaimed. The stories also work within East Asia: last year, Joe Bosco, an anthropologist at the Chinese University of Hong Kong, took several of his students to Taipei for a study tour. After a week of eating Taiwanese restaurant food, Bosco's charges began to complain that they missed home-style cooking. "Okay," Bosco said, "where do you want to eat tonight?" The students all said, "McDonald's!"

Next to Godliness

In China's increasingly affluent cities, parents now worry more about what their children eat outside the home. Rumors frequently sweep through Beijing and Shanghai with the same story line: migrants from the countryside set up a roadside stall selling *youtiar*, deep-fried dough sticks eaten with rice gruel for breakfast. To expand the batter, they add industrial detergent to the mix, creating a powerful poison that kills everyone who eats it. Families of the deceased rush back to the scene to discover that the stall has disappeared; the local police are more interested in silencing the survivors than pursuing the culprits. Such stories are, of course, unverifiable, but they carry a "truth" that resists official denials, much like urban legends in the United States. Last summer's [1999] food scare in Belgium over dioxin-laced eggs and the recent British mad-cow fiasco were well covered in the Chinese media, feeding the anxieties of urbanites with no reliable system of consumer protection.

McDonald's appeals to China's new elites because its food is safe, clean, and reliable. Western intellectuals may scoff at McDonald's for its unrelenting monotony, but in many parts of the world (including China) this is precisely what consumers find so attractive. Why else would competitors go to such extremes to imitate McDonald's? In Beijing one can find fast-food restaurants with names such as McDucks, Mcdonald's, and Mordornal. In Shanghai a local chain called Nancy's Express used a sign with one leg of the double arches missing, forming an "N." Another popular chain of noodle shops, called Honggaoliang (Red sorghum), advertises itself with a large "H" that bears an uncanny resemblance to the "Golden Arches." All over China, competitors dress their staff in McDonald's-style uniforms and decorate their restaurants in yellow. Corporate mascots inspired by Ronald McDonald – clowns, ducks, cowboys, cats, hamburger figures, mythic heroes, and chickens – parade along the sidewalks of Chinese cities. Local fast-food chains frequently engage in public exhibitions of cleanliness: one worker mops the floors and polishes the windows, all day long, every day. The cleaners usually restrict their efforts to the entryway, where the performance can best be seen by passersby.

So Lonely

During McDonald's first three years in China, Communist Party officials could barely restrain their enthusiasm over this new model of modernization, hygiene, and responsible management. By 1996, however, media enthusiasm cooled as state authorities began to promote an indigenous fast-food industry based on noodles, barbecued meats, soups, and rice pots. Now that McDonald's, Kentucky Fried Chicken, and Pizza Hut had shown the way, party officials reasoned, local chains should take over the mass market. (No such chain has seriously challenged McDonald's, but a Shanghai-based restaurateur has fought a much-reported "battle of the chickens" with KFC.)

Meanwhile, China faces yet another family revolution, this one caused by the graying of the population. In 1998, 10 percent of China's people were over 60; by 2020, the figure is expected to rise to approximately 16 percent. In 2025, there will be 274 million people over 60 in China—more than the entire 1998 US population. Since Beijing has made few provisions for a modern social-security system, the implications are profound. The locus of consumer power will soon shift generations as the parents of today's little emperors retire. Unlike the current generation of retirees – the survivors of Maoism – China's boomers will not be content with 1950s-level pensions, and they cannot expect their children to support them. Like their counterparts in the American Association of Retired Persons, future retirees in China are likely to be a vociferous, aggressive lot who will demand more state resources.

So what will happen to child-centered industries? If its experience in Hong Kong is any guide, McDonald's will survive quite handily as a welcoming retreat from the isolation and loneliness of urban life. The full ramifications of China's single-child policy will not be felt for another 20 years. Having one grandchild for every four grandparents is a recipe for social anomie on a truly massive scale. The consequences of China's demographic time bomb can already be seen on the streets of Hong Kong, where the family began to shrink decades ago. Tens of thousands of retirees roam Hong Kong's air-conditioned shopping malls, congregate in the handful of over-crowded parks, and turn their local McDonald's during the midmorning hours into a substitute for the public gardens, opera theaters, and ancestral halls that sheltered their parents. What stands out at McDonald's is the isolation among Hong Kong elders as they try to entertain themselves. Americans may be bowling alone and worrying about the decline of family life, but in early 21st-century Hong Kong, no one even seems concerned about the emergence of a civil society that ignores the elderly.

Whose Culture Is It, Anyway?

Is McDonald's leading a crusade to create a homogenous, global culture that suits the needs of an advanced capitalist world order? Not really. Today's economic and social realities demand an entirely new approach to global issues that takes consumers' perspectives into account. The explanatory device of "cultural imperialism" is little more than a warmed-over version of the neo-Marxist dependency theories that were popular in the 1960s and 1970s – approaches that do not begin to capture the complexity of today's emerging transnational systems.

The deeper one digs into the personal lives of consumers anywhere, the more complex matters become. People are not the automatons many theorists make them out to be. Hong Kong's discerning consumers have most assuredly not been stripped of their cultural heritage, nor have they become the uncomprehending dupes of transnational corporations.

In places like Hong Kong, it is increasingly difficult to see where the transnational ends and the local begins. Fast food is an excellent case in point: for the children who flock to weekend birthday parties, McDonald's is self-evidently local. Similarly, the Hong Kong elders who use McDonald's as a retreat from the loneliness of urban life could not care less about the company's foreign origin. Hong Kong's consumers have made the "Golden Arches" their own.

One might also turn the lens around and take a close look at American society as it enters a new millennium. Chinese food is everywhere, giving McDonald's and KFC a run for their money in such unlikely settings as Moline and Memphis. Mandarin is fast becoming a dominant language in American research laboratories, and Chinese films draw ever more enthusiastic audiences. Last Halloween, every other kid in my Cambridge neighborhood appeared in (Japanese-inspired) Power Ranger costumes, striking poses that owe more to Bruce Lee than to Batman. Whose culture is it, anyway? If you have to ask, you have already missed the boat.

6

Of Hamburger and Social Space: Consuming McDonald's in Beijing

Yunxiang Yan

In a 1996 news report on dietary changes in the cities of Beijing, Tianjin, and Shanghai, fast-food consumption was called the most salient development in the national capital: "The development of a fast-food industry with Chinese characteristics has become a hot topic in Beijing's dietary sector. This is underscored by the slogan 'challenge the Western fast food!'"[1] Indeed, with the instant success of Kentucky Fried Chicken after its grand opening in 1987, followed by the sweeping dominance of McDonald's and the introduction of other fast-food chains in the early 1990s, Western-style fast food has played a leading role in the restaurant boom and in the rapid change in the culinary culture of Beijing. A "war of fried chicken" broke out when local businesses tried to recapture the Beijing market from the Western fast-food chains by introducing Chinese-style fast foods. The "fast-food fever" in Beijing, as it is called by local observers, has given restaurant frequenters a stronger consumer consciousness and has created a Chinese notion of fast food and an associated culture.

From an anthropological perspective, this chapter aims to unpack the rich meanings of fast-food consumption in Beijing by focusing on the fast-food restaurants as a social space. Food and eating have long been a central concern in anthropological studies.[2] While nutritional anthropologists emphasize the practical functions of foods and food ways in cultural settings,[3] social and cultural anthropologists try to explore the links between food (and eating) and other dimensions of a given culture. From Lévi-Strauss's attempt to establish a universal system of meanings in the language of foods to Mary Douglas's effort to decipher the social codes of meals and Marshal Sahlins's analysis of the inner/outer, human/inhuman metaphors of food, there is a tradition of symbolic analysis of dietary cultures, whereby foods are treated as messages and eating as a way of social communication.[4] The great variety of food habits can be understood as human responses to material conditions, or as a way to draw boundaries between "us" and "them" in order to construct group identity and thus to engage in "gastro-politics."[5] According to Pierre Bourdieu, the different attitudes toward foods, different ways of eating, and food taste itself all express and define the structure of class relations in French society.[6] Although in Chinese society ceremonial banqueting is frequently used to display and reinforce the existing social structure, James Watson's analysis of the *sihk puhn* among Hong Kong villagers – a special type of ritualized banquet that requires participants to share foods from the same pot – demonstrates that foods can also be used as a leveling device to blur class boundaries.[7]

As Joseph Gusfield notes, the context of food consumption (the participants and the social settings of eating) is as important as the text (the foods that are to be consumed).[8] Restaurants thus should be regarded as part of a system of social codes; as institutionalized and commercialized venues, restaurants also provide a valuable window through which to explore the social meanings of food consumption. In her recent study of dining out and social manners, Joanne Finkelstein classifies restaurants into three grand categories: (1) "formal spectacular" restaurants, where "dining has been elevated to an event of extraordinary stature"; (2) "amusement" restaurants, which add entertainment to dining; and (3) convenience restaurants such as cafes and fast-food outlets.[9] Although Finkelstein recognizes the importance of restaurants as a public space for socialization, she also emphasizes the antisocial aspect of dining out. She argues that, because interactions in restaurants are conditioned by existing manners and customs, "dining out allows us to act in imitation of others, in accord with images, in responses to fashions, out of habit, without need for thought or self-scrutiny." The result is that the styles of interaction that are encouraged in restaurants produce sociality without much individuality, which is an "uncivilized sociality."[10] Concurring with Finkelstein's classification of restaurants, Allen Shelton proceeds further to analyze how restaurants as a theater can shape customers' thoughts and actions. Shelton argues that the cultural codes of restaurants are just as important as the food codes analyzed by Mary Douglas, Lévi-Strauss, and many others. He concludes that the "restaurant is an organized experience using and transforming the raw objects of space, words, and tastes into a coded experience of social structures."[11] Rick Fantasia's analysis of the fast-food industry in France is also illuminating in this respect. He points out that because McDonald's represents an exotic "Other" its outlets attract many young French customers who want to explore a different kind of social space – an "American place."[12]

In light of the studies of both the text and context of food consumption, I first review the development of Western fast food and the local responses in Beijing during the period 1987 to 1996. Next I examine the cultural symbolism of American fast food, the meanings of objects and physical place in fast-food restaurants, the consumer groups, and the use of public space in fast-food outlets. I then discuss the creation of a new social space in fast-food restaurants. In my opinion, the transformation of fast-food establishments from eating place to social space is the key to understanding the popularity of fast-food consumption in Beijing, and it is the major reason why local competitors have yet to successfully challenge the American fast-food chains. This study is based on both ethnographic evidence collected during my fieldwork in 1994 (August to October) and documentary data published in Chinese newspapers, popular magazines, and academic journals during the 1987–96 period. Since McDonald's is the ultimate icon of American fast food abroad and the most successful competitor in Beijing's fast-food market, McDonald's restaurants were the primary place and object for my research, although I also consider other fast-food outlets and compare them with McDonald's in certain respects.[13]

Fast-Food Fever in Beijing, 1987 to 1996

Fast food is not indigenous to Chinese society. It first appeared as an exotic phenomenon in novels and movies imported from abroad and then entered the everyday life of ordinary consumers when Western fast-food chains opened restaurants in the Beijing market. *Kuaican*, the Chinese translation for fast food, which literally means "fast meal" or "fast eating," contradicts the ancient principle in Chinese culinary culture that regards slow eating as healthy and elegant. There are a great variety of traditional snack foods called *xiaochi* (small eats), but the term "small eats" implies that they cannot be taken as meals. During the late 1970s, *hefan* (boxed rice) was introduced to solve the serious "dining problems" created by the lack of public dining facilities and the record number of visitors to Beijing. The inexpensive and convenient *hefan* – rice with a small quantity of vegetables or meat in a styrofoam box – quickly became popular in train stations, in commercial areas, and at tourist attractions. However, thus far boxed rice remains a special category of convenience food – it does not fall into the category of *kuaican* (fast food), even though it is consumed much faster than any of the fast foods discussed in the following pages. The intriguing point here is that in Beijing the notion of fast food refers only to Western-style fast food and the new Chinese imitations. More important, as a new cultural construct, the notion of fast food includes nonfood elements such as eating manners, environment, and patterns of social interaction. The popularity of fast food among Beijing consumers has little to do with either the food itself or the speed with which it is consumed.

American fast-food chains began to display interest in the huge market in China in the early 1980s. As early as 1983, McDonald's used apples from China to supply its restaurants in Japan; thereafter it began to build up distribution and processing facilities in northern China.[14] However, Kentucky Fried Chicken took the lead in the Beijing market. On October 6, 1987, KFC opened its first outlet at a commercial center just one block from Tiananmen Square. The three-story building, which seats more than 500 customers, at the time was the largest KFC restaurant. On the day of the grand opening, hundreds of customers stood in line outside the restaurant, waiting to taste the world-famous American food. Although few were really impressed with the food itself, they were all thrilled by the eating experience: the encounter with friendly employees, quick service, spotless floors, climate-controlled and brightly-lit dining areas, and of course, smiling Colonel Sanders standing in front of the main gate. From 1987 to 1991, KFC restaurants in Beijing enjoyed celebrity status, and the flagship outlet scored first for both single-day and annual sales in 1988 among the more than 9,000 KFC outlets throughout the world.

In the restaurant business in Beijing during the early 1980s, architecture and internal decoration had to match the rank of a restaurant in an officially prescribed hierarchy, ranging from star-rated hotel restaurants for foreigners to formal restaurants, mass eateries, and simple street stalls. There were strict codes regarding what a restaurant should provide, at what price, and what kind of customers it should serve in accordance with its position in this hierarchy. Therefore, some authorities in the local dietary sector deemed that the KFC decision to sell only fried chicken in such an elegant environment was absurd.[15] Beijing consumers, however, soon learned that a clean, bright, and comfortable environment was a common feature of all Western-style fast-food restaurants that opened in the Beijing market after KFC. Among them, McDonald's has been the most popular and the most successful.

The first McDonald's restaurant in Beijing was built at the southern end of Wangfujing Street, Beijing's Fifth Avenue. With 700 seats and 29 cash registers, the restaurant served more than 40,000 customers on its grand opening day of April 23, 1992.[16] The Wangfujing McDonald's quickly became an important landmark in Beijing, and its image appeared frequently on national television programs. It also became an attraction for domestic tourists, a place where ordinary people could literally taste a piece of American culture. Although not the first to introduce American fast food to Beijing consumers, the McDonald's chain has been the most aggressive in expanding its business and the most influential in developing the fast-food market. Additional McDonald's restaurants appeared in Beijing one after another: two were opened in 1993, four in 1994, and ten more in 1995. There were 35 by August 1997, and according to the general manager the Beijing market is big enough to support more than a hundred McDonald's restaurants.[17] At the same time, Pizza Hut, Bony Fried Chicken (of Canada), and Dunkin' Donuts all made their way into the Beijing market. The most interesting newcomer is a noodle shop chain called Californian Beef Noodle King. Although the restaurant sells Chinese noodle soup, it has managed to portray itself as an American fast-food eatery and competes with McDonald's and KFC with lower prices and its appeal to Chinese tastes.

The instant success of Western fast-food chains surprised those in the local restaurant industry. Soon thereafter, many articles in newspapers and journals called for the invention of Chinese-style fast food and the development of a local fast-food industry. April 1992 was a particularly difficult month for those involved in this sector: two weeks after the largest McDonald's restaurant opened at the southern end of Wangfujing Street, Wu Fang Zhai, an old, prestigious restaurant at the northern end of Wangfujing Street, went out of business; in its stead opened International Fast Food City, which sold Japanese fast food, American hamburgers, fried chicken, and ice cream. This was seen as an alarming threat to both the local food industry and the national pride of Chinese culinary culture.[18]

Actually, the local response to the "invasion" of Western fast food began in the late 1980s, right after the initial success of KFC. It quickly developed into what some reporters called a "war of fried chickens" in Beijing. Following the model of KFC, nearly a hundred local fast-food shops featuring more than a dozen kinds of fried chicken appeared between 1989 and 1990. One of the earliest such establishments was Lingzhi Roast Chicken, which began business in 1989; this was followed by Chinese Garden Chicken, Huaxiang Chicken, and Xiangfei Chicken in 1990. The chicken war reached its peak when the Ronghua Fried Chicken company of Shanghai opened its first chain store directly opposite one of the KFC restaurants in Beijing. The manager of Ronghua Chicken proudly announced a challenge to KFC: "Wherever KFC opens a store, we will open another Ronghua Fried Chicken next door."

All of the local fried chicken variations were no more than simple imitations of the KFC food. Their only localizing strategy was to emphasize special Chinese species and sacred recipes that supposedly added an extra medicinal value to their dishes. Thus, consumers were told that the Chinese Garden Chicken might prevent cancer and that Huaxiang Chicken could strengthen the yin-yang balance inside one's body.[19] This strategy did not work well; KFC and McDonald's won out in that first wave of competition. Only a small proportion of the local fried chicken shops managed to survive, while KFC and McDonald's became more and more popular.

Realizing that simply imitating Western fast food was a dead end, the emerging local fast-food industry turned to exploring resources within Chinese cuisine. Among the pioneers, Jinghua Shaomai Restaurant in 1991 tried to transform some traditional Beijing foods into fast foods. This was followed by the entry of a large number of local fast-food restaurants, such as the Beijing Beef Noodle King (not to be confused with the California Beef Noodle King). The Jinghe Kuaican company made the first domestic attempt to develop a fast-food business on a large scale. With the support of the Beijing municipal government, this company built its own farms and processing facilities, but it chose to sell boxed fast foods in mobile vans parked on streets and in residential areas.[20] Thus it fell into the pre-existing category of *hefan* (boxed rice) purveyors. Although the price of boxed fast foods was much lower than that of imported fast food, the boxed fast foods did not meet consumers' expectations of fast food. The Jinghe Kuaican Company disappeared as quickly as it had emerged. In October 1992, nearly a thousand state-owned restaurants united under the flag of the Jingshi Fast Food Company, offering five sets of value meals and more than 50 fast-food items, all of which were derived from traditional Chinese cuisines. This company was also the first fast-food enterprise to be run by the Beijing municipal government, thus indicating the importance of this growing sector to the government.[21] The Henan Province Red Sorghum Restaurant opened on Wangfujing Street in March 1996, immediately across the street from the McDonald's flagship restaurant. Specializing in country-style lamb noodles, the manager of Red Sorghum announced that twelve more restaurants were to be opened in Beijing by the end of 1996, all of which would be next to a McDonald's outlet. "We want to fight McDonald's," the manager claimed, "we want to take back the fast-food market."[22]

By 1996 the fast-food sector in Beijing consisted of three groups: The main group was made up of McDonald's, KFC, and other Western fast-food chains. Although they no longer attracted the keen attention of the news media, their numbers were still growing. The second group consisted of the local KFC imitations, which managed to survive the 1991 "chicken war." The most successful in this group is the Ronghua Chicken restaurant chain, which in 1995 had eleven stores in several cities and more than 500 employees.[23] The third group included restaurants selling newly created Chinese fast foods, from simple noodle soups to Beijing roast duck meals. Many believe that the long tradition of a national cuisine will win out over the consumers' temporary curiosity about Western-style fast food.

Thus far, however, Chinese fast food has not been able to compete with Western fast food, even though it is cheaper and more appealing to the tastes of ordinary citizens in Beijing. Red Sorghum was the third business to announce in public the ambitious goal of beating McDonald's and KFC (after the Shanghai Ronghua Chicken and Beijing Xiangfei Chicken), but so far none have come close. By August 1996 it was clear that Red Sorghum's lamb noodle soup could not compete in the hot summer with Big Mac, which was popular year-round.[24]

The lack of competitiveness of Chinese fast food has drawn official attention at high levels, and in 1996 efforts were made to support the development of a local fast-food sector.[25] Concerned experts in the restaurant industry and commentators in the media attribute the bad showing of the Chinese fast-food restaurants to several things. In the mid-1990s, at least: (1) the quality, nutritional values, and preparation of Western fast foods were highly standardized, while Chinese fast foods were still prepared in traditional ways; (2) Chinese fast-food establishments did not offer the friendly, quick service of Western fast-food restaurants; (3) the local establishments were not as clean and comfortable as the Western fast-food restaurants; and (4) most important, unlike McDonald's or KFC, Chinese restaurants did not employ advanced technologies or modern management methods.[26] From a Marxist perspective, Ling Dawei has concluded that the race between imported and local fast foods in Beijing is a race between advanced and backward forces of production; hence the development of the local fast-food industry will rest ultimately on modernization.[27]

There is no doubt that these views have a basis in everyday practice; yet they all regard food consumption as purely economic behavior and fast-food restaurants as mere eating places. A more complete understanding of the fast-food fever in Beijing also requires close scrutiny of the social context of consumption – the participants and social settings, because "The specific nature of the consumed substances surely matters; but it cannot, by itself, explain why such substances may seem irresistible."[28]

The Spatial Context of Fast-food Consumption

As Giddens points out, most social life occurs in the context of the "fading away" of time and the "shading off" of space.[29] This is certainly true for fast-food consumption. Fast-food restaurants, therefore, need to be examined both as eating places and as social spaces where social interactions occur. A physical place accommodates objects and human agents and provides an arena for social interactions, and it follows that the use of space cannot be separated from the objects and the physical environment.[30] However, space functions only as a context, not a determinant, of social interactions, and the space itself in some way is also socially constructed.[31] In the following pages I consider, on the one hand, how spatial context shapes consumers' behavior and social relations, and how, on the other hand, consumers appropriate fast-food restaurants into their own space. Such an inquiry must begin with a brief review of Beijing's restaurant sector in the late 1970s in order to assess the extent to which Western fast-food outlets differ from existing local restaurants.

Socialist canteens and restaurants in the 1970s

Eating out used to be a difficult venture for ordinary people in Beijing because few restaurants were designed for mass consumption. As mentioned earlier, the restaurants in Beijing were hierarchically ranked by architecture, function, and the type and quality of foods provided. More important, before the economic reforms almost all restaurants and eateries were state-owned businesses, which meant that a restaurant was first and foremost a work unit, just like any factory, shop, or government agency.[32] Thus a restaurant's position and function were also determined by its administrative status as a work unit.

Generally speaking, the restaurant hierarchy consisted of three layers. At the top were luxury and exclusive restaurants in star-rated hotels, such as the Beijing Hotel, which served only foreigners and privileged domestic guests. At the next level were well-established formal restaurants, many of which specialized in a particular style of cuisine and had been in business for many years, even before the 1949 revolution. Unlike the exclusive hotel restaurants, the formal restaurants were open to the public and served two major functions: (1) as public spaces in which small groups of elites could socialize and hold meetings; and (2) as places for ordinary citizens to hold family banquets on special, ritualized occasions such as weddings. At the bottom of the hierarchy were small eateries that provided common family-style foods; these were hardly restaurants (they were actually called *shitang*, meaning canteens). The small eateries were frequented primarily by visitors from outlying provinces and some Beijing residents who had to eat outside their homes because of special job requirements. The majority of Beijing residents rarely ate out – they normally had their meals at home or in their work-unit canteens.

In the 1950s the development of internal canteens (*neibu shitang*) not only constituted an alternative to conventional restaurants but also had a great impact on the latter. Most work units had (and still have) their own canteens, in order to provide employees with relatively inexpensive food and, more important, to control the time allotted for meals. Because canteens were subsidized by the work units and were considered part of employees' benefits, they were run in a manner similar to a family kitchen, only on an enlarged scale. The central message delivered through the canteen facilities was that the work unit, as the representative of the party-state, provided food to its employees, just as a mother feeds her children (without the affectionate component of real parental care). The relationship between the canteen workers and those who ate at the canteens was thus a patronized relationship between the feeder and the fed, rather than a relationship of service provider and customers. The tasteless foods, unfriendly service, and uncomfortable environment were therefore natural components at such public canteens, which prevailed for more than three decades and still exist in many work units today.

The work-unit mentality of "feeding" instead of "serving" people also made its way into restaurants in Beijing because, after all, the restaurants were also work units and thus had the same core features as all other work units – that is, the dominating influence of the state bureaucracy and the planned economy. Commercial restaurants also shared with the work-unit canteens the poor maintenance of internal space, a limited choice of foods, the requirement that the diner pay in advance, fixed times for meals (most restaurants were open only during the short prescribed lunch and dinner times), and of course, ill-tempered workers who acted as if they were distributing food to hungry beggars instead of paying customers.[33] It is true that the higher one moved up the ladder of the restaurant hierarchy the better dining environment and service one could find. But in the famous traditional restaurants and the star-rated hotel restaurants, formality and ritual were most likely the dominating themes. Still, until the late 1980s it was not easy for ordinary people to enjoy dining out in restaurants.

In contrast, Western fast-food restaurants offered local consumers a new cultural experience symbolized by foreign fast food, enjoyable spatial arrangements of objects and people, and American-style service and social interactions.

The cultural symbolism of fast food

It is perhaps a truism to note that food is not only good to eat but also good for the mind. The (Western) fast-food fever in Beijing provides another example of how in certain circumstances customers may care less about the food and more about the cultural messages it delivers. During my fieldwork in 1994 I discovered that although children were great fans of the Big Mac and french fries, most adult customers did not particularly like those fast foods. Many people commented that the taste was not good and that the flavor of cheese was strange. The most common complaint from adult customers was *chi bu bao*, meaning that McDonald's hamburgers and fries did not make one feel full: they were more like snacks than like meals.[34] It is also interesting to note that both McDonald's and KFC emphasized the freshness, purity, and nutritional value of their foods (instead of their appealing tastes). According to a high-level manager of Beijing McDonald's, the recipes for McDonald's foods were designed to meet modern scientific specifications and thus differed from the recipes for Chinese foods, which were based on cultural expectations.[35] Through advertisements and news media reports, this idea that fast foods use nutritious ingredients and are prepared using scientific cooking methods has been accepted by the public. This may help to explain why few customers compared the taste of fast foods to that of traditional Chinese cuisine; instead customers focused on something other than the food.

If people do not like the imported fast food, why are they still keen on going to Western fast-food restaurants? Most informants said that they liked the atmosphere, the style of eating, and the experience of being there. According to an early report on KFC, customers did not go to KFC to eat the chicken but to enjoy "eating" (consuming) the culture associated with KFC. Most customers spent hours talking to each other and gazing out the huge glass windows onto busy commercial streets – and feeling more sophisticated than the people who passed by.[36] Some local observers argued that the appeal of Chinese cuisine was the taste of the food itself and that, in contrast, Western food relied on the manner of presentation. Thus consumers would seem to be interested in the spectacle created by this new form of eating.[37] In other words, what Beijing customers find satisfying about Western fast-food restaurants is not the food but the experience.

The cultural symbolism that McDonald's, KFC, and other fast-food chains carry with them certainly plays an important role in constructing this nonedible yet fulfilling experience. Fast food, particularly McDonald's fast food, is considered quintessentially American in many parts of the contemporary world. In France, the most commonly agreed "American thing" among teenagers is McDonald's, followed by Coca-Cola and "military and space technologies."[38] In Moscow, a local journalist described the opening of the first McDonald's restaurant as the arrival of the "ultimate icon of Americana."[39] The same is true in Beijing, although the official news media have emphasized the element of modernity instead of Americana. The high efficiency of the service and management, fresh ingredients, friendly service, and spotless dining environment in Western fast-food restaurants have been repeatedly reported by the Beijing media as concrete examples of modernity.[40]

Ordinary consumers are interested in the stories told in news reports, popular magazines, and movies that the Big Mac and fried chicken are what make Americans American. According to a well-known commentator on popular culture in Beijing, because of the modernity inherent in the McDonald's fast-food chain, many American youths prefer to work first at McDonald's before finding other jobs on the market. The experience of working at McDonald's, he argues, prepares American youth for any kind of job in a modern society.[41] To many Beijing residents, "American" also means "modern," and thus to eat at McDonald's is to experience modernity. During my fieldwork I talked with many parents who appreciated their children's fondness for imported fast food because they believed it was in good taste to be modern. A mother told me that she had made great efforts to adapt to the strange flavor of McDonald's food so that she could take her daughter to McDonald's twice a week. She explained: "I want my daughter to learn more about American culture. She is taking an English typing class now, and I will buy her a computer next year." Apparently, eating a Big Mac and fries, like learning typing and computer skills, is part of the mother's plan to prepare her daughter for a modern society.

Inspired by the success of the cultural symbolism of McDonald's and KFC, many Chinese fast-food restaurants have tried to use traditional Chinese culture to lure customers. As I mentioned in the preceding section, almost all local fried-chicken outlets during 1990–91 emphasized the use of traditional medicinal ingredients and the idea of health-enhancing food.[42] Others used ethnic and local flavors to stress the Chineseness of their fast foods, such as the Red Sorghum's promotion of its lamb noodle soup.[43] And some directly invoked the nationalist feelings of the customers. For instance, Happy Chopsticks, a new fast-food chain in Shenzhen, adopted "Chinese people eat Chinese food" as the leading slogan in its market promotion.[44] The power of cultural symbolism in the fast-food sector also has made an impact on the restaurant industry in general: the cultural position of the restaurant business is regarded as an important issue, and the debate about the differences between Western and Chinese cuisine continues in professional journals.[45]

A place of entertainment for equals

According to older residents, in addition to different cuisine styles, traditional restaurants in pre-1949 Beijing also differed in their interior decorations, seating arrangements, and interactions between restaurant employees and customers. During the Maoist era, such features were considered inappropriate to the needs of working-class people and thus gradually disappeared. Under the brutal attack on traditional culture during the Cultural Revolution period, some famous restaurants even replaced their old names with new, revolutionary names, such as Workers and Peasants Canteen (*Gongnong shitang*). As a result, by the late 1970s most restaurants looked similar both inside and out, which, combined with the canteen mentality in restaurant management and poor service, turned Beijing restaurants into unpleasant eating places.

When KFC and McDonald's opened their outlets in Beijing, what most impressed Beijing consumers was their beautiful appearance. As mentioned earlier, both the first KFC and first McDonald's are located near Tiananmen Square in the heart of Beijing, and both boast that they are the largest outlets of their kind in the world, one with a three-floor, 500-seat building and the other with a two-floor, 700-seat building. The statues of Colonel Sanders and Ronald McDonald in front of the two establishments immediately became national tourist attractions.

Once inside the restaurants, Beijing customers found other surprises. First, both McDonald's and the KFC restaurants were brightly lit and climate-controlled. The seats, tables, and walls were painted in light colors, which, together with the shiny counters, stainless-steel kitchenware, and soft music in the background, created an open and cheerful physical environment – a sharp contrast to traditional Chinese restaurants. Moreover, social interaction at McDonald's or KFC was highly ritualized and dramatized,[46] representing a radical departure from the canteen-like restaurants in Beijing. Employees wore neat, brightly colored uniforms, and they smiled at customers while working conscientiously and efficiently. As one observant informant remarked, even the employee responsible for cleaning the toilets worked in a disciplined manner. In his study of restaurants in Athens, Georgia, Allen Shelton commented: "The spectacle of McDonald's is work: the chutes filling up with hamburgers; the restaurant and the other diners are secondary views."[47] In contrast, both the work and the restaurant itself constituted the spectacle at McDonald's and KFC in Beijing.

One of the things that most impressed new customers of the fast-food outlets was the menu, which is displayed above and behind the counter, with soft backlighting and photographic images of the food. The menu delivers a clear message about the public, affordable eating experience that the establishment offers. This was particularly important for first-timers, who did not know anything about the exotic food. Another feature is the open, clean, kitchen area, which clearly shows the customers how the hamburgers and fried chickens are prepared. To emphasize this feature, Beijing's McDonald's also provides a five-minute tour of the kitchen area on customer request.

The Western fast-food restaurants also gave customers a sense of equality. Both employees and customers remain standing during the ordering process, creating an equal relationship between the two parties. More important, the friendly service and the smiling employees give customers the impression that no matter who you are you will be treated with equal warmth and friendliness. Accordingly, many people patronize McDonald's to experience a moment of equality.[48] The restaurants also seem to convey gender equality and have attracted a large number of female customers (I will return to this point later).

All these details in internal space are important in understanding the success of McDonald's and KFC in Beijing: objects have a voice that originates in those who use them, just as the scenery on a stage shapes the movements of an actor.[49] The impact of spatial context on people's behavior in McDonald's restaurants is well addressed by Peter Stephenson. He observed that some Dutch customers lost their cultural "self" in such a culturally decontextualized place because "there is a kind of instant emigration that occurs the moment one walks through the doors, where Dutch rules rather obviously don't apply."[50] Rick Fantasia observed that French customers undergo similar changes or adjustments in behavior in McDonald's outlets in Paris.[51] Given the sharper and deeper cultural differences between American and Chinese societies, it is natural to expect the cultural decontextualization to be even stronger in Beijing's McDonald's and KFC restaurants.

The interesting point is that, owing to the powerful appeal of modernity and Americana projected by McDonald's and KFC, when experiencing the same "instant emigration," Beijing customers seem to be more willing to observe the rules of American fast-food restaurants than their counterparts in Leiden or Paris. For instance, in 1992 and 1993 customers in Beijing (as in Hong Kong and Taiwan) usually left their rubbish on the table for the restaurant employees to clean up: people regarded McDonald's as a formal establishment at which they had paid for full service. However, during the summer of 1994 I observed that about one-fifth of the customers, many of them fashionably dressed youth, carried their own trays to the waste bins. From subsequent interviews I discovered that most of these people were regular customers, and they had learned to clean up their tables by observing the foreigners' behavior. Several informants told me that when they disposed of their own rubbish they felt more "civilized" (wenming) than the other customers because they knew the proper behavior. My random check of customer behavior in McDonald's and in comparably priced and more expensive Chinese restaurants shows that people in McDonald's were, on the whole, more self-restrained and polite toward one another, spoke in lower tones, and were more careful not to throw their trash on the ground. Unfortunately, when they returned to a Chinese context, many also returned to their previous patterns of behavior. As a result, the overall atmosphere in a Western fast-food outlet is always nicer than that in Chinese restaurants of the same or even higher quality.[52]

A multidimensional social space

In part because of the cultural symbolism of Americana and modernity and in part because of the exotic, cheerful, and comfortable physical environment, McDonald's, KFC, and other foreign fast-food restaurants attract customers from all walks of life in Beijing. Unlike in the United States, where the frequenters of fast-food restaurants are generally associated with low income and simple tastes, most frequenters of fast-food restaurants in Beijing are middle-class professionals, trendy yuppies, and well-educated youths. Unfortunately, there has yet to be a systematic social survey of Chinese fast-food consumers. Nevertheless, according to my field observations in 1994, a clear distinction can be drawn between those who occasionally partake of the imported fast foods and those who regularly frequent fast-food restaurants.

Occasional adventurers include both Beijing residents and visitors from outlying provinces and cities. It should be noted that a standard one-person meal at McDonald's (including a hamburger, a soft drink, and an order of French fries, which is the equivalent of a value-meal at McDonald's in the (United States) cost 17 renminbi (rmb) ($2.10) in 1994 and 21 rmb ($2.60) in 1996.[53] This may not be expensive by American standards, but it is not an insignificant amount of money for ordinary workers in Beijing, who typically made less than 500 rmb ($60) per month in 1994. Thus, many people, especially those with moderate incomes, visited McDonald's restaurants only once or twice, primarily to satisfy their curiosity about American food and culinary culture. A considerable proportion of the customers were tourists from other provinces who had only heard of McDonald's or seen its Golden Arches in the movies. The tasting of American food has recently become an important part of the tourist beat in Beijing; and those who partake of the experience are able to boast about it to their relatives and friends back home.

There are also local customers who frequent foreign fast-food outlets on a regular basis. A survey conducted by Beijing McDonald's management in one of its stores showed that 10.2 percent of the customers frequented the restaurant four times per month in 1992, in 1993 the figure was 38.3 percent.[54] The majority of customers fell into three categories: professionals and white-collar workers; young couples and teenagers; and children accompanied by their parents. Moreover, women of all age groups tended to frequent McDonald's restaurants more than men.

For younger Beijing residents who worked in joint-venture enterprises or foreign firms and had higher incomes, eating at McDonald's, Kentucky Fried Chicken, and Pizza Hut had become an integral part of their new lifestyle, a way for them to be connected to the outside world. As one informant commented: "The Big Mac doesn't taste great; but the experience of eating in this place makes me feel good. Sometimes I even imagine that I am sitting in a restaurant in New York or Paris." Although some emphasized that they only went to save time, none finished their meals within twenty minutes. Like other customers, these young professionals arrived in small groups or accompanied by girl/boy friends to enjoy the restaurant for an hour or more. Eating foreign food, and consuming other foreign goods, had become an important way for Chinese yuppies to define themselves as middle-class professionals. By 1996, however, this group had found other types of activities (such as nightclubs or bars), and gradually they were beginning to visit foreign fast-food restaurants for convenience rather than for status.

Young couples and teenagers from all social strata were also regular frequenters of McDonald's and KFC outlets because the dining environment is considered to be romantic and comfortable. The restaurants are brightly-lit, clean, and feature light Western music; and except during busy periods they are relatively quiet, making them ideal for courtship. In 1994, McDonald's seven Beijing restaurants had all created relatively isolated and private service areas with tables for two. In some, these areas were nicknamed "lovers' corners." Many teenagers also considered that, with only the minimum consumption of a soft drink or an ice cream, fast-food establishments were good places simply to hang out.

As in many other parts of the world, children in Beijing had become loyal fans of Western fast food. They were so fond of it that some parents even suspected that Big Mac or fried chicken contained a special, hidden ingredient. The fast-food restaurants also made special efforts to attract children by offering birthday parties, dispensing souvenirs, and holding essay contests, because young customers usually did not come alone: they were brought to McDonald's and KFC by their parents or grandparents. Once a middle-aged woman told me that she did not like the taste of hamburgers and that her husband simply hated them. But their daughter loved hamburgers and milkshakes so much that their entire family had to visit McDonald's three to five times a month. It is common among Beijing families for children to choose the restaurant in which the whole family dines out. Fast-food outlets were frequently the first choice of children.

A gender aspect of fast-food consumption is highlighted in He Yupeng's 1996 study of McDonald's popularity among female customers. In conducting a small-scale survey at four restaurants in Beijing – a formal Chinese restaurant, a local fast-food outlet, and two McDonald's outlets – He found that women were more likely than men to enjoy dining at fast-food restaurants. According to his survey, while 66 percent of the customers (N=68) at the formal Chinese restaurant were men, 64 percent of the customers (N=423) at the local fast-food outlet were women. Similar patterns were observed in the two McDonald's restaurants, where women constituted 57 percent of a total of 784 adult customers.[55] The most intriguing finding of this survey was that women chose McDonald's because they enjoyed ordering their own food and participating in the conversation while dining. Many female customers pointed out that in formal Chinese restaurants men usually order the food for their female companions and control the conversation. In contrast, they said, at a McDonald's everyone can make his or her own choices and, because smoking and alcohol are prohibited, men dominate less of the conversation.[56]

Furthermore, the imported fast-food restaurants provide a venue where women feel comfortable alone or with female friends. Formal Chinese restaurants are customarily used by elite groups as places to socialize and by middle-class people as places to hold ritual family events such as wedding banquets. In both circumstances, women must subordinate themselves to rules and manners that are androcentric, either explicitly or implicitly (the men order the dishes; the women do not partake of the liquor). These customs reflect the traditional view that women's place is in the household and that men should take charge of all public events. There is a clear division between the private (inside) and the public (outside) along gender lines.

A woman who eats alone in a formal Chinese restaurant is considered abnormal; such behavior often leads to public suspicion about her morality and her occupation. For instance, a young woman I interviewed in a McDonald's outlet in 1994 recalled having lunch alone in a well-known Chinese restaurant frequented mostly by successful businessmen. "Several men gazed at me with lascivious eyes," she said, "and some others exchanged a few words secretly and laughed among themselves. They must have thought I was a prostitute or at least a loose woman. Knowing their evil thoughts, I felt extremely uncomfortable and left the place as quickly as I could." She also commented that even going to a formal Chinese restaurant with female friends would make her feel somewhat improper about herself, because the "normal" customers were men or men with women. But she said that she felt comfortable visiting a McDonald's alone or with her female friends, because "many people do the same." This young woman's experience is by no means unique, and a number of female customers in McDonald's offered similar explanations for liking the foreign fast-food restaurants. Several elderly women also noted the impropriety of women dining in formal Chinese restaurants, although they were less worried about accusations about their morals.[57]

In his survey, He Yupeng asked his respondents where they would choose to eat if there were only a formal Chinese restaurant and a McDonald's outlet. Almost all the male respondents chose the former, and all the female respondents chose the latter. One of the main reasons for such a sharp gender difference, He argues, is the concern of contemporary women for gender equality.[58] The new table manners allowed in fast-food restaurants, and more important, the newly appropriate gender roles in those public places, seem to have enhanced the image of foreign fast-food restaurants as an open place for equals, thus attracting female customers.

The appropriation of social space

Finally, I would point out that Beijing customers do not passively accept everything offered by the American fast-food chains. The American fast-food restaurants have been localized in many aspects, and what Beijing customers enjoy is actually a Chinese version of American culture and fast foods.[59] One aspect of this localization process is the consumers' appropriation of the social space.

My research confirms the impression that most customers in Beijing claim their tables for longer periods of time than Americans do. The average dining time in Beijing (in autumn 1994) was 25 minutes during busy hours and 51 minutes during slack hours. In Beijing, "fastness" does not seem to be particularly important. The cheerful, comfortable, and climate-controlled environment inside McDonald's and KFC restaurants encourages many customers to linger, a practice that seems to contradict the original purpose of the American fast-food business. During off-peak hours it is common for people to walk into McDonald's for a leisurely drink or snack. Sitting with a milk-shake or an order of fries, such customers often spend 30 minutes to an hour, and sometimes longer, chatting, reading newspapers, or holding business meetings. As indicated earlier, young couples and teenagers are particularly fond of frequenting foreign fast-food outlets because they consider the environment to be romantic. Women in all age groups tend to spend the longest time in these establishments, whether they are alone or with friends. In contrast, unaccompanied men rarely linger after finishing their meals. The main reason for this gender difference, according to my informants, is the absence of alcoholic beverages. An interesting footnote in this connection is that 32 percent of my informants in a survey among college students (N = 97) regarded McDonald's as a symbol of leisure and emphasized that they went there to relax.

Beijing consumers have appropriated the restaurants not only as places of leisure but also as public arenas for personal and family ritual events. The most popular such event is of course the child's birthday party, which has been institutionalized in Beijing McDonald's restaurants. Arriving with five or more guests, a child can expect an elaborate ritual performed in a special enclosure called "Children's paradise," free of extra charge. The ritual begins with an announcement over the restaurant's loudspeakers – in both Chinese and English – giving the child's name and age, together with congratulations from Ronald McDonald (who is called Uncle McDonald in Beijing). This is followed by the recorded song "Happy Birthday," again in two languages. A female employee in the role of Aunt McDonald then entertains the children with games and presents each child with a small gift from Uncle McDonald. Although less formalized (and without the restaurant's active promotion), private ceremonies are also held in the restaurants for adult customers, particularly for young women in peer groups (the absence of alcohol makes the site attractive to them). Of the 97 college students in my survey, 33 (including nine men) had attended personal celebrations at McDonald's: birthday parties, farewell parties, celebrations for receiving scholarships to American universities, and end-of-term parties.

The multifunctional use of McDonald's space is due in part to the lack of cafes, tea houses, and ice-cream shops in Beijing; it is also a consequence of the management's efforts to attract as many customers as possible by engendering an inviting environment. Although most McDonald's outlets in the United States are designed specifically to prevent socializing (with less-comfortable seats than formal restaurants, for instance) it is clear that the managers of Beijing's McDonald's have accepted their customers' perceptions of McDonald's as a special place that does not fit into pre-existing categories of public eateries. They have not tried to educate Beijing consumers to accept the American view that "fast food" means that one must eat fast and leave quickly.[60] When I wondered how the management accommodated everyone during busy periods, I was told that the problem often resolved itself. A crowd of customers naturally created pressures on those who had finished their meals, and more important, during busy hours the environment was no longer appropriate for relaxation.

In contrast, managers in Chinese fast-food outlets tend to be less tolerant of customers who linger. During my fieldwork in 1994 I conducted several experimental tests by going to Chinese fast-food outlets and ordering only a soft drink but staying for more than an hour. Three out of four times I was indirectly urged to leave by the restaurant employees; they either took away my empty cup or asked if I needed anything else. Given the fact that I was in a fast-food outlet and did all the service for myself, the disturbing "service" in the middle of my stay was clearly a message to urge lingering customers to leave. I once discussed this issue with the manager of a Chinese fast-food restaurant. He openly admitted that he did not like customers claiming a table for long periods of time and certainly did not encourage attempts to turn the fast-food outlet into a coffee shop. As he explained: "If you want to enjoy nice coffee and music then you should go to a fancy hotel cafe, not here."

Concluding Remarks: Dining Place, Social Space, and Mass Consumption

In the United States, fast-food outlets are regarded as "fuel stations" for hungry yet busy people and as family restaurants for low-income groups. Therefore, efficiency (speed) and economic value (low prices) are the two most important reasons why fast foods emerged as a kind of "industrial food" and remain successful in American society today. These features, however, do not apply in Beijing. A Beijing worker who loads the whole family into a taxi to go to McDonald's may spend one-sixth of his monthly income; efficiency and economy are perhaps the least of his concerns. When consumers stay in McDonald's or KFC restaurants for hours, relaxing, chatting, reading, enjoying the music, or celebrating birthdays, they take the "fastness" out of fast food. In Beijing, the fastness of American fast food is reflected mainly in the service provided; for consumers, the dining experience is too meaningful to be shortened. As a result, the American fast-food outlets in China are fashionable, middle-class establishments – a new kind of social space where people can enjoy their leisure time and experience a Chinese version of American culture.

As I emphasize repeatedly throughout this chapter, eating at a foreign fast-food restaurant is an important social event, although it means different things to different people. McDonald's, KFC, and other fast-food restaurants in Beijing carry the symbolism of Americana and modernity, which makes them unsurpassable by existing standards of the social hierarchy in Chinese culture. They represent an emerging tradition where new values, behavior patterns, and social relationships are still being created. People from different social backgrounds may enter the same eating place/social space without worrying about losing face; on the contrary, they may find new ways to better define their positions. For instance, white-collar professionals may display their new class status, youngsters may show their special taste for leisure, and parents may want to "modernize" their children. Women of all ages are able to enjoy their independence when they choose to eat alone; and when they eat with male companions, they enjoy a sexual equality that is absent in formal Chinese restaurants. The fast-food restaurants, therefore, constitute a multivocal, multidimensional, and open social space. This kind of all-inclusive social space met a particular need in the 1990s, when Beijing residents had to work harder than ever to define their positions in a rapidly changing society.[61]

By contrast, almost all local competitors in the fast-food sector tend to regard fast-food restaurants merely as eating places, and accordingly, they try to compete with the foreign fast-food restaurants by offering lower prices and local flavors or by appealing to nationalist sentiments. Although they also realize the importance of hygiene, food quality, friendly service, and a pleasant physical environment, they regard these features as isolated technical factors. A local observer pointed out that it is easy to build the "hardware" of a fast-food industry (the restaurants) but that the "software" (service and management) cannot be adopted overnight.[62] To borrow from this metaphor, I would argue that an understanding of fast-food outlets not only as eating places but also as social space is one of the "software problems" waiting to be resolved by the local competitors in the fast-food business.

Why is the issue of social space so important for fast-food development in Beijing? It would take another essay to answer this question completely; here I want to highlight three major factors that contribute to fast-food fever and are closely related to consumers' demands for a new kind of social space.

First, the trend of mass consumption that arose in the second half of the 1980s created new demands for dining out as well as new expectations of the restaurant industry. According to 1994 statistics released by the China Consumer Society, the average expenditure per capita has increased 4.1 times since 1984. The ratio of "hard consumption" (on food, clothes, and other necessities of daily life) to "soft consumption" (entertainment, tourism, fashion, and socializing) went from 3:1 in 1984 to 1:1.2 in 1994.[63] In 1990, consumers began spending money as never before on such goods and services as interior decoration, private telephones and pagers, air conditioners, body-building machines, and tourism.[64] As part of this trend toward consumerism, dining out has become a popular form of entertainment among virtually all social groups, and people are particularly interested in experimenting with different cuisines.[65] In response to a survey conducted by the Beijing Statistics

Bureau in early 1993, nearly half of the respondents said they had eaten at Western-style restaurants (including fast-food outlets) at least once.[66] A central feature of this development in culinary culture is that people want to dine out as active consumers, and they want the dining experience to be relaxed, fun, and healthful.

In response to increasing consumer demands, thousands of restaurants and eateries have appeared in recent years. By early 1993 there were more than 19,000 eating establishments in Beijing, ranging from elegant five-star hotel restaurants to simple street eateries. Of these, about 5,000 were stateowned, 55 were joint ventures or foreign-owned, and the remaining 14,000 or so were owned by private entrepreneurs or independent vendors (getihu).[67]

These figures show that the private sector has played an increasingly important role in the restaurant business. Unlike the state-owned restaurants, some private restaurants have used creativity to meet consumers' demands for a new kind of dining experience. The best example is the emergence of country-style, nostalgic restaurants set up by and for the former sent-down urban youths. In these places customers retaste their experience of youth in the countryside: customers choose from country-style foods in rooms and among objects that remind them of the past. Like customers in McDonald's or KFC, they are also consuming part of the subculture and redefining themselves in a purchased social space. The difference is that the nostalgic restaurants appeal only to a particular social group, while the American fast-food outlets are multivocal and multidimensional and thus attract people from many different social strata.

The rise of new consumer groups is the second major factor that has made the issue of social space so important to understanding fast-food fever in Beijing. Urban youth, children, and women of all ages constitute the majority of the regular frequenters of American fast-food restaurants. It is not by accident that these people are all newcomers as restaurant customers – there was no proper place for them in the pre-existing restaurant system, and the only social role that women, youth, and children could play in a formal Chinese restaurant was as the dependents of men. Women's effort to gain an equal place in restaurant subculture was discussed earlier, so here I briefly examine the place of youth and children.

Young professionals emerged along with the development of the market economy, especially with the expansion of joint-venture and foreign-owned business in Beijing in the 1990s. To prove and further secure their newly obtained social status and prestige, the young elite have taken the construction of a different lifestyle seriously, and they often lead the trend of contemporary consumerism in Chinese cities. Urban youth may be less well off than young professionals, but they are equally eager to embrace a new way of personal life. According to a 1994 survey, the purchasing power of Beijing youth increased dramatically over the previous decade, and nearly half of the 1,000 respondents in the survey had more than 500 rmb per month to spend on discretionary items.[68] With more freedom to determine their lifestyles and more economic independence, these youngsters were eager to establish their own social space in many aspects of life, including dining out.[69] A good example in this connection is the astonishing popularity among young people in mainland China of pop music, films, and romance novels from Hong Kong and Taiwan.[70]

The importance of teenagers and children in effecting social change also emerged in the late twentieth century, along with the growth of the national economy, the increase in family wealth, and the decline of the birth rate. The single-child policy – which is most strictly implemented in the big cities – has created a generation of little emperors and empresses, each demanding the attention and economic support of his or her parents and grandparents. Parental indulgence of children has become a national obsession, making children and teenagers one of the most active groups of consumers. Beijing is by no means exceptional in this respect. According to Deborah Davis and Julia Sensenbrenner, ordinary working-class parents in Shanghai normally spend one-third of their monthly wages to provide their children with a lifestyle that is distinctly upper middle class in its patterns of consumption. For many parents, toys, trips, fashionable clothes, music lessons, and restaurant meals have become necessities in raising their children. This suggests a significant change in patterns of household expenditure, and accordingly there is an urgent need to meet the market demands and special tastes of this important group of consumers.

The emerging importance of women, youth, and children as consumers results from a significant transformation of the family institution in contemporary Chinese society, which is characterized by the nuclearization of the household, the centrality of conjugality in family relations, the rising awareness of independence and sexual equality among women, the waning of the patriarchy, and the rediscovery of the value of children.[71] As far as fast-food consumption is concerned, the link between new groups of independent consumers and shifts in family values is found in other East Asian societies as well. After analyzing the relationship between the McDonald's "takeoff" in five cities (Tokyo, Hong Kong, Taipei, Seoul, and Beijing) and the changes in family values (especially the rising status of teenagers and children), Watson concluded: "More than any other factor... McDonald's success is attributable to the revolution in family values that has transformed East Asia."[72]

A third important factor in the success of Western fast-food enterprises is the new form of sociality that has been developing in market-controlled public places such as restaurants. A significant change in public life during the post-Mao era has been the disappearance of frequent mass rallies, voluntary work, collective parties, and other forms of "organized sociality" in which the state (through its agents) played the central role. In its place are new forms of private gatherings in public venues. Whereas "organized sociality" emphasized the centrality of the state, the official ideology, and the submission of individuals to an officially endorsed collectivity, the new sociality celebrates individuality and private desires in unofficial social and spatial contexts. The center of public life and socializing, accordingly, has shifted from large state-controlled public spaces (such as city squares, auditoriums, and workers' clubs) to smaller, commercialized arenas such as dancing halls, bowling alleys, and even imaginary spaces provided by radio call-in shows. The new sociality has even emerged in conventionally state-controlled public spaces, such as parks, and has thus transformed them into multidimensional spaces in which the state, the public, and the private may coexist.

Restaurants similarly meet the demand for a new kind of sociality outside state control – that is, the public celebration of individual desires, life aspirations, and personal communications in a social context. As indicated above, in earlier decades the socialist state did not encourage the use of restaurants as a social space in which to celebrate private desires or perform family rituals. Rather, by institutionalizing public canteens in the workplace, the state tried to control meal time and also change the meaning of social dining itself. This is particularly true in Beijing, which has been the center of national politics and socialist transformation since 1949. Any new form of social dining was unlikely to develop from the previous restaurant sector in Beijing, which consisted primarily of socialist canteens. It is thus not accidental that by 1993 nearly three-quarters of the more than 19,000 eating establishments in Beijing were owned by private entrepreneurs (local and foreign) or were operating as joint ventures.[73] McDonald's and other foreign fast-food restaurants have been appropriated by Beijing consumers as especially attractive social spaces for a new kind of socializing and for the celebration of individuality in public. Moreover, consuming at McDonald's and other foreign fast-food outlets is also a way of embracing modernity and foreign culture in public.

To sum up, there is a close link between the development of fast-food consumption and changes in social structure, especially the emergence of new social groups.[74] The new groups of agents demand the creation of new space for socialization in every aspect of public life, including dining out. Fast-food restaurants provide just such a space for a number of social groups. The new kind of sociality facilitated by fast-food restaurants in turn further stimulates consumers' demands for both the food and the space. Hence the fast-food fever in Beijing during the 1990s.

NOTES

1   Liu Fen and Long Zaizu 1986.
2   For a general review, see Messer 1984.
3   See, e.g., Jerome 1980.
4   See Douglas 1975; Lévi-Strauss 1983; and Sahlins 1976.
5   See Harris 1985; Murphy 1986; and Appadurai 1981.
6   Bourdieu 1984, pp. 175–200.
7   Watson 1987. For more systematic studies of food in China, see Chang 1977 and E. Anderson 1988.
8   See Gusfield 1992, p. 80.
9   Finkelstein 1989, pp. 68–71.
10 Ibid. p. 5.
11 Shelton 1990, p. 525.
12 See Fantasia 1995, pp. 213–15.
13 For an anthropological study of sociocultural encounters at McDonald's in Hong Kong Taipei, Beijing, Seoul, and Tokyo, see chapters in Watson, ed., 1997.
14 See Love 1986, p. 448.
15 See Zhang Yubin 1992.
16 See New York Times, April 24, 1992. For a detailed account, see Yan 1997a.
17 See China Daily, September 12, 1994; and Service Bridge, August 12, 1994.
18 See Liu Ming 1992; Mian Zhi 1993.
19 Duan Gang 1991.
20 Zhang Zhaonan 1992a.
21 See Zhang Zhaonan 1992b; You Zi 1994; and Zhang Guoyun 1995.

22 Yu Bin 1996; "Honggaoliang yuyan zhongshi kuaican da qushi" 1996.

23 Yu Weize 1995.

24 See Liu Fen and Long Zaizu 1986.

25 The development of Chinese fast food is incorporated into the eighth national five-year plan for scientific research. See Bi Yuhua 1994; see also Ling Dawei 1996.

26 For representative views on this issue, see Guo Jianying 1995; Huang Shengbing 1995; Jian Feng 1992; Xiao Hua 1993; Ye Xianning 1993; Yan Zhenguo and Liu Yinsheng 1992a; and Zhong Zhe 1993.

27 Ling Dawei 1995.

28 Mintz 1993, p. 271.

29 Giddens 1984, p. 132.

30 See Sayer 1985, pp. 30–31.

31 See Lechner 1991; Urry 1985.

32 For a comprehensive study of the work-unit system, see Walder 1986.

33 In prereform Beijing even the hotel restaurants and guesthouse canteens were open only during "proper" meal times. So if a visitor missed the meal time, the only alternative was to buy bread and soft drinks from a grocery store.

34 For more details on the results of the survey, see Yan 1997a.

35 See discussions in Xu Chengbei 1994.

36 *Zhongguo shipinbao* (Chinese food newspaper), November 6, 1991.

37 *Jingji ribao*, September 15, 1991.

38 Fantasia 1995, p. 219.

39 Ritzer 1993, pp. 4–5.

40 Every time McDonald's opened a new restaurant in the early 1990s, it was featured in the Chinese media. See e.g., *Tianjin qingnianbao* (Tianjin youth news), June 8, 1994; *Shanghai jingji ribao* (Shanghai economic news), July 22, 1994; *Wenhui bao* (Wenhui daily), July 22, 1994. See also Han Shu 1994; Xu Chengbei 1993, p. 3.

41 Xu Chengbei 1992. In fact, I applied to work in a McDonald's outlet in Beijing but was turned down. The manager told me that the recruitment of employees in McDonald's involves a long and strict review process, in order to make sure that the applicants' qualifications are competitive.

42 The relationship between medicine and food has long been an important concern in Chinese culinary culture. See E. Anderson 1988, pp. 53–6.

43 See Yu Bin 1996; and "Honggaoliang yuyan" 1996.

44 Liu Guoyue 1996.

45 See Zhao Huanyan 1995; Xu Wangsheng 1995; Xie Dingyuan 1996; and Tao Wentai 1996.

46 For an excellent account, see Kottak 1978.

47 Shelton 1990, p. 520.

48 *Gaige Daobao* (Reform herald), no. 1 (1994), p. 34.

49 See Douglas and Isherwood 1979.

50 Stephenson 1989, p. 237.

51 Fantasia 1995, pp. 221–2.

52 For an interesting study of eating etiquette in southern China, see Cooper 1986, pp. 179–84. As mentioned near the beginning of this chapter, Finkelstein offers an interesting and radically different view of existing manners and custom in restaurants. Since manners and behavior patterns are socially constructed and imposed on customers, they make the "restaurant a diorama that emphasizes the aspects of sociality assumed to be the most valued and attractive" (Finkelstein 1989, p. 52). Accordingly, customers give up their individuality and spontaneity and thus cannot explore their real inner world in this kind of socially constructed spatial context (ibid., pp. 4–17).

53 The 1994 figure comes from my fieldwork; the 1996 figure is taken from Beijing Dashiye Jingji Diaocha Gongsi (Beijing big perspective economic survey company), quoted in "Kuaican zoujin gongxin jieceng" (Fast food is coming closer to salaried groups), *Zhongguo jingyingbao*, June 21, 1996.

54 Interview with General Manager Tim Lai, September 28, 1994.

55 He Yupeng 1996.

56 Ibid. p. 8.

57 See Yan 1997a.

58 He Yupeng 1996, pp. 8–9.

59 See Yan 1997a.

60 According to John Love, when Den Fujita, the founder and owner of McDonald's chain stores in Japan, began introducing McDonald's foods to Japanese customers, particularly the youngsters, he bent the rules by allowing his McDonald's outlets to be a hangout place for teenagers. He decorated one of the early stores with poster-sized pictures of leather-jacketed members of a motorcycle gang "one shade removed" from Hell's Angels. Fujita's experiment horrified the McDonald's chairman when he visited the company's new branches in Japan. See Love 1986, p. 429.

61 Elsewhere I have argued that Chinese society in the 1990s underwent a process of restructuring. The entire Chinese population – not only the peasants – was on the move: some physically, some socially, and some in both ways. An interesting indicator of the increased social mobility and changing patterns of social stratification was the booming business of name-card printing, because so many people changed jobs and titles frequently and quickly. Thus consumption and lifestyle decisions became more important than ever as ways for individuals to define their positions. For more details, see Yan 1994.

62 Yan Zhenguo and Liu Yinshing 1992b.

63 See Xiao Yan 1994.

64 See, e.g., Gao Changli 1992, p. 6; Dong Fang 1994, p. 22.

65 Gu Bingshu 1994.

66 *Beijing wanbao*, January 27, 1993.

67 *Beijing qingnianbao* (Beijing youth daily), December 18, 1993.

68 Pian Ming 1994.

69 For a review of changes in consumption and lifestyles among Chinese youth, see Huang Zhijian 1994.

70 See Gold 1993.

71 On changing family values and household structure, see chapters in Davis and Harrell 1993. For a detailed study of the rising importance of conjugality in rural family life, see Yan 1997b.

72 Watson 1997, p. 19.

73 See *Beijing qingnianbao*, December 18, 1993.

74 See especially Mintz 1994; see also sources cited in notes 2 to 13.

REFERENCES

Anderson, Eugene. 1988. *The Food of China*. New Haven, Conn.: Yale University Press.

Appadurai, Arjun. 1981. "Gastro-Politics in Hindu South Asia." *American Ethnologist* 8, no. 3: 494–511.

Bi Yuhua. 1994. "Kuaicanye zhengshi chengwei xin de redianhangye" (Fast food officially becoming a new hot sector). *Shichang bao* (Market news), September 19.

Bourdieu, Pierre. 1984. *Distinction: A Social Critique of the Judgement of Taste*. Cambridge, Mass.: Harvard University Press.

Chang, Kwang-chih, ed. 1977. *Food in Chinese Culture: Anthropological and Historical Perspectives*. New Haven, Conn.: Yale University Press.

Cooper, Eugene. 1986. "Chinese Table Manners: You Are How You Eat." *Human Organization* 45: 179–84.

Davis, Deborah, and Stevan Harrell, eds. 1993. *Chinese Families in the Post Mao Era*. Berkeley: University of California Press.

Dong Fang. 1994. "Zhongguo chengshi xiaofei wuda redian" (The five hot points in Chinese urban consumption). *Jingji shijie*, no. 1.

Douglas, Mary. 1975. "Deciphering a Meal." In *Myth, Symbol, and Culture*, edited by Clifford Geertz. New York: W. W. Norton.

Douglas, Mary, and Baron Isherwood. 1979. *The World of Goods*. New York: Basic Books.

Duan Gang. 1991. "Kuaican quanji hanzhan jingcheng" (Fast food chickens are fighting with each other in Beijing). *Beijing Youth Daily*, April 2.

Fantasia, Rick. 1995. "Fast Food in France." *Theory and Society* 24: 201–43.

Finkelstein, Joanne. 1989. *Dining Out: A Sociology of Modern Manners*. New York: New York University Press.

Gaige daobao (Reform herald), no. 1 (1994), p. 34.

Gao Changli. 1992. "Woguo jiushi niandai chengxian duoyuanhua xiaofei qushi". (Consumption trends are diversified in China during the 1990s). *Shangpin pingjie* (Review of commodities), no. 10.

Giddens, Anthony. 1984. *The Constitution of Society: Outline of the Theory of Structuration*. Berkeley: University of California Press.

Gold, Thomas B. 1993. "Go with Your Feelings: Hong Kong and Taiwan Popular Culture in Greater China." *China Quarterly* 136 (December): 907–25.

Gu Bingshu. 1994. "Waican: dushi xin shishang" (Eating out: a new fashion in cities), *Xiaofeizhe*, no. 3: 14–15.

Guo Jianying. 1995. "Tantan kuaican de fuwu" (On service in the fast food sector) *Fuwu jingji* (Service economy), no. 2: 27–8.

Gusfield, Joseph. 1992. "Nature's Body and the Metaphors of Food." In *Cultivating Differences: Symbolic Boundaries and the Making of Inequality*, edited by Michele Lamont and Marcel Fournier. Chicago: University of Chicago Press.

Han Shu. 1994. "M: changsheng jiangjun" (M [McDonald's]: the undefeated general). *Xiaofei zhinan* (Consumption guide), no. 2: 10–11.

Harris, Marvin. 1985. *Good to Eat: Riddles of Food and Culture*. New York: Simon and Schuster.

He Yupeng. 1996. "Zuowei nuxin ripin de Beijing maidanglao" (McDonald's as feminine food in Beijing). Paper presented at the conference "Changing Diet and Foodways in Chinese Culture," Chinese University of Hong Kong, Hong Kong, June 12–14.

"Honggaoliang yuyan zhongshi kuaican da qushi" (The red sorghum predicts the trend of Chinese fast food). 1996. *Zhongguo jingyingbao* (Chinese business). June 11.

Huang Shengbing. 1995. "Kuaican xiaofie xingwei de bijiao yanjiu" (Comparative study of fast food consumption behavior). *Xiaofei jingji*, no. 5: 33–4.

Huang Zhijian. 1994. "Yi ge juda de qingnian xiaofei shichang" (A huge market of youth consumers). *Zhongguo qingnina yanjiu* (China youth studies), no. 2: 12–16.

Jerome, N. W., ed. 1980. *Nutritional Anthropology: Contemporary Approaches to Diet and Culture*. New York: Redgrave.

Jian Feng. 1992. "Zhongshi kuaican, na chu ni de mingpai" (Chinese fast food, show your best brand). *Shichang bao*, November 10.

Kottak, Conrad. 1978. "Rituals at McDonald's." *Journal of American Culture* 1: 370–86.

Lechner, Frank. 1991. "Simmel on Social Space." *Theory, Culture and Society* 8: 195–201.

Lévi-Strauss, Claude. 1983. *The Raw and the Cooked*. Chicago: University of Chicago Press.

Ling Dawei. 1996. "Nuli ba zhongshi kuaican gao shang qu" (Endeavor to develop Chinese fast food). *Zhongguo pengren*, no. 6: 4–5.

——. 1995. "Zhongxi kuaican jingzheng zhi wo jian" (My views on the competition between Chinese and Western fast foods). *Xinshiji zhoukan* (New century weekly), November.

Liu Fen and Long Zaizu. 1986. "Jing, jin, hu chi shenmo?" (What are people eating in Beijing, Tianjin, and Shanghai?). *People's Daily* (overseas edition), August 9.

Liu Guoyue. 1996. "Shenzhen kuaican shichang jiqi fazhan" (The fast food market in Shenzhen and its development). *Zhongguo pengren*, no. 8: 20–2.

Liu Ming. 1992. "Guoji kuaicancheng de meili" (The charming international fast food city). *Zhongguo shipinbao* (Chinese food newspaper), July 13.

Love, John. 1986. *McDonald's: Behind the Arches*. New York: Bantam Books.

Messer, Ellen. 1984. "Anthropological Perspectives on Diet." *Annual Review of Anthropology* 13: 205–49.

Mian Zhi. 1993. "Xishi kuaican fengmi jingcheng; zhongshi kuaican zemmaban?" (Western fast food is the fashion; what about Chinese fast food?). *Lianai, hunyin, jiating* (Love, marriage, and family), no. 6: 10–11.

Mintz, Sidney. 1994. "The Changing Role of Food in the Study of Consumption." In *Consumption and the World of Goods*, edited by John Brewer and Roy Porter. London: Routledge.

Murphy, Christopher. 1986. "Piety and Honor: The Meaning of Muslim Feasts in Old Delhi." In *Food, Society, and Culture*, edited by R. S. Khare and M. S. A. Rao. Durham, NC: Carolina Academic Press.

Pian Ming. 1994. "Jingcheng qingnian qingxin gaojia shangpin" (Beijing youth are keen on expensive commodities). *Zhonghua gongshang shibao* (China industrial and commercial times), July 16.

Ritzer, George. 1993. *The McDonaldization of Society*. Newbury Park, Calif.: Pine Forge.

Sahlins, Marshall. 1976. *Culture and Practical Reason*. Chicago: University of Chicago Press.

Sayer, Andrew. 1985. "The Difference That Space Makes." In *Social Relations and Spatial Structures*, edited by Derrek Gregory and John Urry. London: Macmillan.

Shelton, Allen. 1990. "A Theater for Eating, Looking, and Thinking: The Restaurant as Symbolic Space." *Sociological Spectrum* 10: 507–26.

Stephenson, Peter. 1989. "Going to McDonald's in Leiden: Reflections on the Concept of Self and Society in the Netherlands." *Ethos* 17, no. 2: 226–47.

Tao Wentai. 1996. "Guanyu zhongwai yinshi wenhua bijiao de ji ge wenti" (Issues in comparing Chinese and foreign culinary cultures). *Zhongguo pengren*, no. 8: 26–8.

Urry, John. 1985. "Social Relations, Space and Time." In *Social Relations and Spatial Structures*, edited by Derek Gregory and John Urry. London: Macmillan.

Walder, Andrew G. 1986. *Communist Neo-Traditionalism: Work and Authority in Chinese Industry*. Berkeley: University of California Press.

Watson, James. 1997. "Introduction: Transnationalism, Localization, and Fast Foods in East Asia." In *Golden Arches East: McDonald's in East Asia*, edited by James Watson. Stanford, Calif.: Stanford University Press.

——. 1987. "From the Common Pot: Feasting with Equals in Chinese Society." *Anthropos* 82: 389–401.

——, ed. 1997. *Golden Arches East: McDonald's in East Asia*. Stanford University Press.

Xiao Hua. 1993. "Da ru Zhongguo de yangkuaican" (The invasion of Western fast food), *Jianting shenghuo zhinan* (Guidance of family life), no. 5.

Xiao Yan. 1994. "Xiaofei guannian xin qingxie" (New orientations of consumption perception). *Zhongguo xiaofeizhe bao* (China consumer news), September 12.

Xie Dingyuan. 1996. "Pengren wangguo mianlin tiaozhan" (The kingdom of cuisine is facing a challenge). *Zhongguo pengren*, no. 2: 27–9.

Xu Chengbei. 1994. "Kuaican, dacai, yu xinlao zihao" (Fast food, formal dishes, and the new and old restaurants). *Jingji ribao* (Economic daily), September 17.

——. 1993. "Cong Maidanglao kan shijie" (Seeing the world from McDonald's). *Zhongguo pengren*, no. 8.

——. 1992. "Maidanglao de faluu" (McDonald's law). *Fazhi ribao* (Legal system daily), September 9.

Xu Wangsheng. 1995. "Zhongxi yinshi wenhua de qubie" (The differences between Chinese and Western culinary cultures). *Zhongguo pengren*, no. 8: 28–30.

Yan, Yunxiang. 1997a. "McDonald's in Beijing: The Localization of Americana." In *Golden Arches East: McDonald's in East Asia*, edited by James Watson. Stanford, Calif.: Stanford University Press.

——. 1997b. "The Triumph of Conjugality: Structural Transformation of Family Relations in a Chinese Village." *Ethnology* 36, no. 3: 191–212.

——. 1994. "Dislocation, Reposition and Restratification: Structural Changes in Chinese Society." In *China Review 1994*, edited by Maurice Brosseau and Lo Chi Kin. Hong Kong: Chinese University Press.

Yan Zhenguo and Liu Yinsheng. 1992a. "Yangkuaican chongjipo hou de chensi" (Pondering thoughts after the shock wave of Western fast food). *Shoudu jingji xinxibao* (Capital economic information news), December 3.

——. 1992b. "Zhongguo kuaican shichang shu zhu chenfu?" (Who will control the fast food market in China?). *Shoudu jingji xinxibao*, December 8.

Ye Xianning. 1993. "Jingcheng kuaican yi pie" (An overview of fast food in Beijing), *Fuwu jingji*, no. 4.

You Zi. 1994. "Jingcheng zhongshi kuaican re qi lai le" (Chinese fast food has become hot in Beijing). *Jingji shijie* (Economic world), no. 6: 60–1.

Yu Bin. 1996. "Zhongwai kuaican zai jingcheng" (Chinese and foreign fast foods in Beijing). *Zhongguo shangbao* (Chinese commercial news), June 20.

Yu Weize. 1995. "Shanghai Ronghuaji kuaican liansuo de jingying zouxiang" (The management directions of the Shanghai Ronghua Chicken fast food chain). *Zhongguo pengren* (Chinese culinary art), no. 9: 19–20.

Zhang Guoyun. 1995. "Zhongshi kuaican, dengni dao chuntian" (Chinese fast food, waiting for you in the spring). *Xiaofei jingji* (Consumer economy), no. 3: 54–6.

Zhang Yubin. 1992. "Xishi kuaican jishi lu" (Inspirations from Western fast food) *Zhongguo shipinbao* (Chinese food newspaper), September 4.

Zhang Zhaonan. 1992a. "Gan yu yangfan bi gaodi" (Dare to challenge the foreign fast food). *Beijing wanbao* (Beijing evening news), September 13.

——. 1992b. "Kuaicanye kai jin Zhongguo budui" (The "Chinese troops" entering the fast food sector). *Beijing wanbao*, October 9.

Zhao Huanyan. 1995. "Shilun fandian yingxiao zhong de wenhua dingwei" (On the cultural position of the restaurant business). *Fuwu jingji* (Service economy), no. 8: 10–11.

Zhong Zhe. 1993. "Meishi kuaican – gongfu zai shi wai" (American fast food – something beyond foods). *Xiaofeizhe* (Consumers), no. 2.

Part II

Gentrification, Yuppification, and Domesticating Tastes

Introduction

Part II, "Gentrification, Yuppification, and Domesticating Tastes," presents case studies that explore personal food preferences and tastes in the context of larger political, economic, and cultural trends. The articles by Maris Gillette, William Roseberry, and Susan Terrio show how consumer niches are created not just through socioeconomic forces, but also through selective taste preferences – "taste" in its cultural rather than biological sense. Ultimately, each of these authors delve into the processes by which status distinctions are created, taking their lead from the work of Pierre Bourdieu (*Distinction: A Social Critique of the Judgement of Taste*, Harvard University Press, 1984). Gillette found that Chinese Muslims strictly adhere to dietary prohibitions against pork and foods made by non-Muslims, at least in respect to adult consumption. Children are another matter: Industrially manufactured snacks that have not been touched by human hands are deemed to be "clean" and therefore suitable for children (although adult Muslims avoid such items). Moreover, the image of Western culture associated with industrial manufacturing renders these products particularly desirable be-cause young Chinese consumers (of all ethnic and religious backgrounds) see them as expressions of globalization. Similarly, in his article on American coffee trends, Roseberry explains how upwardly mobile and financially successful con-sumers fostered a boom in yuppie coffee shops in the United States. Starbucks is now a global corporation, largely on the strength of its association with the American digerati. Susan Terrio pursues a related theme by analyzing artisanal chocolates in France as a response to concerns with establishing and marketing an authentically French national identity, distinct from the supranational European identity being created through the European Union (EU). The recent EU row over the regional "ownership" of common food names (Parmesan cheese, Brussels sprouts) reinforces Terrio's point that cuisine closely parallels ideas about ethnic and national identity.

The articles by Eriberto Lozada, Melissa Caldwell, and Purnima Mankekar also pursue issues of food preferences and raise questions about the processes by which these "tastes" acquire meaning, familiarity, and sentimentality. All three authors grapple with domestication as a form of localization, which draws attention to familiarization and homeland. In his article on the domestication of Kentucky Fried Chicken (KFC) in China, Lozada shows how a foreign transnational has become fully integrated into the local consumer economy and has spawned a host of local imitators. Caldwell's article on McDonald's in Russia takes the topic of domestication further and argues that consumers have drawn on uniquely Russian processes of localization to reorient attitudes toward McDonald's. Finally, Mankekar's study of Indian grocery stores in California's Silicon Valley pushes the theme of domestication to a further exploration of how sensory experiences and memories of home are themselves embodied in and evoked by transnational food products.

7

Children's Food and Islamic Dietary Restrictions in Xi'an

Maris Boyd Gillette

One warm spring afternoon in 1995, I rode my bicycle over to Aifeng's house, as I did several times a week during the eighteen months I stayed in Xi'an.[1] Aifeng had plans to visit a wholesale market, and asked me to accompany her. With an extra hand to carry packages, she would be able to buy more of the items her family needed. I had gone shopping with Aifeng many times, but in the past we had stayed in the Muslim district, where Aifeng lived. Just behind her house was a small street market where ten to twelve farmers from the nearby countryside gathered daily to sell fruit and vegetables. This time, however, we rode our bicycles for ten minutes outside of the Muslim district until we reached a busy wholesale market just east of the Xi'an city wall.

The market was a large, concrete-paved lot studded with several roofed, wall-less edifices and encircled by small shops. In the stores, under the covered areas, and out in the open, several dozen vendors displayed boxes and bags of packaged food, soap, paper products, and other factory-produced goods. Aifeng had clearly visited the market many times before; she knew exactly where to buy the cheapest bulk toilet paper and laundry detergent. I helped her load the household goods she bought onto our bicycles and then followed her toward the food vendors.

Although the offerings were plentiful, Aifeng bought only two types of food. She meticulously checked through the many brands of factory-produced, individually packaged instant noodles (*fangbian mian*) for sale until she finally found a large box labeled *qingzhen*, or "pure and true." The term *qingzhen* possesses many meanings in China, but it most frequently refers to food that meets Islamic standards for dietary purity.[2] Like the vast majority of the Muslim district's residents, Aifeng kept a *qingzhen* diet. Aifeng also purchased some packaged snacks for her granddaughter, a one-and-a-half-year-old girl who, along with her father (Aifeng's son) and mother, lived in the upper two floors of Aifeng's house. A vast array of mass-produced, packaged snacks, including candied nuts, puffed rice, chocolates, crisps, biscuits, and hard candies, were for sale at the market. Aifeng purchased enough of these foods to fill two large bags. Later, when we returned to her house, she immediately gave some to her granddaughter, and offered others to her school-age nieces who had stopped to visit.

It was not until months later that I realized the significance of our trip to the wholesale market. At the time I simply noted what goods Aifeng had bought; only afterward did I realize that, unlike the instant noodles she had purchased, the snacks she had bought for her grandchild were not marketed as *qingzhen*. Furthermore, while Aifeng had spent a great deal of time studying the labels of the instant noodle packages, she had paid very little attention to the labels of the snacks she bought for her granddaughter. Based on everything I had seen and been told about the Muslim district and its residents, Aifeng had violated the local standards for Islamic dietary observance by purchasing food for her granddaughter that was not *qingzhen*.

Such an act was difficult to reconcile with what I knew of Aifeng and her family. Aifeng sold *qingzhen* stuffed breads (*baozi*) in a small restaurant she operated with her family on Barley Market Street (*Damaishi jie*) in the Muslim district. She was intimately familiar with which foods were *qingzhen* and which were not, and was careful to adhere to the Islamic dietary proscriptions. In fact, Aifeng was a devout Muslim whose religious observance went far beyond the minimum level of eating *qingzhen*. Although her business and family obligations prevented her from worshiping five times a day (as stipulated in the Qur'an), she nevertheless donated money, food, and other goods regularly to the mosque, upheld Islamic precepts of dress, fasted during Ramadan, and worshiped at the mosque whenever she could. Given the importance she placed on being a Muslim, why did she buy snacks for her granddaughter that were not *qingzhen*?

Children's Food in China

... [F]loodways in the People's Republic of China (PRC) have undergone significant transformations in the wake of Deng Xiaoping's economic reforms. One obvious effect of the reform policies has been the appearance of a variety of new foods on the market, including the mass-produced, packaged snack foods discussed here. These foods have had a profound impact on the nutritional intake of PRC citizens, particularly that of children. The consumer practices surrounding these new foods also indicate that important changes have occurred in the character and quality of family relations: the balance of power between older and younger generations appears to be shifting.

Both of these phenomena have affected the Xi'an Muslim district. During June 1997, I asked Peng, an eleven-year-old resident, to record his total dietary intake for seven days. Peng's food diary revealed that he ate mass-produced snacks similar to those Aifeng purchased for her granddaughter on a daily basis. Peng's high-school-age brother was the only other member of his immediate (nuclear) family who ever ate these foods, but he and his parents agreed that Peng's consumption far outstripped his brother's, at that time and in the past. This pattern matched the eating practices of other children I observed during eighteen months of field research in the Xi'an Muslim district in 1994 and 1995.

Peng was able to eat these snacks because his parents were providing him with "occasional" spending money that amounted to three yuan a day, a fact they had not fully appreciated until we examined his food diary together. They and Peng's brother assured me that Peng was the first member of their family ever to receive what was, in effect, an allowance. The qualitative (and quantitative) shift in parent–child relationships suggested by Peng's intake of the mass-produced foods was replicated in families throughout the Muslim district.

The consumption of mass-produced snack foods described here differs from the other studies in this book in its religious and ethnic implications. In the Xi'an Muslim district, the new snacks mark an ideological and empirical transformation in local Islamic observance and ethnic practice. They represent a significant modification of the centerpiece of Chinese Muslims' collective identity, namely food preparation and eating habits.

Chinese Muslims or Hui

The Xi'an Muslim district is a small ethno-religious enclave containing approximately 30,000 Chinese Muslims. The vast majority of the district's residents are members of the "Hui nationality" (*Huizu*), one of the PRC's 55 officially recognized minority groups (*shaoshu minzu*). Altogether China's minorities make up 8.04 percent of the total population. The Hui are the third largest minority nationality, and the largest of the eleven minorities officially designated as Muslim (Gladney 1991:26–7).

China's minority nationalities have received considerable scholarly attention in recent years, both inside and outside China. Of concern to many American social scientists have been the ways in which "nationality" (*minzu*) designation relates to ethnic affiliation (see, e.g., Gladney 1998, 1991, 1990; Lipman 1997; Harrell, ed., 1995; Harrell 1990; McKhann 1995). According to the government, China's nationalities conform to the Stalinist criteria for "nationality" status, possessing common territorial, linguistic, economic, and psychological traits (Jin 1984; see also Gladney 1998), but the widely dispersed and linguistically and occupationally diverse group known as the Hui fails to meet a single one of the official criteria. Their status as a nationality rests entirely on a historical perception of difference stemming from their Muslim heritage and Islamic observance (Lipman 1997, 1987; Gladney 1991).

Observance of the Islamic dietary restrictions, or eating *qingzhen*, forms a core element of Hui collective identity. The best understood and most familiar aspect of *qingzhen* food consumption is the Hui abstinence from pork. This marker of difference is fundamental and basic: Chinese of all ages, classes, and "nationality" affiliations referred to it when they learned that I studied the Hui. Invariably any mention of Chinese Muslims evoked the remark, "Hui do not eat pork."

A variety of scholarly works have discussed the importance of the pork taboo and *qingzhen* food consumption to maintaining ethnic boundaries between the Hui and China's majority nationality, the Han. One foundational study of this divide is Barbara Pillsbury's article "Pig and Policy" (1975), which is based on ethnographic research conducted on Taiwan. The most important study of *qingzhen* in the PRC is Dru Gladney's *Muslim Chinese* (1991), which explores the concept of *qingzhen* in four distinct Muslim communities. Gladney's work reveals the centrality of *qingzhen* to Hui identity, as well as the critical role that official policies have played in causing a meaningful ethnic identity to coalesce around the "Hui nationality" label.

Qingzhen

While Gladney's study demonstrates that the concept of *qingzhen* is not limited to dietary practices, when I asked residents of the Xi'an Muslim district to explain what *qingzhen* meant, most people responded by talking about food. Many Hui stated the most important characteristic of *qingzhen* food was that it was "particularly clean" (*tebie ganjing*), or sometimes "clean and sanitary" (*ganjing weisheng*). Food can be clean in several respects, and one of the most fundamental is in its content. As Jishu, imam of one of the local mosques, put it, *qingzhen* means "Hui must eat clean things." He said that the foods proscribed in the Qur'an, namely pork, alcohol, blood, and animals that have not been slaughtered in the Islamic fashion, were "dirty" and Hui could not eat them.

Residents of the Muslim district stressed that pork was especially dirty. They believed that the pig was a disease-carrying animal with filthy habits, living in dirt and eating trash. Jiqing, a gatekeeper at a local mosque, exemplified the dirtiness of pigs by the speed at which pork rots. According to him, if a person took a piece of pork and a piece of lamb and left them out for a week, when she or he returned to examine the two meats the pork would be maggoty and disgusting, but the lamb would still be "good," that is, dry and edible. This explanation of pork's dirtiness also appears in a pamphlet for sale in one of the district's Muslim products stores (Ma Tianfang 1971).

Xi'an Hui were extremely concerned with keeping pork away from food, cooking utensils, and the house. Many residents talked about how important it was for Hui not to eat anything that had touched pork or come into contact with lard. Chen, who worked in the public showers owned by one of the mosques, spoke at length about Hui fears that pork products would "pollute" (*ran*) their food. The contaminating power of pork made it impossible for Hui to use cooking or eating utensils that had ever contained it. For this reason, she said, "We are not willing to eat one mouthful of your food, nor drink one mouthful of your tea."

As Chen's remarks suggest, fears about coming into contact with pork products, or even utensils or dishes that had once contained pork, caused the Muslim district's residents to avoid any food that was not prepared by Muslims. Doing so meant refraining from patronizing non-Hui restaurants or food stalls and refusing to eat or drink at the homes of non-Hui. In this way, the pork taboo negatively affected Han food businesses. More deeply felt, however, were its effects on social situations that involved Hui and Han. If Hui visited a Han home, they did not accept any food or drink from their host. This refusal to consume was a striking violation of hospitality in the Chinese setting, where visiting should include both the offer and the receipt of at least a small quantity of food or beverage. Even a cup of hot tea, the most common form of hospitality offered to guests in China, was unacceptable to a Chinese Muslim guest in a Han house. The very cup in which the tea was served, if it belonged to a Han, would cause most Xi'an Hui to refuse it, for they believed that simple washing could not cleanse Han dishes of the residue of pork.[3]

In addition to food content, food preparation techniques also played an important part in determining which foods were *qingzhen* and which were not. Yan, who worked in her family's restaurant, stressed the care that Hui took with food preparation when explaining *qingzhen*. She pointed out that Hui washed vegetables, dishes, and hands in separate basins, and kept different types of food segregated and "in order" (*fenjie*). Other Hui, both men and women, explained *qingzhen* by indicating that Hui washed frequently, and paid close attention when they cooked. One man noted that the character for *qing* has the ideographic representation of water in it, which, he said, shows that Hui "rely on water" (*yi shui wei zhu*).

To a large extent, *qingzhen* was equated with being Muslim. To make *qingzhen* food, one woman told me, you must have "washed a major ablution" (*xi guo da jing*), that is, washed yourself according to the proper Islamic procedure. As Jiqing explained, the *qingzhen* signs food entrepreneurs hung over their establishments showed that the cook was a "believer" (*mumin*). To produce *qingzhen* foods, one had to be Muslim, and in Xi'an, being Muslim meant being Hui – as evidenced by the local habit of using the terms "Muslim" (*Musilin*) and "Hui" (*Huimin*) interchangeably. *Qingzhen* encapsulated the essence of being Muslim in the Chinese context. It was central to local conceptions of identity: as Yan put it, "*Qingzhen* means Hui."

Non-*qingzhen* Food and Western Food

The foods that Aifeng bought for her granddaughter and that Peng consumed were diverse in flavor and ingredients. Most were new arrivals to the area; residents said that the vast majority of such mass-produced snacks had been available in the area for only ten years. One exception to this was soda. Mingxin, a butcher, remembered seeing Chinese-made sodas for sale in the late 1970s. At that time a soda cost eleven *fen* per bottle, a price no ordinary person could afford; only the children of cadres and important people drank it.[4] Nevertheless, although soda had been present for a longer period, Mingxin placed it in the same category as chocolate, biscuits, and hard candies: all were "foreign" foods, produced in "foreign" factories or made by "foreign" machines. He pointed out that even though many Chinese factories produced such foods, they "had learned about them from the West." Mingxin was not alone in perceiving a great variety of new foods on the market as products of "the West" – meaning Europe and the United States – even though many of them were manufactured in Asia. This perception was widespread in the Muslim district, especially with regard to snacks wrapped in machine-made packages.

In Xi'an the number of foods actually imported from the West was limited, and their high prices tended to prevent most Hui from buying them. The majority of mass-produced snacks that locals ate were made in China. Many foreign-brand foods available in Xi'an were produced in Chinese factories, some of which were located in Shaanxi province. By 1997, even such well-known "Western" products as Coca-Cola were made and bottled in Shaanxi.

Residents of the Xi'an Muslim district identified certain foods as Western based primarily on what they learned from the media and large department stores and supermarkets. Hui regarded some foods as Western because they saw them being served and consumed in media representations of the United States, Canada, and Europe. Television programs, both those made in the United States and those made in China about the West, played an important role in educating locals about Western foods and foodways. In addition, movies, news programs, and newspaper articles all made "the West" a meaningful category in the imaginations of my informants, none of whom had ever traveled to the United States or Europe.

Xi'an's Chinese Muslims also learned about Western foods from the products available in department stores, wholesale markets, convenience stores, and a few supermarkets. Supermarkets (*chaoji shichang*) were a new phenomenon in Xi'an when I arrived in January 1994. A Hong Kong firm called the Seastar Overseas Company (*Haixing haiwai gongsi*) had recently opened two supermarkets near the city center when I arrived; by the time I left in August 1995, at least two more stores had opened in Xi'an. One of these supermarkets was quite close to the Muslim district, and attracted some of its residents. This supermarket, the many department stores that lined the main streets surrounding the district, the small convenience stores scattered throughout the area, and the nearby wholesale markets sold a variety of packaged, mass-produced foods.

Between 1994 and 1997 the available products included such beverages as Coca-Cola, Sprite, Tang fruit drink, Nestlé powdered milk, and Nestlé instant coffee, and such foods as Snickers, M&M's, McVitie's Digestive Biscuits, and several kinds of Keebler cookies and crackers, many of which, such as mango-flavored sandwich cookies, I had never seen before. These foods were originally developed in Europe and the United States, and had spawned a variety of Japanese and Hong Kong imitations. The Hong Kong brands, especially Khong Guan and Garden biscuits and crackers, were particularly popular in Xi'an. Many PRC companies also sold Western food spinoffs in Xi'an, such as carbonated drinks, crackers, crisps, cookies, ice cream bars, and candy.

In addition to brand-name promotions, media representations also contributed to the development of stereotypes about Western foods and their ingredients. Butter and milk in particular were regarded as typical of Western food. Even in snacks produced locally, the presence of dairy ingredients lent them an aura of foreign-ness and luxury. For Hui in their thirties and older, dairy products symbolized a high standard of living. Mingxin remembered craving milk as a child, when little was available and his family was too poor to buy it. He commented that low levels of milk production were partially to blame in the past, but since the reform period began in 1978, China's cows had been "science modernized" (*kexue xiandaihua*) and so dairy products were both readily available and affordable.

A number of Xi'an enterprises sold foods such as fresh yeast bread and cakes containing ingredients that caused Hui to regard them as "Western." Unlike the packaged, preserved factory food, local restaurants and bakeries made these foods daily and sold them fresh. However, Chinese Muslims generally refused to consume them; most would only eat the locally made "Western" foods that other Hui produced. No one I knew ate food from the American fast-food chain Kentucky Fried Chicken, the Han Chinese fast-food chains that sold hamburgers, hot dogs, pizza, fried chicken, and the like, or the many bakeries outside the Muslim district that produced yeast bread and oven-baked cakes. Hui also abstained from carbonated beverages that came from soda fountains rather than cans or bottles. They justified their abstinence on the grounds that these locally produced Western foods were not *qingzhen* since they were not made by Hui.

As the preceding discussion makes clear, a number of foods identified as "Western" did not fall into the category of foods Hui were willing to eat. When foods were made in local restaurants and food stalls, residents of the Muslim district would eat only those foods made by Muslims. This was because, "Western" or not, foods made by Hui were by definition *qingzhen*. What was more perplexing was that Hui also ate foods that were produced in factories and thus not made by Hui. Three factors made these foods acceptable: they were not made with pork, they were perceived to be Western, and they were the product of industrial production techniques that did not involve the extensive use of the hands.

An event from Aifeng's and my shopping trip shows the importance of the first two criteria. After Aifeng had purchased her food, I began sorting through the piles to buy some for myself. As I looked at the offerings, I was drawn to a different sort of food than Aifeng was. What was to me more exotic and novel were the factory-produced versions of traditional Chinese food like mung bean cakes (*lüdougao*) and peanut cakes (*huashengsu*).[5] Seeing me rummaging through the boxes and sacks, Aifeng came over to examine what I planned to buy. When she saw the factory-made mung bean cakes, she shook her head. "We can't eat those," she said. "They aren't *qingzhen*."

Clearly Aifeng placed mass-produced mung bean cakes in a different category from the packaged snacks she had bought for her daughter. What caused her to perceive the cakes and the instant noodles with which she took such care to purchase a *qingzhen* brand as requiring attention to *qingzhen*? The answer lies in their familiarity. The mung bean cakes and noodles were the result of industrial food production techniques, but they were recognizably Chinese. They were foods that Hui knew how to make, and ones that were commonly prepared and consumed throughout China. Aifeng knew that when non-Muslims prepared mung bean cakes or noodles they made them with lard; only Hui made such foods with vegetable oil. Her experience and upbringing told Aifeng that she could only consume traditional Chinese foods if they were made by Hui. Even factory-produced "traditional" foods were associated with pork, unless they were certified *qingzhen*. Aifeng and her neighbors recognized factory-produced foods such as mung bean cakes and noodles as part of a local universe in which foods were either Hui and edible or Han and inedible. Western mass-produced foods, however, stood outside of this realm.

Young Consumers

Many residents of the Muslim district bought Western industrial foods, but although many Hui adults purchased them, few actually consumed them. Most of these foods were eaten by children. By and large, Hui adults limited their intake of mass-produced foods to carbonated beverages, coffee, and juice-based drinks. None of these beverages were popular with adults over thirty, and they did not form a part of most adults' daily food intake. Generally, such beverages were used to host visitors and guests. Soda, for example, was an indispensable part of any formal banquet at a restaurant, and was also served with the meals that Hui provided for guests at circumcisions, engagements, and weddings. When the Barley Market Street Anti-Alcohol Association, a grassroots organization dedicated to keeping alcohol out of the Muslim district, hosted a public rally, it provided soda to everyone who attended. Most families I knew kept bottles of soda or boxes of juice drink on hand in the refrigerator for guests, especially during the summer, when temperatures in Xi'an soared well over 100 degrees Fahrenheit.

The other mass-produced Western food that occasionally formed part of the adult Hui diet was candy. Like the Western beverages, mass-produced candies were not eaten daily by the Hui adults I knew but rather were offered to guests. Packaged candies were placed out on trays for guests to eat casually during the lengthy celebrations of life-cycle rituals or brought out for important visitors. Candy also constituted an item of exchange during marriage transactions. Families whose children became engaged or married participated in formal rites of gift-giving (similar to those described in Yan 1996:176–209). In the Muslim district, these exchanges frequently involved food. For example, at one stage during the marriage process, the bride's family presented the groom's family with gifts of nuts, dates, and other fancy snack foods (*gaodian*). A wide variety of traditional pastries were used on this occasion, but packaged hard candy also frequently constituted one of the items exchanged.

Despite these gift exchange and hosting practices, most Hui adults found "Western" foods unpalatable. A frequent comment Hui adults made was that they "could not get accustomed" (*buxiguan*) to the taste of candy, soda, or other Western foods. In general, locals complained that Western foods were "too sweet" and "not filling" (*chi bu bao*). Hui used these foods for gift exchanges and hospitality because they were novel, expensive, and associated with the West and what the West represented, not because they thought the foods tasted good.

Hui children, on the other hand, ate factory-made Western food in large quantities. Parents and grandparents regularly purchased packaged Western snacks for children to eat between meals. Many families I knew kept supplies of these foods at home. Aifeng frequently fed this type of mass-produced snack to her granddaughter when the little girl cried or if she started playing with something Aifeng did not wish her to play with – in short, when Aifeng wanted to distract her. Peng's father bought large cases of soda for his sons; he explained that offering this treat was one way he rewarded his children and encouraged them to work hard in school.

Most parents enabled their children to eat snack foods by giving them spare change. I frequently saw children run up to their parents and ask for a few *mao*.[6] The parents' usual response was to hand over a little money and send the children away. Children spent this money at the small, family-run convenience stores in the area, quite a few of which were near primary and middle schools. Among school-age children, trips to the convenience store occasioned comparisons about who had tried which snacks, queries about which snacks contained toys, and judicious expressions of preferences. Children frequently ate these foods in or around school property, and the schoolyard formed an important venue for the dissemination of knowledge about new snacks.

Some Chinese Muslims questioned the propriety of consuming Western foods. Jishu, an elderly imam, refused to drink carbonated beverages or eat any foods associated with the West because he believed they were not *qingzhen*. Although he did not criticize others for eating these foods, he said that he hoped his abstinence would inspire other Hui to emulate him. Most ordinary Hui avoided offering Western food to imams and members of the community considered to be particularly devout. For example, at the weddings, funerals, and engagements I attended, imams and other "men of religion" were not served Western soft drinks, though lay guests were. Nor did the banquets provided by the mosques for collective religious rituals (such as the annual summertime mourning ritual for the Hui massacred in Shaanxi during the late nineteenth century or the wintertime celebration of the Prophet's Birthday) include any foods associated with the West: no factory-produced snacks, canned or bottled beverages, or local Hui-produced yeast breads or cakes.[7]

"Neutral" Foods

For most Chinese Muslims, mass-produced Western foods were neither *qingzhen* nor taboo. Instead, they fell into an amorphous category of their own. The apparent neutrality of mass-produced Western foods derived in part from the absence of pork or lard in such products. For example, on one occasion I asked Peng's father if Hui could eat chocolate. He responded with a puzzled look. "Of course," he replied. "Chocolate? There is nothing in that (*mci sha*)." "Nothing" meant no pork; neither chocolate nor the other foods Hui considered Western were made with pork or lard.

On another occasion I spoke with Aifeng's daughter Xue, a young woman in her twenties who worked in a department store, about Western foods. Xue had traveled to Beijing with her co-workers on a trip sponsored by her work unit; when she described her visit, she complained about how difficult it was for her to find food that she could eat while she and her co-workers, who were all Han, were sightseeing. Because her Han colleagues ate in places that were not *qingzhen*, she often went hungry. Indeed, she chose to sit outside during meals, so concerned was she to avoid violating *qingzhen*. After listening to her remarks, I asked her whether she could eat in Western restaurants like Kentucky Fried Chicken: did the *qingzhen* food taboo apply to such places? Xue replied that she could not enter or eat in fast-food restaurants because they were not *qingzhen*. And what about the ice cream bars they sold on the street, I asked, could she eat those? What about when she was thirsty? "About some foods it is hard to say (*shuo bu qing*)," she responded. "I could eat an ice cream bar, or drink a soft drink, or even eat packaged biscuits (*binggan*) if they didn't have lard in them."

Intrigued by the neutrality of mass-produced Western foods, I visited Zenglie, a retired professor of Hui history whose family lived in the district. Zenglie characterized these snacks as one stage in a historical development whereby Hui came to eat foods that were once avoided. It used to be, Zenglie said, that Hui would not drink water that did not come from wells owned by Hui; now everyone drank the water that came through the pipes the government installed. Sweets (*tianshi*) and non-alcoholic beverages (*yinliao*) were also foods that had once been prohibited. However, Zenglie noted, in the past such foods were all made by hand. Now they were made in factories, so Hui could eat them.

The Food Industry and Food Production

Industrial production clearly played an important role in rendering the new foods acceptable to Hui. Such foods differed from the vast majority of edibles sold and consumed in the area: most foods available in Xi'an during the mid-1990s were hand-made. "Hand-made" in this context signified more than just the degree of personalization this phrase denotes in the contemporary United States. Rather, it refers to the absence of almost every kind of foodprocessing machine or tool, and to the extensive and intensive use of hands in all forms of food preparation.

As described above, cleanliness figures highly in the Hui concept of "pure and true." Hui criticized Han for being dirty, not just because they consumed pork, but also because they regarded Han as less than sanitary. Several Hui commented to me that Han did not wash their hands after using the toilet, and that Han washed their hands in water Hui considered stagnant. Given the nature of local food-preparation techniques, these sanitation practices assumed a high degree of importance.

Noodles were one of the most popular foods for sale on the streets of Xi'an, both inside and outside the Muslim district. They were sold in establishments that ranged from fancy hotel restaurants to tiny street stalls seating fewer than ten customers. In most restaurants and stalls, noodles were made to order; the urbanites I knew criticized and avoided establishments that sold pre-prepared dried noodles. In the Muslim district, as on many of Xi'an's smaller streets and alleys, fresh noodles were almost always made in the customer's presence. Though noodles could be pulled, rolled, or cut in an assortment of shapes and sizes, all involved significant use of the hands.

Typically, noodle preparation began with making the dough. The cook poured flour and water into a large basin, and then stirred the mixture with chopsticks. As the dough thickened, the cook abandoned the chopsticks in favor of hands. Once the right proportions of flour and water were achieved, the dough was removed from the basin and kneaded by hand. Kneading took anywhere from ten to twenty minutes. Then, if the cook were preparing cut noodles – the simplest sort to prepare – he or she flattened the dough with a rolling pin, using his or her hands to stretch the flattened dough. Once the dough had reached the desired thinness, the cook cut it with a knife. He or she would stop after cutting the right amount of dough for a single bowl, pick it up, and put it to the side in a pile. This process would continue until all the dough was cut.

Once cut, the noodles were ready for boiling. When a customer appeared, the cook would grab one of the piles of noodles with his or her hands and throw them into a big wok filled with water that was heated by a large, round coal-burning stove that was probably made from an oil drum. After a few minutes, the noodles were removed with chopsticks, placed in a bowl, and seasoned to the customer's taste. If the customer wanted them with meat, the cook would cut a few slices of pre-cooked meat, pick them up by hand, and place them in the customer's bowl. Then green bean threads, cilantro, and onions would be added, also by hand. Finally, the cook would ladle broth into the bowl, and serve it to the customer.

Noodles were by no means the only sort of food made by Xi'an restaurateurs that involved the use of hands, nor did noodle preparation involve the most intensive use of the hand. Steamed stuffed buns (*baozi*), dumplings (*jiaozi*), stovetop-baked flat-bread (*tuo tuo mo*), and most other foods sold on the streets of Xi'an all required hands-on preparation. Only a couple of the hundreds of food stalls in the Muslim district possessed machines for food preparation; most enterprises hired multiple laborers to hasten and increase food production.

The contrast is clear: foods that Hui made were produced by hand, on site, while the customer watched; packaged foods, on the other hand, were made by machine, in distant locations, and away from the consumer's gaze. The physical distance between where mass-produced foods were made and where they were consumed, the invisibility of the production process, and the use of machines all contributed to the Hui tendency to regard these foods as neutral.

Industrial processing also defamiliarized food by rendering its products signifi-cantly different in appearance from the foods that Chinese made by hand (see Hendry 1993 for a discussion of the transformative effects of wrapping in Japan). The mass-produced foods were sealed in plastic, glass, or aluminum. Their wrappers were air-tight and leak-proof; they were packaged with expensive materials that could not be produced in the Muslim district. Local packaging was much more casual. Hand-made foods were wrapped in paper and tied with string, or put into flimsy plastic bags tied by their handles. Often consumers would bring their own dishes or bowls to transport their purchases home. Indeed, much of the hand-made food produced in Xi'an was consumed on the spot rather than taken home.

Ingredients and food type also contributed to the strangeness of "Western" factory-made foods. They were standardized in color and shape. Many were dyed. Some were dried and coated; as a category they tended to be crisp. By contrast, hand-made Hui foods were irregularly shaped and varied in size. They were made without artificial colorings, and they tended to be soft.

Consuming Modernity

Mass-produced Western food was alien: encased in sealed containers, made by unfamiliar and unseen production techniques, containing ingredients that were rarely used in local cuisine. Unlike the mass-produced mung bean cakes, they were not "Chinese" but visually, texturally, and orally exotic and foreign. Their "Western" quality was an important reason why Hui consumed them. In the eyes of many Chinese Muslims, the West represented wealth, advanced technology, science, and modernity. By eating the Western factory foods, Hui linked themselves to progress, scientific knowledge, and prosperity.

Largely because of the images and stories of the West transmitted since the economic reforms, Xi'an Hui regarded the West as modern, advanced, liberal, and wealthy. Purchasing and eating food that was Western allowed Hui to assume something of these qualities. Local residents used Western food to make a statement about their cosmopolitanism and familiarity with things foreign. While most adult Hui did not like the taste of ice cream, soda, chocolate, or potato chips, many liked to think of themselves, and liked to be thought of, as modern, progressive, and aware of the world outside China. One way of creating this image was to purchase Western foods, give them as gifts, keep them around the house, feed them to children, and serve them to honored guests. Since only two Hui families made Western-style foods, very little hand-made Western food was available in the Muslim district. Furthermore, the yeast bread and cake these families produced were highly perishable and limited in variety. Hui who wanted to use the contents of their pantry to create a modern, affluent image had little choice but to buy factory-made products, even though they did not meet some of the criteria for *qingzhen*.

Factory-made Western food had the added attraction of being intimately tied to industry, and through this to science and modernity. Things scientific had an immense power in the Muslim district. Residents referred to the Qur'an as "extremely scientific" when justifying their belief in Islam, and "scientific" methods of Islamic education, which involved the use of language cassettes, were privileged over the "old" methods of rote memorization. Hui associated science with development, improved sanitation, and high standards of living. The "advanced technology," as one resident termed it, through which factory-made foods were produced, enhanced their attractiveness.

The modern, scientific aspect of Western factory-made food was particularly important for children. Adult Hui wanted their children to succeed in contemporary society. They wanted their children to have wider experiences than they had had, and to ascend higher on the social ladder. This desire was most obviously manifest through the stress parents placed on their children's education. Parents willingly paid extra money to send their children to better schools, enroll them in extra tutorials, or hire private tutors. Providing their children with Western mass-produced food was another means parents used to prepare their children for the modern world. Through these foods parents hoped to introduce their children to things foreign and equip them to live in an industrialized, technologically advanced, cosmopolitan world.

The French sociologist Pierre Bourdieu writes that "taste classifies, and it classifies the classifier" (1984:6). Xi'an Hui wanted to be classified as modern. Their pursuit of secular education, their enthusiasm for living in high-rise apartments, their preference for religious education that used the technologies of modern life such as language cassettes and videotapes, their desire to make the pilgrimage to Mecca and enjoy the experiences of foreign travel such as riding in airplanes – all demonstrate that residents of the Muslim district approved of and wanted to participate in modernization (see Gillette 2000 for further discussion). Consumption of packaged, mass-produced Western foods was yet another arena in which they pursued modernity. In this case, what was occurring in Xi'an was not the "logical conformity" of taste to social position that Bourdieu describes (1984:471; see also 1990) whereby people prefer goods and services that express their existing social position. Rather, Hui consumption of Western mass-produced foods is an instance of people developing a taste, or instilling a taste in their children, for what they wanted to be: advanced, cosmopolitan, modern.

The Government and Mass Production

Consumption of mass-produced foods was also part of an ongoing reconfiguration of the relationship between the Shaanxi provincial government and Chinese

Muslims, both with the Muslim district and with the wider community of Hui residents elsewhere in Xi'an and Shaanxi. During the summer of 1996, one high-level provincial official told me that the government's Religion and Nationalities Bureau was debating a policy that would certify factories as *qingzhen*. Four criteria had been decided upon: in factories officially designated as *qingzhen*, the "cook" must be Hui (he did not elaborate upon who, in the factory production process, would be considered the cook); the ingredients must not contain pork or pork products; leaders of the factory must be Hui; and at least 25 percent of the factory workers must be Hui. This last point was revised during the week I was visiting; a few days after our initial conversation this official told me that the percentage of factory workers who must be Hui had been increased to 45 percent. He explained that if this policy went into effect, it would apply to many enterprises, including those that did business with Islamic countries. Fears that Muslims from outside China would disapprove of the criteria had caused the provincial government to raise the required percentage of Hui employees. By June 1997, this policy to regulate *qingzhen* had passed through all the necessary administrative channels, but no actions to implement the policy had yet occurred.

The provincial government's debates about certifying factories as *qingzhen* took place in the context of a more general effort to define the meaning of *qingzhen* in secular terms. A few years prior to these debates, the city government's Religious and Nationalities Department created criteria for certifying hand-made Hui foods as *qingzhen* (see Gillette 1997:108–37). Although residents of the Muslim district linked *qingzhen* closely to religion, the government sought to use nationality-based criteria to redefine *qingzhen* as a category based on nationality affiliation. In both the city and the provincial government's eyes, membership in one of the officially created Muslim nationalities determined which foods and which food producers were *qingzhen*.

The Shaanxi provincial government's proposed policy raised questions about the significance of contemporary *qingzhen* labeling, at least for me. Did the instant noodles Aifeng selected, which were advertised as *qingzhen*, adhere to the standards for "pure and true" that had been set by local Chinese Muslims, or did they more closely resemble the secular definitions propounded by the government? Such labeling had enormous potential to mask food preparation practices that diverged widely from those considered clean in the district. By allowing factories to market their industrial products as *qingzhen*, the government added another level of complexity to the Hui evaluation and use of mass-produced foods: did *qingzhen* mean Islamically pure, made by a member of the Hui nationality, or made in a factory whose employees were mostly non-Muslim? The government's actions also foregrounded the puzzling question: to what extent can a machine be considered *qingzhen*?

Hui and Han Eat Together

Local standards of *qingzhen* have shifted in the Xi'an Muslim district. The availability of mass-produced Western foods was transforming what *qingzhen* meant, particularly with regard to children's food consumption. Hui attitudes toward mass-produced foods suggest that *qingzhen* was still defined in opposition to Han, but not in opposition to the West or what the West represented, namely, science and modernization.

This phenomenon reaffirms Bourdieu's insight about social identity, that "difference is asserted against what is closest, which represents the greatest threat" (1984:479). To Xi'an Hui, the food of their next-door neighbors, the Han, was quintessentially polluted. However, they did not feel the same way about factory produced Western food, even if it was made by machines operated by Han. In part, their attitude reflected that the Hui, like nearly everyone else in China, wanted to modernize. Eating Western mass-produced food was one means of achieving a progressive and scientifically advanced image. Most Chinese Muslims elevated the goal of modernization over strict adherence to *qingzhen* guidelines. To reach this goal, *qingzhen* was being reinterpreted solely as that which was not Han, rather than that which was Muslim.

The need for such redefinition was a relatively recent development. Throughout most of the Muslim district's thousand-year history, residents had limited contact with the West. Beginning in the 1980s, however, opportunities to encounter the West through the media and through interactions with foreign visitors to Xi'an increased dramatically. In addition, many more Western products became available than ever before. Xi'an Hui associated such products with "the good life" they saw in media representations and in the material lifestyles of foreign tourists. They embraced this image of wealth and modernity by consuming food they perceived as "Western." Western foods were carefully categorized as distinct from Han food, even when both were made through mechanized factory production.

The consumption of mass-produced Western foods connected Hui with consumers of similar products in the United States, Europe, Japan, and elsewhere. As Jack Goody writes, "processed food is more or less the same in Ealing as in Edinburgh" (1982:189). However, eating this food has not led to cultural homogeneity (see also J. Watson, ed., 1997). While the Hui treatment of candy and crisps may resemble that found in the United States, for example as a snack for children, in other ways it differed markedly. Residents' use of candy and yeast breads as part of the formal engagement presents given by the groom's family to the bride's family, for example, was a practice not found in mainstream American society. More important, Western food in the Muslim district possessed a significance it did not have outside China. One difference was that Western food was not regarded as suitable for regular meals, even in forms that most Americans consider to be substantial, such as yeast bread. Instead, it was closely linked to children and to childish practices such as snacking. Another difference was its special value and quality. Coca-Cola in the United States is quite ordinary and inexpensive, but in Xi'an it was a prestige food, served to honored guests in homes and at banquets.

Despite the sharp distinction Hui made between themselves and Han, and the care they took to avoid mass-produced foods that were considered "traditional Chinese," the consumption of Western mass-produced foods made it easier for Hui to interact with Han. For although Hui adults differentiated between Han foods and Western mass-produced foods, the snacks they allowed their children to eat, and the soft drinks they drank, were also found in the homes and mouths of Han. These foods provided a common ground for Hui and Han to eat together. Hui visitors at Han households could accept Han hospitality if offered a can of soda rather than a cup of tea. If food was the most important factor that kept Hui separate from Han, then the consumption of Western, mass-produced foods diminished the differences between Hui and Han, particularly for children. One wonders where and how the boundary between Hui and Han will be drawn when the children of the 1990s have grown up.

NOTES

1   Based on discussion with my informants, I have chosen to use personal names without family names in this chapter. Xi'an is a city of about two million in Shaanxi Province, one of the five provinces that comprise northwest China.
2   Other meanings of *qingzhen* that residents of the Muslim district reported included honesty in business, belief in Islam, and observance of a Muslim lifestyle.
3   While Hui refuse Han hospitality, Han accept Hui food and drink, freely consuming Hui foods and using Hui cookery. See Pillsbury 1975 for a discussion of this issue with reference to the Hui on Taiwan.
4   A *fen* is one one-hundredth of a yuan.
5   These "cakes" do not resemble Western oven-baked cakes at all. They are made of seeds and nuts compressed into squares, and are not baked.
6   One *mao* is one-tenth of a yuan.
7   The annual mourning for what is known as the "Hui Uprising" (*Huimin qiyi*) takes place in the Muslim district on the seventeenth day of the fifth lunar month of the Chinese calendar. See Gillette n.d. and Ma Changshou 1993 for further information on this late nineteenth-century massacre. The Prophet's Birthday occurs on the twelfth of the third lunar month of the Islamic calendar, but was always celebrated in January in Xi'an.

REFERENCES

Bourdieu, Pierre. 1984. *Distinction: A Social Critique of the Judgement of Taste*. Cambridge, Mass.: Harvard University Press.
——. 1990. "Social Space and Symbolic Power." In *In Other Words: Essays Towards a Reflexive Sociology*, 123–39. Stanford: Stanford University Press.
Gillette, Maris. 1997. "Engaging Modernity: Consumption Practices Among Urban Muslims in Northwest China." Ph.D. dissertation, Harvard University.
——. 2000. *Between Mecca and Beijing: Modernization and Consumption Among Urban Chinese Muslims*. Stanford: Stanford University Press.
——. N.d. "Recalling 19th-Century Violence: Social Memory Among Urban Chinese Muslims." Unpublished manuscript.
Gladney, Dru. 1990. "The Ethnogenesis of the Uighur." *Central Asian Survey* 9, no. 1:1–28.
——. 1991. *Muslim Chinese: Ethnic Nationalism in the People's Republic*. Cambridge, Mass.: Council on East Asian Studies, Harvard University.
——. 1998. "Clashed Civilizations? Muslim and Chinese Identities in the PRC." In Dru Gladney, ed., *Making Majorities: Constituting the Nation in Japan, Korea, China, Malaysia, Fiji, Turkey and the United States*, 106–31. Stanford: Stanford University Press.
Goody, Jack. 1982. *Cooking, Cuisine, and Class: A Study in Comparative Sociology*. Cambridge: Cambridge University Press.

Harrell, Stevan. 1990. "Ethnicity, Local Interests, and the State: Yi Communities in Southwest China." *Comparative Studies in Society and History* 32, no. 3:515–48.

Harrell, Stevan, ed. 1995. *Cultural Encounters on China's Ethnic Frontiers*. Seattle: University of Washington Press.

Hendry, Joy. 1993. *Wrapping Culture*. Oxford: Clarendon Press.

Jin Binggao. 1984. "Discussion of the Production and Effect of the Marxist Definition of Nationality" (Shilun makesizhuyi minzu dingyi de chansheng jiqi yingxiang). *Central Minorities Institute Newsletter* (Zhongyang minzu xueyuan xuebao) 3:64–7.

Lipman, Jonathan. 1987. "Hui-Hui: An Ethnohistory of the Chinese-Speaking Muslims." *Journal of South Asian and Middle Eastern Studies* 11, nos. 1 and 2 (combined):112–30.

——. 1997. *Familiar Strangers: A History of Muslims in Northwest China*. Seattle: University of Washington Press.

Ma Changshou. 1993. *Records of the Historical Investigation into the Shaanxi Hui Uprising of the Tongzhi Period* (Tongzhi nianjian Shaanxi Huimin qiyi lishi diaocha jilu). Xi'an: Shaanxi People's Publishing House.

Ma Tianfang. 1971. *Why Do Muslims Not Eat Pork?* (Huimin wei shenme buchi zhurou?). Booklet printed in Taiwan.

McKhann, Charles. 1995. "The Naxi and the Nationalities Question." In Stevan Harrell, ed., *Cultural Encounters on China's Ethnic Frontiers*, 39–62. Seattle: University of Washington Press.

Pillsbury, Barbara. 1975. "Pig and Policy: Maintenance of Boundaries Between Han and Muslim Chinese." In B. Eugene Griessman, ed., *Minorities: A Text with Readings in Intergroup Relations*, 136–45. Hinsdale: Dryden Press.

Watson, James L., ed. 1997. *Golden Arches East: McDonald's in East Asia*. Stanford: Stanford University Press.

Yan, Yunxiang. 1996. *The Flow of Gifts: Reciprocity and Social Networks in a Chinese Village*. Stanford: Stanford University Press.

8

The Rise of Yuppie Coffees and the Reimagination of Class in the United States

William Roseberry

Let us begin at Zabar's, a gourmet food emporium on Manhattan's Upper West Side. We enter, make our way through the crowd waiting to place orders in the cheese section, move quickly past the prepared foods, linger over the smoked fish, then arrive at the coffees. There, in full-sized barrels arranged in a semicircle, we find a display of roasted coffee beans for sale – Kona style, Colombian Supremo, Gourmet Decaf, Blue Mountain style, Mocha style, "French Italian," Vienna, Decaf Espresso, Water Process Decaf, Kenya AA – and a helpful clerk waiting to fill our order, grind the beans to our specification, and suggest one of a small selection of flavored syrups.

Given Zabar's reputation for quality and excess, this is a rather modest selection as coffee now goes. The evidence of plenty and waste can be found in the size of the barrels and the quantity of roast beans available for sale and spoilage. But the real spot to spend money is upstairs, where the brewers, grinders, and espresso coffee-makers are sold – from simple Melitta drip cones and carafes to the more serious Krups Semiprofessional Programmatic ($349) or the Olympia Caffarex ($1,000). Zabar's collection of coffee is not especially distinguished. They eschew the trend toward flavors (raspberry, almond, chocolate, amaretto, vanilla, and the like, in various combinations), offering instead a few prepackaged coffees in flavors and small bottles of flavored syrups for those customers who prefer them. But only two of their coffees are sold as specific varietals, Colombian Supremo and Kenyan AA. The rest are "styles" that suggest a geographic place without having anything to do with it. Kona style can include beans from El Salvador, Blue Mountain style, beans from Puerto Rico, and so on.

If I visit the deli across the street from my apartment, I can choose from a much wider variety of coffees, 43 in all, including Jamaican Blue Mountain, Venezuela Maracaibo, German Chocolate, Swedish Delight, Double Vanilla Swedish Delight,

Swiss Mocha Almond, and Decaf Swiss Mocha Almond, to name just a few. These are displayed in burlap bags that take up much more space than coffee sections used to occupy when my only choices were Maxwell House, Folgers, Chock Full o' Nuts, El Pico, and Medaglia d'Oro. And they require the assistance of a clerk to weigh, bag, and grind the coffee.

As I walk down the street, virtually every deli offers a similar variety, generally in minibarrels, though sometimes the barrels are distributed in apparently casual abundance throughout the store so that I can also select breads, spreads, teas, chocolates, and cheeses as I decide which among the many roasts, varietals, styles, or flavors I will choose this week. I no longer need the gourmet shop – though such shops, which proliferated in the 1980s, continue to thrive, concentrated in cities but also present in suburban towns and shopping malls – to buy what coffee traders call "specialty" coffees; nor do I need to be a gourmet to buy and enjoy them (or better said, I need not be a gourmet to look, act, and feel like one). I can go to the corner deli or the major supermarket, where even Maxwell House and A&P have joined the "specialty" trend.

Surely these developments are "good." Specialty coffees taste better than mass-market coffees. They offer pleasure in many ways: the aroma, ambience, and experience of the coffee shop or even the deli itself (indeed, part of the experience of a place like Zabar's is the succession of smells); the casual conversation with the shop owner or dinner guest about varietals, roasts, preparation methods; the identification with particular places through consumption – Copenhagen or Vienna, Jamaica or the Celebes; or the inclusion of coffee purchasing, preparation, and consumption in a widening spectrum of foods – including wines, beers, waters, breads, cheeses, sauces, and the like – through which one can cultivate and display "taste" and "discrimination." Moreover, the expansion of specialty coffees marks a distinct break with a past characterized by mass production and consumption. The move toward these coffees was not initiated by the giants that dominate the coffee trade but by small regional roasters who developed new sources of supply, new modes and networks of distribution that allowed, among other things, for consumers to buy coffee directly (well, not *directly*) from a peasant cooperative in Chiapas or Guatemala. New coffees, more choices, more diversity, less concentration, new capitalism: the beverage of postmodernism.

Proper understanding of the proliferation of specialty coffees requires consideration of the experiences and choices of the consumer in the coffee shop and at the dinner table, but it also requires consideration of the methods, networks, and relations of coffee production, processing, distribution, and sale in the 1980s, as well as a placement of those methods, networks, and relations within a wider history.

This essay concentrates on that second range of questions, on what might be termed the *shaping* of taste. I begin with two historical issues – first, the complex relation between the recent rise of specialty coffees and an earlier period characterized by standardization and mass-marketing, and second, the specific history of specialty coffees themselves. In considering both, I deal with coffee in particular, but what was happening with coffee marketing and consumption was not at all unrelated to what was happening with many other food commodities. I then turn to a range of questions that might be termed sociological: How has the turn toward specialty coffees been organized? What has been the position and role of the giant corporations that dominated the coffee trade during the period of standardization? Who have been the innovators and "agents" of change in the move toward specialty coffees? How have they organized themselves? How have they reimagined and reorganized the market? What kinds of class and generational maps of United States society have they used in their reimagination of the market? How have they imagined themselves, and the class and generational segments they target as their market niche, in relation to a wider world of coffee producers?

These more historical and sociological questions raise issues for anthropological interpretation. Can the study of changing marketing and consumption patterns of a single commodity at a particular moment – even a mundane commodity produced for everyday and routine consumption – shed some light on a wider range of social and cultural shifts? We have a good example of such an analysis in Sidney Mintz's *Sweetness and Power* (1985), an exploration of the growing and changing presence of sugar in the English diet from the 17th through 19th centuries, linked – explicitly and necessarily – to industrialization and the growth of a working class, changing modes of life, consumption, and sociality in growing cities in England, and to the establishment of colonial power, plantation economies, and slave labor in the Caribbean. The range of issues considered here is more modest, but it shares Mintz's conviction that "the social history of the use of new foods in a western nation can contribute to an anthropology of modern life" (1985:xxviii).

A distinctive feature of the essay is that the data come largely from two trade journals, *World Coffee and Tea (WC&T)* and *Coffee and Cocoa International (C&CI)*. These journals raise several questions, the first of which is methodological – the use of trade journals in relation to other possible methods and sources, including ethnographic ones. The journals give us access to the preoccupations, diagnoses, and strategies of a range of actors in the coffee trade – growers, traders, roasters, distributors, and retailers large and small, in producing as well as consuming countries. In one sense, they share a common interest: to increase coffee consumption and maximize profits. In many other senses, their interests and their stakes in the coffee trade differ.

If we are trying to understand these actors – their interpretations and intentions, their images of the social world in which they act, their disagreements and disputes, and their actions – trade journals constitute a central, readily available, and underused source. But their use raises a second related and interesting issue of the trade journal as text. The articles in the journals speak to a particular kind of public – in this case, to an assumed community of "coffeemen." The anthropologist who would use these articles for other purposes has the strong sense that he (in this case) is eavesdropping, or – to return to the text – peering over the shoulder of the intended reader.

Connections and Contrasts

We understand and value the new specialty coffees in relation to "the past," though in fact more than one past is being imagined. On the one hand, specialty coffees are placed in positive relation to the past of, say, two decades ago, when most coffee in the United States was sold in cans in supermarkets, the roasts were light and bland, the decaffeinated coffees undrinkable, the choices limited to brand and perhaps grind, and the trade dominated by General Foods and Procter and Gamble. On the other hand, the new coffees seem to connect with a more genuine past before the concentration and massification of the trade. The identification of particular blends and varietals recalls the glory days of the trade; the sale of whole beans in barrels or burlap bags recalls that past (for a present in which the "containerization" in international shipping has rendered such bags obsolete) at the same time that it gives the late-20th-century gourmet shop the ambience of the late-19th-century general store. This identification is further effected with the tasteful display of old coffee mills, roasters, and brewing apparatus on the store shelves. Coffee traders themselves share these identifications. Alan Rossman, of Hena "Estate Grown" Coffee, explained to *World Coffee and Tea* in 1981:

> I am a second generation coffeeman and, through direct experience, remember when there was a certain pride in the coffee business. We used to wonder why, in earlier days, there were so many second generation coffeemen around. And it was because there was an art to coffee then.... Today, the ballgame has changed and suddenly the password in coffee has become "cheaper, cheaper!"
>
> All of a sudden ... comes along somebody who's interested in quality. He doesn't care that he may have to sell it at twice the price of canned coffee, he's only interested in quality. All we're doing today is copying what our fathers and grandfathers did years and years ago.... Specialty coffee has revived the pride that was lost somewhere along the line and it is the main reason why I, who was born and raised in the coffee business, really enjoy now being part of that business. [*WC&T* 1981b:12]

In the same issue of *World Coffee and Tea*, the journal enthused:

> And so it seems that the coffee trade in the US has come full circle, returning to its roots and the uncomplicated marketing of coffee in bins, barrels and the more modern method of lucite containers. As they did in the early days of coffee consumption, American consumers, in ever-growing numbers, are blending their own coffee, grinding it at home and brewing it fresh each day. [*WC&T* 1981b:12]

Similarly, the journal notes that specialty coffees appeal to consumers who prefer "natural," "whole," and "fresh" foods. Imagining yet another past, the same journal nervously tracks the latest government reports on the effects of caffeine or methylene chloride. But to what extent is the new also a return? Upon what pasts have the specialty coffees actually built?

In an important essay, Michael Jimenez (1995) describes the processes through which coffee was transformed from an elite and expensive beverage, with annual per capita consumption in the United States at three pounds in 1830, to a relatively inexpensive drink consumed in working-class homes and at factory "coffee breaks" across the country by 1930. Much of his analysis concerns the first three decades of the 20th century, by which time coffee was widely distributed and consumed.

Of special relevance is Jimenez's analysis of the emergence of a more concentrated and consolidated coffee trade in the first three decades of [the 20th] century, one that had developed a central directing (though not controlling) authority and imposed standardized notions of quality and taste in the creation of a national market. Jimenez shows that we cannot understand transformations in the coffee trade without understanding a broad range of economic and social transformations in the history of American capitalism – the industrial revolution of the late 19th century and the creation of a more homogeneous proletariat; the development of national markets and modes of distribution; the revolution in food production, processing, and distribution that resulted in the creation of the supermarket, among other things (indeed, the histories of the supermarket and of standardization in the coffee trade are contingent); the revolution in advertising; the concentration and consolidation of American industry; and so on. In all this, the particular history of the standardization of coffee for mass markets is not unrelated to the history of standardization, indeed "industrialization," of foods in general in the 19th and 20th centuries (see Goody 1982:154–74).

The process of standardization and concentration begun before the depression was consolidated over the succeeding decades, especially after World War II, during which we can locate two new developments. The first involved the creation of international control instruments and agreements, beginning in World War II and culminating in the creation of the International Coffee Organization and an International Coffee Agreement signed by producing and consuming countries, through which export quotas were imposed upon producing countries. Though room was allowed for new producers (especially from Africa) to enter the market, entry and participation were controlled. With such instruments, and with the widening production and consumption of solubles, the trend toward coffee of the lowest common denominator continued.

The second postwar development involved the long-term decline in consumption beginning in the 1960s. Through the 1950s, consumption was essentially flat, with minor fluctuations. From 1962, one can chart a consistent decline. In that year, 74.7 percent of the adult population was calculated to be coffee drinkers; by 1988 only 50 percent drank coffee (see Table 8.1). Even those who drank coffee were drinking less. In 1962, average coffee consumption was 3.12 cups per day; by 1980 it had dipped to 2.02 cups and by 1991 had dropped to 1.75, which represented a slight increase over the 1988 low of 1.67 (WC&T 1991:14). Worse, in the view of "coffeemen," consumption was increasingly skewed toward an older set. At the beginning of the 1980s, they worried that they had not been able to attract the 20- to 29-year-old generation, who seemed to identify coffee drinking with the settled ways of their parents and grandparents. According to their calculations, 20- to 29-year-olds drank only 1.47 cups per day in 1980, while 30- to 59-year-olds drank 3.06 cups, and those over 60 drank 2.40 (WC&T 1980:22).

Differentiation and the Identification of Market Niches

The long-term trend toward decline was exacerbated by the effects of the July 1975 frost in Brazil, after which wholesale and retail prices rose precipitously. In response, various consumer groups began to call for boycotts, and coffee purchases declined sharply. Congressional hearings were called to investigate the coffee trade, and the General Accounting Office conducted an official inquiry and published a report.

Table 8.1 Percentage of US population drinking coffee, 1962–88. Redrawn and simplified after *WC&T* 1989a.

Year	Percentage drinking
1962	74.7
1974	61.6
1975	61.6
1976	59.1
1977	57.9
1978	56.7
1979	57.2
1980	56.6
1981	56.4
1982	56.3
1983	55.2
1984	57.3
1985	54.9
1986	52.4
1987	52.0
1988	50.0

At the beginning of the 1980s, then, many "coffeemen" had reason to worry. Kenneth Roman Jr., president of Ogilvie and Mather, a major advertising and public relations firm which carried the Maxwell House account, offered them some advice. In an interview with the editors of *World Coffee and Tea*, he commented,

> Coffee is a wonderful product. I believe, however, that we have got to stop selling the product on price. We must sell coffee on quality, value and image. I believe coffee has a potential for this marketing approach and I know we can do it. But we must get started now....
>
> Once you start selling a product on price, you end up with a lot of money being put into price promotions . . . and you forget the basic things like the fact that coffee tastes good, that it smells and looks nice, that it's unique....
>
> We are entering the "me" generation. The crucial questions "me" oriented consumers will ask, of all types of products, are: What's in it for me? Is the product "me"? Is it consistent with my lifestyle? Does it fill a need? Do I like how it tastes? What will it cost me? Is it necessary? Can I afford it? Is it convenient to prepare? How will it affect my health? [*WC&T* 1981a:35]

In a speech to the Green Coffee Association of New York, Roman suggested ficti-tious couples and individuals who could serve as markers of distinct market niches and suggested that "coffeemen" should develop different coffees to appeal to specific niches. The first couple was "the Grays," a dual-income couple in their mid-thirties, for whom coffee is a "way of life" and who prefer to buy their coffee in a gourmet shop. Others included "the Pritchetts," in their late fifties and watching their pennies, for whom price is the most important question; "Karen Sperling," a single working woman in her thirties who does not want to spend much time in the kitchen and for whom a better instant coffee should be developed; "the Taylors," in their sixties and worried about caffeine, for whom better decaffeinated coffees should be developed; and "Joel," a college student who does not drink coffee. "We don't know yet what to do about Joel.... Finding the right answer to that question will be the toughest, and probably the most important task coffee marketers will face in the 80s" (*WC&T* 1981a:76–7).

Kenneth Roman was inviting "coffeemen" to envision a segmented rather than a mass market, and to imagine market segments in class and generational terms. In his scheme were two groups that were to be the targets of specialty coffee promotions – the yuppie "Grays" and the mysterious "Joel," who prefers soft drinks. These two segments mark what were to become two strains of an emerging specialty business – the marketing of quality varietals, on one hand, and the promotion of flavored coffees, the equivalent of soft drinks, on another.

Roman was describing the virtues of product diversification to a trade that had grown on the basis of standardization. Yet the standardization itself was a bizarre development, having been imposed upon a product that "naturally" lends itself to diversity. Even during the period of concentration among roasters and packagers, the export–import trade was organized around a complex grading hierarchy, first according to type (arabica or robusta), then according to place, processing methods, and shape, size, and texture of the bean. Coffees are graded first according to a hierarchy from Colombian arabica, other milds, Brazilian, to robustas. They are traded and may be sold by the place of their origin or export (varietals such as Guatemalan Antigua, Kona, Blue Mountain, Maracaibo); once traded, they may be blended with coffees from other locales or of other grades. Both varietals and blends can then be subjected to different roasts, imparting different, more or less complex aromas and tastes to the coffee. From the point of production through traders, export firms, importers, warehousers, roasters, and distributors, the grading hierarchy with significant price differentials prevails. In their attempt to capture and service a mass market in the 20th century, the giant roasters had bought their coffee through these grading differentials, then proceeded to obliterate them in the production of coffee of the lowest common denominator.

The giants had never controlled the whole trade, however. In addition to the major roasters and their distribution network through grocery stores, smaller "institutional" roasters were scattered throughout the country, servicing restaurants, cafes, offices, vendors, and the like. At the beginning of the 1980s, fewer than 200 roasting and processing companies operated in the United States, with four of them controlling 75 percent of the trade (*C&CI* 1982:17). In addition, a small network of specialty, "gourmet" shops could be found, primarily in coastal cities like New York and San Francisco. In the retrospective view of "coffeemen," these shops began to attract new customers and expand business in the wake of the 1975 freeze, when coffee prices expanded across the board and consumers faced with paying $3 a pound for tasteless coffee began searching for something "better" and found that "quality" coffee that used to cost three times supermarket prices was now only about a dollar more.

This, in turn, provided stimulus for others to enter the gourmet trade, perhaps including specialty coffees as one of a range of foods in a gourmet shop. For this expanding number of retailers, supply was a problem. They were dealing in small lots of a product that was imported, warehoused, and sold in bulk, and were entering a trade that was highly concentrated. As the specialty trade expanded, the critical middlemen were the roasters, who could develop special relationships with importers willing to deal in smaller lots. The roasters, in turn, would supply a network of specialty stores. Location mattered, as a relatively dense concentration of specialty traders, roasters, retailers, and customers developed on the West Coast, especially in Seattle and the San Francisco Bay Area. The roasters best situated to take advantage of the situation were institutional roasters who began to develop specialty lines as subsidiaries of their restaurant supply business. These regional roasters, and others new to the trade, quickly became the control points of an expanding gourmet trade, developing new supplies, roasts, and blends; taking on regular customers among shop owners; running "educational" seminars to cultivate a more detailed knowledge of coffee among retailers, expecting that they in turn would educate their customers; and so on. An early gourmet-market idea popular with retailers was the "gourmet coffee of the day," sold by the cup, allowing the retailer to drain excess inventory and acquaint customers with different blends and roasts at the same time.

One of the most important difficulties for the roaster was the establishment of a regular supply of green coffee. Here the problem was less one of quality than of quantity: major importers and warehousers were reluctant to break lots into shipments below 25 to 50 bags (of 60 kilograms each), but a small to medium-sized roaster dealing with several varietals needed to buy in lots of about 10 bags each. While a collection of green coffee traders in the Bay Area (B. C. Ireland, E. A. Kahl, Harold L. King, Royal Coffee) specialized in the gourmet trade and traded in smaller lots, New York traders were slow to move into the new markets (Schoenholt 1984a:62). As late as 1988, Robert Fulmer of Royal Coffee complained, "Demand for quality has happened faster than producers can react. The New York 'C' market is becoming irrelevant, because it's not representative of what people want" (C&CI 1988a: 18–22).

Although the trend still represented a very small percentage of total coffee sales in the United States by the early 1980s, traders and roasters had begun to take notice. A scant seven months after Kenneth Roman discussed the need to identify a segmented market and diversify coffee products, *World Coffee and Tea* issued a report on "the browning of America," pointing to an exponential growth in the segment of the coffee trade devoted to specialty lines, with annual growth rates approaching 30 to 50 percent. The journal estimated total US sales of specialty coffees for 1980 to be 14 million pounds (WC&T 1981b:12). Over the 1980s growth was phenomenal: *Coffee and Cocoa International* reported sales of 40 million pounds in 1983 (C&CI 1985), after which further reports were presented in value of the trade rather than the number of bags – $330 million in 1985 (C&CI 1986), $420 million in 1986, $500 million in 1987, by which time specialty coffee constituted 8 percent of total trade, and so on (C&CI 1988b).

The expansion of specialty coffees was coincident with a number of technological and commercial developments that require brief mention. First, the "containerization" revolution in international shipping has drastically cut the amount of time coffee is in transit from producing countries to consuming countries (from 17 to 10 days for a typical Santos-to-New York run), and has transformed warehousing practices in the United States, cutting warehouse storage times from an average of six months to an average of 10 to 14 days. Speed in transfer and the development of direct and immediate relationships with roasters have become critical, and the widespread use of containers has allowed distributors to relocate from the coasts to interior cities, enhancing flexibility in supply and distribution (Coe 1983).

Changing relationships between roasters, traders, and bankers were also involved in the gourmet boom. The combination of high inflation and interest rates of the late 1970s and early 1980s affected the way in which "coffeemen" could think about financing their trade. By the early 1980s, banks were less willing to finance purchases of large lots that would be warehoused for several months and encouraged their clients to buy smaller lots and maintain lower inventories. "It's a different world now," Mickey Galitzine of the Bank of New York commented to *World Coffee and Tea* (1983a:21), "and I'm not sure we can go back. People have adjusted to this new situation and are now buying in a different pattern. They're simply used to buying less."

They were buying less, but still buying in lots that were large and risky enough to concern the specialty roaster. Institutional roasters could roast, grind, and package large lots and not worry about freshness. Specialty roasts, to be sold in whole beans, required freshness and had to be distributed and sold quickly. The roaster therefore had to develop an extensive network of retailers but was limited to particular regions because of the difficulties in shipping whole roast beans and maintaining freshness. Here the development of valve packaging made it possible for roasters to keep roasted beans fresh longer, extending the time available for shipping, storage, and selling. The beans could be packed in 250-gram bags for direct retail sale or in 15- or 25-pound bags for retail storage. Indeed, the deli across the street from me buys its 43 varieties from a single roaster in 15-pound valve bags, transferring the coffee to burlap bags for presentation and sale.

New Actors, New Institutions

Throughout the 1980s, the "quality" segment of the coffee market, highest in prices and profit margins, was booming while total coffee consumption declined. This constitutes such a perfect response to market decline, and such an obvious response to the suggestions of Kenneth Roman, that we might expect a central directing power – "Capital," or at least "The Coffee Interest." But the initiative toward specialty coffees occurred outside of and despite the controlling interests of the giants like General Foods, Procter and Gamble, and Nestlé, who ignored the growth of specialty coffees and seemed to regard them as a fad until they captured a significant percentage of the market. Their reticence might be explained by the fact that the giants were part of large food conglomerates likely to be less threatened by a long-term decline in coffee consumption than the smaller institutional roasters, who were forced to develop new markets in order to survive.

This is not to say that the emergence of specialty coffees was completely free from direction and organization. I have pointed to *some* of the larger commercial, financial, and technological changes with which the move to specialty coffees was associated. In addition, the coffee trade viewed the new developments with interest and excitement. We have seen the notice taken by trade journals from the early 1980s. *World Coffee and Tea* began tracking developments quite closely, with frequent reports on the trade and profiles of particular roasters or retailers. In 1984, the journal also began an irregular column, "The Gourmet Zone," by Donald Schoenholt, followed in the early 1990s by a regular column with various contributors, "The Specialty Line." *Coffee and Cocoa International* viewed developments from a greater distance but enjoyed profiling particular gourmet retailers for their readers. Most importantly, a group of roasters and retailers formed the Specialty Coffee Association of America (SCAA) in 1982. As with the earlier formation of the National Coffee Association (and later the International Coffee Organization), the importance of such trade associations needs to be emphasized. They provide an important directing organization that can lobby the government, speak for the trade, identify economic and political trends, engage in promotional campaigns, provide information and training for entrepreneurs entering the trade, and so on.

In association with the National Coffee Service Association, the SCAA appealed to the Promotion Fund of the International Coffee Organization and received a $1.6 million grant to promote specialty coffees, especially among the young (*WC&T* 1983b). The money was funneled through the Coffee Development Group (CDG), which promoted specialty coffees throughout the 1980s. One of their early activities involved joint sponsorship of coffeehouses on college campuses (Columbia University being one of the first), at which coffee brewed from specialty roasts and blends would be sold. The CDG would specify the amount of coffee that had to be included in each pot brewed (*WC&T* 1988). Some, such as the shop at the University of Southern California, even experimented with iced cappuccino, sold in cold drink "bubblers" (*WC&T* 1989b).

In addition to promotional efforts, the SCAA has pursued other goals as well, including the dissemination of information on green market conditions and the development of networks among roasters, retailers, and traders. By 1989, the group held its first convention, and each annual convention demonstrates the phenomenal growth of the association. Its conventions now attract over 3,000 people, and it claims to be the largest coffee association in the world.

Many of the association's members are new to the coffee trade, and they bring with them a formation quite unlike that which characterized second- and third-generation "coffeemen." For one thing, many begin with a lack of knowledge about the basics of coffee production, processing, and marketing. This is reflected in a new tone in *World Coffee and Tea*, which increasingly offers articles giving basic and introductory information of various aspects of the coffee trade, recently advising new entrepreneurs that "historic and geographic background is an essential element to a comprehensive knowledge of coffee. If you're selling Colombian coffee, you should have some idea about where Colombia is located and what kinds of coffee it produces" (McCormack 1994:22). It is also reflected in the kinds of workshops and training sessions offered at annual conventions of the SCAA, popularly known as Espresso 101 or Roasting 101 or Brewing 101.

The presence of new entrepreneurs is also reflected in new sets of social, political, and ethical concerns that would have been anathema to earlier generations of "coffeemen." Among them is a growing interest in social and environmental issues and the creation by coffee roasters of such organizations as Equal Exchange and Coffee Kids, and companies like Aztec Harvests ("owned by Mexican co-op farmers"). As the founder of Coffee Kids, Bill Fishbein, expresses the problem:

> This disparity that exists between the coffee-growing world and the coffee-consuming world is rooted in the centuries and remains the true inheritance of 500 years of colonialism. Although no one in today's coffee industry created the existing situation, everyone, including importers, brokers, roasters, retailers, and consumers are left with this legacy either to perpetuate or address. [Fishbein and Cycon 1992:14]

William McAlpin, a plantation owner in Costa Rica, gives voice to an older generation that dismisses these concerns along the paternalistic lines one expects from a plantation owner proud of the livelihood he has provided for "our residents," but also observes:

> I am always amused to see that many of these same people, who are involved in the final stages of selling specialty coffee, while proclaiming that they support this or that charity or political action squad, are careful to avoid mentioning that the usual mark-up by the specialty coffee trade is from 400% to 600% of the price paid for delivered green coffee. . . .
>
> From the producer's point of view, it seems truly ironic that a product that takes a year to grow, and that requires thousands of worker hours of difficult, delicate, and often dangerous work, should be so remarkably inflated by someone who simply cooks and displays the coffee. [McAlpin 1994:7]

In any case, both dimensions of the formation of the new coffee men and women find expression and are given direction by the SCAA. In addition to the workshops and training seminars, one can see this in their annual choice of a plenary speaker. At its second convention, held in San Francisco, the SCAA arranged a group tour of wineries and invited a wine merchant to give the plenary address, in which he offered advice based on the success of a beverage that the trade journals have most frequently taken as the model to be emulated. For the 1993 convention, the association invited Ben Cohen of Ben and Jerry's Ice Cream. Of his address, *World Coffee and Tea* reported:

> Ben Cohen urged the members of the coffee industry to integrate the 1960s values of peace and love with running their businesses. . . .
>
> Cohen pointed out that coffee is a very political commodity and called on the members of the special coffee industry to:
>
> * purchase coffee from the Aztec Cooperative because a high percentage of the money goes back to the farmers; "buy it, tell your customers about it, and let them choose whether or not they want to pay the higher price," Cohen said.
>
> * buy organic coffees; and
>
> * participate in Coffee Kids by using a coin drop or donating a percentage of sales.
>
> "Use these steps to build your image as a socially conscious business," Cohen explained, "and make it your point of difference in a highly competitive business." [WC&T 1993:7]

Flexibility and Concentration

As the smaller roasters captured the new market niche, they expressed both surprise and concern about the activities of the giants, sometimes assuming that the market was theirs only as long as the giants stayed out (e.g., *WC&T* 1984:12). Some of the roasters' and retailers' fears were realized in September 1986 when both General Foods and A&P introduced specialty lines for sale in supermarkets – General Foods with Maxwell House Private Collection and A&P with Eight O'Clock Royale Gourmet Bean in 14 varieties, "all designed to appeal to the former soft drink generation." At the time, Karin Brown of General Foods commented, "Gourmet is the fastest-growing segment of the market – large enough to make sense for General Foods' entry now" (*C&CI* 1986:9).

By the time the giants began to enter the market, the groundwork for a certain kind of standardization and concentration among the newcomers had already been laid. In coastal cities, the isolated gourmet food shop was already competing with chains of gourmet shops operating in minimalls, which could, if they chose, develop their own roasting capacities. In addition, some roasters (the best known and most aggressive of which has been Starbucks of Seattle) had begun to move beyond regional distribution chains and develop national markets. While structural changes, from the technologies of shipping, warehousing, and packaging to the credit policies of banks, were significant, we need to also consider some of the characteristics of the gourmet beans themselves.

As the gourmet trade expanded, participants viewed two new developments with excitement or alarm, depending on their respective commitment to traditional notions of "quality." As noted above, the quality of coffee "naturally" varies according to several criteria – type of coffee tree and location of cultivation (varietals), method of processing, size and texture of bean, and degree of roasting. With the expansion of the specialty trade, two new modes of discrimination were introduced – "styles" and "flavors." Because the availability of particular varietals is uncertain (a hurricane hits Jamaica, wiping out Blue Mountain coffee, or a trader cannot provide Kenya AA in lots small enough for a particular roaster because larger roasters can outcompete, and so on), and the price of varietals fluctuates accordingly, roasters attempt to develop blends that allow them flexibility in using a number of varietals interchangeably. "Peter's Blend" or "House Blend" says nothing about where the coffee comes from, allowing the roaster or retailer near perfect flexibility, but so again does the sale of "Mocha style" or "Blue Mountain style." At the beginning of this trend, J. Gill Brockenbrough Jr. of First Colony Coffee and Tea complained, "It is more and more difficult all the time to find the green coffee we need. . . . But there really is no such thing as a 'style' of coffee, either it *is* or it *isn't* from a particular origin" (*WC&T* 1981b:15). Donald Schoenholt of Gillies 1840 elaborated in his column, "The Gourmet Zone," in *World Coffee and Tea*:

> In the past I have pointed out the practice of labeling "varietals" with the code word "style," a habit which has come to replace good judgment too often these days. But now it appears we have a new phenomenon added to the good-humored diversity of

specialty coffee labeling: the gentle art of selling the same coffee by whatever varietal label the customer orders.

One well-known trade executive states his customers understand that substitutions are made from time-to-time when varietals are unavailable. A well-known roaster/ retailer avoids buying varietal selections, following instead the accepted tradition of buying for cup qualities alone. He offers his patrons distinctive tastes in varietal labeled blends – Colombian Blend, Kenya Blend, Jamaica Blue Mountain style, etc.

Where the wholesale or retail clientele understand a merchant's practices and honorable intent, both the above-mentioned methods of labeling have been accepted. The problem arises where a merchant's intent is to mislead, through unbridled use of a stencil machine, creating labels just for the sake of inventing variety where none exists. Where no effort or skill is used, the public is presented with cut-rate mislabeled coffees.

A recent inspection of a grocer in the New York area sadly proved a point: Virtually every American roast coffee on display was the same item under different label, purchased from a discount roaster offering all American roast beans, regardless of origin, in the same $2.60 per lb. price range. [Schoenholt 1984b:39]

A second, related development was the emergence of coffee flavors that can be sprayed on recently roasted beans. C. Melchers and Company of Bremen began operating in the United States in 1982, offering an ever-expanding variety of liquid flavors for coffee and tea. Each flavor is composed of 20 to 60 "natural" and "artificial" (chemical) ingredients, and Melchers is adept at developing different combinations to produce "unique" flavors for particular roasters (WC&T 1983c:16, 18). Viewing this trend, Larry Kramer of Van Cortland Coffee observed, "Specialty coffee is becoming the Baskin Robbins of the specialty food trade." Actually, as we have seen, it turned out that Ben and Jerry's would have been more to the point. Some roasters and retailers refused to deal in such coffees. Complained Paul Katzeff of Thanksgiving Coffee, "People who drink good coffee drink it because they enjoy the flavor of real coffee. . . . I doubt that flavored coffees bring in drinkers who never drank coffee before" (WC&T 1982:20). Despite such expressions of dismay, the move toward flavored coffees has continued apace; roasters and retailers alike recognize that flavors are popular, that they are attracting new coffee drinkers, especially among the "former soft drink generation" that had seemed lost to coffee consumption at the beginning of the 1980s – Kenneth Roman's "Joel," about whom "we don't know yet what to do." Increasingly popular in both retail shops and espresso bars are flavored syrups that, in addition to imparting an apparent "Italian" elegance, grant the small retailer more flexibility. A smaller number of blends, varietals, and roasts can be kept in stock, along with a few bottles of syrup, and customers can add or mix their own flavors.

Style and flavor can, in turn, be combined in various ways, so that one can buy Blue Mountain style vanilla or almond, Mocha style chocolate cream or amaretto, and so on. If we further combine with different roasts, throw in the possibility of caffeinated or water process decaffeinated, the possibilities for variety are almost endless. Critically important, however, is that the variety is *controllable*. To the extent that roasters and retailers are able to create criteria of variability and quality that are removed from the "natural" characteristics and qualities of the coffee beans themselves, they generate for themselves extraordinary flexibility. In extreme cases, they "invent variety where none exists," as Schoenholt complains. Here we find a consumer who acts and feels like a gourmet but is buying coffee that is not far removed from Maxwell House Private Collection. More generally, they create, define, and control their own forms of variety. Specialty "coffeemen" constantly emulate and consult wine merchants and hope that consumers will select coffee with the same discrimination and willingness to spend money they demonstrate when buying wine, but the Baskin Robbins (or Ben and Jerry's) model may not be too much of an exaggeration.

Ironically, controllable variety also makes the specialty trade subject to concentration, whether from the outside as giants create their own "Private Collection" and "Royale Gourmet Bean" lines or from internal differentiation, expansion, and concentration among smaller roasters. Variety, too, can be standardized, especially if the varieties have little to do with "natural" characteristics.

The Beverage of Postmodernism?

In his study of the transformation of coffee production and consumption in the early 20th century, Michael Jimenez suggests that coffee is the beverage of US capitalism. Indeed, as we consider the place of coffee as a beverage of choice in working- and middle-class homes and in factory canteens, the role of coffee traders in the emergence of a practical internationalism, and the processes of standardization and concentration that restructured the coffee market, we see that the coffee trade was subject to and participant in the same processes that made a capitalist world.

This is not to suggest, of course, that coffee exists in some sort of unique relationship with capitalism, but that it provides a window through which we can view a range of relationships and social transformations. The processes of standardization and industrialization were common to many foods in the 20th-century United States, and coffee would therefore be one of many foods through which one could examine the transformation industrialization wrought in such broad areas as the structure of cities, the remaking of work and domestic life and organization, or more specific concerns, such as the rise of advertising or the supermarket. Here, Jimenez's work on coffee in the United States complements Mintz's work on sugar in England (1985). Yet coffee and sugar belong to a small subset of commodities that can illuminate capitalist transformations in other ways in that they link consumption zones (and the rise of working and middle classes that consumed the particular products in ever increasing numbers) and production zones in Latin America, the Caribbean, Africa, and Asia (and the peasants, slaves, and other rural toilers who grew, cut, or picked the products). For these commodities once inadequately termed "dessert foods" and now increasingly called "drug foods," Sidney Mintz offers a more arresting phrase – coffee, sugar, tea, and chocolate were "proletarian hunger killers" (1979).

Might we, in turn, now consider coffee to be the beverage of postmodernism? That is, can an examination of shifts in the marketing and consumption of one commodity provide an angle of vision on a wider set of social and cultural formations and the brave new world of which they are a part? That I can walk across the street and choose among a seemingly endless variety of cheeses, beers, waters, teas, and coffees places me in a new relationship to the world: I can consume a bit of

Sumatra, Darjeeling, France, and Mexico in my home, perhaps at the same meal. Such variety stands in stark contrast to the stolid, boring array of goods available two decades ago. We live now in an emerging era of variety and choice, and the revolution in consumption seems to indicate, and in some ways initiate, a revolution in production. As with coffee, so with other food products: the moves toward product diversification often came not from the established and dominant corporations but from independents whose initiatives have undercut and undermined the established practices and market share of those corporations. We might see this as the extension of the Apple Computer model of entrepreneurialism to other realms.

David Harvey elaborates:

> The market place has always been an "emporium of styles" . . . but the food market, just to take one example, now looks very different from what it was twenty years ago. Kenyan haricot beans, Californian celery and avocados, North African potatoes, Canadian apples, and Chilean grapes all sit side by side in a British supermarket. This variety also makes for a proliferation of culinary styles, even among the relatively poor. . . .
>
> The whole world's cuisine is now assembled in one place in almost exactly the same way that the world's geographical complexity is nightly reduced to a series of images on a static television screen. This same phenomenon is exploited in entertainment palaces like Epcot and Disneyworld; it becomes possible, as the US commercials put it, "to experience the Old World for a day without actually having to go there." The general implication is that through the experience of everything from food, to culinary habits, music, television, entertainment, and cinema, it is now possible to experience the world's geography vicariously, as a simulacrum. The interweaving of simulacra in daily life brings together different worlds (of commodities) in the same space and time. But it does so in such a way as to conceal almost perfectly any trace of origin, of the labour processes that produced them, or of the social relations implicated in their production. [1989:299, 300]

A more complete understanding of coffee marketing and consumption in the 1980s and 1990s requires that we make some attempt to examine the world of production concealed by the emporium of styles. We might begin by maintaining an understanding of coffee as "the beverage of United States capitalism" but placing the history of that beverage within two periods of capitalist accumulation.

In David Harvey's view, much of 20th-century capitalism was dominated by a "Fordist" regime of accumulation; since the mid-1970s a new regime has emerged, which he labels "flexible accumulation." The Fordist regime can be seen to begin in 1914, with the imposition of assembly line production, and it has dominated the post-World War II period. The Fordist regime was founded on mass production and industrial modes of organization, based in a few key industries (steel, oil, petrochemicals, automobiles), characterized by the presence of both organized management and organized labor with negotiated, relatively stable pacts between them. These industries, in turn, were subject to state regulation and protection of markets and resources, and they produced standardized commodities for mass markets. With the financial crises of the 1970s, the stabilities of the Fordist regime came to be seen as rigidities. Harvey sees the regime of flexible accumulation emerging in partial response. His description of the innovations characteristic of flexible accumulation concentrates on many features that we have already encountered in our discussion of specialty coffees – the identification of specialized market niches and the production of goods for those niches as opposed to the emphasis on mass-market standardized products; the downsizing of plants and production processes; the shrinking of inventories so that producers purchase smaller quantities and practice just-in-time production; the revolution in shipping and warehousing technologies to cut shipping times; the reconfiguration of financial markets; and so on.

In this regard, it is interesting to place the period considered by Jimenez and the period examined in this essay next to each other. Both concern decades that saw, if we follow Harvey's analysis, experimentation with new regimes of accumulation. But if we return to a history more specific to coffee, both also began with a perceived problem – stagnation in consumption in the first, long-term decline in the second. Both began with evident consumer dissatisfaction and governmental investigation (in the form of congressional hearings). In both, the coffee trade, in the individual actions of its fragmented members and in the programs of its directing centers, devised strategies to respond to perceived crises that, as it happens, neatly correspond with the forms, methods, and relations of emerging regimes of accumulation.

As I visit the gourmet shop, it might be a bit disconcerting to know that I have been so clearly targeted as a member of a class and generation, that the burlap bags or minibarrels, the styles and flavors of coffee, the offer of a "gourmet coffee of the day," have been designed to appeal to me and others in my market niche. But such are the circumstances surrounding my freedom of choice. In an influential essay on the global cultural economy, Arjun Appadurai has suggested the emergence of a new "fetishism of the consumer" and claims that commodity flows and marketing strategies "mask...the real seat of agency, which is not the consumer but the producer and the many forces that constitute production.... The consumer is consistently helped to believe that he or she is an actor, where in fact he or she is at best a chooser" (1990:307). While I think Appadurai's larger claims regarding the radical disjuncture between the present global cultural economy and earlier moments and forms require careful and skeptical analysis (Roseberry 1992), the recent history of coffee marketing and consumption seems to support his understanding of consumer fetishism.

That is to say, my newfound freedom to choose, and the taste and discrimination I cultivate, have been shaped by traders and marketers responding to a long-term decline in sales with a move toward market segmentation along class and generational lines. While I was thinking of myself as me, Kenneth Roman saw me as one of "the Grays." How many readers of this essay have been acting like "Joels"? This is not, of course, to say that we enter the market as mere automatons; clearly, we have and exercise choices, and we (apparently) have more things to choose from than we once did. But we exercise those choices in a world of structured relationships, and part of what those relationships structure (or shape) is both the arena and the process of choice itself.

Another, inescapable part of that world of structured relationships is a set of connections with the world of production and of producers. My vicarious experience of the world's geography is not *just* a simulacrum; it depends upon a quite real, if mediated and unacknowledged, relationship with the rural toilers without whom my choice could not be exercised. How has the brave new world of choice and flexibility affected them?

For both Fordist and flexible accumulation regimes, the mode of mobilizing labor is critical – the importance of a stable core of organized labor and labor relations under Fordism and its virtual opposite under flexible accumulation, which seems to remove labor as much as possible from core to peripheral (temporary, seasonal, occasional, or contracted) labor supplies that can be engaged and disengaged as needed. Some of the innovations that I have discussed in relation to the coffee market have involved such shifts in labor relations (e.g., the move toward contain-erization in international shipping, which revolutionized distribution in the United States and allowed importers to bypass the docks and warehouses of coastal cities, cutting the need for labor and the power of the unions of longshoremen and warehousemen).

As we turn from the United States to the manifold points of production, we find that the changes can be quite dramatic, though their shape and consequences remain uncertain and can only be suggested here. Throughout the post-World War II period, the coffee trade was regulated by a series of international coffee agreements, the first of which was the Pan American agreement during the war, and the longest lasting of which was the International Coffee Agreement (ICA) administered by the Inter-national Coffee Organization (ICO), formed in 1963. Through the agreements, producing and consuming countries submitted to a series of quotas that could be adjusted and even suspended from year to year – as particular countries suffered hurricanes, droughts, or frosts or other countries entered the market and signed the agreement – but that nonetheless imposed a series of (let us call them Fordist) rigidities on international trade. They also provided a series of protections for individual producing countries and regions, regulating both prices (which fluctuated but with highs and lows that were less dramatic) and market share.

The agreements were never especially popular among "coffeemen," who profess a free trade philosophy, and they encountered increasing opposition in the 1980s. Specialty traders wanted to develop new sources of supply, emphasizing arabicas and deemphasizing robustas, which had an important place in mass-market blends and soluble (instant) coffees but found little acceptance in specialty markets. Unfor-tunately for the specialty traders, the percentages of arabicas and robustas offered on the world market were fixed by the ICA; fortunately for robusta producers, their livelihoods were relatively protected by that same agreement.

The ICA was due for renewal and extension in 1989, but the various members of the ICO encountered difficulties in resolving their differences. Two countries were especially insistent on their needs – Brazil, which wanted to maintain its 30 percent share, and the United States, which pressed two concerns: (1) the troublesome practice among producing countries of discounting prices to nonmember consuming countries (essentially those within the then-existing socialist bloc), and (2) the inflexibility of the quotas that, they argued, prevented traders and consumers from acquiring more of the quality arabicas. Because the differences could not be re-solved, the ICA was suspended in mid-1989, ushering in a free market in coffee for the first time in decades.

The immediate effects were dramatic for producing countries. Prices plummeted and quickly reached, in constant dollar terms, historic lows. Exporting countries that could do so expanded exports in an attempt to maintain income levels in the face of declining unit prices, and importers took advantage of the low prices and expanded stocks. In addition to the general price decline, robusta producers were especially disadvantaged, as prices for robusta dipped below \$.50 per pound and farmers faced a world market that no longer wanted their product. Robusta is grown primarily in Africa, and African producers and economies were devastated.

By 1993, under the leadership of Brazil and Colombia, along with Central American arabica producers, a coffee retention plan was signed that called for the removal of up to 20 percent of production by participants in the plan. The plan was the first step toward a new Association of Coffee Producing Countries in which both Latin American and African countries participated, and it has succeeded in spurring a price recovery. It remains a fragile coalition, however, and by the time it had been formed the market had been completely restructured. Most importantly, because market prices had fallen below the level of production costs, only the strong – those who could weather a prolonged depression – survived. The weak disappeared from the coffee scene.

The free market vastly increased the flexibility of coffee traders and "peripheralized" the labor of coffee growers in a direct and immediate way. My freedom to choose in the deli across the street or the gourmet shop a few blocks away is implicated with the coffee trader's freedom to cut off the supply (and therefore the product of the laborer) from, say, Uganda or the Ivory Coast. To the extent that "coffeemen" have been successful in creating styles, so that I think I am drinking coffee from a particular place but the coffee need not have any actual association with that place, I will not even be aware of the processes of connection and disconnection in which I am participating. "The beverage of US capitalism," indeed!

Conclusion

Resolution of the issues raised by this analysis would take us beyond our sources. My aim is to draw out certain implications and perspectives resulting from the angle of vision pursued herein, but also to point toward questions and perspectives that could be pursued in supplementary and complementary analyses – other chapters, so to speak.

This essay's perspective on the shaping of market trends and taste may raise the specter of manipulation by unseen, but powerful, forces. In an important discussion of the Frankfurt School's approach to culture industries in general and to consumption patterns in particular, Stephen Mennell observes:

> The problem with the use of words like "manipulation" by the Frankfurt School and other critics is that it suggests that those in powerful positions in industry – the culture industry or the food and catering industries – *consciously* and with malevolent intent set out to persuade people that they need and like products of inferior or harmful quality. It fails to draw attention to the unplanned, unintended, vicious spiral through which supply and demand are usually linked. [1996:321]

There is, of course, plenty of evidence from the trade journals that conscious action on the part of a range of actors in the coffee trade to persuade people that they need and like certain products – leaving aside the question of intent and the quality of the products – is *precisely* what they do. But it is also clear from the sources that they do not act in concert, that there is no single controlling interest (despite obvious power relations), that there has been ample room for new interests and actors, that these actors, big and small, often do not know what they are doing, and that in their bumbling experimentation they have stumbled on some strategies that work. They work not because there is a manipulable mass out there waiting to be told what to drink but because there is a complex, if specific, intersection between the shaping actions of various actors in the coffee trade and the needs, tastes, and desires of particular groups of consumers and potential consumers.

We gain access to that intersection by means of a discussion of *class*. We have seen that Kenneth Roman preached market segmentation along class and generational lines. His own suggestion of segments was relatively simple, even crude – divided by very broad distinctions of class and generation, with some sense of gender differentiation, but each of the segments was implicitly white. Theorists of niche marketing have since gone much further in dividing national populations into class, racial, ethnic, and generational groups than Roman would have imagined in the early 1980s, as books like *The Clustering of America* (Weiss 1988) make clear. That these distinctions, however crude, are being made, and that they *work* for the purposes for which they are intended, is worth some reflection.

The point, of course, is that when market strategists *imagine* a class and generational map that includes people like "the Grays" and "Joel," they are not trying to create categories out of thin air. They are doing – for different purposes – what sociologists and anthropologists used to do: trying to describe a social and cultural reality. The imagined map works only if there are indeed such groups "out there," so to speak, and that the map needs to work is the whole point.

That there is a complex relationship between class and food consumption is often remarked, first in the obvious sense that particular groups occupy differential market situations in terms of their ability to purchase certain foods, and second in the uses various groups make of foods and food preferences in marking themselves as distinctive from or in some sense like other groups. In the case of specialty coffee, one of its interesting features is that it is *not*, or is not meant to be, a "proletarian hunger killer." Looking further afield, it is worth comment that the other proletarian hunger killers of the 19th and 20th centuries – with the exception of sugar, which does not lend itself to such multiple distinctions except in combination with other substances – are also caught up in the move toward variety and at least the illusion of quality. In one sense this signals the return to "dessert food" status, but there are other senses that need to be considered.

The original market segment toward which specialty coffee, tea, and chocolate were directed was that of "the Grays" – urban, urbane, professional men and women who distinguished themselves through consumption and who consumed or hoped to consume variety and quality, as well as quantity. If they fashioned themselves through consumption, an interesting feature of the movement is that among the commodities in which they demanded variety and quality were the old proletarian hunger killers. In doing so, they almost certainly did not imagine themselves in connection either with proletarians or with the rural toilers who grew, cut, or picked what the yuppies chose to consume.

The identifications they were making were rather more complex and may connect with the commodities' "prehistory," as it were, representing a kind of preindustrial nostalgia. Each of the proletarian hunger killers entered European social history as expensive goods from exotic locales, affordable and consumable only by a privileged few, not in homes but in the courts, or, increasingly in the 17th and 18th centuries, in coffee houses (Schivelbusch 1992; Ukers 1935). They became proletarian hunger killers as their costs of production, processing, and shipping dropped, as available quantities increased dramatically, and as they became items of domestic and routine consumption. The class and cultural identification of this yuppie segment, then, is not so much bourgeois as courtly, genteel, cosmopolitan. It could be seen to represent an attempt to re-create, through consumption, a time before mass society and mass consumption. It could be seen, then, as a symbolic inversion of the very economic and political forces through which this particular class segment came into existence. Here, close attention to class-conditioned patterns of consumption can provide another window onto the cultural history of US capitalism.

But the story does not end here. Over the past decade, the consumption of yuppie coffees has broken free from its original market segment, as the coffees are more widely available in supermarkets and shopping malls and are more widely consumed. We have seen that the processes of production and distribution have been subject to concentration and centralization from above and below as Maxwell House and Eight O'Clock Coffee have introduced gourmet coffees and as new chains as different from each other as Starbucks and Gloria Jean's move into central positions at the coffee shop end. This movement, in which a class-conditioned process of marketing, promotion, and consumption escapes class locations, and apparent variety and quality are standardized and mass-marketed, has obvious limits. Gourmet coffees can be standardized, and their processes of production and marketing concentrated, but it is unlikely that these coffees will ever become truly mass-market coffees. Their continued success will depend upon the processes of social and cultural differentiation they mark, even as the social locations of groups of consumers are blurred. It will also depend upon the continued existence, at home and abroad, of a world of exploitative relationships, evidenced in the social relations through which coffee is produced, the engagement of coffee-producing regions under free-market conditions, and the processes of standardization and concentration to which gourmet coffee production and marketing have been subjected. Coffee remains, as Ben Cohen expressed it, a "very political commodity."

REFERENCES

Appadurai, Arjun
1990 Disjuncture and Difference in the Global Cultural Economy. *Theory, Culture and Society* 7:295–310.
Coe, Kevin
1983 Changes in Store. *Coffee and Cocoa International* 10(5):39–41.
C&CI (*Coffee and Cocoa International*)
1982 High Hopes for the Promotion Drive. *Coffee and Cocoa International* 9(2):14–17.

1985 Major Growth Seen for Gourmet Coffee Market. *Coffee and Cocoa International* 12(1):5.

1986 Giants Clash in Specialty Brands War. *Coffee and Cocoa International* 13(5):9.

1988a The California Trade: A West Coast View. *Coffee and Cocoa International* 15(5): 18–22.

1988b $500m Gourmet Market to Expand, Says Study. *Coffee and Cocoa International* 15(6):6.

Fishbein, Bill, and Dean Cycon

1992 Coffee Kids. *World Coffee and Tea*, October: 14–15, 28.

Goody, Jack

1982 Cooking, Cuisine, and Class: A Study in Comparative Sociology. Cambridge: Cambridge University Press.

Harvey, David

1989 The Condition of Postmodernity. Oxford: Basil Blackwell.

Jimenez, Michael

1995 From Plantation to Cup: Coffee and Capitalism in the United States, 1830–1930. *In* Coffee, Society, and Power in Latin America. William Roseberry, Lowell Gudmundson, and Mario Samper Kutschbach, eds. Pp. 38–64. Baltimore, MD: Johns Hopkins University Press.

McAlpin, William J.

1994 Coffee and the Socially Concerned. *World Coffee and Tea*, July: 6–7.

McCormack, Tim

1994 Teaching Consumers about Coffee. *World Coffee and Tea*, July: 21–3.

Mennell, Stephen

1996 All Manners of Food: Eating and Taste in England and France from the Middle Ages to the Present. 2nd edition. Urbana: University of Illinois Press.

Mintz, Sidney

1979 Time, Sugar, and Sweetness. *Marxist Perspectives* 2:56–73.

1985 Sweetness and Power: The Place of Sugar in Modern History. New York: Viking.

Roseberry, William

1992 Multiculturalism and the Challenge of Anthropology. *Social Research* 59:841–58.

Schivelbusch, Wolfgang

1992 Tastes of Paradise: A Social History of Spices, Stimulants, and Intoxicants. New York: Vintage.

Schoenholt, Donald N.

1984a The Gourmet Zone. *World Coffee and Tea*, September: 62–3.

1984b The Gourmet Zone. *World Coffee and Tea*, November: 39.

Ukers, W. H.

1935 All about Coffee. 2nd edition. New York: Tea and Coffee Trade Journal Company.

Weiss, Michael J.

1988 The Clustering of America. New York: Harper and Row.

WC&T (World Coffee and Tea)

1980 US Coffee Drinking Slips after Slight Gain; Young Still Not Drinking. *World Coffee and Tea*, November: 21–2.

1981a Ad Man Cautions Coffee Men to Modernize Coffee's Image; Sees Coffee as Drink of '80s. *World Coffee and Tea*, January: 35, 76–8.

1981b America's Coffee Renaissance Explodes with Excitement as Specialty Coffee Trade Booms. *World Coffee and Tea*, August: 10–15.

1982 Specialty Coffee '82: A Look at Some Trends. *World Coffee and Tea*, August: 16–28.

1983a Bankers Cite Changes in Coffee Business Due to World Economy. *World Coffee and Tea*, November: 20–2.

1983b CDG Receives ICO Grant: Specialty Coffee Task Force Formed. *World Coffee and Tea*, August: 11.

1983c Coffee, Tea Flavorings Play Important Role in US Gourmet Scene. *World Coffee and Tea*, August: 16–18.

1984 Quality, Fresh Product Keep Sales Booming in the Gourmet Segment. *World Coffee and Tea*, August: 8–14.

1988 College Coffeehouses Flourish. *World Coffee and Tea*, August: 10.

1989a United States of America, Percentage Drinking Coffee, 1962 to 1988. *World Coffee and Tea*, March: 14.

1989b Decaffeinated and Soluble Constantly Experiment to Improve Market Share. *World Coffee and Tea*, March: 11–15.

1991 Depressed Prices Lead to Continued Building of Stocks by Consumers. *World Coffee and Tea*, September: 12–16.

1993 SCAA '93–The Largest Coffee Event in History! *World Coffee and Tea*, June: 6–7.

9

Crafting *Grand Cru* Chocolates in Contemporary France

Susan J. Terrio

C'est un magasin où le chocolat règne en maître, traité par un maître. C'est du travail cent pour cent artisanal au sens "artist" du terme, qui sait tirer de la sublime fève d'Amérique la substantifique splendeur.[1]

– *Le guide des croqueurs de chocolat*, 1988

I noted the display of Parisian master chocolatier Michel Chaudun in the window of his seventh arrondissement confectionery boutique when I arrived to interview him in late October 1990. It featured the lush tropical flora, tools, and raw materials associated with third-world cacao harvests. A framed text above assured customers that "notre chocolat provient des plus grands crus de cacaos du monde" (our chocolate comes from the best cacao bean growths in the world). Next to this was a basin of liquid dark chocolate, specialized handicraft tools, and *Le guide des croqueurs de chocolat (The guide of chocolate eaters)* listing the "170 best chocolatiers of France," including Michel Chaudun. A photocopy of the guide page devoted to Michel Chaudun revealed that his chocolates rated an 18 out of 20.

Michel Chaudun greeted me at the door and ushered me into his tiny, elegant boutique. Inside, dark chocolate candies with evocative names like Esmeralda and Véragua were invitingly displayed on an open central island. A small hand-printed sign indicated the price per kilo: 340F, or roughly $68. A stunning array of confectionery art, from baby bottles to life-size animals, was shelved alongside porcelain and crystal figurines, next to chic confectionery gift boxes. The boutique décor combined neutral earthen tones and rich woods with an abundant use of mirrors. Through a door separating the boutique from the adjacent workshop a young craftsman, Chaudun's only full-time worker and former apprentice, could be seen preparing a batch of house specialities. Next to him were newly coated rows of glossy, ebony-black chocolate bonbons. The intoxicating aroma of chocolate permeated the boutique whenever the workshop door opened.

Along its complex trajectory from cultivation and harvest in the third world to processing and consumption in the first world, chocolate is transformed and differentiated into many culturally relevant categories of food. In France these include breakfast breads, snacks, drink mixes, dessert cuisine, specialty candies which are sold as gifts, for personal consumption, and for ranking in connoisseur tastings, and finally, confectionery art.

In the 1980s Belgian producers of chocolate candies made a swift and successful incursion into the French market by specifically targeting the specialized niche dominated until then by French artisanal chocolatiers. Over the same period, European Community (EC) representatives prepared for the Maastricht Treaty by proposing a set of European norms of chocolate production which threatened to undercut existing French legislation. Facing the intensified international competition of the 1980s and heightened fears of increasingly centralized regulation, French chocolatiers and cultural taste makers attempted to stimulate new demand for craft commodities by promoting "genuine," "grand cru," or "vintage" French chocolate.[2] Despite the publication of a plethora of works on the logic of consumption in late capitalist societies and a recent volume on the increasing demand for culturally authentic, handicraft goods from developing nations among first-world consumers, little is known about the economic and sociocultural dimensions of craft commodity production in advanced capitalism.[3] Few studies have examined the complex process whereby craft objects are culturally marked and endowed with social, aesthetic, and economic value as they are produced, exchanged, and consumed in postindustrial centers.

The exploration of the relationship between the elaboration of chocolate as a cultural commodity and the affirmation of national identity is important to consider in the wake of EC unification. The 1992 ratification of the Maastricht Treaty by a slim margin of French voters and the hostility it continues to generate among many British people are only two examples of the ambivalence engendered by the creation of a unified Europe. One of the strategies chosen by EC bureaucrats to forge a closer union among factious member nations has been to create a pan-nationalism grounded in a common European culture and shared cultural symbols (Shore and Black 1992).

Attempts in Brussels to build and impose a universal European culture threatened to undermine a notion of French culture defined in identical terms. A universalist notion of civilization still survives in France and is strongly linked to the view that French culture itself best embodies it (Rigby 1991). Many French people see their achievements in literature, philosophy, and the arts, both high and popular, as evidence of this. Moreover, the French state and its representatives take seriously the protection of their language and cultural forms from intrusive foreign influences. Current debates on the ubiquitous spread of English and the effect of European norms on traditional foods such as cheese illustrate this. Thus, even as France asserts her diplomatic, political, and economic presence in the "new" Europe, the arena of culture remains highly charged and contested.

On the eve of 1993, French chocolatiers and taste makers responded to repeated calls for European uniformity in various areas by invoking the uniqueness of their cultural products as exemplified in the specifically French "art" of chocolate making. This art was grounded in superior aesthetic standards and in the preeminence of French culinary arts and skilled artisanship, both constituent elements and potent emblems of French culture. Thus French chocolate, one of the commodities that connote the value of traditional craft production and the prestige of haute cuisine, provides a means of investigating the production of taste and its relation to key elements at the core of contemporary French culture.

Artisanal Chocolate Production: The Past as Present

It is perhaps wise to begin with a description of contemporary chocolate businesses and a brief discussion of the evolution of both the craft and French patterns of confectionery consumption. Despite a continuous restructuring of the craft since chocolate was introduced to France in the late 16th century, the arrival of Belgian chocolate franchise outlets in France in the 1980s was reported as a unique event. It served as an important catalyst in the creative reinvention of chocolate candies as prestige cultural commodities. The organization of artisanal chocolate businesses like Chaudun's reveals the continuing salience of certain "traditional" work and social forms such as skilled craft production and independent entrepreneurship. Family members, both blood relations and in-laws, control daily business operations, which usually include two complementary and mutually reinforcing activities: sales and production. These businesses also adhere to a strictly gendered division of labor according to which men generally produce goods in the private space of the workshop and women sell them in the public sphere of the adjacent boutique. Skill is transmitted largely through experiential training and work is organized hierarchically, according to skill and experience, under the authority of the craftsman-owner in the workshop and his wife in the boutique.

Through their window displays and boutique interiors, French chocolatiers actively capitalize on the enduring association between contemporary artisanal production and the idealized, aestheticized image of a "traditional," premodern France.[4] This image evokes a "simpler," "better" time when family workshops provided the exclusive context within which a solidaristic community of uniformly skilled masters guaranteed the production of quality goods. French masters like Chaudun celebrate contemporary craftsmanship while linking it to a rich past of preindustrial guild traditions. Chaudun's elaborate pieces of confectionery art recall the masterpieces (chefs d'oeuvre) completed as a necessary rite of passage in French craft guilds and journeymen brotherhood associations *(compagnonnage)* (Coornaert 1966; Sewell 1980). The small size of Chaudun's boutique evokes the traditional artisanal shop and its place in a distinctively French national tradition of small-scale, skillbased family modes of entrepreneurship. The display of raw materials and artisanal tools reinforces, for the consumers' benefit, the human labor embodied in the goods. House candies are handmade on the premises by Michel Chaudun. The creation and prominent public presentation of individually named candies, as well as the culinary guide rating his chocolates, invoke a renowned French gastronomic heritage based on taste and aesthetics. Chaudun is not only a master craftsman but also a master chef.

At the same time, Chaudun's business is a testament to the changes that have transformed the craft of artisanal chocolate production. Progressive mechanization over the course of the 19th and 20th centuries provoked a two-stage restructuring of the craft. Initially, small- and medium-sized family chocolatiers who mechanized their workshops displaced craftsmen manually producing chocolate from cacao beans. These small-scale family producers were in turn definitively displaced by large-scale industrial manufacturers. By the 1950s the skills associated with the production of chocolate from cacao beans had shifted entirely to industrialized mass production. The craft of chocolate production was redefined and its skills came to center exclusively on the fabrication of dipped chocolate candies, molded chocolate figurines and, most recently, confectionery art. Currently, artisanal chocolatiers occupy a specialized niche within a fully industrialized sector; they purchase industrially manufactured blocks of chocolate and transform them into a personalized line of goods.[5]

In France, chocolate candies are purchased primarily as gifts and distributed to relatives, friends, and colleagues at significant social occasions. The purchase of artisanal candies is embedded within stylized gifting relations and remains closely linked to seasonal and ceremonial occasions such as private rite-of-passage observances and religious holidays such as Christmas and Easter. Until quite recently, French customers of family confectionery businesses purchased equal numbers of dark and milk chocolate candies as gifts, chose from fewer house specialities, saw virtually no confectionery art, and had no specialized culinary guides with which to rate the best French chocolates. A series of developments in the 1980s coalesced to effect considerable change.

During the 1970s and 1980s, competition increased and patterns of confectionery consumption changed. The purchase of artisanally produced candies for distribution as gifts increased modestly in the 1970s but stagnated at virtually the same level in the 1980s (Casella 1989). In contrast, the sale of mass-produced chocolate products registered a significant increase. Over the same period, foreign multinationals, including the American (Mars) and the Swiss (Lindt) companies, came to dominate the French market for mass-produced chocolate products.

In addition, from the early 1980s on, Belgian franchise outlets specifically targeted the market for confectionery gifts by selling mass-produced chocolate candies in store fronts that closely resembled French artisanal boutiques.[6] Belgian chocolates retailed for one-half to one-third the price of French artisanal candies and between 1983 and 1990 captured 48 percent of the confectionery gift market (Mathieu 1990). The success of the Belgians touched a raw nerve among French chocolatiers and cultural taste makers.[7] Belgian firms appropriated the presentational forms of French chocolates (sold in elegant confectionery boutiques), their cultural value to consumers (linked to gifting relations and ceremonial consumption), and specialized French trade terms (used to distinguish among types of candies and to assign evocative names to them).[8] Mass-produced in Belgium for export, these candies were sold by franchise owners who had no training and little or no contact with the family entrepreneurs of the local craft community.

The French were dismayed by the increasing popularity and market share of candies they judged to be of inferior quality and taste. According to them, Belgian candies are too large (*gros*), too sweet (*sucré*), and too full of fillers (*gras*). They contrast French candies made from pure, dark, bittersweet chocolate with the larger milk and white chocolate products that predominate *chez les Belges* (in Belgian shops). In postindustrial societies such as France, cuisine defines a critically important area where economic power and cultural authority intersect. French cuisine has long enjoyed a preeminent reputation among the cuisines of the world; continuing dominance of the culinary world order is a matter of national pride. Yet in this context what counts as French taste and confectionery savoir faire is not at all clear. As Dorinne Kondo (1992:177) notes for Japanese fashion, "nation" and "culture" are problematized for French artisans when chocolates produced by foreign competitors gain French market share. How can one speak of a distinctive French chocolate when the French are just as likely to eat bars made by Mars or Lindt or to offer gifts of bonbons made by Belgian franchises as they are French candies?

Persistent concerns related to chocolate mirrored the tenor of wider debates on the central themes of French national identity. These themes include French competitiveness, economic power, political stature, and, especially, cultural autonomy in new European and world orders.

Demand, Commoditization, and Craft

Recent anthropological analyses move away from a preoccupation with production to privilege exchange and consumption as well as the social life of objects themselves.[9] Some of these accounts emphasize the nature of commoditization as a process that extends from production through exchange to consumption.[10] Commodities and exchange are defined in ways that mute the reified contrasts between gift and commodity exchange. Nevertheless accounts of both gift and commodity exchange in advanced capitalist contexts usually center on only one type of commodity, mass-produced objects. This scholarship ignores both the existence and commodity status of craft objects as well as their particular suitability for gift exchange in these contexts.

The growing exchange of "traditional" craft commodities in global markets suggests that their purchase and consumption may be an essential feature of the present world economy (Nash 1993). Yet the mechanisms that underlie the demand for and consumption of craft commodities produced in postindustrial centers require further study. Craft commodities acquire and shed culturally specific meanings and symbolic value as they are circulated and consumed. While closely tied to local contexts, the exchange and consumption of craft commodities is also mediated by complex, shifting class and taste distinctions which are in turn shaped by global developments. Few studies address the question of how and to what extent the demand for craft objects is linked to taste-making processes such as rapid fashion shifts, direct political appeals, and the development of late capitalism itself.

If the globalization of markets and transnational consumerism characterize the continuing expansion of industrial capitalism, then this development also engenders a contradictory trend. This trend is manifest in the reassertion of local, culturally constituted identities, places, work practices, and commodities as a source of distinction and authenticity in the face of rapid change and the perceived homogeneity of transnationalism (Harvey 1989). Claims of cultural authenticity in advanced capitalism are often linked to an ideal, aestheticized premodern past as well as the groups, labor forms, and products associated with it.[11] Indeed it is the politics of cultural authenticity in the globalization of markets that enables "genuine," locally produced craft work and commodities to be maintained, revived, and/or reinvented precisely because they can be commoditized and sold as such.

What makes the chocolates sold in French boutiques "authentic" and those retailed in Belgian franchises "inauthentic"? How are these labels linked to changing habits of taste and the status struggles associated with them? In a cultural model of consumption where elite habits are disseminated downward and taste makers have heightened power to manipulate taste, chocolatiers and taste makers collaborated to codify and promote a new set of expert criteria for determining both the quality and the authenticity of "vintage" chocolates (Harvey 1989; Zukin 1991). The French differentiate and validate their chocolates through reference to a definitive taste standard adapted from wine connoisseurs. In the pursuit of social distinction, connoisseurship plays an important role. It drives demand for the prestige goods associated with it by reinforcing their rarity and conferring cultural capital on those who consume them. In this game of newly formulated rules of chocolate connoisseurship, consumers demonstrate that they are worthy of symbolically appropriating the objects they purchase through their mastery and display of esoteric taste protocols (Bourdieu 1984).

Moreover, in advanced capitalist societies where consumers have little if any direct experience with production, which itself is a symbol of alienation, Chaudun's chocolates are incarnated signs. Unlike mass-produced commodities, they do not require significant cultural work on the part of consumers to be moved symbolically from the realm of the standardized, impersonal commodity into the realm of personalized gift relations (Carrier 1990). Craft commodities do this cultural work for consumers; they make visible both a particular form of production (linking the conception of a product to its execution) and its attendant social relations. They are imbued with and are the bearers of the social identities of their makers and for this reason retain certain inalienable properties (Mauss 1990 [1925]; Weiner 1992). Produced in limited quantities, using traditional methods and/or materials, they evoke uninterrupted continuity with the past. The historicities of these goods, even if invented or altered, give them special value for both use and gift exchange. This is what makes them "authentic" and distinguishes them from the "fake" or "inauthentic" chocolate made from identical materials. The silver jewelry made by Navajo Indians, the confections crafted by Japanese artisans, the pottery produced by Onta craftsmen, and the French candies crafted by master chocolatiers all have cultural authenticity in this sense.

If Chaudun's "art" exemplifies the principles of Veblenian consumption, it also reveals the extravagance and power of the potlatch (cf. Tobin 1992). Craftsmen like Chaudun spend many hours sculpting and molding pieces of confectionery art commissioned by both individual and corporate clients. Coaxed from the most perishable and delicate of media, chocolate art costing hundreds of dollars must be destroyed in order to be eaten. In some instances these pieces are publicly displayed only to be ceremoniously shattered and then distributed to those present.

The Gentrification of Chocolate Taste

Although Pierre Bourdieu's (1984) exhaustive account of French consumption succeeds in rescuing taste from essentialist doctrines of aesthetics by linking it to
culture, his treatment of both culture and taste remains largely arbitrary and static.
In the end, objects are constitutive elements of a tight, circular model of social and
cultural reproduction which perpetuates established class hierarchies. Not considered is the capacity of objects to play a role in blurring or subverting status
continuities rather than merely reinforcing them. Neither is the impact of cultural
taste makers on demand and the process of commoditization.

In France, the considerable interest in culinary arts is signified by a huge gastronomic literature, tourist guides, cooking demonstrations, and exhibits. These
sources provide consumers with comprehensive rules governing the choice of ingredients, appropriate implements, correct preparation techniques, aesthetic presentation, and the ordering and consumption of different dishes in restaurants. In France
as well as other postindustrial economies, rising levels of per capita income and
greater disposable income have produced a broader middle class of consumers with
the financial means to adopt a "reflexive" attitude toward the consumption of goods
in general and food in particular (Zukin 1991). Their search for differentiation and
authenticity in the consumption of food is reflected in the growing international
demand for gourmet cuisine. It is a cuisine dominated by the latest French culinary
trends. In what has been called "the gentrification of taste," distinctive regional
culinary styles and local foodstuffs are rediscovered and marketed by taste makers,
restaurateurs, and retailers (Bestor 1992). The aesthetic presentation of locally and
regionally produced foodstuffs in new taste combinations appeals to sophisticated
urbanites who want food that has both cultural authenticity and cachet. The
formulation of a new French standard in chocolate consumption exemplifies the
gentrification of taste.

The new standard was organized around the basic principles informing the
nouvelle cuisine style of cooking that dominated the French culinary establishment
in the 1970s. Like nouvelle cuisine, this standard emphasized healthful eating habits
and dietetic concerns. It also mandated fresh, natural ingredients, novel but simplified flavorings, and the production of "good-for-you" dark chocolates made with
little sugar. The new standard emerged in the late 1970s and early 1980s and was
widely disseminated in gastronomic texts destined for the general public, in craft
publications compiled for customers, and in newspaper and magazine articles, travel
guides, television and radio interviews, public craft events, chocolate tastings, and
boutique displays.[12]

According to this standard, only bittersweet chocolate, rated according to the
percentage of pure cacao, constitutes a refined commodity as opposed to a sweet
milk or white chocolate. The use of the term *cacao* here is significant. In French one
word, *cacao*, glosses both the raw material (cacao bean) and the processing phases
that yield cocoa and chocolate. The promotion of "les plus grands crus de cacao"
thus implies control over the entire production process from cultivation to finished
product, while simultaneously lending the authority of the internationally accepted
reference standard of French wines to expert judgments of chocolate.

In the new game of chocolate connoisseurship in which taste makers manipulate new fashions, consumers emulate celebrated chocolatiers and Parisian gastronomes. The life history of one chocolatier closely associated with the new standard, Robert Linxe, illustrates the French cultural specificity of this process.

Linxe is an acknowledged master chef, chocolatier, and gastronome. He came from a working-class background and perfected his craft through the traditional means of apprenticeship in several different confectionery houses and long years of hands-on work experience. In 1954 Linxe purchased a Parisian pastry business in decline, building it into a highly successful operation over more than 20 years. Anxious to specialize in chocolate, Linxe sold his first business and in 1977 opened the House of Chocolate in a very fashionable area of Paris, the Faubourg Saint-Honoré.[13]

Linxe's new business attracted considerable media attention. Because of the importance of seasonal confectionery gift purchases in France and the high sales volume at these times (between 35 and 50 percent of annual sales are generated at Christmas), French chocolatiers are always showcased in special media features during December and before Easter. At a time when most French chocolatiers sold roughly equal numbers of milk and dark chocolate candies, Linxe proposed a house line of specialities which included 23 dark candies and only four milk chocolates. He also subverted and remade traditional work practices in the family artisanal boutique. At a time when most craftsmen remained in the private space of the family workshop, Linxe moved freely between the workshop and the public space of the boutique. He took a highly visible role in both production and sales by personally advising customers on the choice and proper consumption of their chocolates. Linxe took the lead in "reeducating French palates" by offering guided tastings of his candies within his boutique.

Reeducating French Palates

Throughout my fieldwork craftspeople and taste makers explained the success of Belgian franchises by alluding to an overall assault on traditional French taste standards in food. They insisted that this began in the early 1970s with the proliferation of foreign fast-food chains like McDonald's, currently the largest restaurant chain in France. They bemoaned the fact that French palates had been deformed (*déformés*) by exposure to the questionable composition of foreign chocolates mass-produced from cheap substitute ingredients. In 1990 an article dealing specifically with the Belgian "invasion" appeared in the national daily *Le Monde* (December 20). Quotes from Parisian craftspeople stressed the need to reeducate French palates and to defend a distinctive French art of chocolate production and taste.

As my fieldwork progressed, it demanded my personal investigation of chocolate taste – as aesthetic judgment, cultural standard, and sentient experience. Paul Stoller (1994) has recently argued that ethnography has long privileged visual metaphors and has, as a result, failed to document the full range of sensory perception or "the savory sauces of ethnographic life." My personal apprenticeship in taste and understanding of the craft, its practitioners, and the tastes distinguishing "vintage" French chocolates from Belgian "imitations" demanded the education of my own palate. Through guided repetition, my "good taste" in chocolate was habituated and embodied.

Since 1977, Linxe has conducted literally dozens of interviews which have been widely disseminated through national and international media. Linxe agreed to an interview – of which a tasting is an integral part – and after a tour of his flagship Saint-Honoré boutique and workshop, we sat down. Linxe looked at me over his glasses and announced that the best part had arrived – the tasting. I had fully expected and even greatly anticipated a chocolate tasting, yet as I waited for him to get the chocolates, I felt my palms begin to sweat and unruly butterflies begin to flutter in my stomach. The tasting was designed to instill new taste criteria as well as to test my judgment as a discriminating consumer of chocolate. At the time I was well aware of the new taste standard.

During six months of preliminary fieldwork in 1989 I had conducted some informal experiments in which I entered French artisanal boutiques and specifically requested sweet milk chocolates in order to observe the reaction of the salespeople. What shocked me as I sat in Linxe's boutique was my fear of failing as well as my eagerness to demonstrate my possession of cultural capital in chocolate consumption. As Linxe returned bearing a silver tray with six chocolate candies (four coated with dark chocolate and two with milk chocolate) and a bottle of cool water, I knew I would never admit to liking sweet milk chocolate.

Before beginning Linxe abruptly asked me, in a tone that only allowed for a positive response, "Vous aimez le chocolat?" Being reassured that I liked chocolate, he described the forthcoming experience as an "apprenticeship in taste allowing those palates which are receptive to learn to discriminate among different kinds of chocolate and to appreciate the best." Just then a saleswoman interrupted us saying that there was an important call for Monsieur. He hesitated, looked at me apologetically, and excused himself, urging me to begin on my own. He promised to question me on my preferences.

When I was left alone staring at the candies my mind went back to a description of his house specialities I had read in *The guide of chocolate eaters*. Linxe had served as technical adviser to an exclusive club of Parisian chocophiles, Le Club des Croqueurs du Chocolat, that published the guide. Created in 1982, the club's founding members included gastronomes Claude Lebey and Sylvie Girard, fashion designer Sonia Rykiel, social historian Jean-Paul Aron, and wine connoisseur Nicolas de Rabaudy. Club members promoted French chocolates by regularly organizing elegant chocolate tasting soirées during which they sampled and rated candies from all over the country. The results were published in *The guide*, which in 1988 was widely available in both specialty and mass-distribution book outlets. In his preface, Claude Lebey outlined the criteria informing the ratings:

> We want to make perfectly clear that our taste leads us to favor dark chocolates over milk chocolate and...that we generally prefer candies with a high dark chocolate content which corresponds to the current taste standards of chocolate connoisseurs. [1988:5–6]

This preface also included specialized oenological terminology for evaluating quality chocolates. Like wine connoisseurs, consumers were urged to marshal four senses in the quest for fine chocolates. They were advised "to look for a shiny coating, to smell the deep and powerful chocolate bouquet, to feel the creamy texture on the palate and to taste the subtle combination of bitter and sweet notes in the composition" (1988:9).

Reading it for the first time, I had been struck by the inclusion of the newest Belgian franchises. It seemed paradoxical that a guide published to highlight "true," grand cru (French) chocolates should even include "cheap" foreign imitations. However, Belgian candies served as a perfect foil to the highly rated candies produced by French masters and received the poorest ratings.

> It is obvious that a certain public exists for these attractive sweets which do not have much in common with the powerful subtleties of the Aztec cacao bean. In fact, one should really think of a name other than chocolate for these candies. [1988:152]

As I sat facing the row of tiny, ten-gram candies, I remembered that Linxe was the only chocolatier to receive a rating of 19 out of 20. I tried without success to recall the descriptions his house specialities received in that review. I took several deep breaths and began slowly to sample the candies, mindful of Linxe's parting counsel to "allow the chocolate to melt slowly so that my palate could fully absorb it." I had begun with the dark chocolate bonbons and had only tasted two when Linxe returned. He immediately took charge, briefly describing the basic ingredients and principal flavorings of the candies before I tasted them. "This chocolate is a superb bittersweet *ganache*, a creamy dark chocolate center made with the freshest cream, butter, and finely ground morsels of pure, dark chocolate and then coated in dark chocolate. The center is delicately flavored with lemon. It's sublime... very long on the palate." After we had finished, the analysis began. Which candy did I prefer? Could I say why?

I chose the first dark chocolate I had tasted, a ganache with a bittersweet dark center and dark chocolate coating, in part because it had left the most distinct gustatory impression. To my delight, and profound relief, Linxe emitted an appreciative "ah" saying, "Madame, I congratulate you on your excellent taste. The candy you chose is one of the most famous of my house specialities, the Quito." He added, "Someone who knows how to judge good wine is also able to judge a good chocolate... a good chocolate is long on the palate, full-bodied, has the correct degree of acidity, a rich, balanced bouquet, and a wonderful finish."

This oenological encounter powerfully illustrates how taste is produced and reproduced. The point is not that I was nervous in the company of native experts or that I finally acquired good taste in chocolate. Rather, it is to show how consumers, even foreign anthropologists acutely aware of the processes at work, can be drawn into mastering, displaying, and ultimately, replicating taste protocols. It also reveals the interplay of culture and power. If North Americans who hold dominant class positions see themselves as culturally invisible (Rosaldo 1989:202–4), in France the reverse holds true. The culture that members of the dominant bourgeois class see themselves as exemplifying is the source and sign of their power. It is their cultured practices that separate them from the uncultured, even "barbarous" habits of lower classes (Bourdieu 1984). At the same time, the popularization of an elite standard means that it will not remain the unique preserve of the dominant classes.

All consumers who internalize and reinforce the standard by buying and giving the right chocolates to family and friends can achieve some measure of social distinction. By virtue of their good taste they become more cultured and more French.

And what is the impact of the ethnographer? My documentation of this standard may have the unintended outcome of both validating it and hastening mass consumption of prestige candies. It may also unwittingly serve the interests of Parisian craft leaders who, involved in difficult, ongoing negotiations with bureaucrats in Paris and Brussels over issues ranging from training to new norms of chocolate production and labeling, sent me an urgent request for a copy of my dissertation in September 1994. This example also underscores the complexity of doing fieldwork in sites where the people we study not only read but selectively appropriate and disseminate portions of what we write for validation of their own strategic ends.

Authentic Taste and Artisanal Savoir-faire

Their access to public media allows famous masters to play an important role in defining and celebrating the special skills that distinguish them as craftsmen from industrial producers. This differentiation has involved adroitly manipulating the knowledge of the transformations that a commodity like chocolate undergoes between cultivation and consumption. Knowledge about both the production and consumption of commodities has "technical, mythological and evaluative components and ... [is] susceptible to mutual and dialectical interaction" especially as the complexity and distance of their flows increases (Appadurai 1986:41). As noted above, French artisans no longer select, blend, and process cacao beans. All purchase industrially produced blocks of chocolate. Yet few French consumers know this, and Parisian chocolatiers like Linxe and Chaudun make creative use of an oenological model, which gives the impression that their knowledge of and involvement in the productive process extends from the choice of the best vintages of beans to their transformation and presentation in the family boutique. Craftsmen on the local level have enthusiastically followed this lead.

As Linxe explained in a 1989 radio interview, "there are different types of cacao beans each from a different place, each with a climate and soil which endows it with particular properties" (*Champs-Elysées*, série 8, numéro 5). In asserting their skill as expert "alchemists," chocolatiers invoke a system for blending cacao beans that closely parallels that of the highest quality officially classified growths or estates (les grands crus) in the Bordeaux winegrowing region. While no such classification or regulation of cacao bean plantations exists, French chocolatiers nevertheless assure consumers that they select only the best vintages from renowned domains in South America.[14]

They also remind consumers that industrially produced candies are "mummified" with preservatives and lack the "purity" and originality of handcrafted candies. The authenticity of their candies is linked to traditional methods passed down intergenerationally from father to son which privilege manual versus mechanized production and guarantee goods freshly made on the premises.

In postindustrial societies like France, craft can serve as a metaphor for an alternative set of cultural values and work practices in contrast to the dominant norm.[15] In these settings the persistence, reinvention, or creation of traditional craft cultural forms, work practices, and communities can be a means to reassert cultural distinctiveness and identity in response to rapidly changing circumstances (Harvey 1989). Master craftsmen can be celebrated as symbols of local and/or national cultural values. Craft commodities can be marketed on the basis of the nostalgia for an aestheticized, preindustrial work ethos. Here tradition serves as a model of the past that changes constantly because it is continually reinvented and reconstructed from the vantage point of the present. Indeed, the uses of the past outlined in the next section reveal it to be a social construction strongly mediated and shaped by persistent contemporary concerns.[16]

Stimulating Chocolate Consumption: The Uses of the Past

Culturally constructed stories or mythologies about commodity flows acquire particular intensity as the spatial, cognitive, and institutional distances between production and consumption increase (Appadurai 1986:48). This intensity is reflected in the recently constructed mythology surrounding chocolate as an exotic New World substance. This mythology aimed to alter the symbolic associations and culturally constituted uses of chocolate as a device to stimulate consumption. In the early 1980s chocolate began to be marketed as a food that appealed to the childlike hedonist within the consumer. It was promoted as a healthy and irresistible food to be eaten spontaneously whenever the urge arose. Currently many chocolatiers display and refer customers to a recent publication by a French doctor entitled *The Therapeutic Virtues of Chocolate* (Robert 1990) which debunks all the persistent "myths" regarding chocolate's deleterious side effects.

The French make an astute use of the past and play on an enduring fascination with the exoticism of the inhabitants, customs, and cuisines of the New World and the Orient. Drawing selectively on historical accounts left by European explorers and missionaries, French chocolatiers and taste makers have recreated an exoticized history of the discovery, production, and consumption of chocolate in the New World. This reinvented history both celebrates and replicates a number of primitivist tropes. It involves a timeless, exotic story set in a dangerous land dominated by primal impulses, bizarre customs, and ludic excess (Said 1978). This history centers on the "primitive" methods, "strange" spices (such as hot pepper), and "curious" uses of chocolate in the New World as well as on its introduction and reception into European court society. It highlights the process whereby the unruly substance that served as a bitter, spicy drink to Aztec nobles at Montezuma's court was "domesticated" and made appetizing to the delicate "civilized" palates of European aristocratic elites, particularly women. While chocolatiers celebrate the transformation from raw to cooked they also promote chocolate as a substance that fuses nature and culture. Superior-tasting chocolate is bittersweet, both exotic and refined. Although linked to a new standard of refinement, quality French chocolate leads true aficionados to abandon cultural convention in favor of hedonistic indulgence.

In most representations of chocolate there are consistently recurrent elements. These include indigenous legends and rituals related to chocolate use during the time of the Aztecs. The most popular is the Indian origin myth, which describes the divine provenance of cacao trees in the Garden of Eden and their transportation to mortal men by the Indians' plumed serpent god Quetzalcoatl. In some accounts this myth is inevitably accompanied by a recounting of the worship of Quetzalcoatl in elaborate Aztec fertility rites marked by "violent orgies" (Constant 1988; Robert 1990).

Aztec imagery figures prominently in the symbols and rituals adopted by a number of contemporary craft associations. One such organization, La Confrérie des Chocolatiers Français, stages elaborate public induction ceremonies in which Brotherhood elders don brown velour robes and a headdress with an effigy of Quetzalcoatl, who is described as "the Aztec god of chocolate."

Another recurrent theme highlights the primitive production methods used by the Aztecs. Virtually all of the chocolate gastronomic texts published in the 1980s feature the same image of an American primitive with chocolate tools which appeared in a 17th-century scholarly work centering on the three substances new to Europe: coffee, tea, and chocolate (Dufour 1685). Selective portions of this text are quoted to provide testimony to the contrast between a crudely processed, spicy American drink and the sweet, refined beverage perfected by Europeans.

At the same time, French representations of chocolate consumption by Aztec nobles at Montezuma's court recall visions of ritualistic excess and the agonistic expenditure associated with the potlatch (Bataille 1985; Baudrillard 1981). In these treatments chocolate is a food of erotic temptation, both irresistible and dangerous – irresistible because of its divine taste and the aphrodisiac properties attributed to it by both Aztec and European aristocratic elites. Many accounts relate selected portions of the eyewitness account of Montezuma I's court provided by a member of Cortez's entourage (Diaz del Castillo 1803[1572]). At a local craft-sponsored conference on the history of chocolate in the New World attended by 250 people in the southwest city of Pau in February 1991, one of the featured speakers gave his version of conspicuous consumption at the Aztec court: "I must tell you that Montezuma had a prodigious appetite and capacity for chocolate. It is said that he was served about 50 cups of frothy chocolate in golden cups which were used once and then thrown away." In the question-and-answer period that followed he was asked if chocolate really is an aphrodisiac. His reply: "Well, I'll respond indirectly to that question by telling the audience that Montezuma is reputed to have had 100 wives and he was served chocolate before each visit to the harem in order to be in good form."

In these representations chocolate is also dangerous because of its addictive properties. French accounts of chocolate consumption glorify the breakdown of willpower and playfully hint at the bizarre excesses to which an acquired habit for fine chocolate can lead, especially if it is thwarted. A number of gastronomic accounts relate the unsuccessful attempt of a Catholic bishop in colonial Mexico to stop what he considered to be the blasphemous practice of Spanish noblewomen so attached to their chocolate that they had it served to them during morning mass.[17] The bishop forbade the taking of chocolate in church on pain of excommunication. Soon after, he became ill and died after drinking poisoned chocolate served him by one of his disgruntled parishioners.

Examples of prodigious consumption of chocolate among aristocrats in the past are interspersed with those of contemporary social elites.[18] The fashion designer Sonia Rykiel has frequently spoken of her chocoholism in published interviews. When I interviewed her in 1989 she claimed to be "pursued" by chocolate and described it as "a drug and a mystery you shouldn't try too hard to solve." Dark, evocatively named chocolates like "Montezuma," "Caracas," and "Aztec" evoke and invite new consuming passions; they suggest self-pleasuring, playful indulgence, and conspicuous leisure. French consumers are invited to join in the play and to follow the lead of accomplished masters and taste makers in sophisticated urban centers who indulge their taste for grand cru chocolates.

Conclusion

The recent conjuncture of the rise of a broader middle-class group of French consumers with the means to purchase expensive, handcrafted chocolates as gifts and for their own consumption, on the one hand, and the appearance of foreign franchises selling mass-produced candies in settings that replicate French artisanal boutiques, on the other, is a unique one in the history of the craft. The swift proliferation of these franchises changed the terms of the dialogue between French consumers and artisanal producers. The issue of exclusivity that had informed this dialogue in the past, when chocolate was a rare and costly luxury reserved for elite consumption, gave way to the issue of authenticity (Appadurai 1986:44). Authenticity in this context is determined by culturally elaborated judgments involving connoisseurship, taste, and correctness.

In contemporary postindustrial economies like that of France, discriminating consumers want distinctive goods that are both culturally genuine and esoteric. Yet in these settings the only way to preserve or recreate the elite resonance of commodities that can be mass-produced is to elaborate the criteria of authenticity surrounding them. Through this elaboration and dissemination of an esoteric taste standard, French chocolatiers and cultural taste makers have differentiated authentic French chocolates handcrafted in French workshops by master craftsmen from foreign imitations. As *bricoleurs* they adapted a number of relevant elements of French culture in order to transform traditional craft candies into dessert cuisine with enhanced value and cachet for both individual consumption and gift exchange. Informing the cultural authenticity of these commodities are oenological criteria of connoisseurship in taste, a culinary discourse of freshness, purity, and aesthetics, and a French heritage of skilled craftsmanship and family entrepreneurship.

The craft commodities displayed in French boutiques like Chaudun's draw their power and value from their symbolic loading. Both craft and cuisine are potent, manipulable symbols of French culture on which numerous ideas can be projected and validated. In postindustrial economies marked by the "production of volatility" (Harvey 1989) handcrafted commodities satisfy the nostalgia for and appeal of the localized goods and modes of production associated with a traditional past. Chaudun's chocolates are both locally produced and distinctly French. The very persistence of skilled craftsmen and family modes of entrepreneurship in these economies means they can be absorbed within and designated as unique manifestations of a unified national culture. They can be enshrined as part of the nation's historic patrimony and redefined as genuine, living cultural forms.

The reconception of French chocolates as culturally genuine food occurred amid the uncertainty generated by the impending unification of the European community.

Attempts to forge Europeanness in the name of a universal culture were especially problematic given the existence of a notion of French culture also defined as universal and embodied in French cultural achievements from literature to cuisine. Belgian candies, marketed as if they were freshly made, locally crafted French goods, were particularly threatening because they represented an incursion into sensitive cultural terrain. The proposed implementation of European production norms for chocolate only heightened fears of increased cultural homogeneity in the name of Europe. The promotion of signature candy recipes and confectionery art were a reassertion of French cultural integrity as it is manifest in the culinary arts, master craftsmanship, and aesthetic standards.

The selective appropriation, reinvention, and exoticization of the historical origin and uses of chocolate in the New World also serve this purpose. By constructing a specifically French history of chocolate and celebrating its transformation from a primitive, foreign foodstuff to a refined French one, chocolatiers and connoisseurs reinforce received notions concerning French taste even as these notions are used to promote new confectionery criteria for determining it. In the skilled hands of French craftsmen, chocolate is sweetened but retains the powerful taste of its wild, natural origins. It is domesticated yet remains inextricably linked to the consuming habits of elites redefined as both cultured and hedonistic.

Preliminary French studies of confectionery consumption patterns (Casella 1989; Mathieu 1990) as well as surveys I conducted among producers and consumers during 1990–91 revealed that French consumers embraced the new standard by routinely specifying dark, semisweet chocolates in both personal and gift purchases. It remains to be seen if they will continue to indulge, even satiate, their appetite for the chocolates of masters like Linxe and Chaudun whose art, according to *The guide*, fully reveals the "powerful subtleties of the Aztec cacao bean" (1988).

NOTES

1 Author's translation: This is a boutique where chocolate is master, crafted by a master. It is 100 percent artisanal work in the artistic sense of the term, which excels in drawing out the full-bodied splendor of the sublime American [cacao] bean.
2 Here *taste maker* refers to food critics, chefs, restaurateurs, journalists, social and artistic elites, and intellectuals such as social historians with access to visual and print media in France and the power to shape taste.
3 Some important works on consumption in advanced capitalist contexts include Appadurai 1986; Baudrillard 1981; Bourdieu 1984; Harvey 1989; Jameson 1984; Miller 1987; Sahlins 1976; Tobin 1992; and Zukin 1991. See Nash 1993 for an analysis of craft goods in the world market.
4 Historically France has been a preeminent nation of small manufacture, skilled artisanship, and craft associations such as guilds. France's reputation in luxury craft production was established through the worldwide export of French perfume, fashion, porcelain, sculpted furniture, wine, and cuisine. French artisanship also enjoys a positive resonance because smallscale, skill-based modes of family entrepreneurship dominated trade and industry well into the 20th century.

5 Attempts to depict the size of the French artisanal chocolate industry result in different statistics. The number of French businesses specializing in chocolate production and employing fewer than ten employees totals 720. If one considers small and medium-sized businesses (up to 50 employees), this number increases to 3,500 (Mathieu 1990).

6 It is important to distinguish among the Belgian franchises in question. These do not include the Godiva chocolate franchises firmly implanted in the French market. The new Belgian firms include Léonidas, Daskalidès, Jeff de Bruges, and Neuville.

7 Although there was wide agreement for action among chocolatiers throughout France, Parisians were the first to act for several reasons. First, Paris has historically been and continues to be the most important chocolate center by virtue of its power as a dominant culinary center and because of the amount of chocolate produced annually there. In 1990, 149,306 tons were produced there, while the second most important regional area produced 95,085 tons. Also, Belgian franchises opened first there and maintained a large presence. For example, of the 100 Léonidas franchises in France in 1990, almost one-quarter were located in Paris (Casella 1989).

8 French craftspeople give individual names to each of the house candies they create and produce. These names remain constant over the life of the candy. Recall Chaudun's Esmeralda above.

9 See Appadurai 1986; Baudrillard 1981; Douglas and Isherwood 1981; Miller 1987; Sahlins 1976; and Tobin 1992.

10 See Appadurai 1986; Bestor 1992; and Kopytoff 1986.

11 See Badone 1991; Bestor 1992; Moeran 1984; and Tobin 1992.

12 A partial list of this new chocolate literature includes *The guide of chocolate eaters* 1988; Constant 1988; Girard 1984; and Robert 1990.

13 The trajectories of famous craftsmen like Robert Linxe and nouvelle cuisine chefs Michel Guérard and Paul Bocuse suggest a radical reconfiguration of the French culinary landscape beginning in the 1970s (Zukin 1991:208–10). This new landscape is tied to the worldwide expansion of gourmet cuisine as a new form of cultural consumption. In less than a decade, Linxe built an international reputation by creating a small chain of exclusive chocolate boutiques in Paris, Tokyo, and New York.

14 Yet French industrial producers of chocolate have continued to use predominantly West African beans cultivated on plantations in their former colonies, blending these with smaller proportions of the rarer South American beans. The complete omission of Africa in the story of French chocolate effectively elides a problematic colonial past and in so doing reenacts the very dynamics of colonialism.

15 See Ennew 1982; Harevan 1992; Kondo 1990; and Moeran 1984.

16 A large body of anthropological and historical scholarship centers on the invention of tradition and the politics of memory; see Connerton 1989; Halbwachs 1968; Handler and Linnekin 1984; and Hobsbawm and Ranger 1983. In France the field of memory has received the most systematic attention from historians – both "new history" Annales historians (Nora 1993) and those whose work examines the World War II Vichy period (Rousso 1990). Rousso's analysis of the tension between a "voluntarist" memory which commemorates and an "implicit" memory which elides is useful here. Memory omissions reveal much about the symbolic construction of nation, craft, and commodity.

17 This incident was reported in a virtually identical manner in the gastronomic texts listed above. It is taken from Thomas Gage, English chronicler of Mesoamerican Indian life in the colonial period (1958[1648]:143–5).

18 See the correspondence of the well-known chronicler of 17th-century French court life, Madame de Sévigné.

REFERENCES CITED

Appadurai, Arjun, ed.
  1986 The Social Life of Things: Commodities in Cultural Perspective. Cambridge: Cambridge University Press.
Badone, Ellen
  1991 Ethnography, Fiction, and the Meanings of the Past in Brittany. *American Ethnologist* 18(3):518–45.
Bataille, Georges
  1985 Visions of Excess: Selected Writings, 1927–39. A. Stoekl, ed. Theory and History of Literature, No. 14. Minneapolis: University of Minnesota Press.
Baudrillard, Jean
  1981 For a Critique of the Political Economy of the Sign. St Louis: Telos Press.
Bestor, Theodore C.
  1992 The Raw, the Cooked, and the Industrial: Commoditization and Food Culture in a Japanese Commodities Market. Paper presented at the Department of Anthropology Colloquium at New York University. New York, NY.
Bourdieu, Pierre
  1984 Distinction: A Social Critique of the Judgement of Taste. R. Nice, trans. Cambridge, MA: Harvard University Press.
Carrier, James
  1990 The Symbolism of Possession in Commodity Advertising. *Man* 25:693–706.
Casella, Philippe
  1989 La profession de chocolatier. Paris: Agence Nationale pour le Développement de l'Éducation Permanente.
Connerton, Paul
  1989 How Societies Remember. Cambridge: Cambridge University Press.
Constant, Christian
  1988 Le chocolat: le goût de la vie. Paris: Nathan.
Coornaert, Emile
  1966 Les compagnonnages en France du moyen âge à nos jours. Paris: Éditions Ouvrières.
Diaz del Castillo, Bernal 1803[1572] The True History of the Conquest of Mexico. Salem, MA: Cushing and Appleton.
Douglas, Mary, and Baron Isherwood
  1981 The World of Goods. New York: Basic Books.
Dufour, Philippe Sylvestre
  1685 Traitez nouveaux et curieux du café, thé et du chocolate. The Hague: Adrian Moetjens.
Ennew, Judith
  1982 Harris Tweed: Construction, Retention and Representation of a Cottage Industry. *In* From Craft to Industry: Ethnography of Proto-Industrial Cloth Production. Esther Goody, ed. Pp. 167–99. Cambridge: Cambridge University Press.
Gage, Thomas
  1958[1648] Thomas Gage's Travels in the New World. J. Eric S. Thompson, ed. Norman: University of Oklahoma Press.
Girard, Sylvie
  1984 Le guide du chocolat et de ses à côtés. Paris: Messidor-Temps.

Guide des croqueurs de chocolat, Le
  1988 Le guide des croqueurs de chocolat (The guide of chocolate eaters). With a preface by Claude Lebey. Paris: Olivier Orban.
Halbwachs, Maurice
  1968 La mémoire collective. Paris: Presses Universitaires de France.
Handler, Richard, and Jocelyn Linnekin
  1984 Tradition, Genuine or Spurious. *Journal of American Folklore* 97(385):273–90.
Harevan, Tamara
  1992 The Festival's Work as Leisure: The Traditional Craftsmen of Gion Festival. *In* Worker's Expressions. J. Calagione, D. Francis, and D. Nugent, eds. Pp. 98–128. Albany: State University of New York Press.
Harvey, David
  1989 The Condition of Postmodernity: An Enquiry into the Origins of Cultural Change. Cambridge: Basil Blackwell.
Hobsbawm, Eric, and Terence Ranger, eds.
  1983 The Invention of Tradition. Cambridge: Cambridge University Press.
Jameson, Frederick
  1984 Postmodernism or the Cultural Logic of Late Capitalism. *New Left Review* 146:53–92.
Kondo, Dorinne
  1990 Crafting Selves: Power, Gender, and Discourses of Identity in a Japanese Workplace. Chicago: University of Chicago Press.
  1992 Aesthetics and Politics in Fashion. *In* Remade in Japan: Everyday Life and Consumer Taste in a Changing Society. J. Tobin, ed. Pp. 176–203. New Haven: Yale University Press.
Kopytoff, Igor
  1986 The Cultural Biography of Things: Commoditization as Process. *In* The Social Life of Things. A. Appadurai, ed. Pp. 64–91. Cambridge: Cambridge University Press.
Mathieu, Johann
  1990 La confiserie du chocolat: diagnostic de l'univers et recherche d'axes de développement. Paris: L'Institut d'Observation et de Décision, Direction de l'Artisanat du Ministère et l'Artisanat et du Commerce.
Mauss, Marcel
  1990[1925] The Gift: The Form and Reason for Exchange in Archaic Societies. W. D. Wells, trans. New York: W. W. Norton.
Miller, Daniel
  1987 Material Culture and Mass Consumption. Oxford: Basil Blackwell.
Moeran, Brian
  1984 Lost Innocence: Folk Craft Potters of Onta, Japan. Berkeley: University of California Press.
Nash, June, ed.
  1993 Crafts in the World Market. Albany: State University of New York Press.
Nora, Pierre, ed.
  1993 Les lieux de mémoire. 7 vols. Paris: Gallimard.
Rigby, Brian
  1991 Popular Culture in Modern France: A Study of Cultural Discourse. London: Routledge.
Robert, Hervé
  1990 Les vertus thérapeutiques du chocolat. Paris: Artulen.

Rosaldo, Renato
  1989 Culture and Truth. Boston: Beacon Press.
Rousso, Henri
  1990 Le syndrome de Vichy: de
  1944 à nos jours. Paris: Éditions du Seuil.
Sahlins, Marshall
  1976 Culture and Practical Reason. Chicago: University of Chicago Press.
Said, Edward
  1978 Orientalism. New York: Vintage.
Sewell, William H., Jr.
  1980 Work and Revolution in France: The Language of Labor from the Old Regime to
  1848. Cambridge: Cambridge University Press.
Shore, Chris, and Annabel Black
  1992 The European Communities and the Construction of Europe. *Anthropology Today*
  8(3):10–11.
Stoller, Paul
  1994 Embodying Colonial Memories. *American Anthropologist* 96:634–48.
Tobin, Joseph J., ed.
  1992 Remade in Japan: Everyday Life and Consumer Taste in a Changing Society. New
  Haven: Yale University Press.
Weiner, Annette
  1992 Inalienable Possessions: The Paradox of Keeping-While-Giving. Berkeley: University
  of California Press.
Zukin, Sharon
  1991 Landscapes of Power: From Detroit to Disney World. Berkeley: University of California Press.

10

Globalized Childhood? Kentucky Fried Chicken in Beijing

Eriberto P. Lozada, Jr.

The social ramifications of transnationalism – the flows of ideas, products, people, capital, and technologies across national boundaries – have become the staple of recent anthropological literature. This interest is based largely on the high visibility of cultural artifacts from transnational corporations, which have left people in very different parts of the world, as one scholar puts it, "increasingly wearing the same kinds of clothes, eating the same kinds of food, reading the same kinds of news-papers, watching the same kinds of television programs, and so on" (Haviland 1994:675). The growing power of such corporations is sometimes considered a major cause of cultural disruption in developing countries, mutating local traditions beyond recognition. In this chapter, I argue that although there are now many visible markers of homogenization because of a more integrated global system of produc-tion and consumption, there has also been a dramatic expansion in particularism, as competing claims for cultural identity and authenticity have become more strident. This particularism can be seen in the ways some of the most crucial decisions affecting transnational corporations are made and then modified within the confines of local societies, through the participation of local people and in adjustment to local social changes.

To elaborate on this argument, I will examine how the US-based Kentucky Fried Chicken (KFC) catered to Beijing children in the 1990s. This focus is mainly warranted by two considerations. First, fast-food restaurants like KFC have been especially successful among children in large Chinese urban centers. Children are often the decision-makers in determining whether an urban family will patronize a KFC restaurant. Moreover, what children eat is a fundamental part of their social-ization, and changes in children's dietary patterns are indicative of changes in their larger social environment (Beardsworth and Keil 1997). In addition, children's consumption of both material and cultural goods is becoming a fiercely contested domain in many parts of the world and among various social groups seeking to implement their particular visions of the future by shaping childhood experiences (Stephens 1995). As an organizational actor, KFC is a part of the social life of Beijing children and influences Chinese experiences of childhood by becoming part of local Beijing life. Before I set up the ethnographic context of KFC in Beijing for analysis, let me make a few remarks about this chapter's theoretical framework.

Transnational Organizations and Chinese Children

Transnational organizations, which provide institutional support for the movement of people, goods, and ideas across national boundaries, have existed as long as there have been nations (Wolf 1982; Hannerz 1992; Huntington 1973).[1] However, in the past such organizations were less influential than other social organizations, for example, the nation-state itself, in shaping the social practices of local communities (Nye and Keohane 1972). Today, local communities are more fully integrated by global communication networks, world trade and market networks, and labor migrations into a global system of interdependence (Sassen 1996; Appadurai 1996; Featherstone 1990). As a result, understanding the social fabric of everyday life now more than ever requires an understanding of how transnational organizations connect local communities with global forces of economic development and social change (Moore 1994, 1987; Strathern, ed., 1995).

In social analyses of transnationalism, scholars have emphasized one of two perspectives. Some studies have focused on what the anthropologist Marilyn Strathern calls the "concrete models of globalization" (Strathern, ed., 1995:159), that is, the structural implications arising from the "world capitalist system" (see, e.g., Wallerstein 1974; Frank 1969; Vallier 1973; Hanson 1980). Studies based on this type of organizational analysis are often problematic because they assume a high level of cultural homogeneity in the organizations being studied and a high degree of passivity in the adaptation by the host cultures. Also, these studies do not fully account for the influences of informal networks within institutional frameworks. A second group of studies has focused on the cultural implications of transnational processes, in such areas as development, public culture, and diaspora identity (see, e.g., Morley and Robins 1995; Gupta 1992; Escobar 1995). However, these studies tend to underestimate the political asymmetries between nation-states and their ability to define and shape transnational issues. They also tend to homogenize the various transnational institutions such as world religious organizations and international business companies.

In this chapter, I will try to avoid the aforementioned problems by combining the strengths of both perspectives and by focusing concretely on a single transnational organization. My basic approach is identifying Kentucky Fried Chicken in Beijing as an entry point of transnationalism into a specific city and, I might add, literally into the gastronomy of the local people. This approach requires an examination of KFC restaurants in Beijing as socially constructed localities of consumption,[2] the commercial success of which depends on understanding how the local society operates. Since the opening of the first Beijing branch in 1987, KFC operations in China have been gradually "domesticated," in the sense that a formerly exotic, imported food has been transformed into a familiar and even intimate type of cuisine. This domestication process bears the accumulative effects of "localization," which in this chapter refers to innovations and modifications made by KFC in reaction to local competition and to a growing understanding of the special place of children in urban China. Localization also refers to the transformed attitudes of KFC patrons, whereby the once-foreign KFC product is incorporated into everyday social life.[3]

Whether or not they have actually eaten at KFC, Chinese boys and girls know about it from various sources, including television and classmates. This awareness does not mean that an opportunity to eat at KFC is equally available to all children, but it does result in KFC's becoming a desired taste, a lifestyle aspiration, and even a measure of "distinction" (Bourdieu 1984:6).[4] In addition, catering to Chinese children has placed special demands upon KFC, one of which originates in the children's less-than-enthusiastic response to KFC's most recognizable symbol – the white-bearded, elderly-looking Colonel Sanders. Chinese children rejected this figure in favor of "Chicky," a youngish, fun-loving, and child-specific KFC icon specifically developed for the Chinese market and introduced there in 1995. Chicky will be further discussed below in analyzing the roles of children, parents, schools, and Chinese mass media in the localization of a transnational implant such as KFC in Beijing.

Chicky or Colonel Sanders?

The first KFC restaurant in China opened in November 1987 at a heavily trafficked and highly visible location at the Qianmen area of Beijing, just south of the Mao Zedong Mausoleum and Tiananmen Square. At that time, this Qianmen KFC was the world's largest fast-food restaurant, seating 500. In its first year, the Qianmen KFC drew between 2,000 and 3,000 customers a day, and subsequently set numerous KFC records. In 1988, for example, it fried 2,200 chickens daily and topped all KFC restaurants in turnover at 14 million yuan. By 1994, KFC had seven restaurants in Beijing, located in high-volume tourist and shopping areas, and 21 other restaurants in cities throughout the country. The KFC restaurants in China became a major source of profit for the international restaurant division of KFC's parent company, PepsiCo, Inc. Based on its success in China, as well as on its overall achievements in East Asia (KFC Asia-Pacific in 1993 provided more than 22 percent of all KFC sales, including those in the domestic United States market), KFC announced in 1994 that it was investing an additional $200 million over the next four years to expand the number of KFC restaurants in China to 200.

My study of KFC in Beijing began in 1994 and continued with visits to Beijing during the following four years while I conducted research in southern China. On a Saturday afternoon in the summer of 1995, I visited a KFC restaurant in Dongsi, a popular shopping and dining area in downtown Beijing. Inside the restaurant's foyer, two children crowded around a KFC-uniformed "children's hostess," trying to tell her their preferences in "flying sticks" – a toy children can spin to make fly. "I don't want the green one, I want the red one," one boy shouted.

It was a busy afternoon for the hostess, as she stood by the door, greeting all the children and handing out flying sticks to each child. She had been standing for several hours, but her easily recognized KFC uniform, the trademark red-and-white shirt with black pants, looked crisp and clean, as if she had just put it on. She hesitated in exchanging the boy's toy. His companion also wanted a red one too, in place of the yellow one. Not wanting to disappoint the children, she reached into her bag and brought out two red ones and gave them to the children. They scampered happily back to their tables, and the hostess, having satisfied two more children, turned to look for others in need of a toy or a smile.

KFC, like other fast-food restaurants, has discovered that children love eating at its restaurants and are its regular customers.[5] Adult customers at its Dongsi branch, who most often came with their families, told me that they visit KFC mainly because their children like it.[6] Parents, when asked what they thought about the food in comparison with other fast-food choices, said that they themselves did not really care which fast-food restaurant they patronized, but that their children chose to come to KFC. Their impression of KFC as a place primarily for children was in line with the company's own promotion of itself among children in China as a "fun and exciting place to eat." This is why the company added special hostesses for children.

The most salient symbol of this focus on children is Chicky, known in Chinese as *Qiqi*, a cartoon character that KFC hopes Chinese children will associate with KFC. Chicky is a white-feathered chicken dressed in big red sneakers, red-and-white striped pants, a red vest marked with the initials KFC, and a blue bow-tie. His blue baseball cap (also with KFC logo) is worn pulled to one side, as is the rage in hip-hop pop culture of the United States; Beijing children see such images in music videos regularly aired on local television. Chicky embodies what KFC hopes is the dining experience of its younger clientele. He is obviously fun-loving, as he winks and dances around, with his baseball cap askew. Chicky is exciting, as he waves from his plane in one restaurant mural. But he also works hard in school. On a back-to-school pencil case given to customers ordering the KFC children's meal in August 1995, Chicky exhorts the young customers to "study hard, play hard" (*renzhen xuexi, kaixin youxi*).

The Chicky character provided a strong contrast to Colonel Sanders, the dominant symbol of KFC on its arrival in China in 1987 – whose statues stood like guardians at the entrance of the first Beijing restaurant. It gradually became clear to local managers that Beijing children had problems relating to the Colonel. They identified him as an elderly and dour grandfather, with his white suit, white hair, and goatee. One general manager reported that children would come into KFC restaurants saying "Grandfather sent us." Managers at KFC's regional headquarters in Hong Kong decided to develop Chicky to set a more playful tone for the place.[7]

The physical layouts of KFC restaurants in Beijing also have been designed with children in mind. Many KFC restaurants are built with a play area for their young customers (though not the Dongsi restaurant, due to space limitations). Furniture is built with children's small scale in mind; the sink for hand-washing is low enough that most six-year-olds can use it without assistance. Also, a space is set aside for a childhood ritual only recently introduced to China, the birthday party. The Dongsi KFC had a raised seating area on the second floor, separated from the other tables by a wooden railing. On one wall, a mural depicted Chicky singing "Happy Birthday" and kicking up his heels. The area could seat about 56 customers, and for birthday parties it was decorated with balloons.

During my visits to Beijing between 1994 and 1997, I found that fast-food restaurants, including KFC, were becoming desirable places for children's birthday parties, and staff members and areas within the restaurants were specially designated to help celebrate these events. Partygoers included parents, relatives, and especially "little friends," as children are often called in China. That KFC restaurants were becoming an integral part of conspicuous consumption in the celebration of children's birthdays is one of many indications that youngsters in Beijing and other Chinese cities were acting as consumers in their own right. Chinese and Western firms were finding more commodities specifically designed for and targeted at this new consumer market.

Eating Kentucky Fried Chicken Versus Glorious China Chicken

The KFC restaurant in Dongsi was a two-story establishment, seating around 250 people. The neighborhood has long been an active market area and is home to a wide variety of retail outlets. On a summer Saturday in 1994,[8] I saw a line of people waiting patiently to be admitted by a restaurant employee wearing a pink-collared polo shirt with the KFC logo. This orderly scene starkly contrasted with the mobs that crowded around nearby bus stops, pushing and shoving to board. The restaurant had large windows allowing passersby to see into the kitchen; the stainless-steel counters and tiled floors reflected high standards of cleanliness. There was a takeout window, for those on the move in Beijing's new fast-paced entrepreneurial environment, with a full menu and pictures of selected items. The menu was comparable to American KFC restaurants, with fried chicken, potatoes and gravy, coleslaw, sodas – including Pepsi Cola, of course, as KFC is a PepsiCo subsidiary. A regular two-chicken-piece meal cost 17.10 yuan ($2.14), while a children's meal went for around 8.80 yuan ($1.10). Inside the airconditioned, brightly lit restaurant, many people gathered around the counters to place their orders, while another crowd clustered around the two sinks toward the back of the restaurant, where signs pointed out the sanitary facilities where customers could wash their hands. Upstairs was a larger seating area, with windows overlooking the street and signs pointing to another set of sinks where patrons could wash up. Uniformed KFC employees were constantly wiping counters, emptying garbage cans, and mopping the walking areas – no easy task given the stream of people walking through the restaurant. On this day, the place was crowded with families – nearly every table had at least one elementary schoolaged child. Managers said in interviews that the restaurant was busy serving an army of children almost every weekend.

Across the street from the Dongsi KFC was "Glorious China Chicken," or *Ronghuaji* in Chinese. Here, too, there was also a line, but it was much shorter. There was a hostess, too, but unlike the one at KFC, she looked bored as she smiled and opened the door for customers. The Ronghuaji restaurant was also airconditioned, but its decor was more reminiscent of a night club. Although the menu did not have as much variety as KFC's, a standard meal was considerably cheaper (8.80 yuan, or $1.10) and the customers got more food (fried rice, soup, and some vegetables). There were also alternatives to fried chicken, such as baked paper-wrapped chicken. Draft beer, a popular item in Beijing restaurants this summer, was also available here. Both the food and the service seemed more "Chinese"; one patron complained in a letter to the editor of a local newspaper about the absence of bathrooms to wash hands after eating greasy chicken, bad service with rushed "hostessing,"[9] and the manager's unpleasant attitude when the customer complained. Nonetheless, Ronghuaji staff (like those at KFC) emphasized cleanliness, or at least the appearance of cleanliness; Ronghuaji staff members were constantly mopping the floor and wiping counters. On that same Saturday afternoon, there were fewer families with children and more groups of young adults eating at the Ronghuaji than at the KFC.

Chicken Frying and Transnational Politicking

The differences between these two restaurants extend beyond such aspects as the age of their customers. Ronghuaji, a Chinese corporation set up in 1989, had strained to emulate the American KFC,[10] whereas in fact KFC in China, as in many other countries, had been introducing changes to adapt to local consumer demands. Although corporate standards of quality, cleanliness, and management have been applied internationally by KFC, there is, in fact, no standardized way of selling chicken. In China, KFC has had to respond to the demands of different local actors (including many levels of Chinese government)[11] within a shifting political economy. Local managers are given a great deal of operational autonomy by Louisville, Kentucky (KFC headquarters), and Purchase, New York (PepsiCo headquarters), to determine the relationship between KFC restaurants and the Chinese government, as long as they achieve "results with integrity" – standards that are spelled out in the KFC Code of Conduct. This localization of authority, providing the means to respond quickly to consumer demand, may be the key to KFC's (and PepsiCo's) international success. PepsiCo has more than 25,000 units and annual sales exceeding $25 billion (KFC accounts for more than 9,000 of those units outside the United States), and oversees the world's largest restaurant system. With the reopening of the Chinese market to foreign investment in the early 1980s, KFC became the first Western restaurant company to enter the People's Republic with the February 1987 establishment of the joint venture Beijing Kentucky Co., Ltd.[12]

Unlike many other American joint ventures in China, KFC launched its operations from the political power center, Beijing, instead of the economic centers of Guangzhou and Shanghai – a difference that Timothy Lane, who was KFC Asia-Pacific president at the time, called the key to KFC's success in China (Evans 1993). One result of this decision, however, was to link KFC's business in China to events in Beijing. For instance, in 1989 in Beijing, the reopening of KFC's Qianmen restaurant, adjacent to Tiananmen Square, occurred just one week after the military suppression of pro-democracy demonstrations in the square on June 3–4 sent many other foreign investors fleeing or sharply curtailing operations in China.[13] After the crackdown, the KFC Qianmen restaurant was used by Chinese troops occupying Tiananmen Square. American popular consciousness of the failed democracy movement, stirred by its dramatic unfolding and then suppression on television, put many American businesses under domestic pressure to cease operations in China. However, KFC reopened its Qianmen restaurant, citing "contractual obligations." In this tense period of US-China relations, there was still an arena less constrained by state control that allowed KFC and its Beijing partners to continue doing business. According to Saskia Sassen (1996), this arena of global capitalism exists only with the complicity of states; in this case, China's commitment to modernization and economic development (and the American desire to expand the capitalist market) created the conditions for KFC to continue selling chicken. In other words, although transnational organizations have a degree of maneuverability in the arena of global capitalism, they are still greatly constrained by state involvement.[14]

KFC is very much decentralized in its operations. On the most local level, its restaurants are either franchises, joint-venture operations, or company-owned stores. Although the franchises and joint ventures retain greater autonomy from KFC control, even the company-owned stores have a good deal of latitude in the way they conduct their business. The devolution of the decision-making process in KFC is driven by the pressures of the fast-food business: chicken goes bad quickly, and there is little time for KFC staff to consult with superiors about decisions. Marketing plans are driven by local assessments of potential consumers and are also executed on the local level. In our discussions, KFC executives consistently recognized the hetero-geneity of local markets.

KFC's flexible structure reinforces the attitude that there are many ways to sell chicken, and that for KFC to succeed in any given society it must be firmly grounded in that society. This is not to say that KFC restaurants are not supported by its transnational networks – Beijing's KFC restaurants draw heavily on PepsiCo's support services. In fact, with the 1995 restructuring of PepsiCo, KFC restaurants now share such services with other PepsiCo restaurants (including Pizza Hut and Taco Bell), with headquarters in Dallas, the home of PepsiCo's snack-food subsid-iary Frito-Lay. However, local managers decide how to draw on these support services. They remain important decision-makers in day-to-day operations and in planning of local strategies.

"Cock Fight": Competing and Learning

With the success of the Beijing KFC restaurants, Chinese companies in other major cities such as Shanghai sought to form joint-venture operations with KFC; after 1988, more than 100 companies across the country wanted to open KFC restaurants (Hua 1990). With plans by a Shanghai group to open a KFC in 1989, as the story goes, two Shanghai entrepreneurs went to Beijing to see what was behind the "KFC Fever." After waiting for more than an hour in line at the Qianmen KFC, they gave up and went to the Dongsi KFC, where they were able to taste some fried chicken.[15]

They concluded that the reasons for KFC's success in Beijing, in addition to advanced processing, quality assurance, and management techniques, were tied to the region itself: northerners were used to eating foods similar to the standard KFC fare, such as potatoes and bread. These two entrepreneurs decided that they would emulate the social and technical practices of KFC, but for Shanghai they would offer fried chicken that was more appealing to the southern Chinese palate. In 1989, they opened the Ronghuaji restaurants in Shanghai to compete head-on with KFC. Chinese newspapers (see, e.g., Qian and Li 1991; Niu 1992; *Liberation Daily*

1990) picked up on the rivalry, labeling it a "cock fight" (*dou ji*), and praised Ronghuaji for scoring its first victory when, in February 1990, under competitive pressure, KFC reduced its prices. This Geertzian "deep play" became a symbol of the cultural struggle between local Chinese foodways and the American fast-food invaders.

With the opening of a Ronghuaji in Beijing in Dongsi in October 1992, the "cock fight" story changed tenor, and instead posed the problem in terms of adapting to a new lifestyle; namely, what are the social costs and benefits of a fast-food culture? Ronghuaji's success in competing with KFC demonstrated that Chinese entrepreneurs could employ Western technology and create an industry with "Chinese characteristics." Moreover, there had been a growing recognition that the mass consumption of KFC and other non-Chinese products served as a marker of China's and, more important socially, individual consumers' success in the world market (Wen Jinhai 1992). Later articles (see, e.g., *Beijing Bulletin* 1994a, 1994b) commenting on the "cock fight" noted that KFC was changing its strategy as domestic conditions changed. For example, when the first KFC restaurant opened in China in 1987, 40 percent of the raw materials for its menu were imported. By 1991, thanks to the local development of the fast-food industry, only 3 percent of the raw materials had to be imported – namely, the Colonel's eleven secret herbs and spices.

These assertions of China's successful adaptation of Western business techniques, made in different ways by entrepreneurs such as the Ronghuaji managers, Chinese joint-venture managers, and government officials, ring like a 1990s version of Chinese reformers' calls a century earlier of "Chinese learning for the essence, Western learning for utility" (cf. Wei and Wang 1994). The point is that KFC did not obliterate China's culinary traditions; instead it stimulated a local discourse on national heritage. Since Ronghuaji opened its first branch in Beijing, competing explanations for the origins of fast food have been offered in the media coverage of the "cock fight." Some claim that the origins of China's fast-food industry can be found thousands of years ago in such foods as stuffed buns (*baozi*) and glutinous-rice rolls (*zongzi*); others trace the origins to more recent traditional foods such as spring rolls, fried dough sticks, and other foods that once could be bought on the streets of any market town. Others argue that fast food is an idea wholly imported from the United States, and is something unique to American culture that has spread throughout the world. Another claim is that fast food in China is linked to the recent explosion of economic development and increased personal consumption.

With the reforms begun in the late 1970s, all economic sectors including agriculture have experienced tremendous growth – resulting in increasing levels of individual consumption. One of the most cited reasons for patronizing fast-food restaurants is the desire to eat Western food – to have a taste of modernity. For Chinese visitors to Beijing, eating at a fast-food restaurant is part of the experience of visiting the nation's capital; the Dongsi KFC made this explicit, by mapping out KFC restaurants and tourist sites in Beijing on a large display outside the restaurant. Out-of-town visitors are readily distinguished from native Beijingers when they pose for family pictures standing next to a life-size statue of Colonel Sanders.

Whatever the origins of fast food in China, the beginnings of a fast-food craze in Beijing were apparent in 1984, when the first Western-style fast-food restaurant opened in the city's Xidan district. The Chinese-owned and operated Yili Fast Food restaurant, which used Donald Duck as its symbol, claimed to be "the first step in solving the food service problem."[16] The restaurant charged 1 yuan for a hot dog, 1.20 yuan for a hamburger, and 4 yuan for fried chicken with french fries. About the same time, Huaqing Snack Food Restaurant opened across from the Beijing railway station, making Chinese-style fast food. Both of these early ventures stood out from other Chinese restaurants that simply served food fast by using updated food-preparation technology imported from abroad – Hong Kong and the United States. The arrival of KFC in 1987 further defined the characteristics of the modern fast-food restaurant: high standards of hygiene and a standardization of food quality and menus. By 1994, fast-food restaurants, both Chinese and foreign, had multiplied in Beijing: McDonald's, Pizza Hut, Brownies (Canadian), Café de Coral (Hong Kong), Vie de France (French), Yoshinoya (Japanese), Million Land House (Chinese), and so on. All are marked by standardized, mechanized cooking and an explicit concern for hygiene; the uniformed staff member mopping the floor, no matter what the style of food, is always highly visible in Beijing fast-food restaurants. The flourishing of these fast-food restaurants coincided with a growing concern among Beijing residents about hygiene when eating out. In summer 1993, soon after the outbreak of the "cock fight," there was a food-poisoning scare in Beijing. KFC and similar fast-food restaurants had the advantage in this situation of offering anxious Chinese consumers a predictable product. Furthermore, with the ability to reliably produce a large amount of food, KFC has also been commissioned by businesses and government agencies to cater large banquets. An American economics professor recounted that whenever he visits Beijing, the Chinese Academy of Social Sciences is sure to give him at least one banquet with KFC products. In summer 1994, KFC began providing free delivery within central Beijing (inside the city's Third Ring Road) for orders of more than 500 yuan ($62.50).

The wide variety of fast-food restaurants with international links like KFC have provided a space for Beijing residents to exercise choice: whether sampling exotic, non-Chinese cuisines, choosing which style of fast food to eat, or selecting items from a menu. Beijingers, for the most part, no longer struggle just to obtain life's necessities. With the maturation of the economic reforms, they can now choose from a wider range of goods and services. The new phenomenon of food "neophilia" reinforces Beijingers' sense of being modern, of having progressed well beyond subsistence (Beardsworth and Keil 1997; Chapter 7, this volume by Maris Gillette). The ability of Beijing residents to choose, especially choosing to eat fast food, can be seen as marking their entry into modernity.[17] At the height of the "cock fight" controversy, one writer lamented: "It is said that the pace of modern society has quickened. Pushed by a rapidly advancing way of life, people hardly have time to pant, let alone to enjoy life. Perhaps it is worth the sacrifice in quality to add to the quantity so that everyone has a chance to enjoy the fast-food culture" (Zhang Xia 1993). The accelerated production of a vast array of consumer goods and services, associated with the capitalist market and modernity, has fostered an ideology of consumer choice in Western societies: "Choice has become the privileged vantage from which to measure all action" (Strathern 1992:36). This ideology means more than having a number of different commodities to choose from; it emphasizes the shift of emphasis from producers to consumers. The former's profit depends on the latter's satisfaction – an idea that is gradually spreading in China's transition to a free-market economy.

Working with Schools and Finding Young Consumers

As mentioned earlier, KFC's most important Chinese customers have been children. To further its recognition among children, KFC has worked to develop partnerships with schools, teachers, and parents. Throughout China, KFC sponsors numerous children's sporting events, essay competitions, and other contests. These events have in turn helped KFC lure more of these young customers (and their parents) into its restaurants: KFC set a one-day sales record on June 1, 1993, International Children's Day.[18] The journalist Susan Lawrence describes the welcome given in May 1994 to John Cranor, then president and chief executive officer of KFC, by 110 Shanghai schoolchildren. Dressed in white wigs, fake goatees, and string ties, they performed the "Colonel Sanders Chicken Dance" at a ceremony marking the opening of the world's nine-thousandth KFC outlet (1994:46). Schools, as KFC appreciates, have a major impact on the socialization of children and in defining ideal forms of childhood. But today's Chinese schools cannot be seen as the extension of the nation-state in shaping students into ideal citizens (in the eyes of the Chinese government) or as a homogeneous system defining cultural standards of childhood (cf. Shirk 1982). The variety of schooling options for Beijing children today reflects the increasing social disparities arising from the booming growth of the Chinese economy (Yan 1992, 1994). The emergence of private schools, catering to a new elite, suggests that Chinese children participate as subjects in these processes of social stratification but are also themselves symbolic objects for adults.[19]

It can be argued that KFC plays an important role in this stratification of Chinese childhood. Meals at fast-food restaurants, while an enjoyable family event from the child's perspective, are considered expensive by average consumers. In 1993, a typical meal for a family of three cost between 18 and 48 yuan, when the average monthly income of a wage-earner was about 400 to 600 yuan (Evans 1993:3). John Cranor of KFC described the company's customers as "aspirational consumers," people with enough disposable income to spend the money for a fast-food meal. However, with the enforcement of the one-child policy, Chinese parents are willing to spend more money on their "little emperors" (*xiao huangdi*) or "little suns" (*xiao taiyang*) for fast-food meals, snacks, and toys. Commentaries abound in the Chinese press on how parents and grandparents are focusing too much attention and too many resources on single children, spoiling them to the point that they grow up without discipline. The popularity of fast food, despite its expense, and changing patterns of consumption must be understood in light of these changes in children's social relationships.

KFC is only one of a number of foreign and domestic organizations competing for children's attention in China.[20] In summer 1994, Yoshinoya distributed prizes such as rulers with magnifying glasses to any customer who purchased at least 25 yuan worth of food. McDonald's (there is one across the street now from the Dongsi KFC) was the leader in the distribution of toys, in Happy Meals, and assorted other souvenirs; at the McDonald's on Wangfujing Street in central Beijing, there was even a separate counter for toy and souvenir purchases. Fast foods were not the only items that children were demanding; children recognize a whole range of brightly packaged snacks by brand name. In a *Beijing Weekly* article discussing changing food consumption patterns, one mother complained that "Every month we spend a third of our income on our child's food, and snacks maybe cover a larger percentage" (Qiu 1994:8). According to the same report, Chinese children spent (or their parents spent for them) $1.25 billion in 1993 on snack food, a category that included KFC chicken.

Besides fast-food restaurants, there are a number of other domains where children and their parents can spend money today that are a recognized aspect of Beijing childhood. Video-game parlors (such as the SegaWorld in Qianmen) are scattered throughout Beijing's shopping districts, including the Dongsi area. Each game cost between one and two yuan in the mid-1990s. Just down the street from the Dongsi KFC were two "Mickey's Corner" stores, the local retailers of Walt Disney products. The Dongsi McDonald's was in the basement of a four-story department store filled with toys, computers, and other wares for children, and bookstores all along Wusi in central Beijing sold books, computer programs, and magazines to help children with their schoolwork. In a survey on children's consumption in Beijing, marketing experts James McNeal and Wu Shushan (1995:14; see also McNeal and Yeh 1997:45–59) discovered that urban children in China influence 69 percent of decisions about consumer purchases and have direct control (through allowances, gifts from parents and grandparents, etc.) of more than $5 billion per year (25 percent of which goes toward the purchase of snacks).

Television is yet another medium that draws Beijing children's attention. Many non-Chinese children's shows (like *Captain Planet, G.I. Joe,* and *Inspector Gadget* from the United States and other cartoons from Japan) are part of the local experience of Beijing children. The influence of these shows is further reinforced with toys, clothing, and other products based on the show. Late-afternoon television is dominated by these children's programs, including locally produced children's game shows in which teams of children compete in various obstacle courses, athletic challenges, or information quizzes with children-only audiences screaming "*Jia you*" (literally "add oil," a phrase that translates into something like "Rah, rah" or "Go for it"). And many commercials airing during children's programming advertise drinks, snacks, computers, and other mostly local products targeted at young consumers.

Children also watch television shows not directly aimed at them as a group, including popular serial dramas, sporting events, musical shows, and news reports. These become part of the local experience, symbolic resources that children can draw upon for their own use.[21] For example, in the summer of 1995, students from several Beijing senior and junior high schools, in conjunction with the China Wildlife Conservation Association, mobilized to save the Wusuli tiger from extinction.[22] They set up booths throughout the city to publicize the danger of extinction and to solicit donations to support a wildlife center. After seeing the students on the news, I went to a shopping area, where I saw young people wearing "Save the Tiger" T-shirts, handing out flyers, and collecting money. When reinforced by children's television shows like *Captain Planet* that promote a similar message, and by news reports of other children's social activism around the world, this kind of campaign becomes part of the socialization of Beijing children in the 1990s.

Conclusion: Globalized Childhood?

The most telling marker of KFC's localization in Beijing is that the company eventually lost its status as a "hot topic" (*remen huati*), meaning that it was no longer a major focus of cultural wars. By 1995, "cock fight" articles had become less salient in media discussions, and Glorious China Chicken had expanded, albeit slowly, with food choices that appealed more strongly to young adults. The novelty of "having a taste of modernity" faded. KFC patrons were more likely to say they ate there because it was convenient (*fangbian*), the children liked it, and it was clean. Symbolically, the Dongsi KFC no longer enjoyed equivalency with Beijing landmarks. In August 1995, the KFC map marking KFC restaurants and Beijing's tourist sites was replaced by a new one sponsored by a Chinese non-fast-food restaurant, which omitted any mention of KFC. Eating at KFC represented a change of eating habits. One man who was accompanied by his young daughter told me, "You can't make KFC chicken at home," in a manner suggestive of Americans eating take-out Chinese dishes. It was still a treat, but not a special one. To some Chinese, particularly older people, KFC products still would "taste foreign," but for children, KFC simply tasted good.

As KFC gained more experience in China, it expanded its offerings to continue attracting customers and to distinguish itself from the growing number of fast-food alternatives. Being Western was no longer enough to ensure success, as KFC became a routine part of the local environment. For example, in 1995, Beijing KFC restaurants offered a spicy chicken sandwich that was not available in KFC restaurants in the United States. With the proliferation of international fast-food restaurants, companies begun to stress the uniqueness of their products. An outlet of the South Korea-based Lotteria chain advertised the "Koreanness" of its fast food in a placard outside the restaurant. There was also a constant bombardment of Lotteria commercials on television, in Korean, showing scenes of happy South Korean customers. The menu highlighted Korean fast-food specialties, such as the bulgogi burger (barbecued beef) and red-bean frozen dessert. Beijing customers became more selective in their consumption, more aware of the differences among fast-food offerings.

In retrospect, Chinese children have played a key role in the "localization" of KFC restaurants, influencing many of the changes in KFC business tactics. KFC has become a fixture of the local environment in the sense that it is part of the local children's experiences and embedded in local social relations. In one sense, children do draw parents into KFC restaurants, to eat fast food, taste modernity, and have fun. In the process they are drawing their elders into an intersection of local society and transnationalism. The children's special relationship with KFC restaurants is reinforced by television shows and other popular media and by their schools, as each enhances awareness of the world outside China and the relationship between their lives and global capitalism.

But this is not a passive relationship in which a transnational organization like KFC dictates lessons to be mastered by the natives. Both local residents and KFC are linked in a network of social relations that include manifestations of the nation-state (through schools, bureaucracies, and so forth), the media, and rival fast-food restaurants like Ronghuaji. As a result, KFC has had to adapt to the expectations and demands of its customers in ways that are not necessarily standard throughout the world KFC organization. In this case, the "periphery" talks back to the "center." With the increased consumption of goods and services for children, KFC has had to ensure that people are interested and supportive of their message. Rather than reflecting a fixed set of practices originating in its world headquarters in Louisville or its regional headquarters in Hong Kong, KFC's branches in Beijing are the sites of consumption where transnational forces are "domesticated," that is, localized with the input of local people, including local managers and young consumers. The invention of the mascot Chicky is a case in point, in that this character was invented specifically for Chinese children. Staffing requirements have also been adjusted, to introduce hostesses catering to young people. Additionally, KFC's outreach programs linked to schools and children's holidays incorporate local employees' understanding of the Chinese educational system.

Beijing children, just as children in most parts of the world, live in a deterritorialized space that can be viewed as a sort of globalized childhood culture; Chicky pencil-boxes with a pinball game on top can appeal to first-graders, whether in Beijing or in Boston. Fast-food restaurants like KFC are favorites among children, and like school they are part of children's social experiences. Many of the same cartoon characters continue to attract young television viewers in both China and the United States. The resulting "culture" is not a single, homogenized global children's culture, because these childhood experiences with consumption exist not in a vacuum but embedded in particular networks of social relations and historical contexts. Particularism becomes possible despite seemingly worldwide practices such as eating at KFC because specificity is produced in the consumption process. At first glance, KFC restaurants in China, as part of a transnational corporation, might seem to be one of those hallmarks of globalism that the anthropologist Daniel Miller refers to as the "new massive and often distant institutions" that catalyze the politics of differentiation (1995:290). On closer inspection, however, the success of KFC restaurants in Beijing has depended on its ability to become local, to become an integral part of Beijing children's social life.

Modernist descriptions of transnational organizations, as discussed earlier, are clearly not reflected in KFC's own business structure. In its decentralized organizational structure, businesspeople are well aware of the organizational traits necessary to succeed in today's globalized economy and the shift of emphasis from production to consumption. Even with global linkages, international support networks, and an arsenal of both financial and symbolic capital, the ability of transnational organizations to succeed in various locations, whether in Beijing or Delhi, hinges on their ability to become intelligible to people in their local social context.

NOTES

1   Studies of transnational processes have also long existed in anthropology, as seen in the earlier concerns of diffusionist and acculturation theorists. Also see the work of Godfrey Wilson and others working out of the Rhodes-Livingston Institute and Manchester

University, and the analysis of earlier anthropological studies of transnationalism in Vincent (1990).

2 I refer to consumption as "a use of goods and services in which the object or activity becomes simultaneously a practice in the world and a form in which we construct our understandings of ourselves in the world" (Miller 1995:30).

3 Following Appadurai's model (1996), localization is the result of the "work of the imagination." According to this model, social groups need to create specificity from a more universal set of abstract ideas or concrete things. In other words, localization is the translation of the social meanings of abstract ideas or concrete things from a general gloss to particular ideas, ideas that make sense in a social group's specific context.

4 This is not to say that all Chinese children share a fixed standard of childhood, nor that their intentions or goals in employing such standards are universal. Instead, I am asserting that eating at fast-food restaurants has become a habitualized aspect of Chinese childhood experience.

5 Raymond 1996.

6 My two fieldwork visits in 1994 and 1995 both took place during the summer when school had let out, so non-weekend observations of customers with children are probably much higher than during the school year.

7 Raymond 1996.

8 Prior to 1994, the official Chinese work week was Monday through Saturday. In 1994, the work week was changed to six days one week, and five days the next. In 1995, the Chinese government officially changed to a five-day work week, Monday to Friday. The day that I am describing is an alternating five-day work week Saturday.

9 "Hostessing" is a fast-food industry euphemism for staff encouragement of customers to eat quickly and not linger at tables. In this case, the staff member directly asked the person to leave his seat (Liang Hui 1992).

10 The first franchise was sold by Colonel Sanders in 1952, and Kentucky Fried Chicken became incorporated in 1955. In 1969, Kentucky Fried Chicken went public, listing on the New York Stock Exchange. Kentucky Fried Chicken was acquired by RJR Nabisco in 1982 and then acquired by PepsiCo in 1986.

11 The relevance of Ferguson's discussion of the state in this case is especially clear, where the state is seen not as a single, unified entity, but as a "relay or point of coordination and multiplication of power relations" (1990:272).

12 "Colonel Sanders' Legacy." Public relations announcement, Kentucky Fried Chicken Corporation. Kentucky Fried Chicken contributed US$630,000 of the initial $1.04 million dollar investment (60 percent), with the Beijing Travel and Tourism Corporation contributing 28 percent and the Beijing Corporation of Animal Products Processing Industry contributing 12 percent.

13 *South China Morning Post*, June 22, 1989.

14 President Clinton's major critique of Bush's foreign policy was his soft line with the Chinese government after the Tiananmen Massacre. In 1993, Kentucky Fried Chicken waited until President Clinton announced his decision to extend the Most Favored Nation Treaty to China before announcing their plans to invest an additional US$200 million in the People's Republic of China. This is an example of what Sassen describes as state complicity in the creation of a transnational arena, an arena that challenges traditional ideas of state sovereignty.

15 The two entrepreneurs cited are Ronghuaji manager Li Yucai and assistant manager Li Yaozhen (*Liberation Daily* 1990).

16 *Hong Kong Standard*, April 16, 1984.

17 McCracken (1988) asserts that the "great transformation" of the West involved not just an "industrial revolution," but also a "consumer revolution" that has shifted Western

ideas about the relationship between the individual and society. McCracken's arguments are congruent with Harvey, Miller, Appadurai, and Strathern's discussion of postmodernity and the shift of emphasis from production to consumption.

18 Susan Lawrence, personal communication.

19 In addition to one-time "sponsorship fees" (costing as much as US$3,600), annual tuition fees and room and board could be as much as $1,550; considering that the average annual Beijing household income is between $1,800 and $3,600, it is obvious that these private schools are only for the well-to-do elite and upper middle class of China (Crowell and Hsieh 1995). Public schools also have large fees; for example, in Guangdong's Jiaoling county, many children could attend the top local high school only after paying a sponsorship fee of 8,000 yuan (approximately US$964).

20 This competition for attention is similar to the role of "drawing attention to" in Stafford's analysis of Angang education/socialization (1995:11–12).

21 This argument is similar to Barth's (1987) discussion of personal uses of communal ritual symbols.

22 Although these are adolescents, they serve as "models" whom younger children aspire to emulate. However, further research is needed to better understand the dynamics between Beijing "youth" (*qingnian*) and "childhood" (*tongnian*).

REFERENCES

Appadurai, Arjun. 1996. *Modernity at Large: Cultural Dimensions of Globalism*. Minneapolis: University of Minnesota Press.

Barth, Fredrik. 1987. *Cosmologies in the Making: A Generative Approach to Cultural Variation in Inner New Guinea*. Cambridge: Cambridge University Press.

Beardsworth, Alan, and Teresa Keil. 1997. *Sociology on the Menu: An Invitation to the Study of Food and Society*. London: Routledge.

Beijing Bulletin (Beijing tongxun). 1994a. "The Fad of Standard Fast Food in Beijing and Its Origin" (Jingcheng zhengshi kuaican re qi laili). Feb.:15–16.

——. 1994b. "The Battle of Fast Food in Beijing: Chicken of Eight Allied Forces" (Jingcheng kuaican zhan: Baguo lianjun ji). Feb.:17.

Bourdieu, Pierre. 1984. *Distinction: A Social Critique of the Judgement of Taste*. Cambridge, Mass.: Harvard University Press.

Crowell, Todd, and David Hsieh. 1995. "Little Emperors: Is China's One-Child Policy Creating a Society of Brats?" *Asiaweek* 21, no. 48 (Dec. 1):44–50.

Escobar, Arturo. 1995. *Encountering Development: The Making and Unmaking of the Third World*. Princeton: Princeton University Press.

Evans, Mark. 1993. "Finger Lickin' Chinese Chicken." *South China Morning Post*, July 26, B3.

Featherstone, Mike. 1990. "Global Culture: An Introduction." In *Global Culture: Nationalism, Globalization, and Modernity*, 1–14. London: Sage.

Ferguson, James. 1990. *The Anti-Politics Machine*. New York: Cambridge University Press.

Frank, Andre G. 1969. "The Development of Underdevelopment." In Andre G. Frank, ed., *Latin America: Underdevelopment or Revolution*, 3–17. New York: Monthly Review Press.

Gupta, Akhil. 1992. "Song of the Nonaligned World: Transnational Identities and the Reinscription of Space in Late Capitalism." *Cultural Anthropology* 7, no. 1:63–79.

Hannerz, Ulf. 1992. *Cultural Complexity: Studies in the Social Organization of Meaning*. New York: Columbia University Press.

Hanson, Eric O. 1980. *Catholic Politics in China and Korea.* Maryknoll: Orbis Books.

Haviland, William A. 1994. *Anthropology.* New York: Harcourt Brace College Publishers.

Hong Kong Standard. 1984. "Beijing Duck Making Way For Hamburgers and Fries." April 19, 19.

Hua Xiaoyu. 1990. "Beijing's Kentucky Fever." *China's Foreign Trade* (Nov.):34–5.

Huntington, Samuel P. 1973. "Transnational Organizations in World Politics." *World Politics* 25:333–68.

Lawrence, Susan. 1994. "Chinese Chicken: Dancing for Fast-Food Dollars." *U.S. News and World Report,* July 18, p. 46.

Liang Hui. 1992. "Ronghua Chicken: Don't Come Back If You Are Unsatisfied" (Ronghuaji: bu manyi ni xiaci bie lai). *China Industrial and Commercial News* (Zhonghua gongshang shibao), Nov. 11, p. 1.

Liberation Daily (Jiefang ribao). 1990. "Ronghua Chicken and Kentucky Fried Chicken" (Ronghuaji yu kendiji), Aug. 16, p. 1.

McCracken, Grant. 1988. *Culture and Consumption: New Approaches to the Symbolic Character of Consumer Goods and Activities.* Bloomington: Indiana University Press.

McNeal, James U., and Chyon-Hwa Yeh. 1997. "Development of Consumer Behavior Patterns Among Chinese Children." *Journal of Consumer Marketing* 14, no. 1:45–59.

McNeal, James U., and Shushan Wu. 1995. "Consumer Choices Are Child's Play in China." *Asian Wall Street Journal Weekly,* Oct. 23, p. 14.

Miller, Daniel, ed. 1995. *Acknowledging Consumption: A Review of New Studies.* New York: Routledge.

Moore, Sally Falk. 1987. "Explaining the Present: Theoretical Dilemmas in Processual Ethnography." *American Ethnologist* 14, no. 4:727–36.

——.1994. "The Ethnography of the Present and the Analysis of Process." In Robert Borofsky, ed., *Assessing Cultural Anthropology,* 362–74. New York: McGraw-Hill.

Morley, David, and Kevin Robins. 1995. *Spaces of Identity: Global Media, Electronic Landscapes, and Cultural Boundaries.* London: Routledge.

Niu Wenxin. 1992. "Focal Points of Beijing: Cock Fight" (Jingcheng re shi: Douji). *China Industrial and Commercial News* (Zhonghua gongshang shibao), Oct. 21, p. 1.

Nye, Joseph S., and Robert O. Keohane. 1972. *Transnational Relations and World Politics.* Cambridge, Mass.: Harvard University Press.

Qian Peijin and Li Jieming. 1991. "Cock Fight in Shanghai" (Douji Shanghai tan). *People's Daily* (Renmin ribao), Sept. 22, p. 1.

Qiu Qi. 1994. "Quick Meals at Home Speed Food Sellers' Growth." *Beijing Weekly,* July 24, p. 8.

Raymond, Linda. 1996. "China Facing the Future: KFC Focuses on 'Little Suns.'" *The Courier-Journal* (Louisville, Ky.) January 21, Business p. 1E.

Sassen, Saskia. 1996. *Losing Control? Sovereignty in an Age of Globalism.* New York: Columbia University Press.

Shirk, Susan L. 1982. *Competitive Comrades: Career Incentives and Student Strategies in China.* Berkeley: University of California Press.

South China Morning Post. 1989. "US Restaurant Chain Reopens in Tiananmen." June 22, B4.

Stafford, Charles. 1995. *The Roads of Chinese Childhood.* Cambridge: Cambridge University Press.

Stephens, Sharon, ed. 1995. *Children and the Politics of Culture.* Princeton: Princeton University Press.

Strathern, Marilyn. 1992. *Reproducing the Future.* New York: Routledge.

——, ed. 1995. *Shifting Contexts: Transformations in Anthropological Knowledge.* New York: Routledge.

Vallier, Ivan. 1973. "The Roman Catholic Church: A Transnational Actor." In Joseph Nye and Robert Keohane, eds., *Transnational Relations and World Politics*, 129–52. Cambridge, Mass.: Harvard University Press.

Vincent, Joan. 1990. *Anthropology and Politics: Visions, Traditions, and Trends*. Tempe: University of Arizona Press.

Wallerstein, Immanuel. 1974. "The Rise and Future Demise of the World Capitalist System: Concepts for Comparative Analysis." *Comparative Studies in Society and History* 16:387–415.

Wei Lilin and Wang Shangcheng. 1994. "An Initial Commentary on the Development of the Chinese Fast-Food Industry" (Fazhan zhongshi kuaicanye chuyi). *Beijing Evening News* (Beijing wanbao), March 22, p. 1.

Wen Jinhai. 1992. "From Kentucky Fried Chicken to McDonald's: An Examination of the Fast-Food Fad" (Cong kendeji dao maidanglao: Kuaican re xianxiang toushi). *Xingyang Daily* (Xingyang ribao), Sept. 19, p. 1.

Wolf, Eric R. 1982. *Europe and the People Without History*. Berkeley: University of California Press.

Yan, Yunxiang. 1992. "The Impact of Rural Reform on Economic and Social Stratification in a Chinese Village." *Australian Journal of Chinese Affairs* 27:1–24.

——.1994. "Dislocation, Reposition, and Restratification: Structural Changes in Chinese Society." In Maurice Brosseau and Lo Chi Kin, eds., *China Review*, 15. Hong Kong: Chinese University Press.

Zhang Xia. 1993. "Too Many Devour Only Fast-food Culture." *China Daily*, April 22, p. 3.

11

Domesticating the French Fry: McDonald's and Consumerism in Moscow

Melissa L. Caldwell

During my yearly research trips to Moscow, I periodically visited my friend Veronika who lives in a small town several hours outside the city. Concerned that Moscow's metropolitan setting was sapping my energy and giving me an atypical view of Russian life, Veronika insisted that these visits and her home-cooked meals would both rejuvenate me and provide a more "authentic" Russian experience. Shortly after arriving at Veronika's apartment in summer 2000, my hostess arranged a large bowl, electric mixer, fresh strawberries from her garden and vanilla ice cream on her kitchen table. She explained that an acquaintance had told her about the latest craze in Moscow: the "milk cocktail" (*molochnyi kokteil*). More commonly known as "milkshakes" to American consumers, these milk cocktails were introduced to Russia by McDonald's in the early 1990s. Given that I am an American and presumably experienced in such matters, Veronika asked me to do the honors. When I was done mixing, my friend called her 85-year-old father, a decorated Second World War veteran, into the kitchen to have a sample. The older man skeptically took his glass and left the room. Within minutes, he returned with an empty glass and asked for a refill.

Today, with more than 75 outlets throughout Russia, McDonald's is a prominent feature in the local landscape. In Moscow, where the majority of restaurants are located, the physical topography of city streets and pedestrian walkways is shaped by large red signs with recognizable golden arches and arrows directing pedestrians and motorists to the nearest restaurant, and local residents use McDonald's restaurants as reference points when giving directions to friends from out of town. Political demonstrators use McDonald's restaurants as landmarks for staging and dispersal areas such as during an anti-government and anti-American demonstration in early October 1998, when marchers first assembled at the McDonald's store at Dobryninskaia metro station and were then joined by additional supporters when the procession went past the outlet at Tretiakovskaia station. Muscovite acquaintances who participated in the demonstration ate lunch beforehand at the McDonald's at Dobryninskaia metro station.[1] Whereas school groups formerly took cultural excursions to sites such as Lenin's tomb, museums and factories, today these same groups take educational tours through McDonald's restaurants and the McComplex production facilities.

Muscovites' experiences of McDonald's offer an instructive intervention into theories about the nature of globalization and the local/global tensions that social scientists have ascribed to transnational movements. Specifically, Muscovites' efforts to incorporate McDonald's into their daily lives complicate the arguments proposed by Giddens (1990, 2000), Ritzer (2004), Tomlinson (1999) and others that the homogenizing effects of global movements such as McDonaldization elide meaning from daily life. Instead, Muscovites have publicly affirmed and embraced McDonald's and its products as significant and meaningful elements in their social worlds. More importantly, however, Muscovites have incorporated McDonald's into the more intimate and sentimental spaces of their personal lives: family celebrations, cuisine and discourses about what it means to be Russian today. In so doing, Muscovites have drawn McDonald's into the very processes by which local cultural forms are generated, authenticated and made meaningful. It is by passing through this process of domestication that McDonald's has become localized.

In this article, I am concerned with the ways in which Russian consumers' experiences with McDonald's depart from local/global paradigms that juxtapose "the global" with an authentic and unquestionably indigenous "local". As I will describe, Russian consumers are blurring the boundaries between the global and the local, the new and the original, through a set of domesticating tactics grounded in flexible ideologies of trust, comfort and intimacy. Through the application of these principles, Russian consumers render McDonald's restaurants and food as locally constituted (and, more importantly, as locally meaningful) phenomena and not simply as transnational entities with local features or as local entities enmeshed in transnational forces. Ultimately, my task in this analysis is to explore how the "local" itself is reinvented through processes of domestication.

This motif of "domestication" calls attention to Russian practices of consumption that link ideas about home and intimacy with ideas about the nation. In Russia, after an initial period in the early and mid-1990s when foreign goods were valued precisely for their *foreignness*, Russian consumers have refocussed their attentions on the merits of domestically produced goods. When making selections in the marketplace, Russian shoppers consider such qualities as the cultural heritage and ethnic background of producers and their products (see also Humphrey, 1999; Patico, 2001). The appeal of the inherent *localness* of goods has only been heightened in the wake of Russia's August 1998 financial crisis, when the mass departure of transnational firms from the country not only created opportunities for domestic companies to meet market demands, but also prompted customers to support local industries for both patriotic and economic reasons. A nationwide "Buy Russia" campaign that explicitly invoked the rhetorics of nationalism and insiderness associated with the segmentary system of *Nash* ("ours") appealed to Russian consumers to give priority to domestically produced goods.[2]

Because the flexible discourse of Nash invokes claims of intimacy and familiarity, it incorporates both the imagined space of the nation, occasionally rendered as *otechestvennyi* (which means "fatherland" and "domestic industry", also "patriotic"), and the physical space of the home, usually rendered as *domashnii* (which means "of the home"), or even more simply as *bytovoi* ("of daily life").[3] An approach that employs this dual sense of "home" is critical for understanding the larger significance of McDonald's induction into Russian social life. At the same time that McDonald's and Muscovites' home lives intersect in intriguing and powerful ways, so that consumers are both taking McDonald's home with them and bringing their home lives to McDonald's, Russians' encounters with McDonald's also reflect their interest in nationally constituted local cultures.

More important, however, while the process of Nash typically evokes a sense of nationalist qualities, Russian consumers also use it more simply to demarcate feelings of intimacy that are not exclusively national. Specifically, the emphasis on sentimental familiarity, trust and comfort that is embodied in the Nash ideology transcends absolute distinctions between local and foreign and instead creates more abstract categories of insider and outsider. As I describe later in this article, the flexible and inclusive nature of Nash emerges clearly when Russians apply it to indicate that their relationships with foreign persons and products are intimate, ordinary and meaningful (see Caldwell, 2004). In this sense, a consideration of domestication as a form of Nashification approximates the process by which goods and values acquire a state whereby they seem natural and ordinary, which Ohnuki-Tierney (1993: 6) describes as "naturalization".

To pursue this theme of domestication, I first consider how recent analyses of globalization and localization approach the issues of meaning and home before turning to the specific case of McDonald's and an examination of the processes by which the company and its products have been incorporated into Muscovites' daily lives. This discussion resonates with other accounts of how transnational food corporations have entered foreign markets by simultaneously responding to local practices and cultivating new local interests oriented to the company's goals (Dunn, 1999; Lozada, 2000; Watson, 1997; Yan, 2000). From this discussion, I address the processes by which Muscovite consumers have encouraged and shaped the company's efforts to "go native" and what these efforts reveal about Russian social practice.

The material on which this article is based derives from a larger ethnographic project on changing consumption practices and food provisioning in Moscow that I conducted between 1995 and 2002.[4] For the particular case study described here, I draw on archival materials; company brochures and advertisements; and personal visits, both alone and with friends, to various McDonald's restaurants in Moscow, the company's production and distribution facilities in a suburb outside the city and other restaurants, cafés and food shops in Moscow. Unless otherwise noted, all ethnographic observations are mine. These data are supplemented by surveys, formal interviews and informal conversations that I conducted between autumn 1997 and autumn 1998 with middle-class Muscovites ranging in age from school-children to elderly pensioners. Approximately 50 university students in Moscow completed written surveys describing their eating habits, food preferences, experiences with foreign foods and views on foreign foods such as McDonald's. I conducted personal interviews with five university students. Group interviews were conducted at three schools in the Moscow region: two sets of interviews with nine children aged five to seven; two sets of interviews with nine children aged eight to 11; and three sets of interviews with 17 children aged 12 to 16. Interview questions focussed on students' eating habits, food preferences and experiences with McDonald's. My conversations with older adults (mid-thirties to mid-sixties) took place more informally over meals and visits to people's homes.

Locality, Home and Meaning in Globalization Theories

Themes of origins, home and homeland have been important in examinations of the intersection of food practices and global systems (Bestor, 2000; Freidberg, 2001; Goldfrank, 1994; Mankekar, 2002; Wilk, 1999). National origins have attracted particular attention as foreign products have been alternately accepted and rejected by local consumers precisely because of the national traits and tastes that are associated with those products (Miller, 1998; Terrio, 2000: 248–56; Wilk, 2002). In her work on foodscapes, Ferrero argues that, "in transnational contexts, ethnic food is also seen as a vehicle for understanding the practices of 'home cooking,' where food practices represent a symbolic and cultural connection with the homeland" (2002: 194).

Issues related to the notion of "home" have also emerged as key themes in localization/globalization studies. The increasing interconnectedness of peoples and cultures throughout the world facilitates the global colonization of local communities so that the individuals who inhabit the realm created by these processes are increasingly caught between the local spaces where they live their everyday lives and the global arenas where they interact with other global citizens (Featherstone, 1995; Ritzer, 2004; Robertson, 1992; Tomlinson, 1999). Through these processes of displacement or deterritorialization, distinctive and meaningful local communities are replaced by "non-places" that are noticeable precisely because they are "forms lacking in distinctive substance" (Ritzer, 2004: 10). Featherstone describes these processes thus: "Localism and a sense of place give way to the anonymity of 'no place spaces', or simulated environments in which we are unable to feel an adequate sense of being at home" (1995: 102). Building on this theme, Giddens notes (1990: 140) that this tension is "a complex relation...between familiarity and estrangement", a feature that Hannerz describes in his observation that cosmopolitans "are never quite at home again in the way real locals can be" (1990: 248). By extending this notion of the non-place, we can see, in Sassen's idea (1991) of the "global city", a similar loss of the familiarity and intimacy that come with a "home town". Thus, local spaces characterized by familiarity and intimacy, such as those embodied in the notion of home, are accessible only via the imagination as an object of nostalgia (Ritzer, 2004; Tomlinson, 1999) or as a new postmodern imagined community (Appadurai, 1990, 1996).

At the same time, global processes present opportunities for localities not only to assert and affirm themselves, but also to recast the global according to locally particular and meaningful ways (Friedman, 1990; Jing, 2000; Metcalf, 2002; Miller, 1995; Watson, 1997; Wilk, 1995, 2002; Yan, 2000). In some cases, social actors refashion imported elements to fit preexisting community standards and practices, such as Watson describes for the assimilation of McDonald's in Hong Kong (1997).

In other cases, these actors appropriate imported elements and give them meaning as signs of local distinctiveness, as Wilk describes for Belizean cuisine (1995, 2002). What is common to both perspectives is that these processes are a "culture's way of making new and unusual things part of itself" (Mintz, 1985: 120–1). Thus, localization involves processes of familiarization, domestication and shared belonging (Featherstone, 1995; Giddens, 1990; Lozada, 2000; Wilk, 2002).

The dynamic interplay between localities and globalities is captured in the notion of "creolization", in which different cultural meanings are fused to create new forms (Friedman, 1994; Hannerz, 1987, cited in Barber and Waterman, 1995). A variation is that proposed by Robertson's idea of "glocalization" (1992: 172) whereby "the universal and the particular" coexist. Barber and Waterman caution, however, that despite Friedman's, Hannerz's and Robertson's visions of diversity and newly created cultural forms, models such as creolization and globalization in fact reify distinctions between "'indigenous' (traditional, local) and 'imported' (modern, global) elements" (1995: 241). This warning raises an important point about the distinction between content and process. Specifically, implicit in localization theories such as those described above is an acceptance that it is possible to identify and preserve the specific cultural practices and beliefs that constitute local cultures. For Watson's subjects, for instance, there is something identifiably and predictably Chinese that is affirmed in the ways in which they interact with McDonald's (see also Lozada, 2000). This insistence on authentic original content also emerges in Bourdieu's (1984) schemas of cultural distinction and Ritzer's (2004) distinction between entities that possess meaning and value and those that do not.

This emphasis on cultural content is insufficient for conveying the complexities of the local/global experience in Russia where the origins of specific goods and behaviors are often less important than the values that Russians attach to them. Even as local and foreign observers depict McDonald's as the ultimate symbol of cultural imperialism (Love, 1986; Luke, 1990), many Russian consumers who support local businesses and commodities have transferred that support to McDonald's.[5] As McDonald's has lost its strangeness and become familiar and comfortable, it has become, in very tangible ways, domesticated. Thus, an approach that focusses on the processes by which the local is invented and rendered familiar is more productive for understanding the case of McDonald's in Moscow. As Appadurai notes (1996: 185), the production of the local is a continuous process of creativity and adjustment (see also Pilcher, 2002). What this means is that although the social processes of localization may be culturally specific, the content of local culture is continually invented.

In the rest of this article, I explore the processes by which Muscovites and McDonald's have collaborated to achieve this domestication. This process of domestication is twofold and reflects the cooperative efforts of McDonald's and Russian consumers. The first section presents a more familiar narrative of how McDonald's interprets local interests and carefully responds to – or exploits – them (Ritzer, 1996). The second section, however, presents an alternative vision of the domestication of McDonald's in Russia. Specifically, by illustrating how Russian customers actively rework McDonald's to fit their own needs and values, this section emphasizes the agency and autonomy of Russian social actors as they engage with global processes.

From the Exotic to the Mundane: Cultivating Friendship, Intimacy and Trust

Within consumption studies of postsocialist societies, McDonald's has emerged as a prime symbol of the processes and stakes at work in negotiations among local, regional, national and global forces (Czeglédy, 2002; Harper, 1999; Shekshnia et al., 2002; Watson, 1997; Yan, 2000). For the specific case of Russia, the for-eign/local tension is particularly significant in light of McDonald's role among Russian institutions and its place within Russian culinary traditions. Throughout Russia's history, food has been both a celebrated aspect of Russian cultural, social and political life and an evocative symbol of national tastes and practices (Glants and Toomre, 1997). This importance was heightened during the Soviet period when, as in other socialist states, control of the food services sector provided a key venue for articulating and implementing political philosophies and social control (Borrero, 1997; Goldstein, 1996; Osokina, 1999; Rothstein and Rothstein, 1997).

Soviet leaders linked their visions of an egalitarian communist society with the goals of producing and distributing sufficient food supplies for the population.[6] To accomplish these tasks, authorities put the entire sphere of food services under state control; the culinary arts were standardized through the professionalization of food workers and the regulation of cuisine. Food production shifted from home kitchens and private restaurants to communal kitchens, state-owned cafeterias and food shops, workplace canteens and cafeterias run by consumers' societies (Borrero, 1997; Rothstein and Rothstein, 1997; see also Fitzpatrick, 1999; Kotkin, 1995). It was within this modernist vision of industrialized food services that privately owned transnational food corporations such as McDonald's first emerged.

After 14 years of negotiations with Soviet authorities, George Cohon, president of McDonald's Canada and *not* McDonald's USA – a distinction that Soviet leaders requested because of political tensions between the Soviet Union and the US – opened Russia's first outlet in 1990. To attract new customers, the company quickly immersed itself in Russian daily life by highlighting not its novelty and foreignness, but its very ordinariness. Specifically, the company crafted itself as a place where ordinary people work and visit. In a continuing effort to cultivate these images of familiarity, responsiveness and accessibility, McDonald's periodically conducts market surveys. In 2000, I sat at a nearby table as a young female employee stopped young adults and asked them a series of questions about how much they would be willing to pay for different food items. The employee questioned respondents about how frequently they visited McDonald's and what they typically purchased. Then, pointing to pictures on a card, she asked respondents how much they would pay for particular items and if a specific price would be too expensive or acceptable.

More revealing, however, are McDonald's explicit efforts to position itself vis-à-vis Russians' cherished principle of Nash as a marker of trust, intimacy and sociality. First, McDonald's acknowledged the value that Russian consumers have historically placed on social networks and concepts of collective responsibility (Caldwell, 2004; Ledeneva, 1998; Pesmen, 2000) by situating itself as a responsive member of the local community. In addition to such activities as sponsoring athletic events and donating profits to a children's oncology program, the company has collaborated with local officials to develop fire safety programs in the city and established a Russian branch of the Ronald McDonald Children's Charity Fund. On a more individual level, McDonald's directly facilitates connections among consumers. In summer 2000, displays in several restaurants invited children to join a collectors' group to exchange toys and meet new people. Children treat the statue of Ronald McDonald that is invariably to be found in each restaurant as a friend with whom they sit and visit.

McDonald's officials next responded to local ideas about health and nutrition as essential qualities of Nash products (see also Gabriel, 2003). Russian consumers articulate food preferences through evaluations of the purity and healthiness of particular foods. Many Russians initially found the anonymity and technological regulation of McDonald's austere and sterile kitchen facilities, as well as the mass manufacture of foodstuffs, unnatural and disquieting.[7] One college student explained his discomfort with McDonald's by equating it to a transnational candy corporation that he had visited; referring to the latter, he commented, "It was too clean". A middle-aged Muscovite friend complained that McDonald's impersonal industrial kitchen was unsanitary, and several high school and university students complained that the types of food served at McDonald's were not as healthy as foods prepared at home.[8]

In contrast, Russians determine the healthiness and authenticity of foods according to where they are produced and by whom. More specifically, consumers privilege fruits and vegetables that are grown on farms in the Russian countryside or in gardens at private summer cottages (*dachas*) and then collected or prepared by friends or relatives. As one college student commented, authentically Russian foods "grow here" and are eaten by Russians. This insistence on territorial origins emerged in the comments of many other informants such as Masha, a middle-aged mother who asserted that Russians are healthy precisely because they eat produce taken directly from the ground. Another college student acknowledged the importance of Russia's organic economy when she commented that Russian products are those grown by peasants. When buying commercial products, Muscovites claim to prefer domestically produced meats and dairy products over American and other products that are known to be filled with additives and preservatives. As part of their daily shopping practices, Muscovites ask salespersons and market vendors to verify the local origins of food items. For their part, salespersons attract customers by volunteering the information that particular products are locally grown or manufactured.

In their responses to these local preferences, McDonald's executives have joined other Russian companies in promoting the local origins of their produce.[9] Using billboards, signs on the sides of freight trucks and tray liners, McDonald's advertises its contract with a Russian agricultural corporation whose name explicitly invokes the symbolic power of the Russian countryside and personal gardening, *Belaia dacha* ("white cottage"). McDonald's thus reassures customers not only that its produce is Russian-grown, but also that it meets "the standards accepted by the Russian Federation" and that it uses "only the highest quality meat without additives and fillers".[10] In 1998, tray liners guaranteed that "The high quality of the products of the firm 'McDonald's' begins with the highest quality ingredients. . . . 'McDonald's' – it is quality!" Finally, special advertising supplements, available in Moscow restaurants in summer 2000, assured customers that McDonald's provides "The taste that you love, the quality that you trust".

McDonald's efforts to cultivate a sense of trust among Moscow consumers emerged most visibly when the company explicitly appropriated the rhetoric of Nash.[11] Russian marketers frequently include the word "Nash" on their brand labels and present Nash goods with images and themes that invoke shared Russian origins and qualities. As such, Nash belongs to a larger discourse about the value of domestic production, such as was seen in a billboard slogan during a recent advertising campaign to promote domestically produced goods that reminded Muscovites, "When we buy domestic, we live better" (*Pokupaem otechestvennoe – zhivëm luchshe*). More significant, however, is that although Nash is more exclusive than labels such as "domestic" or "Russian" because it delineates subgroups within larger national or ethnic groups, it in fact supersedes concrete origins and identities because of its emphasis on trust and familiarity. As Elena, a 28-year-old artist, explained: "[Nash] does not depend on one's nation.... It is a spiritual belief. [Nashi people] are the people to whom I tell my problems. You can switch from foreign [*chuzhoi*] to native [*rodnoi*] in a minute." Elena concluded that Nash conveyed a sense of trust and helpfulness.

By summer 2002, McDonald's had begun invoking the rhetoric of Nash in posters that reminded consumers that the company was "Our McDonald's" (*Nash Makdonalds*). This move enabled McDonald's to position itself within the parameters of the imagined – and, more importantly, *trusted* – collectivity to which its Muscovite customers belonged. Moreover, McDonald's claimed status as a local entity by cultivating what Featherstone sees as the essential features of local culture: "this sense of belonging, the common sedimented experiences and cultural forms which are associated with a place" (1995: 92).

Although Giddens argues that notions of intimacy, familiarity and tradition are themselves products of modernity (1990, 2000), they are nonetheless the markers by which Russians articulate their connections with local culture. It is perhaps more instructive, however, to consider how Russians are autonomous social actors who themselves encourage, accept, shape and discipline this sense of familiarity and intimacy. Rosaldo persuasively describes this process with his ideas about cultural invisibility: "As the 'other' becomes more culturally visible, the 'self' becomes correspondingly less so" (1993: 202). As the Russian McDonald's case illustrates, this process is one that Russian consumers are actively producing and fashioning. In the next section, I turn to a discussion of how Muscovites express their autonomy by creatively incorporating McDonald's into their most intimate and personal activities: their home lives.

Feeling at Home: McDonald's as Comfort Food

Initially, Muscovites' relationship with McDonald's was framed through themes of novelty and exoticness.[12] In 1995, my landlady Anya, a retired geologist, recalled that when McDonald's and the pizza restaurants first opened in Moscow, it was precisely their foreignness that prompted long lines of curious customers.[13] Her brother-in-law expressed a sentiment similar to that I heard from other Muscovites when he commented that he and his teenaged son had tried McDonald's once simply for the experience, but that in general his family did not like the taste of McDonald's food and so had not returned. Several years later, during a dinner conversation on an unrelated topic, a close friend turned to me, asked if I had ever tried McDonald's food and then confessed that he had tried it and could not understand why a person would eat such food more than to try it once. Yet, even as urbanites such as my friends express their dislike for the taste of McDonald's food, they agree that the company has a certain appeal for the uninitiated and uncultured. In a 1998 interview, a Moscow university student remarked, "People from the provinces, the first place they would go, I think, is McDonald's".

Despite these individuals' emphasis on the novelty and social distinctiveness of McDonald's, what is more revealing is a more profound shift in Muscovites' attitudes towards McDonald's. Specifically, for many Muscovites, McDonald's has become so ordinary that it is no longer culturally marked. This shift to invisibility emerged vividly in conversations with schoolchildren and college students about what constituted Russian foods. Intriguingly, in their responses, students often included transnational foods such as McDonald's and Coca-Cola. When asked why they had included these items as "Russian", students typically replied that they simply took them for granted and did not contemplate their origins. One college student put it this way: "I am used to them. They are tasty and easy to buy." In contrast, he said, new or foreign foods were those that he was not used to thinking about and with which he did not have a "mental association": "They do not appear in my mind."

Another example that illustrates this process of domestication is the extent to which Russian consumers have accepted, and even facilitated, the inclusion of McDonald's foods in Russian cuisine. As in many countries, cuisine has occupied an important place in Russian culture and social life (Glants and Toomre, 1997), and Muscovite acquaintances express great pride in being able to prepare authentic Russian dishes.[14] Despite a long culinary history, however, Muscovites' food practices *are* changing as imported foods become more available. As one young woman observed: "In Moscow it is impossible to distinguish between Russian and foreign foods because they are so mixed." A specific example of these changes is evident in the "milkshake craze" that my friend Veronika described when we prepared milkshakes at her home. By the end of the 1990s, milkshakes were available in both fast food and high-end restaurants throughout Moscow as well as at temporary sidewalk food stalls. Even vendors in the lobbies of Moscow's finest theaters and opera houses had added fresh milkshakes to their more typical intermission offerings of elegant chocolates, open-faced sandwiches, topped with smoked fish and caviar, and champagne. Russian restaurant owners now provide French fries with their main courses, and vendors at walk-up sidewalk stands include, among the usual assortment of candy bars, chips and nuts, Russian-made knock-offs named *Big mak* and *gamburgr roial* (as Quarterpounders are called in Russia).

Nevertheless, these examples point only to the spread of foods inspired by McDonald's throughout the commercial sphere. What is more intriguing is the extent to which Muscovites have incorporated McDonald's into their "home cooking" (*domashchnaia pishcha*), a domain that Muscovites consider uniquely Russian. One college student, who said that she was able to identify distinctively Russian foods, explained: "I remember what my grandmother cooked and how my mother cooked." In a similar comment, another student observed: "People who cook at home cook 'Russian' because they buy ingredients and then cook like they did earlier." An academic researcher in his mid-30s stated: "I prefer home cooking [*domashnuiu pishchu*] because home is more comfortable."

What was particularly instructive about these individuals' insistence that foods prepared at home are authentically Russian was that their repertoires of Russian cuisine included imitations of McDonald's foods. Like several middle-aged mothers I interviewed, my landlady Anya periodically attempts to make hamburgers at home to please her children and grandchildren, who want to eat at McDonald's, but are unable, owing to cost or time constraints, to do so. In some cases, cooks have resorted to highly creative culinary reinventions such as the meal described by one of my students. When the student's sister studied in Moscow, her host family offered to make McDonald's hamburgers at home. The promised meal turned out to be fried cabbage between two pieces of bread.[15]

More revealing, however, were the responses I received from schoolchildren whom I interviewed about Russian cuisine in 1998. During two sets of interviews, one at a school in Moscow and another in a town located two hours away and without a McDonald's, I asked nine children aged five to seven to draw pictures of their favorite Russian foods. In response, four out of nine children independently depicted Russian-style fried potatoes (*zharennye kartoshki*), a staple in most families' meals, in recognizable McDonald's French fry boxes. In a similarly illuminating incident at a birthday party I attended, the guest of honor, a friend's four-year-old daughter who loved French fries, could barely contain her excitement at the news that we would have fried potatoes for dinner. When she was presented with the homemade French fries, however, she took one look at them and shrieked in horror: "But they're not McDonald's!"

Collectively, these transformations in local food habits reveal that Muscovites have effectively turned the tables on McDonald's and transformed it not simply into something that is familiar and ordinary, but into something that is authentically indigenous as well as desirable and personally meaningful. More significantly, as the comments and actions of the schoolchildren whom I interviewed illustrate, McDonald's has become the local standard against which Russians' own food practices are measured. In this respect, as McDonald's has been more fully domesticated, it has lost its distinctiveness as something alien and visible and has instead become part of everyday life.

The routinization and habituation of McDonald's into the most ordinary and intimate aspects of Muscovites' daily lives are most vivid within the context of negotiations over the parameters of both domestic and domesticated space. As illustrated in the previous section, Muscovites are taking aspects of McDonald's into their homes. Yet, more and more, they are also taking their home lives into McDonald's, a practice that Muscovite employees facilitate by rarely limiting the amount of time that customers spend in the restaurants. For individuals without accommodation, such as visitors to the city and homeless persons, McDonald's serves as a surrogate home. I have frequently observed visitors using the bathrooms to bathe themselves and to wash out their clothes and dishes. Street children also find the restaurants to be safe havens. The store managers of a central Moscow McDonald's allow these children to sit at the tables and eat food that has been left on diners' trays. On one occasion, I watched as the store manager engaged several homeless children in friendly conversation and offered to help them with their problems. Even Muscovites who have apartments and jobs nearby elect to go to McDonald's to sit and enjoy their homemade lunches (and sometimes even a bottle of beer or two) that they have brought with them into the restaurant.

Other Muscovites have transferred their social lives to McDonald's. Instead of gathering for meals at someone's home, as was a more usual practice during Soviet days when meals in private kitchens were more cost-effective and safe from the prying eyes of others, friends, relatives and colleagues now meet at McDonald's to socialize or conduct business. One friend reported that when she and several other friends tried to organize an outing to a museum, one of the women decided which museum they could visit according to the location of the McDonald's where she wanted them to have lunch. Children and teenagers who live outside Moscow spend their weekends traveling to the city simply to visit McDonald's. During interviews that I conducted with a group of schoolchildren who lived several hours away from Moscow (and the nearest McDonald's), the students excitedly described how frequently they traveled to the city with their friends simply to have dinner at McDonald's. Similarly, several college students confessed that before they had come to Moscow to study, they were unfamiliar with McDonald's. After spending a few months in the city, however, they had quickly begun congregating at McDonald's with their friends for late night meals and conversations.

Birthday parties, which Muscovites generally observe at home or at the family cottage, now represent the most obvious example of these efforts to refashion McDonald's as a domestic and socially significant space. Brightly colored posters and flyers invite children to celebrate their birthdays with a formal party organized and hosted by McDonald's staff.[16] Such events occur regularly throughout the city and, on weekends, the restaurants are often busy with multiple parties taking place simultaneously. During one such party that I witnessed in September 1998, two female McDonald's employees supervised a group of about fifteen 10-year-olds. As several parents chatted and snacked at a nearby table, the children played games, gave presents to the birthday guest, ate hamburgers and French fries and drank sodas. After the party, the two employees cleaned up the area and removed birthday decorations from the walls. Muscovites with more limited resources organize their own birthday parties at McDonald's. I sat near one such party and watched as a group of children chatted and played together at a table that their parents had decorated themselves. The parents first delivered their food orders from the counter and later divided a cake and other sweets that they had brought with them from home.

As these examples show, the emphasis that Muscovites place on the comforts and intimacy associated with home emerges in the ways that they interact with McDonald's. For these individuals, McDonald's occupies an important space within the rituals and ideals that give meaning to their daily lives. As a place invested with meaning, value, delight and, more importantly, heightened sociality, McDonald's is an intrinsically and authentically local space (cf. Giddens, 1990; Ritzer, 2004; Tomlinson, 1999).

The Domestic Other: Creating the New Local

In many ways, Muscovites experiences with McDonald's appear to resonate with the premises underlying the McDonaldization thesis: that the routinizing nature of McDonald's facilitates its insinuation into the organization and regulation of daily life and that McDonald's inherent rationality replaces indigenous, and hence more authentic, meaning with its own set of values and practices. At this point in time, however, it is impossible to predict whether complete McDonaldization will eventually be achieved in Russia. Yet preliminary comparison of McDonald's with other food transnationals in Moscow suggests that, as of now, McDonald's has not yet achieved the same degree of rationality in Muscovites' everyday lives.

Specifically, we can look to the spread of coffee shops and sushi bars (sometimes coexisting in the same café) across Moscow during the past three years. There is an obvious sameness particularly among Russian coffee shops, as managers educate their clientele as to proper (i.e. American-style) coffee etiquette and tastes. The manager of one coffee shop boasted that his goal was to turn his Russian patrons into American coffee connoisseurs. Muscovite consumers have visibly adapted themselves to these changes by substituting cappuccinos and espressos for their more usual afternoon teas or instant coffees and by learning to debate the subtleties of muffins, bagels and other American pastries. Most noticeable is the change in social relations that has accompanied these shifts: previously, afternoon tea was a social occasion when co-workers would stop working for a few moments to sit and socialize with each other. In Moscow's coffee shops, however, it is common to see individuals sitting alone and working on school or work projects while drinking a cup of coffee. In contrast, even as Muscovites treat coffee shops as impersonal and generic settings, they continue to approach McDonald's as a trusted social space where they gather with friends and relax. More importantly, Muscovites are actively manipulating McDonald's by refashioning the eating experience to reflect their own ideas of what constitutes private space and personally meaningful activities. Hence, at this stage, McDonald's has not yet reached the same degree of homogeneity as that pursued and promoted by its competitors.

I have grounded my analysis in an ethnographic perspective (Caldwell, 2004) that proposes that Muscovites are autonomous social agents – even when their choices are constrained by external forces. Thus, by focussing on Muscovite consumers as individuals who actively engage with the institutions and forces with which they coexist, I have drawn attention to the ways in which Muscovites produce and enact the domesticating process of Nash. Although Muscovites may in some ways be complicit partners with McDonald's in this process, it is ultimately these consumers who set the indigenous standards that McDonald's must exploit and satisfy. Finally, because my intent in this article was to highlight the ways in which Muscovites are finding and making meanings within new cultural systems, a focus on the domesticating process of Nash as a particular form of localization calls attention to the ways in which Muscovites do not simply appropriate and refashion foreign elements as familiar and special, as happens in processes of glocalization, but rather reorient their attitudes, feelings and affections in order to experience and know the foreign as something mundane and, hence, part of the local landscape. Despite the power of

McDonald's to position itself as local, Muscovites are the final arbiters of this distinction.

In this article, I have suggested that the uniqueness of McDonald's experience in Russia is evident in the ways that consumers affirm its place in local culture not simply by embracing it as just another part of the ordinary routines of daily life, but more accurately by taking it for granted. For many Muscovites, McDonald's has become, in Rosaldo's terminology, "invisible". Furthermore, at the same time as Muscovite consumers have accepted McDonald's as a local and personally mean-ingful experience, they have privileged it over other, more visibly foreign and uncomfortable, experiences. This quality of domestication emerged clearly when two Muscovite friends, a young middle-class married couple, recounted their driving vacation across the USA. Vera commented that because she and her husband were comfortable with the service and food at the McDonald's near their home in Moscow, they stopped at a McDonald's restaurant along an American interstate, but were surprised to find dirty facilities. They were even more astonished, she added, to discover that the food in the American McDonald's was not as tasty as that in Russia. Ultimately, Vera and her husband decided not to visit another McDonald's while they were on vacation, but to wait until they returned to Russia. As Vera noted, the McDonald's restaurants in Moscow were familiar and trustworthy and thus distinct from their North American prototypes.

By extending values of trust and intimacy to McDonald's, not only are Russian consumers reworking local understandings of such fundamental concepts as the private and the public, the domestic and the foreign, the personal and the popular, but they are also setting the standards that McDonald's must meet in order to flourish. McDonald's is more than a localized or a glocalized entity in Russia. By undergoing a specifically Russian process of localization – Nashification – it has become a locally meaningful, and hence domesticated, entity.

NOTES

1 A photograph that appeared in newspapers throughout the US in 1999 captured the image of an elderly Russian veteran, dressed in a suit adorned with medals, eating at McDonald's following a political parade (Lovetsky, 1999).
2 For a more detailed discussion of these trends, see Caldwell (2002).
3 I thank an anonymous reviewer for adding *bytovoi*.
4 See Caldwell (2002, 2004).
5 Tim Luke describes the McDonaldization of the Soviet Union as the "McGulag Archipel-ago" (Luke, 1990).
6 Food production offers a valuable insight into gender roles and expectations during the Soviet and post-Soviet period, particularly since industrial food production was intended to liberate women from the duties of the domestic realm. Because an extended analysis of this topic is beyond the scope of this article, I would refer interested readers to Goldstein (1996) and the essays in Glants and Toomre (1997).
7 This contrasts sharply with what Yunxiang Yan describes regarding Beijing consumers who see McDonald's as a paragon of nutrition and technoscientific development (Yan, 1997).

8   Cf. Ohnuki-Tierney (1997) for a related perspective on Japan.

9   I discuss this in more detail in Caldwell (2002).

10 These quotations were taken from McDonald's tray liners.

11 See also Humphrey (1995) for a discussion of the ideology of Nash in Soviet and post-Soviet practice.

12 See Campbell (1992) for a discussion of the role that novelty plays in consumer choice.

13 A writer for *Fortune* magazine ironically compared attendance at Moscow's McDonald's to that of another major Moscow attraction, Lenin's tomb. While the 1990 attendance rate at Lenin's tomb decreased to 3.2 million visitors (9,000 daily average), the attendance rate at the new McDonald's just blocks up the street soared to almost 10 million (27,000 daily average). A young Muscovite professional explained her preference for standing in a two-hour line at McDonald's instead of at Lenin's tomb in this way: "At least you can get something to eat here. Who wants to stand in line to see some dead guy?" (Hofheinz, 1990: 11).

14 Moscow's Museum of Public Dining offers a fascinating look at the important role that cuisine has played in Russian culture throughout the last several centuries. Former chefs guide visitors through impressive collections of cooking implements, menus, cookbooks and plastic food displays. As further proof of the value placed on cuisine, several walls in the museum are devoted to pictures honoring chefs and other individuals known for their contributions to Russia's culinary traditions.

15 One reviewer pointed out that the Russian *kotleta* might be analogous to this cabbage hamburger. I agree that this is likely, but it is nonetheless significant that the hostess in this story chose to call her dish a "McDonald's hamburger". I thank Mary Kay Taylor for this story.

16 Compare with Yan's descriptions of birthday parties in Beijing (2000: 216–17).

REFERENCES

Appadurai, Arjun (1990) "Disjuncture and Difference in the Global Cultural Economy", *Theory, Culture & Society* 7: 295–310.

Appadurai, Arjun (1996) *Modernity at Large: Cultural Dimensions of Globalization*. Minneapolis: University of Minnesota Press.

Barber, Karin and Waterman, Christopher (1995) "Traversing the Global and the Local: Fújì Music and Praise Poetry in the Production of Contemporary Yorùbá Popular Culture", in Daniel Miller (ed.) *Worlds Apart: Modernity through the Prism of the Local*, pp. 240–62. London: Routledge.

Bestor, Theodore C. (2000) "How Sushi Went Global", *Foreign Policy* (Dec.): 54–63.

Borrero, Mauricio (1997) "Communal Dining and State Cafeterias in Moscow and Petrograd, 1917–1921", in Musya Glants and Joyce Toomre (eds) *Food in Russian History and Culture*, pp. 162–76. Bloomington: Indiana University Press.

Bourdieu, Pierre (1984) *Distinction: A Social Critique of the Judgement of Taste* (trans. Richard Nice). Cambridge, MA: Harvard University Press.

Caldwell, Melissa L. (2002) "The Taste of Nationalism: Food Politics in Post-socialist Moscow", *Ethnos* 67(3): 295–319.

Caldwell, Melissa L. (2004) *Not by Bread Alone: Social Support in the New Russia*. Berkeley: University of California Press.

Campbell, Colin (1992) "The Desire for the New: Its Nature and Social Location as Presented in Theories of Fashion and Modern Consumerism", in Roger Silverstone and Eric Hirsch (eds) *Consuming Technologies: Media and Information in Domestic Spaces*, pp. 48–64. London: Routledge.

Czeglédy, André P. (2002) "Manufacturing the New Consumerism: Fast-Food Restaurants in Postsocialist Hungary", in Ruth Mandel and Caroline Humphrey (eds) *Markets and Moralities: Ethnographies of Postsocialism*, pp. 143–66. Oxford: Berg.

Dunn, Elizabeth (1999) "Slick Salesmen and Simple People: Negotiated Capitalism in a Privatized Polish Firm", in Michael Burawoy and Katherine Verdery (eds) *Uncertain Transition: Ethnographies of Change in the Postsocialist World*, pp. 125–50. Lanham, MD: Rowman & Littlefield.

Featherstone, Mike (1995) *Undoing Culture: Globalization, Postmodernism and Identity*. London: Sage.

Ferrero, Sylvia (2002) "*Comida Sin Par*, Consumption of Mexican Food in Los Angeles: 'Foodscapes' in a Transnational Consumer Society", in Warren Belasco and Philip Scranton (eds) *Food Nations: Selling Taste in Consumer Societies*, pp. 194–219. New York: Routledge.

Fitzpatrick, Sheila (1999) *Everyday Stalinism: Ordinary Life in Extraordinary Times – Soviet Russia in the 1930s*. New York: Oxford University Press.

Freidberg, Susanne (2001) "On the Trail of the Global Green Bean: Methodological Considerations in Multi-site Ethnography", *Global Networks* 1(4): 353–68.

Friedman, Jonathan (1990) "Being in the World: Globalization and Localization", *Theory, Culture & Society* 7: 311–28.

Friedman, Jonathan (1994) *Cultural Identity and Global Process*. London: Sage.

Gabriel, Cynthia (2003) "Healthy Russian Food Is Not-for-profit", paper presented at the annual Soyuz Symposium, University of Massachusetts, February.

Giddens, Anthony (1990) *The Consequences of Modernity*. Cambridge: Polity Press.

Giddens, Anthony (2000) *Runaway World: How Globalization Is Reshaping Our Lives*. New York: Routledge.

Glants, Musya and Toomre, Joyce (eds) (1997) *Food in Russian History and Culture*. Bloomington: Indiana University Press.

Goldfrank, Walter L. (1994) "Fresh Demand: The Consumption of Chilean Produce in the United States", in Gary Gereffi and Miguel Korzeniewicz (eds) *Commodity Chains and Global Capitalism*, pp. 267–79. New York: Praeger.

Goldstein, Darra (1996) "Domestic Porkbarrelling in Nineteenth-century Russia, or who Holds the Keys to the Larder?", in Helen Goscilo and Beth Holmgren (eds) *Russia, Women, Culture*, pp. 125–51. Bloomington: Indiana University Press.

Hannerz, Ulf (1987) "The World in Creolisation", *Africa* 57(4): 546–59.

Hannerz, Ulf (1990) "Cosmopolitans and Locals in World Culture", *Theory, Culture & Society* 7: 237–51.

Harper, Krista (1999) "Citizens or Consumers? Environmentalism and the Public Sphere in Postsocialist Hungary", *Radical History Review* 74: 96–111.

Hofheinz, Paul (1990) "McDonald's Beats Lenin 3 to 1", *Fortune* 122(15): 11.

Humphrey, Caroline (1995) "Creating a Culture of Disillusionment: Consumption in Moscow, a Chronicle of Changing Times", in Daniel Miller (ed.) *Worlds Apart: Modernity through the Prism of the Local*, pp. 43–68. London: Routledge.

Humphrey, Caroline (1999) "Traders, 'Disorder,' and Citizenship Regimes in Provincial Russia", in Michael Burawoy and Katherine Verdery (eds) *Uncertain Transition: Ethnographies of Change in the Postsocialist World*, pp. 19–52. Lanham, MD: Rowman & Littlefield.

Jing, Jun (ed.) (2000) *Feeding China's Little Emperors: Food, Children, and Social Change*. Stanford, CA: Stanford University Press.

Kotkin, Stephen (1995) *Magnetic Mountain: Stalinism as a Civilization*. Berkeley: University of California Press.

Ledeneva, Alena V. (1998) *Russia's Economy of Favours: Blat, Networking and Informal Exchange*. Cambridge: Cambridge University Press.

Love, John F. (1986) *McDonald's: Behind the Arches*. New York: Bantam Books.

Lovetsky, Dmitry (1999) Photograph, *Christian Science Monitor* (10 May): 6.

Lozada, Eriberto P., Jr (2000) "Globalized Childhood? Kentucky Fried Chicken in Beijing", in Jun Jing (ed.) *Feeding China's Little Emperors: Food, Children, and Social Change*, pp. 114–34. Stanford, CA: Stanford University Press.

Luke, Tim (1990) "Postcommunism in the USSR: The McGulag Archipelago", *Telos* (84): 33–42.

Mankekar, Purnima (2002) "'India Shopping': Indian Grocery Stores and Transnational Configurations of Belonging", *Ethnos* 67(1): 75–98.

Metcalf, Peter (2002) "Hulk Hogan in the Rainforest", in Timothy J. Craig and Richard King (eds) *Global Goes Local: Popular Culture in Asia*, pp. 15–24. Vancouver: University of British Columbia Press.

Miller, Daniel (ed.) (1995) "Introduction: Anthropology, Modernity and Consumption", in *Worlds Apart: Modernity through the Prism of the Local*, pp. 1–22. London: Routledge.

Miller, Daniel (ed.) (1998) "Coca-Cola: A Black Sweet Drink from Trinidad", in *Material Cultures: Why some Things Matter*, pp. 169–87. Chicago, IL: University of Chicago Press.

Mintz, Sidney W. (1985) *Sweetness and Power: The Place of Sugar in Modern History*. New York: Penguin.

Ohnuki-Tierney, Emiko (1993) *Rice as Self: Japanese Identities through Time*. Princeton, NJ: Princeton University Press.

Ohnuki-Tierney, Emiko (1997) "McDonald's in Japan: Changing Manners and Etiquette", in James L. Watson (ed.) *Golden Arches East: McDonald's in East Asia*, pp. 161–82. Stanford, CA: Stanford University Press.

Osokina, Elena (1999) *Our Daily Bread: Socialist Distribution and the Art of Survival in Stalin's Russia, 1927–1941*. Armonk, NY: M.E. Sharpe.

Patico, Jennifer (2001) "Globalization in the Postsocialist Marketplace: Consumer Readings of Difference and Development in Urban Russia", *Kroeber Anthropological Society Papers* 86: 127–42.

Pesmen, Dale (2000) *Russia and Soul: An Exploration*. Ithaca, NY: Cornell University Press.

Pilcher, Jeffrey M. (2002) "Industrial *Tortillas* and Folkloric Pepsi: The Nutritional Consequences of Hybrid Cuisines in Mexico", in Warren Belasco and Philip Scranton (eds) *Food Nations: Selling Taste in Consumer Societies*, pp. 222–39. New York: Routledge.

Ritzer, George (1996) *The McDonaldization of Society: An Investigation into the Changing Character of Contemporary Social Life*. Thousand Oaks, CA: Pine Forge Press.

Ritzer, George (2004) *The Globalization of Nothing*. Thousand Oaks, CA: Pine Forge Press.

Robertson, Roland (1992) *Globalization: Social Theory and Global Culture*. London: Sage.

Rosaldo, Renato (1993) *Culture and Truth: The Remaking of Social Analysis*. Boston, MA: Beacon Press.

Rothstein, Halina and Rothstein, Robert A. (1997) "The Beginnings of Soviet Culinary Arts", in Musya Glants and Joyce Toomre (eds) *Food in Russian History and Culture*, pp. 177–94. Bloomington: Indiana University Press.

Sassen, Saskia (1991) *The Global City: New York, London, Tokyo*. Princeton, NJ: Princeton University Press.

Shekshnia, Stanislav V., Puffer, Sheila M. and McCarthy, Daniel J. (2002) "To Russia with Big Macs: Labour Relations in the Russian Fast-food Industry", in Tony Royle and Brian Towers (eds) *Labour Relations in the Global Fast-food Industry*, pp. 117–35. London: Routledge.

Terrio, Susan J. (2000) *Crafting the Culture and History of French Chocolate*. Berkeley: University of California Press.

Tomlinson, John (1999) *Globalization and Culture*. Chicago, IL: University of Chicago Press.

Watson, James L. (ed.) (1997) *Golden Arches East: McDonald's in East Asia*. Stanford, CA: Stanford University Press.

Wilk, Richard (1995) "Learning to Be Local in Belize: Global Systems of Common Difference", in Daniel Miller (ed.) *Worlds Apart: Modernity through the Prism of the Local*, pp. 110–33. London: Routledge.

Wilk, Richard (1999) "'Real Belizean Food': Building Local Identity in the Transnational Caribbean", *American Anthropologist* 101(2): 244–55.

Wilk, Richard (2002) "Food and Nationalism: The Origins of 'Belizean Food'", in Warren Belasco and Philip Scranton (eds) *Food Nations: Selling Taste in Consumer Societies*, pp. 67–89. New York: Routledge.

Yan, Yunxiang (1997) "McDonald's in Beijing: The Localization of Americana", in James L. Watson (ed.) *Golden Arches East: McDonald's in East Asia*, pp. 39–76. Stanford, CA: Stanford University Press.

Yan, Yunxiang (2000) "Of Hamburger and Social Space: Consuming McDonald's in Beijing", in Deborah S. Davis (ed.) *The Consumer Revolution in Urban China*, pp. 201–25. Berkeley: University of California Press.

12

"India Shopping": Indian Grocery Stores and Transnational Configurations of Belonging

Purnima Mankekar

This paper is a fragment of a larger ethnographic project titled "India Travels," which examines the transnational circulation of public cultures – as embodied in texts, images, and commodities – between India and the US.[1] In this project, I trace how some of the conflicts and contestations about culture occurring in the Indian subcontinent – some of the culture wars about who gets to define the nation and shape national culture – might or might not travel to the diaspora. In a diasporic context, what, for instance, is the difference between the conceptions of Sikhs and Hindus of their respective homelands, and how do these sometimes antagonistic conceptions shape their relationship with India? How do representations of "India" shape the lives of men, women, and youth in the diaspora, the communities they create, and the politics they negotiate? Following Arjun Appadurai, I wish to appropriate "India" as an optic rather than as "a reified social fact or crude nationalist reflex" (1996:18). Throughout, I wish to foreground the ongoing and contested construction of a transnational set of images, discourses, and institutions that engender what different people mean by "India."

In this paper, my primary objective is to examine how grocery stores in the San Francisco Bay Area enable the production and consumption of a range of texts, images, and commodities that participate in this ongoing construction of India and Indian culture. My analysis is based on the following three propositions: (1) Indian grocery stores in the diaspora form a *crucial node* in the transnational circulation of texts, images, and commodities between India and the diaspora; (2) the objects sold in these stores create different *regimes of value* as they move from location to location; (3) *gender* (as it intersects with class and race) offers an important lens to examine the kinds of social practices facilitated by these stores. Rather than address each of these propositions in turn, I will weave them through my argument.

In a review essay on the "futures" of anthropology, Sherry Ortner points out that both the objects and our modes of anthropological enquiry have changed radically: "the field has changed irreversibly" (2000:984, 990). For several years now, it has been evident that ethnographies of local communities, identities, and spaces necessarily involve an interrogation of how the "local" is produced at the intersection of translocal, regional, and global cultural fields (Appadurai 1996; Gupta & Ferguson 1997a; Gupta 1998; Hannerz 1996). Anthropological enquiry has been re-envisioned in terms of efforts to interrogate the conjunction of place, space, and culture through a thorough rethinking of the concept of culture (Appadurai 1996; Gupta & Ferguson 1997b). As we have reconfigured our perspectives on the objects and modes of our enquiry, we have rethought the processes that constitute the texts we produce: from examining the poetics and politics of ethnography to re-examining the relationship between ethnography and other modes of cultural analysis, for instance, literary texts, film and video, and journalism (Behar & Gordon 1995; Clifford & Marcus 1986; Daniel & Peck 1996; Hannerz 2002). Furthermore, fieldwork, so central to the production of anthropological data and theory, has also been reconceptualized in ways that lay bare the nexus between the production of anthropological knowledge and the political projects of colonialism, and the deterritorializations and, indeed, reterritorializations brought about in the wake of international migrations, transnational mass media, and global capitalism (Gupta & Ferguson 1997b). The anthropological analysis of transnational processes presents fruitful challenges and opportunities to reinvigorate and reinvent conventional modes of anthropological enquiry. Again, some excellent models exist: from studying the production of a transnational public sphere in specific parts of the world (for instance, Mayfair Yang's reseach on Shanghai [1997]) to conducting what George Marcus (1998) calls multi-sited ethnographic research by following the movements of migrants and exiles (Roger 1991; Schein 1999) and tracing the circuits of transnational capital (Ong 1999). In this paper I want to explore how tracing the cultural constitution of spaces and objects might enable us to do an ethnography of transnationality. In so doing, I bring the critiques of fieldwork and ethnography cited above into conversation with a longer history of studying objects and commodities in anthropology.[2] Concretely, I am interested in how, in diasporic contexts, Indian grocery stores are sites in which people and objects on the move converge. As particular kinds of social spaces, these stores enable us to study the reconfiguration of gender, class, and race in an interconnected world.

A Brief History of Indians in California

I begin by situating the constitution of Indian communities in the Bay Area in a longer history of immigration from Asia. As pointed out by Lisa Lowe, "immigration has been a crucial locus through which US interests have recruited and regulated both labor and capital from Asia" (1996:7). In addition to being shaped by the US economy's changing needs for labor and capital, immigration policy is refracted by race and national origin. California occupies a distinctive place in the history of immigration from India. The start of the twentieth century witnessed the migration of laborers from Punjab to California and other parts of the West Coast (Leonard

1992), and constituted the first wave of immigrants from the South Asian subcontinent. The Alien Land Laws of 1913, 1920 and 1923 cast all Asians as ineligible for citizenship, and the 1917 Immigration Act explicitly excluded Indians from naturalization. In 1946, the Luce-Cellar Bill repealed the "barred zone" clause of the 1917 Immigration Act. Thereafter, between 1946 and 1965, there was an increase in South Asian immigration into the US. The second wave of South Asian immigration started after the 1965 Immigration and Nationality Act: the entry of Indians in the US rose from 12,296 in 1960 to 51,000 by the end of 1965 (Hing 1993:70, 72). By the 1980s, there were about 20 to 30,000 South Asians emigrating every year (Khandelwal 1995), and in 1985 Indian immigrants ranked third (at 28,498) behind Filipinos and Koreans. According to the 1990 Census, Asian Indians constituted 0.8% of the total population in the nine counties of the Bay Area, with 1.3% in the South Bay and 1.0% in the East Bay. This data, however, is outdated: it accounts neither for the increase in the Indian population in the Bay Area, nor for the substantial numbers of residents who arrived on H-IB visas in the last ten years.

H-IB visas are given to men and women that the Immigration and Naturalization Service of the US government (INS hereafter) classifies as highly-trained workers with skills that satisfy the prevailing needs of the US economy. For more than a decade now, a majority of H-IB visas have been given to computer programmers and software engineers from India, Taiwan, Ireland, Israel, and so on. According to INS statistics, in 1999, 52% of all H-IB visas were given to computer-related professionals. H-IB visa-holders have played a pivotal role in the transformation of the economic and cultural landscape of Silicon Valley – according to the *San Jose Mercury News*, about 100,000 H-IB workers live in Northern California alone. According to the INS, during the first half of 1999, 46% of all computer-related H-IB workers came from India. A majority of the H-IB visa holders are recruited directly from India by employment agencies that hire them out to computer companies. In the Valley, these agencies are known as "body shoppers."

H-IB visa-holders complicate our understanding of the relationship between class, labor, and immigration. H-IB visa-holders are a new breed of migrant worker. Companies usually sponsor the H-IB visas of their employees. H-IB visa-holders are often contracted to the body shoppers who hire them to different companies all over the US. They are well paid by Indian standards, but considerably less than US citizens and permanent residents (according to some estimates, many of them are paid about a third of what US citizens and permanent residents make for the same tasks). Because their visas are the property of their employers – whether computer companies or body-shoppers – their legal status is always precarious, making it difficult for them to change jobs, and of course there is no question of their unionizing or organizing or overtly participating in politics. Most H-IB visa holders seek to eventually gain permanent residency in the US, and quite a few have been successful in doing so. Furthermore, in times of economic crises or "downturns," H-IB visa-holders become extremely vulnerable and are among the first to be fired.

The case of the H-IB visa-holders reveals that, once again, immigration policies enact and produce a tiered hierarchy, sedimented not only by race but also by class, gender, and age: contrast, for instance, the urgency surrounding calls for raising the annual quotas for H-IB visa-holders, with the stagnancy and backlog in all other quotas, especially those pertaining to family reunification, so that parents, less wealthy relatives and the (generally female) spouses of residents now have to wait for years before gaining entry as legal residents. Immigration policies articulate both the needs of the US economy for an "appropriate" labor force, and an imperative to restrict its inflow so as to prevent a so-called "excess" of labor supply (Lowe 1996:13). In an economic context marked by mixed production and flexible accumulation, race emerges yet again not as a fixed singular essence but, as Lowe argues, "as the locus in which economic, gender, sex and race contradictions converge" (1996:26). In general, the racial self-representation of Indians in the Bay Area is overwhelmingly shaped by class. While the number of Indians working in blue collar occupations, the service industry, and in small businesses has increased substantially, the story of this community is now frequently told in terms of the dominant narrative of "Indian success" in the Bay Area, most notably in Silicon Valley. The narrative of Indian success in Silicon Valley – and this story is told largely in cultural-nationalist terms – reinserts them into the dominant racial order; simultaneously and ironically, it contributes to the race-blindness on the part of a majority within this community.[3] It seems to me that the (relative) race-blindness of Indians in Silicon Valley is shaped by specifically *local* political-economic and historical factors in that it might be much harder to sustain in, say, New Jersey or Queens, New York or, for that matter, in other parts of California.

The celebration of the (varied) successes of middle- and upper-class Indians in Silicon Valley must not blind us to the racial foundations of the US economy and the US national imaginary. Bonnie Honig cautions us that the myth of immigrant success reveals the intimate relationship between xenophilia and xenophobia:

> The foreigners whose immigrations to the United States daily reinstall the regime's most beloved self-images are also looked on as threats to the regime. And this is no accident. Their admirable hard work and boundless acquisition put "us" out of jobs. Their voluntaristic embrace of America reaffirms but also endangers "our" way of life. The foreigner who shores up and reinvigorates the regimes also unsettles it at the same time. Nationalist xenophilia tends to feed and (re)produce nationalist xenophobia as its partner (1998:3).[4]

Honig's broader point about the dangers of the myth of the successful immigrant might give us pause as we witness the celebration of the upward mobility of some Indians in the Bay Area and especially in Silicon Valley: first, because there is indeed something unsettling about the always-already foreigner whose upward mobility might leave "us" behind (the "us" in Honig's argument obviously refers to a normative European American Self and not to the foreign Other). More importantly, rather than foreground or even acknowledge the intersection of race and class in the regulation of immigrant labor, these representations of immigrant success have crucial consequences for Indian Americans' own representations of their community as predominantly middle class or upper class. These representations render poor and working-class Indians in America voiceless if not invisible.

But for all their success stories, to what extent are Indians in America deemed assimilable into the dominant racial and cultural order? Race struggles are frequently portrayed as cultural struggles on the part of many Indian Americans, whose unassimilability into the fabric of dominant US national culture allegedly reflects their racial unassimilability. The racial unassimilability of Indians must, however, be situated in a larger ideological context of constructions of Asia and Asian culture in the dominant US national imaginary. As several Asian American scholars have argued, Asia, and Asians in America, have long represented the space of alterity against which dominant notions of citizenship and belonging are constructed in the US. As Lowe points out, "'Asia' has always been a complex site on which the manifold anxieties of the US nation-state have been figured: such anxieties have figured Asian countries as exotic, barbaric, and alien . . . on the other hand, Asian immigrants are still a necessary racialized labor force within the domestic national economy" (1996:4–5).[5] This depiction of Asians seems particularly pertinent to the ambiguous and ambivalent racialization of (some) Indians in the Bay Area, who are portrayed as embodying the quintessentially "American" values of capitalist entrepreneurship, ingenuity, and hard work, and simultaneously, as always-already foreign because of their unassimilability into US "national culture," and their recalcitrance to blending into the so-called melting pot. In what follows, I will examine how, in this political and cultural context, Indian grocery stores might enable men and women of Indian origin to forge community and identity.

India Shopping

I take my title, "India Shopping," from one of the store owners I interviewed in connection with this project. He said to me: "Oh, people don't just come here to buy groceries. They come for the whole package. They come for India shopping." The "India" that is produced and consumed in these stores is a highly contested construct; the kinds of affect this "India" arouses range from fond nostalgia to ambivalence, sometimes even antagonism. I'm especially concerned with how some of the commodities displayed and sold in these grocery stores facilitate the production of the modality of the familiar which, in turn, reveals a complicated set of discourses about nation, community, gender, and family. In other words, through the ways in which Indian grocery stores produce a sense of familiarity for their customers, they provide them not just with the spices, lentils, and other ingredients deemed crucial to Indian cooking, they also make available a range of objects, artifacts, images, and discourses for consumption. The social contexts in which the production and consumption of "India" occurs in these stores is marked, among other factors, by gender hierarchies, regional differences, and class differences.

While the stores I'm going to describe primarily sell groceries, they also sell other goods imported from India – namely, cosmetics, music, religious icons and, in some cases, clothes and jewelry. Most of them also rent videos and DVDs of films and television programs from the South Asian subcontinent. These stores cater to people from all over the South Asian diaspora. It is important to remember that store owners are extremely savvy about the diverse ethnic and national identities of their customers and employ different marketing strategies to target immigrants from other nations in the South Asian subcontinent, including Pakistan (in fact, some of them call themselves Indo-Pak stores rather than Indian stores), and also the Caribbean, East Africa, and other parts of the world where people of South Asian origin have lived. Furthermore, depending on their locations, these stores are

traversed by shoppers and browsers of diverse national, racial, and cultural affiliations, including European Americans.[6] These stores perform different functions for
the latter (from satisfying their curiosity about their new and not-so-new neighbors,
to enabling them to purchase exotic "ethnic Indian" products). Clearly, Indian
grocery stores in the Bay Area are complex social spaces, and the commodities and
texts they display and sell are polyvocal in that they evoke a range of responses for the
men and women who patronize them. In this paper, however, I train my focus on the
memories, longings, and often ambivalent (if not contradictory) structures of feelings
these stores and the commodities and texts they display – what I have termed objects-
in-motion – evoke in men and women who have migrated from India.

How do grocery stores participate in the creation and consumption of discourses
of the homeland for people of Indian origin in the San Francisco Bay Area? As sites
of public culture, Indian grocery stores enable us to track how, in Indian America,
"Culture" is reified in terms of loss or fears of loss – something that has to be
consciously retained, produced, or disavowed. Culture, as Lowe argues, "is the
terrain through which the individual speaks as a member of the contemporary
national collectivity, but culture is also a mediation of history, the site through
which the past returns and is remembered, however, fragmented, imperfect or
disavowed. Through that remembering, that decomposition, new forms of subjectivity and community are thought and signified" (1996:x).

In what follows, I reflect on the cathexis of highly contested pasts onto commodities sold in Indian grocery stores. In so doing, I argue for the importance of objects
to social life. I borrow from Baudrillard's formulation of objects as representational
systems in and of themselves (1981). At the same time, I'd like to hold on to the
materiality of objects by turning to the notion of objectification. Daniel Miller
argues that "values and social relations are not prior to the cultural form they
take, and therefore not reflected by them, but are created in the act by which cultural
forms come into being" (1995c:277). Miller terms this mutual entanglement of
things, values, and social relations objectification. Consumption, therefore, is enmeshed with objectification; as Miller points out, consumption is "a use of goods
and services in which the object or activity becomes simultaneously a practice in the
world and a form in which we construct our understandings of ourselves in the
world" (1995b:30). I, therefore, appropriate the notion of objectification to prob-
lematize distinctions between things, thought, and action.

Since things are inextricable from social life, I find it helpful to trace the trajectories of things-in-motion as they travel from context to context, and to track their role
in meaning-making and in the regimes of value they produce and incite. As pointed
out by Arjun Appadurai, the notion of regimes of value emphasizes that acts of
commodity exchange and consumption do not presuppose "a complete cultural
sharing of assumptions, but rather that the degree of value coherence may be highly
variable from situation to situation, and from commodity to commodity" (1986:15).
Regimes of value are inseparable from other domains of politics, for the consumption of commodities is always-already embedded in other social and semiotic practices. What sorts of regimes of value are created by the consumption of products sold
in Indian grocery stores?

On the one hand, Indian grocery stores in the Bay Area mark the urban landscape
with specific signifiers of ethnicity and "Indian" culture and, hence, enable Indian

communities to represent themselves both to themselves, and to the dominant community (it is not surprising that, in some US cities, the neighborhoods in which these stores are concentrated are known as "Little India"). They also provide spaces where Indians gather and exchange important information about community events, and where many new arrivals learn about neighborhoods, schools, and employment opportunities. This is where some women might exchange recipes, obtain information about religious rituals and, in the stores that also sell clothes, about Indian fashions. Given the social spaces created by these stores, the commodities they sell invoke and produce powerful discourses of "home," family, and tradition (Appadurai 1986; Bonus 1997). I'm especially interested in examining how these stores manufacture *variable* notions of the homeland – what Salman Rushdie calls imaginary homelands – for some people from different parts of India. I will do this by analyzing three aspects of Indian grocery stores: the relationship between food and diasporic memory; brand names and the evocation of nostalgia; the social spaces created by the stores.

Food and Diasporic Memory

Parama Roy points to the intimate relationship between "gustatory and national memories" (n.d.:12), and the power of "nostalgic gastronomy" (n.d.:18) in the semiotics of food for diasporic and migrant subjects. Food acquires a distinctive valence, and a distinctively gendered valence, in diasporic and migrant communities. As markers of cultural continuity/difference, hybridity, and/or assimilation, the gastronomic habits of diasporic subjects become especially fraught areas for contestations and negotiations of gender, community, and kinship. One informant pointed out the importance of being able to buy "suitable" ingredients so that she could cook Indian food for her husband and children. As a busy professional woman, she gave priority to cooking Indian food because, she said, this was one way of maintaining her "culture" abroad. "Language and food are two ways to retain our culture," she explained. "Now that the kids are in school, they're forgetting their Gujarati. But the least I can do is to give them one Indian meal a day." As Roy reminds us, "Food, in the migrant/diasporic subject's cosmos, becomes – whatever it might have been at its place of putative origin – tenaciously tethered to economics simultaneously and irreducibly national and moral" (n.d.:2).

Another woman spoke to me about how, when she first arrived in the US fifteen years ago after marrying a man she didn't know very well, cooking her husband's favorite Indian dishes helped "develop" her marriage. She continued: "It helped me get to know him, his needs. And on weekends we would go together to buy groceries in Jackson Heights [in New York, where the couple lived at that point], and we both looked forward to that." For both these women, and for several others I have interviewed, cooking Indian food was integral to their roles in the family and to their constitution as national and gendered subjects – indeed to their identities as Indian women.[7] As dutiful wives and mothers, they believed they could keep their respective cultures "alive" through the food they cooked, a task made infinitely easier and, in some cases, pleasurable, by being able to buy the necessary groceries at Indian stores.

The relationship between food preparation and ideas of "suitable" or dutiful womanhood is clearer when we hear what some women store-owners told me about their efforts to "teach" younger and second-generation Indian American women how to cook Indian food. One woman store-owner in Berkeley recounted:

> Very often, young women who've grown up here come to my store because they are missing something their mom used to cook. They describe it to me, and I tell them how they can make it in their own apartments. They don't know anything about Indian cooking. But if you're Indian of course you'll want Indian food [note how the longing for Indian food is naturalized – or rather nationalized – here]. Sooner or later you'll miss it. After all how long can you eat hamburgers. It is not in our culture. And then they come to me. I tell them what to buy, how to cook. What basic ingredients to always keep in their kitchen. I tell them how to use short-cuts so it's not necessarily what their mothers cook, because they don't have the time to cook authentic recipes. But it is Indian food that can be made in America. I tell them what to do. It's obvious they've never cooked before.

These words bring together discourses of food, gender, and culture in interesting ways. According to this store-owner, second-generation women, marked as such by their appearance and their accents, would "of course" want to eat Indian food because, despite how they might look or sound, they are, after all, Indian. If, as Miller observes, commodities are "brought to life in the consumption practices of the household" and "enact moral, cosmological and ideological objectifications," the products of grocery stores "create the images by which we understand who we have been, who we are, and who we might or should be in the future" (1995b:35). Furthermore, "Indian food" (clearly, the immense diversity of the culinary traditions of the subcontinent is being collapsed here) enables the reproduction of "culture" in the diaspora. While the recipes these store-owners give to young Indian American women might not be "authentic" (to the extent that they entail improvisation, short-cuts, and the hybrid use of ingredients) they are, nevertheless, deemed "Indian" or at least are "Indian recipes" that can be made in the US.

Notwithstanding this shop-owner's homogenizing of "Indian culture" and "Indian food," most store-owners were, in fact, extremely knowledgeable about the diverse culinary habits of their customers. They were all too aware that they had to cater to a regionally and culturally heterogeneous community. For instance, while earlier, most stores only sold ingredients used in North India, they now made it a point to offer products used in southern Indian cuisines. Store-owners were proud of their niche-marketing practices shaped, in turn, by their knowledge of local demographics and patterns of settlement: as the owner of a chain that has branches in Berkeley and Sunnyvale said to me, "I always keep *gongura* [an ingredient used in Andhra food], in my store in Sunnyvale because there are lots of Telugu-speaking people there. In Berkeley, there aren't that many Telugus [*sic*], so I don't bother." Another store-owner who called his business Indian Bazaar spoke proudly of selling "food from all over India." On the one hand, this is the story of US multiculturalism meeting savvy marketing;[8] at the same time, it also expresses the nationalist "unity in diversity" narrative promoted by the postcolonial Indian state.

Brand-name Nostalgia

Certain commodities sold in Indian grocery stores evoked a range of nostalgic emotions in some of the men and women who consumed them. For most of these men and women, however, nostalgia was not just a simple, romantic longing for the past: it was a complex set of emotions shot through with ambivalence. Indeed, in some cases nostalgia entailed contradictory emotions, sometimes in the same individual who would, at once, feel a sense of loss regarding certain elements of the past, and a sense of relief at having left that past behind. As Daphne Berdahl points out in her analysis of the nostalgia surrounding commodities from the former German Democratic Republic, "In this sense, nostalgia is about the production of a present rather than the reproduction of a past" (1999:202).

Susan Stewart describes nostalgic desire as arising from the "gap between resemblance and identity... nostalgia is enamored of distance, not of the referent itself" (from Naficy 1993:150). Some scholars of diaspora, such as Hamid Naficy, define nostalgia as being about the desire to return to the homeland (1993:148). This definition does not always hold true for Indian migrants in the San Francisco Bay Area. Many of those that I interviewed may or may not want to actually return to India, but felt nostalgic all the same. In their case, nostalgia was not driven by a desire to return to the homeland, whether it is their home-town, their state, or more generally (their conception of) India.

According to Bakhtin, chronotopes enable the interconnection of spatial and temporal relationships. For some customers, the chronotope of grocery stores engendered a nostalgia that keeps alive an ambivalence towards the purported "homeland." As one informant put it, going into Indian stores is like "going into a time warp. It's messy, it's loud. It's fun while you're there. But you can then return home to your clean and quiet house. You don't have to stay there [in the store]." Nostalgia and memory also get transposed or cathected onto some of the products sold in Indian grocery stores (here I refer particularly to products made in India). According to some shop owners and their customers, most Indians go to these stores to buy the same brands that they used in India – popular brands such as Maggi Noodles, Hamam soap, Brahmi Amla hair oil, Glucose biscuits, and Amul Butter. As one of my informants, Sunita Gupta, who had been frequenting stores in Sunnyvale for the past eight years, told me, using these brands "brought back memories of home." Sunita is a thirty-something professional who works in a Silicon Valley company in the area. She spoke of how she always reached for the same products. She always bought Glucose biscuits to have with her morning tea because they reminded her of early mornings in her parents' house:

> Every morning, I would waken to the sounds of tea being served in our living room. My parents used to wake up very early, go for a walk, and then drink their tea when they returned. My father would sit with a pile of newspapers, and my mother would sit beside him, serving tea. I would walk in bleary-eyed, dip my Glucose biscuit into my tea, and sip it slowly. As soon as I was done, I would rush off to get ready for school. My mother would scold me every morning for dawdling over my tea; I would always have to eat my toast on my way to the bus stop. It was a set routine: every morning I would

drink tea with them; my mom would yell at me; I would ignore her and sip my tea, my father and I smiling slyly at each other. No matter what else happened, this happened every single morning, every morning . . . Here, so far away, I still dip my Glucose biscuits into my tea. And I skip breakfast because I never have time to eat before I leave.

Hence, commodities may function as "cultural mnemonics" (Naficy 1993:152), enabling the production and consumption of particular narratives of the past, a past, rooted as it were, in the shifting signifier that is the homeland. Other women I met also described how particular brands of products evoked very specific memories of their childhood in India. Indira, who taught in a primary school in Fremont, spoke of how she always bought Brahmi Hair Oil because, every Sunday, her mother would oil her hair for her. Similarly, every Diwali – which is the Hindu New Year – she bought Mysore Sandalwood Soap because that is what they used in her family on Diwali. As she said, "You're so far away and you want links with those days."

As one of the store-owners exclaimed to me: "There are three reasons why my customers reach for the same brands they used in India: nostalgia, nostalgia, nostalgia!" Through the products they sell, Indian stores enable the cathexis of different fragments of the past on to commodities, enabling both the consumption and (re)production of "Indian culture" in the diaspora. At the same time, it is important to remind ourselves, first, that obviously these commodities do not evoke nostalgia in all customers; second, even among those who nostalgically reach for the same brand names that they consumed in India, the emotions these commodities evokes are quite varied.

Furthermore, nostalgia is predicated on a selective remembering and forgetting of the past (see also Berdahl 1999:198). Thus, the consumption of a particular commodity in the diaspora might lead an individual to remember the warmth and laughter surrounding family gatherings and celebrations in the homeland (rather than the conflicts and family politics surrounding them). I came across several instances of this selective remembering and forgetting soaked in a nostalgia evoked by a favorite brand (for instance, Maggi Noodles or, as in the case above, Glucose Biscuits), but one stands out particularly vividly in my mind. I was interviewing a middle-aged couple in their living room about the role of Indian grocery stores in their lives in the Bay Area, when the man started to speak of how a particular brand of basmati rice brought back nostalgic memories of family celebrations of the Hindu festival Diwali. As the man waxed lyrically about the mountains of food prepared for the occasion, the wife slyly remarked to me that Diwali in her in-laws' home meant that the women of the family would be "stuck" in the kitchen all day preparing the grand meal. "No way am I going to do that here," she added. The gendered division of labor surrounding food preparation in her in-laws' home meant that she could not share in her husband's nostalgia, and selective remembering, of Diwali celebrations of the past.

Evidently, the nostalgia evoked by favorite brands of commodities is neither reflective nor constitutive of any sort of collective memories or identification on the part of customers of Indian origin. In fact, as in the case of Berdahl's informants, nostalgia can "evoke feelings of longing, mourning, resentment, anger, relief, redemption, and satisfaction – often within the same individuals" (1999:203). There are two additional caveats I would like to insert here. As I noted earlier, the meanings attached to products are obviously shaped by the contexts in which these consumption practices occurred. Commodities bought in India acquire a different valence when consumed in the US. Thus, a favorite shampoo was simply a favorite shampoo when used in India; in the diaspora, however, this shampoo acquired particular value because it evoked specific memories of home and childhood. Secondly, I do not intend to paint a fuzzy, soft-focused picture of memories of home or family that are uniformly pleasurable. There are many for whom these memories can evoke sorrow or fear. Indian grocery stores are not just familiar, but for some deeply familial, with all the longing, ambivalence, or terror that the familial can invoke. What resonances or memories might these stores invoke for those for whom the familial is not evocative of pleasure or security? Or when the home is not a safe space?

Retailing the Familiar: The Social Spaces of Indian Grocery Stores

As noted earlier, the anthropological study of transnational processes has proved challenging for practitioners of ethnography. What does it mean to do an ethnography of transnationality? Ortner describes ethnography thus: "Ethnography of course means many things. Minimally, however, it has always meant the attempt to understand another life world using the self – as much of it as possible – as the instrument of knowing. Classically, this kind of understanding has been closely linked with field work, in which the whole self physically seeks to understand. Yet implicit in the recent discussions of ethnography is something I wish to make explicit here: that the ethnographic stance (as we may call it) is as much an intellectual (and moral) positionality, a constructive and interpretive mode, as it is a bodily process in space and time" (1995:173). In this section, I will examine the sensory experience of shopping in these stores, and will trace the kinds of affect produced in these stores for some people of Indian origin in the Bay Area. In addition, I will analyze how Indian grocery stores in the Bay Area create social spaces in which people of Indian origin might forge identity and community. As we will see, these stores create spaces of familiarity that are comforting for some shoppers and that, for others, are fraught with claustrophobia and community surveillance. They are rich sites to observe the everyday practices, customs and rules of social interaction that exist among the Indian diaspora in the San Francisco Bay Area.

Let me begin by recounting my observations of one such store. It had been eight years since I'd last been in Spice Bazaar, an Indian grocery store in Sunnyvale, a community in Silicon Valley that is home to a large number of residents from India. There had been many changes: from a dingy one room, catering to Indian students and professionals in the area, it was now a dingy three-room store. There were tables on the sidewalk displaying vegetables, and as I walked past them, I could smell the tomatoes ripening all-too-rapidly in the blazing July heat. Despite it being a weekday afternoon, the sidewalk was full of people, mostly women of different ages, buying produce. From the way they were dressed, some women looked like they were making a stop there on lunch break from their offices.

But not everyone here was on break from their offices. One elderly woman in a white polyester sari, her white hair pulled back in a severe bun, was going through a huge bin of okra with meticulous care. She would pick each okra, and put it to the snap test: if it snapped under the pressure of her fingers, she would grimace and throw it back into the pile; those that survived the snap test were placed in a plastic bag. As I stood taking in the sights and smells, I noticed a middle-aged couple greeting a salwar-kameez clad younger woman with great enthusiasm: it was obvious that they were friends and had not seen each other for a long time. When she saw the older couple, the younger woman immediately draped her dupatta over her head and bent to touch their feet in a traditional Hindu gesture of showing respect to one's elders: the older woman embraced her and they started to exchange news.

I randomly picked the middle of the three doors leading into the store: it turned out to be the main entrance. On one wall were pasted flyers of all kinds. As I peered at them, I saw flyers for nanny and housekeeping services, posters of upcoming film concerts, advertisements for room-mates, and real estate notices. Lining a second wall were shelves of videotapes and DVDs: the young woman behind the counter with stacks of registers, stared blankly back at me in response to my somewhat timid smile. Intimidated and a bit self-conscious, I walked on: unlike my usual trips to Indian grocery stores, when I rushed in with a list of things to pick up, this time I was determined to browse. Inside, the store was even more crowded than the sidewalk outside. All the spices were on a row of shelves in one of the rooms, lying in what seemed to me to be utter disarray; lentils, icons of Hindu gods, and posters of Sikh gurus were placed together on another shelf. There was music blaring, and one woman, who seemed to be the owner, glared balefully at her customers as she rang in their purchases: with a start I was reminded of the kind of "customer service" I received in stores in my hometown, New Delhi.

It was not just the "customer service" (such as it is) and the apparent disorder that reminded me and several of the people I interviewed of shopping experiences in India. Through the products they offer, their sights and smells, Indian grocery stores enact the semiotics of the familiar in complex ways. The visual clutter is only one part of the sensory stimuli they provide. The dominant impression most people I interviewed had of Indian stores was their distinctive smell. If to other communities, these stores represent sites of (olfactory) alterity, to many Indians who go to these stores, they represented spaces of familiarity. To several men and women I spoke with, Indian grocery stores felt familiar in a foreign land where Indians are marked as alien by the smells we embody. Varsha, a second-generation Indian American woman, described her changing feelings towards the smells of Indian stores thus: "When I was a kid, one of the things I hated was you came out smelling of spices, smelling of India. I used to say, Mom, we can't go anywhere afterwards because we smell like India. But later I started liking the smell, I liked that pungent smell." Another woman pointed out to me, "Its not just the smell of the spices and the dals, it is the smell of the press of people, of Indian bodies."

There are other sensory cues that make Indian stores feel familiar. One woman I spoke with mentioned that she made it a point to go to Spice Bazaar on weekends: "Its just like bazaars in India. There is always music blaring in the background; everybody talks loudly. If the owner wants to check on the price of a particular product, she shouts across the store to someone in the back to look it up. I always have a headache by the time I leave. But it's always fun. It's not like Safeway or Wal-Mart."

In addition to providing the familiar sounds of Indian bazaars, these stores provide other auditory links with the homeland through the music they sell. India Palace is a new chain of stores opened in Sunnyvale and Milpitas (Milpitas is also part of Silicon Valley and, like Sunnyvale, home to a very large Indian community). India Palace is famous for its huge selection of music. I saw three long shelves with CDs and audiotapes, of which two were lined with South Indian film and classical (Carnatic) music. On the top of the shelves were signs declaring "South Indian Music." Tapes and CDs in different southern Indian languages – Tamil, Malayalam, and Telugu – all lay mixed together in stacks. I commented to the saleswoman at the counter that this was a huge collection of music, did they get a lot of customers? Yes, she replied, "these South Indians love their music no matter where they are." The store obviously catered to a large number of people from the southern regions of India, their musics all lumped together under the homogenized category "South Indian music." This display reinforced a system of categorization whereby the music and, by extension, the diverse cultures of southern India were lumped together. This homogenization emphasized the dominance of North Indian assumptions about a normative "Indian culture," and reflected some of the explosive tensions and fractures between regional and ethnic communities in India. The construction of the familiar, in such cases, reinforces (and elides) the tensions and hierarchies present in India around the shaping of a hegemonic national culture.

At the same time that these stores enable a crucial link with their respective homelands through the constitution of spaces of familiarity, not all of these links are pleasurable or nurturing – and gender seems to be a crucial variable in this regard. For some women, the social space of Indian grocery stores represents an extension of the surveillance exercised within the community. Younger, second-generation women have frequently commented to me about how, when they accompany their parents to these stores, they are repeatedly admonished for "immodest" or "loud" behavior. As the nerve-centers or, rather, as gossip-centers of the community, these stores are spaces where some women are subjected to particularly gendered forms of surveillance. Furthermore, as Seema, a colleague in a domestic violence organization, pointed out to me, in instances where women's mobility is restricted by their abusive spouses, they are "allowed" to go by themselves to Indian stores even when they are prohibited from going to "regular" stores, because Indian stores are deemed "safe" by their husbands. On the one hand, the stores provide opportunities for women whose mobility is otherwise curtailed. On the other hand, the very fact that abusive men feel that their wives are unlikely to do anything "inappropriate" while in these stores suggests that they also represent an extension of patriarchal control: the sense of familiarity staged by these stores obviously has a dark side as well.

For example, one informant, Bindu Singh, spoke of how, ten years ago after her divorce from her abusive husband, she was stigmatized by the Indian community in Berkeley where she then lived. She recounted that she had felt like an "outcast" and this sense of stigma was most vivid when she went grocery shopping at the Indian stores lining University Avenue. "I felt everybody's eyes were on me. Maybe I was being paranoid, but I'd walk into a store and I knew everybody was talking about me. The community in Berkeley was very small in those days, and everybody knew what was going on in each other's homes." But, she said, their attitude had changed recently. After her divorce she had seen some very hard years as a single parent to her two children, but she had managed to train herself as a real estate agent and had achieved tremendous success in her profession; furthermore, her children were now grown up, with her son at Stanford and her daughter at UCLA. Having become wealthy and provided a "good upbringing" to her children, she had earned the acceptance of her community members. She said: "[Then] I ignored their stares and now, when I go to their stores or meet them somewhere else, they are so nice to me." "Now they want to ask me for advice," she added sarcastically. From being spaces of surveillance and claustrophobia, these stores had become spaces where Bindu, with her independence and, more importantly, her upward mobility (marked both by her successful career and the fact that her children went to elite colleges), was greeted with grudging respect by her community members.

It should come as no surprise to us that, at the same time that shop-owners insisted that they treat all their customers equally, they and their employees develop ways of identifying the class positions of their customers. As one person told me, "Educated people, the professionals, behave differently from taxi drivers." Indeed, my partici-pant-observation in stores in both Berkeley and Sunnyvale confirmed that most store-owners treated their working-class customers differently. Some store-owners complained that working-class customers tended to haggle more; they also alleged that, in some cases, they had to watch these customers and, in particular, their children carefully because they were afraid they might shop-lift. The owner of Indian Bazaar in Sunnyvale claimed, "We don't have to do this with educated people." Hence, the social contexts in which the production and consumption of "India" occurs in these stores are marked by class differences, highlighting how class fissures communities in the Bay Area. Class distinctions also exist among stores, so that some stores consider themselves more upper class than others. Finally, class distinc-tions exist within stores as well, not just between owners and employees but also, in the case of so-called family-owned stores, between owners and the rest of the family, especially poorer relatives whose labor is exploited.[9]

Conclusion

In this paper, I've argued that Indian grocery stores form a crucial node in the transnational circulation and consumption of commodities and discourses about India. I have been interested in exploring how these grocery stores, the objects-on-the-move they display and sell, and the social spaces they create, might enable us to do an ethnography of transnationality. I have attempted to demonstrate that, as sites of public culture, Indian grocery stores invoke and produce powerful discourses of home, family, and community – all of which are contested, and all of which are gendered in important ways. The commodities displayed and sold in these stores are deeply enmeshed in the social lives and identities of Indians in the Bay Area. Hence, I have been particularly interested in the relationship between commodities and the production of culture in the context of travel. As I have been describing, these stores are important sites for the production of "Indian culture" outside India, forcing us to re-examine the relationship between culture and territory – especially territory as policed by nations and states – in an increasingly interconnected world.

A commodity, as Baudrillard (1981) and Appadurai tell us, is a "thoroughly socialized thing" (Appadurai 1986:6). The semiotics of commodities in Indian grocery stores involve the production and consumption of discourses of culture, family, community, nation, and gender. It should be clear that my analysis of consumption practices is not intended to suggest that consumption is either causative or reflective of social phenomena. Further, rather than dismiss it as the outcome of social manipulation, it might help to conceptualize the desire to consume as produced at the intersection of a range of social relations and longings (Appadurai 1986:29). Nor, as crude theories of fetishization or manipulation imply, do commodities "hide" reality as it "really exists" (as in the consumption equals false consciousness model). For some migrants from India, Indian grocery stores, and the commodities they display and sell, engender a complex set of emotions (ranging from nostalgia to ambivalence to open antagonism) refracted by the haunting presence of the familiar – its loss, its absent presence and, in a few cases, its attempted retrieval – such that it is simultaneously erased and reinscribed through the daily practices of subjects in diaspora. As we have seen, however, for many of my informants, the familiar was not always evocative of pleasure or security: in some cases, it was redolent of surveillance or claustrophobia, and was suffused with ambivalence, if not outright resentment. It is useful, therefore, to bear in mind the polyvocality of the commodities displayed and sold in these grocery stores. Indian grocery stores, the social spaces they create, and the commodities they display and sell inaugurate patterns of sociality that both extend and disrupt hierarchies of value originating in the "homeland," even as they produce heterogeneous relations of power along axes of gender, kinship, community, and race in the diaspora.

NOTES

1   The larger project is based on ethnographic research conducted in two sites in this transnational circuit, New Delhi and the San Francisco Bay Area. My choice of New Delhi and the San Francisco Bay Area as fieldsites was shaped by intellectual and practical factors. My research in New Delhi builds on previous fieldwork; the San Francisco Bay Area is of great historical significance to the history of Indians in the US because some of the earliest South Asian communities in North America were formed here at the turn of century in rural California (Leonard 1992; Takaki 1989). Furthermore, the Bay Area is home to a very diverse Indian community, with residents hailing from all over the subcontinent and ranging from entrepreneurs in Silicon Valley to assembly-line workers.
2   For an anthropological analysis of goods as spheres of exchange and gift-giving see Bohannan (1955) and Gregory (1982) respectively. On the semiotics of material culture, see Sahlins (1976); Hodder (1982); Shanks & Tilley (1986). Important influences on the symbolic analysis of goods may be found in Douglas & Isherwood (1978); Appadurai (1986); and Miller (1995c). See also the special issue of *Ethnos* (64:2, 1999), titled "Objects on the Loose: Ethnographic Encounters with Unruly Artifacts."
3   See also George (1997) and Visweswaran (1997) on race-blindness among South Asians in the US.
4   Insightful as Honig's argument is, it ignores issues of racial inequality and hegemonic constructions of cultural difference. Also, this argument is itself based on an

assimilationist narrative because, contrary to what it presumes, not all immigrants can (or wish to) "embrace" America: for many, the ineffability of racial and cultural difference forestalls such an embrace.

5 See also Palumbo-Liu 1999.

6 This appears to be more true of stores in Berkeley, with its large student population and liberal, multicultural politics, than Milpitas and Sunnyvale where they cater largely to shoppers of South Asian origin rather than to the "mainstream" community. One inform-ant commented to me that "white people look out of place" in stores in Sunnyvale, implying that one didn't see too many European Americans there.

7 Cf. Mankekar 1999 on the discursive constitution of notions of Indian Womanhood in India.

8 Multiculturalism is characterized by the aestheticization and commodification of cultural difference (Lowe 1996:9). It seems to me that while some Indian grocery stores might enable alternative cultural practices resistant to an assimilationsist model of US national culture, they often also reify, aestheticize and commodify ethnic difference. This is par-ticularly true of stores in Berkeley which also cater to European American customers and, hence, feel compelled to represent "Indian culture" to "mainstream" Americans. This appears to be less applicable to stores in Sunnyvale and Milpitas which, as posited above, are not frequented very much by European American customers.

9 See Dhaliwal 1995 and Wadhwani 1998 for excellent analyses of labor politics within Indian family-run stores in the San Francisco Bay Area.

REFERENCES

Appadurai, Arjun. 1986. Introduction: Commodities and the Politics of Value. In *The Social Life of Things: Commodities in Cultural Perspective*, edited by Arjun Appadurai, pp. 3–63. Cambridge: Cambridge University Press.

——. 1996. *Modernity at Large: Cultural Dimensions of Globalization*. Minneapolis: Uni-versity of Minnesota Press.

Baudrillard, Jean. 1981. *For a Critique of the Political Economy of the Sign*. St. Louis: Telos Press.

Behar, Ruth & Deborah Gordon (eds.). 1995. *Women Writing Culture*. Berkeley: University of California Press.

Berdahl, Daphne. 1999. "(N)Ostalgie" for the Present: Memory, Longing, and East German Things. *Ethnos*, 64(2):192–211.

Bohannan, Paul. 1955. Some Principles of Exchange and Investment among the Tiv. *American Anthropologist*, 57:60–70.

Bonus, Enrique. 1994. Marking and Marketing "Difference": Filipino Oriental Stores in Southern California. *Positions*, 5(2):643–669.

Clifford, James & George Marcus. 1986. *Writing Culture: The Poetics and Politics of Ethnography*. Berkeley: University of California Press.

Daniel, E. Valentine & Jeffrey M. Peck (eds.). 1996. *Culture/Contexture: Explorations in Anthropology and Literary Studies*. Berkeley: University of California Press.

Dhaliwal, Amarpal. 1995. Gender at Work: The Renegotiation of Middle-class Womanhood in a South Asian-Owned Business. In *Reviewing Asian America*, edited by Wendy L. Ng et al., pp. 75–85. Pullman: Washington State University Press.

Douglas, Mary & Baron Isherwood. 1978. *The World of Goods*. London: Allen Lane.

George, Rosemary Marangoly. 1997. From Expatriate Aristocrat to Immigrant Nobody: South Asian Racial Straategies in the Southern California Context. *Diaspora*, 6:31–60.

Gregory, Christopher. 1982. *Gifts and Commodities*. London: Academic Press.

Gupta, Akhil. 1998. *Postcolonial Developments: Agriculture in the Making of a Modern Nation*. Durham, NC: Duke University Press.

Gupta, Akhil & James Ferguson. 1997a. *Culture Power Place: Explorations in Critical Anthropology*. Durham, NC: Duke University Press.

Gupta, Akhil & James Ferguson (eds.). 1997b. *Anthropological Locations: Boundaries of a Field Science*. Berkeley: University of California Press.

Hannerz, Ulf. 1996. *Transnational Connections: Culture, People, Places*. London: Routledge.

——. 2002. Among the Foreign Correspondents: Reflections an Anthropological Styles and Audiences. *Ethnos*, 67(1):57–74.

Hing, Bill Ong. 1993. *The Making and Remaking of Asian America through Immigration Policy, 1850–1990*. Stanford, CA: Stanford University Press.

Hodder, Ian. 1982. *Symbols in Action*. Cambridge: Cambridge University Press.

Honig, Bonnie. 1998. Immigrant America?: How Foreignness "Solves" Democracy's Problems. *Social Text*, 16(3):1–27.

Khandelwal, Madhulika. 1995. Indian Immigrants in Queens, New York City: Patterns of Social Concentration and Distribution, 1965–1990. In *Nation and Migration: The Politics of Space in the South Asian Diaspora*, edited by Peter van der Veer. Philadelphia: University of Pennsylvania Press.

Leonard, Karen. 1992. *Making Ethnic Choices: California's Punjabi Mexican Americans*. Philadelphia: Temple University Press.

Lowe, Lisa. 1996. *Immigrant Acts: on Asian American Cultural Studies*. Durham, NC: Duke University Press

Mankekar, Purnima. 1999. *Screening Culture, Viewing Politics*. Durham, NC: Duke University Press.

Marcus, George. 1998. *Ethnography through Thick and Thin*. Princeton: Princeton University Press.

Miller, Daniel (ed.). 1995a. *Acknowledging Consumption*. London: Routledge.

——. 1995b. Consumption as the Vanguard of History. In *Acknowledging Consumption*, edited by Daniel Miller, pp. 1–57. London: Routledge.

——. 1995c. Consumption Studies as the Transformation of Anthropology. In *Acknowledging Consumption*, edited by D. Miller, pp. 264–95. London: Routledge.

Naficy, Hamid. 1993. *The Making of Exile Cultures: Iranian Television in Los Angeles*. Minneapolis: University of Minnesota Press.

Ong, Aihwa. 1999. *Flexible Citizenship: The Cultural Logics of Transnationality*. Durham, NC: Duke University Press.

Ortner, Sherry. 1995. Resistance and the Problem of Ethnographic Refusal. *Comparative Studies in Society and History*, 37(1):173–94.

——. 2000. Some Futures of Anthropology. *American Ethnologist*, 26(4): 984–91.

Palumbo-Liu, David. 1999. *Asian/American: Historical Crossings of a Racial Frontier*. Stanford: Stanford University Press.

Rouse, Roger. 1991. Mexican Migration and the Social Space of Postmodernism. *Diaspora*, 1(1):8–23.

Roy, Parama. n.d. Citizenship, Cinema, and Culinary Communities: The Gastropoetics of the South Asian Diaspora.

Sahlins, Marshall. 1976. *Culture and Practical Reason*. Chicago: University of Chicago Press.

Schein, Louisa. 1999. Diaspora Politics, Homeland Erotics, and the Materializing of Memory. *Positions*, 697–730.

Shanks, Michael & Christopher Tilley. 1986. *Re-Constructing Archaeology*. London: Routledge.

Stewart, Susan. 1984. *On Longing: Narratives of the Miniature, the Gigantic, the Souvenir, the Collection*. Baltimore: Johns Hopkins University Press.

Takaki, Ronald. 1989. *Strangers from a Different Shore: A History of Asian Americans*. New York: Penguin.

Visweswaran, Kamala. 1997. Diaspora by Design: Flexible Citizenship and South Asians in u.s. Racial Formations. *Diaspora*, 6:1:5–29.

Wadhwani, Anita. 1998. Working Overtime. *India Currents*. Dec. 98–Jan. 99:44–6.

Yang, Mayfair Mei-Hui. 1997. Mass Media and Transnational Subjectivity in Shanghai: Notes on (Re)Cosmopolitanism in a Chinese Metropolis. In *Ungrounded Empires: The Cultural Politics of Modern Chinese Transnationalism*, edited by Aihwa Ong & Donald Nonini, pp. 287–322. New York: Routledge.

Part III

The Political Economy of Food

Introduction

Part III, "The Political Economy of Food," presents a series of articles that deal directly with current political negotiations over food and eating and their consequences. Warren Belasco and Jeffrey Pilcher each analyze political ideologies and movements that are embedded within food practices. Belasco reads something as ordinary as bread as a text on Americans' cultural politics. Jeffrey Pilcher looks at the industrialization of tortillas and how this process has affected United States–Mexico relations. In her article on feeding programs for Chinese athletes, Susan Brownell describes the ways in which the Chinese state has disciplined its citizens, and established status distinctions through differential access to food resources. Hans Buechler and Judith-Maria Buechler map the transition from state socialism to market capitalism in (the former) East Germany – showing how bakers and consumers of bread are affected by economic forces that are beyond their control.

The articles by Robert Paarlberg, Sarah Phillips, and Harriet Ritvo grapple with the symbolic (and concrete) dangers posed by the global traffic in food commodities. Robert Paarlberg unravels the complex politics of genetically modified food, specifically grain crops. He shows that scientific opinion is often ignored when governments seek to protect indigenous producers and, often incidentally, national consumers. Sarah Phillips takes us to post-Chernobyl Ukraine and investigates Ukrainians' concerns with radiation poisoning in the aftermath of one of the late twentieth century's most dangerous incidents. Her account raises serious questions about the ability of financially strapped governments to protect the natural environment and, by extension, the world food supply. Harriet Ritvo tracks a similar issue, mad cow disease, that has traumatized Europe and fostered a new form of consumer activism. Europeans today (like many Japanese and, increasingly, American consumers) no longer trust bureaucratic regulators or scientific experts, given their singular failure to avert the mad cow catastrophe. Future developments in the global food system will be conditioned by these deep social and psychological anxieties.

13

Food and the Counterculture: A Story of Bread and Politics

Warren Belasco

Throughout North America and Western Europe, the neo-bohemian youth movement known as the counterculture turned to natural and organic foods in the late 1960s. While this "countercuisine" is still associated with mass-mediated stereotypes of forlorn hippies scratching away in weedy communal gardens ("Easy Rider," 1969) and of dubious New Age repasts of mashed yeast with alfalfa sprouts ("Annie Hall," 1977), it is my argument that the countercuisine represented a serious and largely unprecedented attempt to reverse the direction of dietary modernization and thereby align personal consumption with perceived global needs. If there was a paradigm animating countercultural foodways, it was nicely expressed in the triad of no-nonsense "laws" propounded in *The Whole Earth Catalog* in 1968:

> Everything's connected to everything.
> Everything's got to go somewhere.
> There's no such thing as a free lunch.[1]

For the more conscientious advocates of the countercuisine, food was a way of integrating the world, seeing the social consequences of private actions, and reminding us of our moral responsibilities. Or, as one Berkeley community gardener put it in 1969, food was an "edible dynamic" – a visceral, lived daily link between the personal and the political.[2]

Thirty years after my first brown-rice-with-tofu experience, I still maintain this holistic world view in my food research and teaching. Thus in my courses, "American Food," and "The American Food Chain," I tell students that eating is more than a private, physiological act. It connects us to people and places all over the world – past, present, and future. As an example, I invite them to think about the simple act of toasting and eating a slice of packaged white bread. Growing that wheat helped some Midwestern farmers pay their bills while also polluting their water supply with fertilizers and pesticides, eroding their soil, and, if they used irrigation, lowering their region's water table. The land used to grow the wheat had been acquired – or seized – long ago from other living creatures, human and otherwise, and converted to growing a grass that had originated as a weed in the Middle East and had been gradually domesticated and improved by countless generations of gatherers, peasants, farmers, and, only just recently, scientists. Turning the wheat into bread required the coordinated efforts of numerous companies specializing in food transportation, storage, processing, and marketing, as well as others involved in manufacturing and selling farm equipment.

By extending the bread's shelf life, the plastic wrapping lowered costs and increased profits for corporate processors, distributors, and supermarkets. That packaging also helped to put thousands of neighborhood bakers out of business. Making the plastic from petrochemicals may have helped to foul Cancer Alley in Louisiana and, if the oil came from the Middle East, may have helped to pay for the reconstruction of Kuwait, which was destroyed several years ago by an Iraqi army also financed by petrochemical bread wrappers. The copper in the toaster and electrical wiring may have been mined during the Pinochet dictatorship in Chile or Mobutu's Zaire or Bruce Babbitt's Arizona. The electricity itself probably came from a power plant burning coal, a source of black lung, acid rain, and global warming. And so on.... All of this – and more – was involved in making toast. And we have not even mentioned the butter and jam![3]

Since my students already tend to patronize me as a quaint 1960s relic, I do not tell them that my interdisciplinary, global interest in food did in fact originate in the late 1960s and early 1970s, when I was a student at the University of Michigan. This perspective came not so much from my coursework – historians rarely looked at food back then – but from what I was doing off campus. It was in that period that I, like several million other young people, was discovering the political implications of playing with our food. At the coop house where I cooked in 1968, I learned how upset my straighter housemates could be if I left the meat out of the lasagna, injected the roast beef with red dye, or served octopus instead of tuna salad. In 1970 my wife and I met our first macrobiotic, who seemed irritatingly self-righteous and mystical; but soon we too turned vegetarian and came to appreciate the provocative power of refusing steak at the family dinner table. Reading Frances Moore Lappe's *Diet for a Small Planet*, we learned about protein complementarity and the ecological inefficiency of feeding precious grains to cattle. Hoping to secede from the System (or at least from the supermarket), we found *The Tassajara Bread Book* and started baking.[4] *Mother Earth News* and *Organic Gardening* showed us how to make raspberry jam, pickle cucumbers, and grow all the corn and tomatoes we could ever eat on our 20-by-20-foot, chemical-free plot at the nearby community garden. We also brewed dark ale, picked purple clover for wine, and grew our own cannabis. At the anarchistic natural foods coop on South State Street, we bagged our grains, sliced our own cheddar, toted up our bill, and paid whatever we wanted. The new Sikh restaurant in downtown Ann Arbor taught us about vegetable tempura, curried squash soup, and tantric meditation. Cookbook writers Ellen Ewald and Anna Thomas showed us how to make tasty ethnic dishes while saving the Earth.[5] At noisy demonstrations and concerts we scarfed free brown rice and beans served by radical communes dedicated to nourishing "the Revolution." And when, in 1974, someone accidentally mixed fire retardant in dairy cattle feed, we, like every milk drinker in Michigan, learned that in a complex food system, everything really is connected and that there can be no complete escape to nature or self-sufficiency.

My radicalized food awareness translated into sustained scholarship a decade later, when I started a study of the hegemonic process – the way mainstream institutions handle subcultural dissent and deviancy.[6] How does an urban-industrial-capitalist society profit from discontent with urban-industrial-capitalist society? For case studies in what I called "retailing revolt," I chose to examine the fate of blue jeans, "rock 'n' roll," and natural foods. (It does seem that many food studies begin not out of intrinsic interest in food but because of interest in what specific foods can tell us about something else – gender, labor relations, class, ethnicity, imperialism, capitalism, or, in my case, the cooptation of cultural rebellion.) More or less by chance, I started with the food chapter, which soon became a whole book about the counterculture's confrontation with the food industry.[7]

In my research, I tried to set my own nostalgia and amnesia aside and went back to the food-related documents of the late 1960s, especially the Library of Congress's vast collection of countercultural cookbooks, periodicals, catalogs, guides, broadsides, and memoirs. Even today, as I scan this often feverish material with the somewhat sedated perspective of a middle-aged teacher with his own rebellious children, I am still impressed by the core insights of the underground food writers, organic farmers, chefs, entrepreneurs, and consumer activists who articulated the "digestible ideology"[8] of dietary radicalism. Unlike some journalists and historians, I do not dismiss the countercuisine as the latest silly manifestation of the "nuts among the berries" health food faddism that, according to critics, has deceived and diverted gullible Americans since Sylvester Graham, John Harvey Kellogg, Horace Fletcher, and Gaylord Hauser.[9] While postwar crusaders like Adele Davis and J. I. Rodale established some continuity between the earlier health food movement and the countercuisine, it is my argument that the latter was motivated less by concerns about personal vitality or longevity (the traditional health food focus) than by radical politics and environmentalism. Or, just as much food scholarship is really about something other than food, the hip food rebellion was an expression of concerns that extended far beyond the kitchen and dinner table. Alienated by modern culture and anxious about future planetary survival, practitioners of the countercuisine looked to the past for ways to reverse the unsustainable tendencies of the global food supply system.

Using bread as an example, I will first sketch some of the countercultural food-related beliefs, practices, and institutions as they emerged in the late 1960s (content). Then I will speculate about why the countercuisine emerged at that particular time (context). Again focusing on bread, I will briefly overview what happened to the countercuisine over the next few decades (change), and then I will suggest why this all should matter to us today (the moral).

Content

Drawing largely on anthropological sources, I define a cuisine as a set of socially situated food behaviors with these components: a limited number of "edible" foods (*selectivity*); a preference for particular ways of preparing food (*technique*); a distinctive set of flavor, textural, and visual characteristics (*aesthetics*); a set of rules for consuming food (*ritual*); and an organized system of producing and distributing the food (*infrastructure*). Embedded in these components are a set of ideas, images, and values (*ideology*) that can be "read" just like any other cultural "text."[10]

While the countercultural food arrangements I am "reading" were never as well-established and formalized as those of China or France, I do consider them to be intelligible enough to merit the use of the word cuisine.[11] Thus, as every parent who confronted a newly vegetarian teenager discovered, the countercuisine was highly selective, elevating vegetable protein over animal, "natural" foods over those deemed to be "poisoned" by chemicals and processing. Food preparation techniques tended to be labor- and time-intensive, requiring some willingness to make dishes "from scratch" using low-tech manual implements – in opposition to the dominant corporate cuisine's reliance on "quick and easy" automated convenience. The aesthetic principles of taste, texture, and presentation were adapted largely from ethnic styles, particularly Mediterranean, Latin American, and Asian dishes. I use the word "adapted" advisedly because in true post-modern style, the countercuisine was more interested in improvisational creativity than in antiquarian authenticity. (For attracting new recruits, the aesthetic eclecticism of Mexican-Italian Blintzes and sweet-and-sour spaghetti sauce was probably a clear marketing improvement over the earlier health food movement, whose cookbooks favored the ascetic banality of cottage cheese patties and walnut-squash loaf.) Similarly, rituals of consumption tended to be informal, irreverent, and spontaneous – the use of fingers or simple implements (especially chopsticks), much sharing, and a deliberate inattentiveness to matters of time, order, dress, microbial contamination, or conventional decorum. Finally, from the very start many participants in the countercuisine were intensely interested in setting up an alternative infrastructure of organic farms (some operated communally, some individually), farmers' markets, cooperative stores, natural foods processors, group houses, vegetarian restaurants and groceries – as well as an increasingly sophisticated informational distribution system of periodicals, newsletters, cookbooks, guides to simple living, and think tanks devoted to agricultural, nutritional, and entrepreneurial research. This elaborate but decentralized infrastructure of alternative institutions most differentiated the countercuisine from the earlier health food underground, whose primary institutions consisted mainly of a few supplement manufacturers, retail outlets, private clinics, and quasi-religious publishers.[12]

As for an underlying ideology, I have detected three major themes that intertwined to give shape and coherence to countercultural food writings and practices. A consumerist theme targeted foods to be avoided, especially chemicalized "plastic" foods. A therapeutic theme had to do with positive concerns for pleasure and identity, particularly a hunger for craftsmanship, leisure, and tradition. Concerned with the integration of self, nature, and community, an organic motif addressed serious issues of production and distribution, that is, how to reconcile private consumption with wider planetary needs.

To illustrate how these three themes intersected, I will focus on one of the distinctively countercultural food practices that emerged in the late 1960s: the baking of whole wheat bread. When hip cooks began to experiment with soybean stroganoff, curried brown rice, or sesame-garbanzo latkes, they also started to bake the dark, heavy, whole-grained loaves described in books like *The Tassajara Bread Book, The Moosewood Cookbook*, and *Laurel's Kitchen*.[13] While the breads were not always very successful, they were a central part of the rebellion. By baking and eating these breads, you were signifying what you were against (consumerist self-protection) and what you were for (therapeutic self-enhancement). In short, bread was part of an oppositional grammar – a set of dichotomies between the devitalized, soft, suburbanized world of Wonder Bread and the vital, sturdy, nutrient-dense peasant world of whole grained breads. In addition to straddling these consumerist and therapeutic elements, this set of dichotomies also pointed towards a holistic or organic sense of how the food system operated.

Plastic versus natural

Wonder Bread was commonly derided as "plastic bread:" tasteless, completely standardized and homogenized, rendered indestructible – indeed virtually embalmed – by chemical additives and plastic wrapping. Homemade whole wheat breads were, on the other hand, "natural." Natural had two components. First, it meant a lack of additives, preservatives, chemicals, "poisons"; because it lacked these adulterants, it seemed more alive and life-sustaining. Sourdough was particularly intriguing because it was made from breathing cultures passed down from one generation to another – an expression of the transcendent vital force (much like yogurt cultures, unprocessed beer, and ripened cheese). The second aspect of natural referred to time: It was old-fashioned, traditional, nostalgic – the opposite of the highly rationalized, multinational food industry. The nostalgia tended to look back to ethnic, regional, peasant societies – all seemingly more honest, simple, and virtuous than the bureaucratic urban-industrial state. Thus, in its most romantic sense natural stood for a free form, eccentric, rough-hewn, unstandardized state of mind – a primitive, folksy resistance to the banal, dehumanizing, massifying tendencies of modern culture.[14]

White versus brown

Paralleling the natural-plastic dichotomy was the opposition between White and Brown: The counterculture did not have much good to say about whiteness, whether in food, clothes, or politics. As one underground newspaper put it, "Don't eat white, eat right, and fight." Whiteness meant Minute Rice, Cool Whip, instant mashed potatoes, white sugar, peeled apples, white tornadoes, white collar, white bucks, bleached cotton, whitewash, white trash, white coats, and, of course, Wonder Bread. Wonder Bread came in for special attack because it was so symbolically rich. Long advertised as the builder of strong bodies in eight ways, Wonder was the best-selling brand. A first cousin by corporate marriage to that other expression of tasteless modern culture, the Twinkie, Wonder Bread's manufacture could be taken to represent the white flight of the 1950s and 1960s. To make clean bread, ITT's bakers removed all colored ingredients (*segregation*), bleached the remaining flour (*suburban school socialization*), and then, to prevent discoloring decay, added strong preservatives and stabilizers (*law enforcement*). Brown bread, on the other hand, may have had a shorter shelf life, but at its peak it seemed hardier, more resilient, more full of innate character. You found this color contrast everywhere. If you visited an underground food coop, you found a preference for brown in everything, from eggs, rice, and sugar to the brown paper bags, wrappers, and signs. The color contrast thus externalized white radicals' alienation from sanitized suburban life – and expressed a neo-primitivist fascination with cultures and struggles of brown people throughout the world.[15]

Convenience versus craft

A virtue of brown bread was that it took some time and skill to produce, and this leads to another important contrast, convenience versus craft. Wonder Bread represented the ultimate in labor-saving convenience, which was (and is) the food industry's main product and primary hope for global expansion. It saved time, effort, attention, and money – it even took virtually no time or effort to chew. Sliced white bread thus may have been one of the world's wonders, but the costs in taste seemed enormous. Thanks to the nutrients added back after processing, it may have been "biochemically adequate" but was spiritually vacuous.

Baking your own bread was a considerably less-efficient way to get nutrients, but that was almost the point. Like most Bohemians, hippies wanted to get off the fast track of modern life, to focus on the here and now. Bread baking was a form of craft therapy and meditation: a way to focus attention, a chance to slow down and spend a few hours in intimate contact with the textures, aromas, and chewy sensuality of creating something from scratch. After tasting her first homebaked loaf, hippy cookbook writer Ita Jones (*The Grub Bag*) wrote that she had to bake her own even if it took a whole afternoon – indeed precisely because it took a whole afternoon. "There's no return to the days when I thought that three cluttered hours were preferable to three, long, calm, warm fragrant ones."[16] Those last adjectives – long, calm, warm, fragrant – captured the nostalgic spirit of the counterculture's fascination with traditional crafts, and I believe that if you scratch the surface of the current vogue for artisan and hearth breads, you will find that same hunger for a mythic world of village butchers, bakers, and candlestick makers.

Product and process

Finally, closely related to the contrast between convenience and craft was the one between product and process. Mainstream consumer culture put a premium on the end product; how it got to you did not really matter. For the sake of time-saving efficiency, the consumer was alienated from the act of production. The counter-cuisine, on the other hand, focused on the process – the opportunity to learn by doing, even from the failures. An underground newspaper's food column – called "Bread Bakin': A Garden of Kneadin'" – put it this way: "Don't be discouraged by a few bricks, or even a lot of bricks – they're all building blocks." It was more important how you got there, what you learned along the way, than what you actually wound up with. Hip food writers liked to quote Kahlil Gibran: "If a man bakes bread with indifference, he bakes a bitter loaf that feeds but half his hunger." But if you really paid attention to the process of baking bread, you would nourish both stomach and soul.[17]

For the most serious politically minded, this attention to process also resulted in a radical ecological analysis of global food networks. This was the organic theme, the growing awareness of ecological connections between field and fork, production and consumption. In addition to presenting recipes, hip food writers sometimes asked hard questions about the way the wheat was grown, milled, and marketed. Who grew it, what chemicals did they use, where did the water come from, how were farm workers treated, how did the grain conglomerates treat the wheat growers, what ties did the mass-market bread corporations like Wonder's ITT have to the Vietnam War, and so on? Attention to process revealed that the production and distribution of bread, like all food, was intensely political. Similarly, in light of the corporate food system's need to range widely and freely around the globe for the cheapest sources of raw materials, thinking about where one's food came from could become a rather subversive act.[18]

If there was a theme emerging from much of this countercultural experimentation with bread and other foods, it was the one of responsibility: By eating "organically" raised foods (that is, those produced with concern for environmental impact), consumers showed they understood that their eating behavior had roots and consequences – implications not just for their own health but also for the state of the economy, environment, and, ultimately, the planet. (Again, Stewart Brand's "Three Laws.") Out of the ferment of the late 1960s countercuisine came a host of activist nutritionists, agricultural economists, New Age therapists, and radical academics who pushed the analysis.[19] And then there were all the hip business people who combined their social and environmental consciousness with old-fashioned entrepreneurial hustle to establish the organic farms, coops, farmers' markets, natural foods supermarket chains, New American Cuisine restaurants, and designer bread boutiques that feed some of us today.[20]

Context

What *was* going on in the 1960s? Why this rejection of mainstream white bread cuisine and culture? There were two contexts for this rebellion – a mounting dissatisfaction with the prevailing nutritional paradigm coupled with a repositioning of the oppositional left. Harvey Levenstein has clearly documented how the New Nutrition arose in the early part of this century and achieved conventional wisdom status after World War II.[21] As expressed by most nutritionists, agronomists, and food technologists, this modernist paradigm had several main tenets.

First, when evaluating whether a diet is "adequate," the whole is less than its parts. That is, as long as you get the right biochemical nutrients – amino acids, vitamins, minerals, and so on – it does not matter what final form they take. Thus, enriched white bread is nutritionally equivalent to whole wheat. A good diet is more a matter of statistics than of taste or tradition.

Second, a healthy diet is a "well-balanced" one, composed of hefty doses of animal protein from two of the four "basic" food groups; such a high-fat, resource-intensive diet is the envy and goal of "developing" peoples all over the world.

Third, America has the cheapest, safest, most varied food supply – and for all of that we should thank our modern food industry, with all its agrichemicals and labor-saving farm machinery, food processing, and mass-marketing. Chemicals are our friends. Moreover, only through such high tech production can we ever hope to feed a rapidly expanding world population.

Fourth, conversely, the supposedly good old days before chemicals and agribusiness were really terrible, characterized by the three "P's": plagues, pestilence, and pellagra. Contrary to nostalgia, Grandma did not know best when it came to providing safe, wholesome food; and neither did Old MacDonald, the family farmer, nor the friendly Mama-Papa corner grocery. Information about what constitutes good food should be left to science, not tradition.[22]

This consensus – fondly referred to as the Golden Age by food technologists – crested in the 1950s and early 1960s as marketers successfully rolled out a host of fabricated, synthesized, plastic-wrapped products, as women's magazines taught suburban cooks how to whip up "gourmet" meals using processed foods (my favorite is the "Eight-Can Casserole") and as the nation's much-loved President Eisenhower unapologetically scarfed hash on a tray in front of the TV set.[23] It was also the heyday of the agrichemicals that helped American farmers achieve yield increases that were unimaginable just a decade earlier. Pushing the modernist envelope, technological utopians of the 1950s predicted a push-button future of fully automated farms, restaurants, and kitchens that would "liberate" humanity once and for all from the drudgery of food production and preparation.[24]

These modernist fantasies were not confined to the science-fiction pulp magazines and Sunday supplements. One notable case of technocratic hubris was the widespread belief held by many highly regarded food policy analysts that, in the near future, a crowded world could readily be fed by foods synthesized from chlorella, a high-protein microalgae that, under laboratory conditions, was able to convert upwards of 20 percent of sunlight to usable nutrients.[25] (Conventional "higher" plants like corn and soy, on the other hand, were able to "capture" less than 1 percent.) By "industrializing" photosynthesis, algae manufacturers would be able to bypass inefficient higher plants and anachronistic family farms altogether. Instead, air-conditioned, fully automated "skyscraper farms" would raise algae on raw sewage in enclosed ponds and then pipeline the protein-rich green "scum" to factories fabricating cheap hamburgers, pasta, and animal feed. As for the slimy taste problem – chlorella had what flavorists termed a high "gag factor" – algae's proponents placed great faith in the culinary skills of food engineers. As Cal Tech biologist James Bonner put it in 1957, "the craft of food technology" would soon be able to create "wholly satisfactory" steaks made entirely from vegetable protein flavored with "tasty synthetics" and "made chewy by addition of a suitable plastic matrix." True, such foods might not be up to elite gourmet standards, but Bonner predicted that in the ultra-utilitarian, modernized future, "human beings will place less emotional importance on the gourmet aspects of food and will eat more to support their body chemistry."[26] Here, then, was the apotheosis of what Harvey Levenstein calls the New Nutrition – the progressive-era belief that in a truly efficient world, one would eat just to live, and what one ate would be dictated by biochemical analysis, not frivolous aesthetics.

Unfortunately for the proponents of algae – and for food technology in general – in the 1960s the biochemical paradigm came under assault from a variety of directions. First, the more affluent, urbane, liberal segments of the general public became less receptive to dietary modernism. Inspired by the three "J's" – Julia Child, John

F. Kennedy, and jet travel – the new gourmets of the 1960s awakened to food's social and aesthetic dimensions. A renewed interest in roots encouraged many to try traditional ethnic and regional cuisines. Conversely they became more resistant to modernistic advice to eat just for biochemical efficiency, especially as consumer advocates questioned the safety of additives that preserved, fortified, and flavored highly processed foods.[27] By the end of the decade, many Americans could appreciate social critic Lewis Mumford's blast at "the brave new world of totalitarian technics." According to Mumford, promoters of algae and other processed panaceas ignored food's role in enhancing conversation, pleasure, and the landscape. The "pathological technical syndrome" of the efficiency experts was "based on a desire to displace the organic with the synthetic and the prefabricated with the scientifically controlled." The world needed more small farms, Mumford suggested, and with that a greater sensitivity to localness and diversity.[28]

Mumford's advocacy of small-scale, decentralized farming had strong roots in American populist culture, but for most of [the twentieth] century proponents of modern agribusiness had successfully argued that the only way to keep up with rapid population growth (the Malthusian trap) was through extensive industrialization and consolidation of agriculture. The Malthusian threat loomed large in the 1960s, as world population increased at an unprecedented rate of 2.5 percent a year – leading to warnings of impending food wars not just from the apocalyptic Paddock brothers and Paul Ehrlich but also from the Food and Agriculture Organization of the United Nations (FAO), National Academy of Sciences, and US Department of Agriculture (USDA).[29] While the USDA encouraged further agricultural rationalization as a way to feed a hungry world, doubts mounted about the safety and efficacy of modern farming's primary tools, especially pesticides, synthetic fertilizers, subsidized irrigation projects, and heavy machinery that destroyed soil while bankrupting over-mortgaged farmers.[30]

Concerns about the environmental impact of modern agriculture dovetailed with new worries about another key tenet of the reigning nutritional paradigm: the necessity and superiority of animal protein. Most of America's postwar agricultural productivity gains went not into feeding the world's hungry but into producing the corn and soybeans that fattened cattle, which in turn fattened consumers of steaks and fast-food hamburgers. Mainstream food marketers responded to the cholesterol scare of the 1960s with a proliferation of low-calorie, low-fat products, but disaffected youth looked for more comprehensive, subversive solutions. Thus, in the late 1960s a Berkeley graduate student, Frances Moore Lappe went to the library to look for research on feed-grain ratios, protein complementarity, and the ecological impact of animal production. The result – *Diet for a Small Planet* – was perhaps the best-selling book of the countercuisine. Lappe's basic point was simple: By feeding grains to farm animals, Americans were literally throwing away most of their food. A grain-fed North American steer ate twenty-one pounds of vegetable protein for every pound of protein it delivered to the steak eater. In addition to squandering food and clogging our arteries, the animal industry depleted soil, water, and energy resources – all of which would be in short supply in a world whose population was doubling every few decades.[31]

Lappe's argument was by no means new. For many years Malthusians had been saying that rapid population growth, coupled with degradation of farmlands, threatened to reduce Anglo-American beef eaters to "coolie rations" – an "Asian" peasant cuisine based on grains and legumes, with little or no animal protein. But rather than advocate a reduction in steak consumption, most Malthusians urged a reduction in the number of steak consumers, that is, birth control. (Or, as an alternative way to stave off an involuntarily vegetarian future, Cornucopians pushed high-tech agriculture.)[32] Where Lappe differed was not in her statistics but in her willingness to advocate the once unthinkable route – the diet of grains and beans. Calling the scaremongers' bluff, Lappe suggested that perhaps those "coolie rations" were not so unpalatable after all! To prove it, after presenting her research, she provided tasty peasant recipes – and headed off to become "the Julia Child of the Soybean Circuit."

Lappe's book sold millions of copies because her holistic, ecological perspective on meat struck a responsive chord with a young white, largely middle-class audience who shared her need to "think globally, act locally" – the working motto of the new environmental movement. Environmentalism filled an oppositional void left by dissatisfaction with the civil rights and antiwar movements, far-leftist revolutionary socialism, and the druggy urban counterculture. Whereas liberal white youths had once rallied to the cause of racial integration, by the end of the decade that movement had been taken over by exclusionary Black Power advocates. The antiwar movement was also in a rut, especially after the Democratic Convention debacle of 1968 produced the election of Richard Nixon and the lunatic rantings of the Weathermen. While demonstrations continued, peaceful protest was sporadic and only partially effective; yet the confrontational "street-fighting" tactics of the "revolutionary" left were dangerously counterproductive. The internal disputes of assorted Marxist-Leninist factions seemed irrelevant to more pressing worries about oil spills, urban smog alerts, insecticides like DDT in breast milk, poisoned birds, and burning industrial rivers, not to mention the warnings of overpopulation and famine. This sense of impending catastrophe also induced many young people to think twice about the hip drug culture, which by the end of the decade was producing far too many "bad trips." If civilization was about to collapse, perhaps the best hip survivalist strategy was to toughen up, cleanse the body of "poisons," and eat right. Thus, *The Last Whole Earth Catalog* recommended a natural foods cookbook (*Passport to Survival*): "Emergency procedures and forethoughts stored here will serve you come holocaust, catastrophe, or unemployment."[33]

In this polarized, apocalyptic climate of 1968–70, environmentalism emerged as a peaceful, pastoral, pragmatic alternative. Environmentalism gave dissidents a safe cover; even *Time* and President Nixon praised Earth Day (April 22, 1970). But underneath its placid feel-good surface, ecology could be, in the words of one popular text, "the subversive science"; for to fix the mess that industrial society had created, everything would have to be changed. As eco-poet Gary Snyder put it, "You can't be serious about the environment without being a revolutionary."[34] Like the women's movement that emerged at about the same time, environmentalism improved on the "revolutionary" rhetoric surrounding other leftist activities by requiring that you walked the way you talked. Environmentalism entailed more than attending demonstrations and reading radical tracts; you had to change the way you lived: transportation, housing, energy use, and, most of all, food.

Of all the household reforms dictated by ecological living, dietary change seemed the most radical and least cooptable step (especially for young people who did not yet have large investments in energy-hogging cars, houses, and appliances). Dietary radicalism could be lived 365 days a year, three times a day. If, as all leftists knew, the personal was political, what could be more personal than eating? And what could be more political than challenging America's largest industry, the food business? Given the deep-seated, ultra-conservative nature of socialized food habits, radical dietary change required considerable self-scrutiny and self-sacrifice. It was also quite inconvenient, since finding natural foods and preparing them involved effort and skill – hence the strong push to establish an alternative infrastructure to supply and inform the countercuisine. But those who successfully completed the transition could experience the consumerist security of avoiding "poisons," the therapeutic high of a newfound identity, and the organic tranquility that came from living in tune with planetary needs in the long run.

Change

Of course, it did not quite work out as the countercuisine's rhapsodists hoped. The hegemonic incorporation process soon came into play and much of the natural foods movement was safely contained by a food industry that, if anything, is more consolidated, chemicalized, and globalized now than it was in the 1960s. It is safe to say that corporate food executives were not too thrilled by the more subversive aspects of the countercuisine – particularly the emerging radical analysis of the food system. Organic agriculture, in particular, underwent very strong ridicule in the early 1970s, as journalists echoed the claims of industry-subsidized food scientists that, without agrichemicals, millions would starve. The news media also belittled the organic movement's preference for localized, small-scale production and distribution, which was obviously contrary to the multinational direction of the food industry. But food marketers also appreciated that some of the hip critics struck a deep chord in middle-class urban culture – especially the nostalgia for slower, simpler, more honest and intimate times wrapped up in the interest in natural and ethnic foods and the lost craftsmanship of cooking and baking. Also, as the news media highlighted mounting scientific debate about the old nutritional paradigm, more Americans in the 1970s began to worry about pesticides, additives, meat, and cholesterol. In the 1980s the US government's Dietary Guidelines would reinforce some of these health concerns – particularly the negative consumerist uneasiness about fat, sugar, and sodium. Reports about the protective qualities of fiber seemed to confirm the countercuisine's veneration of brown breads, whole grains, and fresh vegetables.[35]

Consumer "demographics" also impressed food marketers. The fact that these nostalgic, health-conscious consumers tended to come from the more affluent part of the population made it even more imperative that the food industry respond in some way, as modern marketing theory was coming to appreciate the virtues of market segmentation. Gone were the days when a company could try to capture a single mass market with one product – say Kellogg's Corn Flakes or Continental Baking's Wonder Bread. Now it appeared that they would need to cater to different "segments" and especially to the people with the more upscale demographics. If the richer half or third of the population wanted natural, old-fashioned foods, then the modern food industry would just have to give it to them – perhaps not quite the same stuff that the hip gourmets of Berkeley were creating but a close enough facsimile to appease most patrons of suburban supermarkets and casual theme-restaurant chains. And that is how we got some of the products that now take up considerable supermarket shelf space, such as natural cereals, the granolas and granola bars, yogurts, ethnic frozen dinners, veggie burgers, salad bars with alfalfa sprouts and sunflower seeds, Celestial Seasonings herbal teas, Ben and Jerry's ecologically right-eous premium ice cream, and "lite" versions of virtually everything.[36]

Rather than recapitulate the full progression from countercuisine to Lean Cuisine, I will focus on the evolution of those early hippy wholewheat "bricks" into what the food industry calls "variety or specialty breads," the consumption of which sur-passed that of plain white bread among the more affluent shoppers of the 1980s. The incorporation process was gradual. At first, mass-market bread companies simply tried to coopt countercultural symbols: the loaves in brown wrappers with key words like "natural," "wholesome," and "whole-grained," even though the whole wheat was only a tiny percentage of the flour and the extra fiber sometimes came from wood pulp. Or the old-fashioned, craftsman-like feel of "rustic" or "country" breads from Pepperidge Farm, an acquisition of Campbell's Soup. Or the vaguely ethnic or European aura of Stella D'Oro, Lender's, or Entenmann's, all also acquired by major food conglommerates.[37]

While these packaged baked goods captured some of the look of tradition, they lacked the texture, aroma, and taste. Filling that niche were new "boutique" baker-ies, many of them established and staffed by ex-hippies who, once the counterculture disbanded in the early 1970s, professionalized their food interests by traveling to Europe to study with top chefs and bakers who were catering to similar longings felt elsewhere in the West. Returning home, they showed Americans what real peasant bread tasted like, first in the California-Cuisine style of panethnic bistros (also set up by countercuisine veterans) that dotted the chic gourmet ghettoes of coastal cities, university towns, and upper-class resorts, and then (in the later 1980s and 1990s) in their own craft bakeries, which retailed rustic sourdough, sesame semolina, and savory olive breads for four to six dollars a loaf.[38] Ironically, by importing these Old World foods, they furthered the culinary globalization of foodways that had begun with the Columbian Exchange, if not before.

The middle class's flirtation with these "artisan breads" was a bit unsettling for packaged bread manufacturers. Instead of reviving the once-ubiquitous neighbor-hood "made-from-scratch" bakeries, the new hip bread boutiques probably acceler-ated their disappearance, for supermarkets responded with their own in-store bakeries, which increased from about 2,000 in 1972 to over 30,000 today (com-pared with around 350 of the independent boutiques). Retailing limp baguettes for 99 cents or pale imitations of seven-grain bread for $1.98, the in-store bakeries now account for about half of the nation's $18 billion sales of baked goods. Like the supermarket produce sections, which also boomed in response to affluent shoppers' demand for healthier foods, these in-store bakeries are quite profitable, for the fresh-baked variety loaves command a higher price than packaged breads, although they do not cost a lot more to produce.[39]

The supermarket in-store unit is the corner bakery of our day and has some of the same appeal on the surface: the personal, over-the counter service, the inviting racks of warm loaves and sugary confections, the cute awnings, free samples, and most important, the freshly baked aroma that pervades the whole store. Sometimes you can even see what looks like an oven and thus vicariously participate in the baking process, much as diners at chic restaurants with exposed demonstration kitchens think they are watching dinner being cooked. But it is mostly an illusion. There simply are not enough scratch bakers left to staff every supermarket, and no big chain wants to pay the high costs of training and keeping them, so most of the skilled mixing work – and much of the baking, too – is done at centralized wholesale locations, often in highly automated German tunnel ovens that are capable of turning out fairly sophisticated crusty loaves and flat breads. (As is always the case when labor is too expensive or troublesome, Fordist automation rules.) If anything is actually baked in the store, it is usually from frozen dough, or more likely it is a pre-cooked "par-baked" loaf that is heated (or "finished") just enough to provide the warmth and yeasty smell. And the crunchiness of the crust can be adjusted by the type of plastic bag it is sold in.[40]

The main reason for this persistence of the status quo is that convenience – the food industry's strongest suit – still sells. While consumers have shown a nostalgia for craftsmanship, most really do not want to spend much time or energy baking, or even shopping for bread. (Similarly, while many of us envy the impressive health profile of the traditional Mediterranean diet, few want the hard labor that went along with it.) Most consumers would rather buy a finished product that looks as if a skilled craftsman did it; and to save time, they would just as soon buy it in the same supermarket where they pick up their milk, laundry detergent, and drug prescription.

To be sure, the truly discerning (and richest) bread gourmets may still take the time to patronize the boutiques, where the craftsmanship, quality, and freshness are real – and there is no doubt that these are increasing. Some industry observers see a potential for as many as 3,000 more over the next few years. But it is doubtful that they will remain independent for long as they undergo the same pressures for conglomeration that drives the mainstream food industry. A few franchise operations are already underway, and it is likely that we will soon see a shakeout and consolidation similar to what has happened in premium ice cream, bagels, and coffee. Indeed, one gourmet bread franchiser recently stated that he hopes to do for bread what Starbuck's has done for coffee. So beware the illusion of the folksy corner bakery. The retail units may have righteous populist names like Northern Plains, Prairie Grain, and Montana Gold, but they will be centralized corporate affairs ripe for eventual takeover by the really big players – General Mills, Campbell's, Phillip Morris, and so forth. True, McDonald's aborted its recent Hearth Express experiment in which unwrapped, locally baked loaves of "hearth breads" were sold along with take-out roasted chicken and meat loaf, but just because McDonald's backed off does not mean that Boston Market or T. G. I. Friday's will do the same. Like the processors and supermarkets, the restaurant chains are very interested in high-profit variety breads.[41]

But why should I care about these trends? If we, the upper-middle-class writers and readers of this volume, can find and afford this great bread, is not that what counts? I suppose the answer is "yes," if one is content with a purely privatistic, myopic view of food. But, as this chapter shows, I am too much a child of the 1960s. I keep thinking about the global picture. As my hippy mentors wrote, it is not the product, it is the process. If we think only about the end product rather than the process by which it was made, then the food industry will always be able to come up with products that at least superficially cater to our worries about health, skill, tradition, and community. But if we start asking questions about the process by which grain was transformed into the bread that sustains and entertains us, then we are not likely to be so easily appeased. What actually is in this stuff anyway? Is it really so wholesome? Who baked it and under what conditions? Thinking about process means asking why a peasant bread costs $5.00, while real peasants abroad cannot buy plain wheat and poor people here can barely afford store-bought white bread. And it means asking about environment and agriculture: Where did the plastic bag come from and where will it go after I discard it? How will the greenhouse effect affect grain production? Is our global seed stock genetically diverse enough to withstand the inevitable attack of the next pesticide-resistant fungus or fly? Did the farmer get a fair share of the profits? And down the road will that farmer's land be in good enough condition to feed our grandchildren's grandchildren? These are the questions that really matter.[42] And no amount of postmodern marketing wizardry will answer them or make them go away.

NOTES

1   *The Last Whole Earth Catalog* (Menlo Park, Calif.: Portolo Institute, 1971), 43.
2   "People's Pods," *Good Times*, July 24, 1969, p. 14.
3   What I am describing here is an analysis of product's "ecological wake." For more on this type of environmental auditing, see Alan Durning, *How Much is Enough? The Consumer Society and the Future of the Earth* (New York: Norton, 1992); Mathis Wackernagel and William Rees, *Our Ecological Footprint: Reducing Human Impact on the Earth* (Barioola Island BC: New Society Publishers, 1996); Martin Teitel, *Rain Forest in Your Kitchen: The Hidden Connection between Extinction and Your Supermarket* (Washington, DC: Island Press, 1992); Alessandro Bonanno, et al., *From Columbus to Conagra: The Globalization of Agriculture and Food* (Lawrence: University Press of Kansas, 1994); Geoff Tansey and Tony Worsley, *The Food System: A Guide* (London: Earthscan, 1995). Two particularly fine historical audits of individual foodstuffs are Sidney W. Mintz's *Sweetness and Power: The Place of Sugar in Modern History* (New York: Viking, 1985), and the chapters on grain and meat in William Cronon's *Nature's Metropolis: Chicago and the Great West* (New York: Norton, 1991), pp. 97–147, 207–59.
4   Frances Moore Lappe, *Diet for a Small Planet* (New York: Ballantine, 1971); Edward Espe Brown, *The Tassajara Bread Book* (Berkeley: Shambala Publications, 1970).
5   Ellen Buchman Ewald, *Recipes for a Small Planet* (New York: Ballantine, 1973); Anna Thomas, *The Vegetarian Epicure* (New York: Vintage, 1972).
6   On hegemony theory: Dick Hebdige, *Subculture: The Meaning of Style* (London: Methuen, 1979); Stuart Hall, et al., *Resistance through Rituals* (London: Hutchison, 1976); Todd Gitlin, *The Whole World is Watching: Mass Media in the Making and Unmaking of the New Left* (Berkeley: University of Calfornia Press, 1980).
7   Warren Belasco, *Appetite for Change: How the Counterculture Took on the Food Industry* (Ithaca: Cornell University Press, 1993).
8   Berkeley gardener, "People's Pods," 14.

9   For the most biased historical treatment of "food faddism," see Gerald Carson, *Cornflake Crusade* (New York: Rinehart, 1957); Ronald Deutsch, *The Nuts Among the Berries* (New York: Ballantine, 1961). For more recent and balanced appraisals: James C. Whorton, *Crusaders for Fitness: The History of American Health Reformers* (Princeton: Princeton University Press, 1982); Harvey Green, *Fit for America: Health, Fitness, and American Society* (New York: Pantheon, 1986); Ronald G. Walters, *American Reformers, 1815–1860* (New York: Hill and Wang, 1978), 145–72; Harvey Levenstein, *Revolution at the Table: The Transformation aof the American Diet* (New York: Oxford University Press, 1988), 86–97; and Levenstein, *Paradox of Plenty: A Social History of Eating in Modern America* (New York: Oxford, 1993), 178–94. For journalistic treatment of the countercuisine: *Appetite for Change*, 154–82.

10 My understanding of "cuisine" has been shaped particularly by Peter Farb and George Armelagos, *Consuming Passions: The Anthropology of Eating* (Noston: Houghton Mifflin Co., 1980), 190–8; Elizabeth Rozin, "The Structure of Cuisine," in Lewis M. Barker, ed., *The Psychobiology of Human Food Selection* (Westport CT: AVI Publishing, 1982), 189–203; Roland Barthes, "Toward a Psychosociology of Contemporary Food Consumption," in Robert Forster and Orest Ranum, eds., *Food and Drink in History* (Baltimore: Johns Hopkins University Press, 1979), 166–73; Charles Camp, *American Foodways* (Little Rock: August House, 1989).

11 The "reading" of the countercuisine in the rest of this section is drawn from Belasco, *Appetite for Change*, 15–108.

12 On the countercultural infrastructure in general: John Case and Rosemary C. R. Taylor, eds., *Co-ops, Communes, and Collectives: Experiments in Social Change in the 1960s and 1970s* (New York: Pantheon, 1979).

13 Brown, *Tassajara Bread Book*; Mollie Katzen, *The Moosewood Cookbook* (Berkeley: Ten Speed Press, 1977); Laurel Robertson, Carol Flinders, and Bronwen Godfrey, *Laurel's Kitchen* (New York: Bantam Books, 1978).

14 Belasco, *Appetite for Change*, 37–42.

15 *Ibid.*, 48–50. In a sense the neo-primitivistic attraction to brown-ness had deeper roots in the ambivalence of affluent Westerners towards the fruits of their own political and economic mastery of third-world societies. Thus, in the 1920s rich metropolitan intellectuals on both sides of the Atlantic found themselves attracted to black music (jazz), sexuality (Josephine Baker), and pigments themselves (Coco Chanel's tanning craze). Jan Nederveen Pieterse, *White on Black: Images of Africa and Blacks in Western Popular Culture* (New Haven: Yale University Press, 1992).

16 Ita Jones, "Grub Bag," *Liberation News Service* #135, January 30, 1969, p. 4; Belasco, *Appetite for Change*, 50–4.

17 mother bird, "Bread Bakin': A Garden of Kneadin'," *Northwest Passage*, January 10, 1972, p. 4; Belasco, *Appetite for Change*, 46–8.

18 Belasco, *Appetite for Change*, 32–4, 68–76. Claude Fischler makes a related point in "The Mad Cow Crisis," in Raymond Grew, ed., *Food in Global History* (Boulder, Co: Westview Press, 1999): the modern food system's vast distance between process and product leads to considerable consumer distrust and anxiety, but while Fischler tends to dismiss such sentiment as verging on paranoia, I see it as merited and, if channelled constructively, politically useful.

19 Examples of early radical analysis of the food system by countercuisine veterans: Jim Hightower, *Eat Your Heart Out: Food Profiteering in America* (New York: Crown Publishers, 1975); Catherine Lerza and Michael Jacobson, eds., *Food for People, Not for Profit* (New York: Ballantine Books, 1975); Frances Moore Lappe, *Diet for a Small Planet* (New York: Ballantine, 1971); Gene Marine and Judith Van Allen, *Food Pollution: The Violation of Our Inner Ecology* (New York: Holt, Rinchart and Winston,

1972); Joan Dye Gussow, ed., *The Feeding Web: Issues in Nutritional Ecology* (Palo Alto: Bull Publishing, 1978). Post-countercultural think tanks devoted to alternative approaches include: Michael Jacobson's Center for the Study of Science in the Public Interest, Frances Moore Lappe's Institute for Food and Development Policy, Wes Jackson's Land Institute, John Todd's New Alchemy Institute, and Amory and Hunter Lovins' Rocky Mountain Institute.

20   On hip entrepreneurs: Belasco, *Appetite for Change*, 94–108. Two of the most influential hip businesses of the 1980s and 1990s: Alice Water's Chez Panisse, the Berkeley training school for countless environmentally aware chefs and bakers, and Whole Foods, the quasi-organic/gourmet supermarket chain from Austin that is rapidly expanding throughout the United States.

21   Levenstein, *Revolution at the Table*, especially 72–85, 147–60; *Paradox of Plenty*, 3–23, 53–130; Ross Hume Hall, *Food for Nought: The Decline in Nutrition* (New York: Vintage, 1976); Laura Shapiro, *Perfection Salad: Women and Cooking at the Turn of the Century* (New York: Farrar, Straus, and Giroux, 1986); Gussow, ed., *The Feeding Web*, 119–204.

22   For the response of nutritional "orthodoxy" to the countercuisine: Belasco, *Appetite for Change*, 111–31.

23   Jane and Michael Stern, *Square Meals*, 274; Levenstein, *Paradox of Plenty*, 120; Gerry Schremp, *Kitchen Culture: Fifty Years of Food Fads* (New York: Pharos Books, 1991), 1–96.

24   On agricultural yields: Lester Brown, et al., *Vital Signs: The Trends that are Shaping Our Future* (New York: Norton, 1994), 29; Gilbert C. Fite, *American Farmers: The New Minority* (Bloomington: Indiana University Press, 1981), 80–197. For technological utopian visions: Robert Brittain, *Let There Be Bread* (New York: Simon and Schuster, 1952); Jacob Rosin and Max Eastman, *The Road to Abundance* (New York: McGraw-Hill, 1953); Victor Cohn, *1999: Our Hopeful Future* (Indianapolis: Bobbs-Merrill, 1956); Joseph J., Corn, ed., *Imagining Tomorrow: History, Technology, and the American Future* (Cambridge: MIT Press, 1986).

25   For a fuller treatment of the chlorella story: Warren Belasco, "Algae Burgers for a Hungry World? The Rise and Fall of Chlorella Cuisine," *Technology and Culture* (July 1997).

26   *Proceedings of "The Next Hundred Years": A Symposium* (New York: Seagram's, 1957), 31.

27   Levenstein, *Paradox of Plenty*, 131–43; Jane and Michael Stern, *American Gourmet* (New York: Harper Collins, 1991); Warren Belasco, "Ethnic Fast Foods: The Corporate Melting Pot," *Food and Foodways*, 2 (1987), 1–30; Rachel Carson, *Silent Spring* (Boston: Houghton Mifflin, 1962); Beatrice Trum Hunter, *Consumers Beware! Your Food and What's Been Done to It* (New York: Simon and Schuster, 1971).

28   Lewis Mumford, "Closing Statement," in *Future Environments of North America*, F. Fraser Darling and John P. Milton, eds. (Garden City, NY: Natural History Press, 1966), 724–5.

29   Paul Ehrlich, *The Population Bomb* (New York: Bantam, 1968); William and Paul Paddock, *Famine 1975! America's Decision: Who Will Survive?* (Boston: Little Brown, 1967); P. V. Sukhatme, "The World's Hunger and Future Needs in Food Supplies," *Journal of the Royal Statistical Society*, 124:4 (1961), 463–525; National Academy of Sciences, *Resources and Man* (San Francisco: W. H. Freeman, 1969), 43–108; Joseph W. Willett, "A Single Chariot with 2 Horses: The Population and Food Race," *Contours of Change* (Washington: USDA, 1970), 247–50.

30   Carson, *Silent Spring*; Hightower, *Eat Your Heart Out*, 154–217; Hall, *Food for Nought*, 88–205.

31   Lappe tells her story in *Diet for a Small Planet: Tenth Anniversary Edition* (New York: Ballantine, 1982).

32   Earlier Malthusian warnings about the Asian population/culinary menace are discussed in Walter B. Pitkin, *Must We Fight Japan?* (New York: Century, 1921); Edward M. East, *Mankind at the Crossroads* (New York: Charles Scribner's Sons, 1924); William Vogt, *The Road to Survival* (New York: William Sloane Associates, 1948). Cornucopian versions: J. Russell Smith, *The World's Food Resources* (New York: Henry Holt, 1919); Robert J. McFall, "Is Food the Limiting Factor in Population Growth?," *The Yale Review*, January 1926, pp. 297–316; E. E. DeTurk, ed., *Freedom from Want: A Survey of the Possibilities of Meeting the World's Food Needs in Chronica Botanca*, 2:4 (1948), 207–84. For an excellent overview of the food/population debate, see Joel E. Cohen, *How Many People Can the Earth Support?* (New York: Norton, 1995).

33   *The Last Whole Earth Catalog* (Menlo Park, CA: Portola Institute, 1971), 198; Belasco, *Appetite for Change*, 15–42.

34   Peter R. Jannsen, "Where the Action Is," *Ecotactics: The Sierra Club Handbook for Environmental Activists*, John G. Mitchell, ed. (New York: Pocket Books, 1970), 55; Paul Shepherd and David McKinley, eds., *The Subversive Science – Essays Toward an Ecology of Man* (Boston: Houghton Mifflin, 1969).

35   Belasco, *Appetite for Change*, 109–99.

36   *Ibid.*, 185–251.

37   "Analysis of Baked Goods," *Food Engineering*, August 1980, 81–2; Danielle K. Mooney, *Mass-Merchandised Healthy Foods: Markets, Trends* (Stamford CT: Business Communications Co., 1982), 62–9; "Easing of Bread Ad Ban Asked," *Advertising Age*, June 27, 1983, p. 16. Kenneth Wylie, "Bread Returns to Its Humble Beginnings," *Advertising Age*, May 3, 1984, p. M62; "It's Natural, It's Organic, Or Is It?" *Consumer Reports*, July 1980, p. 411; Belasco, *Appetite for Change*, 218–24, 229–36.

38   "New Restaurant-Bakery Combinations Taking Off," *Nation's Restaurant News*, February 3, 1986, p. 1; Florence Fabricant, "Fresh from the Baker: A New Staff of Life," *The New York Times*, November 11, 1992, p. C1; Danielle Forestier, Joe Ortiz, Steven Sullivan, "The Making of the Ultimate Loaf," panel at the symposium, "Bread: A Language of Life," California Academy of Sciences, San Francisco CA, March 2, 1996.

39   Doug Krumrei, "Great Harvest of Specialty Breads," *Bakery Production and Marketing*, September 1994, p. 44; "Instore Bakeries: the Top 10 Categories," *Supermarket Business*, June 1994, p. 89; "Let the Good Times Roll," *Bakery Production and Marketing*, June 24, 1995, p. 1; Roseanne Harper, "Bred to Rise," *Supermarket News*, January 30, 1995, p. 21.

40   Dan Malovany, "How New Products Drive Automation," *Bakery Production and Marketing*, June 24, 1995, p. 18; Pat Lewis, "Evolution of In-Store Bakeries," *Supermarket News*, December 28, 1992, p. 70; "Savor the Flavor," *Bakery Production and Marketing*, March 24, 1995, p. 42.

41   "Doing for Bread What Starbucks Has Done for Coffee," *Brandweek*, April 10, 1995, p. 30; "Bake Shop Bonanza," *Restaurant Hospitality*, September 1994, p. 78; Louise Kramer, "McDonald's Deep-Sixes Test of Hearth Express Concept," *Brandweek*, July 17, 1995, p.1.

42   For important questions about the global food system: Lester Brown, *Who Will Feed China?* (New York: Norton, 1995); Brown, *Tough Choices: Facing the Challenge of Food Scarcity* (New York: Norton, 1996); Joan Dye Gussow, *Chicken Little, Tomato Sauce and Agriculture: Who Will Produce Tomorrow's Food?* (New York: Bootstrap Press, 1991); Jack Ralph Kloppenburg, *First the Seed: The Political Economy of Plant Biotechnology, 1492–2000* (Cambridge: Cambridge University Press, 1988); Cary Fowler and Pat Mooney, *Shattering: Food, Politics, and the Loss of Genetic Diversity*

(Tucson: University of Arizona Press, 1990); Elizabeth Ann R. Bird, et al., eds., *Planting the Future: Developing an Agriculture that Sustains Land and Community* (Ames: Iowa State University Press, 1995); Lawrence Busch, et al., ed., *Plants, Power and Profit* (Oxford: Basil Blackwell, 1991); Robin Mather, *A Garden of Unearthly Delights: Bioengineering and the Future of Food* (New York: Penguin, 1996).

14

Industrial *Tortillas* and Folkloric Pepsi: The Nutritional Consequences of Hybrid Cuisines in Mexico

Jeffrey M. Pilcher

In January 1999, neoliberal President Ernesto Zedillo eliminated the long-standing subsidy on Mexico's daily staple, corn *tortillas*. It was intended as an efficiency measure to improve competitiveness in the global economy, but many saw the decree as an end to the welfare state that had assured political domination for the ruling party for most of the twentieth century. Nevertheless, as neighborhood *tortilla* factories throughout Mexico City began to close – unable to compete, without the subsidy, against the industrial conglomerate Maseca, a producer of dehydrated *tortilla* flour – Mexicans feared the end of another era: more than two thousand years of eating *tortillas* made from freshly ground corn.[1] This essay will examine the twentieth-century transformation of Mexican cuisine, both the mechanization of Native American *tortilla* making and the introduction of Western-style industrial processed foods. The modernization of food production has been instrumental in drawing *campesinos* into the market economy, but it has done so in a halting and incomplete fashion, creating culinary versions of what Nestor García Canclini termed "hybrid cultures." While this half-baked globalization allowed people to retain elements of rural, often-indigenous identities by "entering and leaving modernity," many paid a high nutritional price, suspended between traditional and modern diets, eating the worst of both worlds.[2]

The modernization of *tortilla* production held enormous promise at the dawn of the twentieth century, because Mexico's subsistence diet involved tremendous work for both male farmers and female cooks. Women labored for hours each morning over the pre-Hispanic *metate* (saddle quern) to feed their families *tortillas*. Despite this backbreaking daily chore, when mechanical mills capable of grinding the moist corn dough began arriving in rural communities in the 1920s and 1930s, women patronized the establishments only with great hesitancy. Their skepticism about the new technology reflected not a reflexive peasant conservatism but justified concerns about the expense of using the mills and about their own identity within the family. The so-called Green Revolution of agricultural modernization was greeted with similar concern by *campesinos* following World War II because of the high cost of hybrid seeds and chemical fertilizers and pesticides, as well as the government's failure to supply adequate irrigation, silos, and transportation. Productivity surged in the 1960s, allowing the government to supply cheap food to urban consumers, thereby helping to hold down the pressure for higher industrial wages. As a result, already low rural incomes plummeted further, driving millions of people to the cities in search of work and adding to the pool of surplus labor. Food policy in Mexico, as in so many postcolonial nations, has therefore sacrificed the countryside in search of industrial development.[3]

The great challenge for Mexico and other emerging countries has been to realize the possibilities of nationalism and industrialization in a democratic manner that preserves the distinctiveness of local cultures. Few areas can claim greater urgency in this regard than food policy. The history of postcolonial Africa and India clearly demonstrates the need for democratic governance of food distribution. Despite a rapidly growing population, India has been spared from famine, not because of the agricultural gains of the so-called Green Revolution but rather through political mechanisms for assuring that the hungriest people get food. Starvation in Africa has meanwhile resulted largely from the actions of armed bands that confiscate and sell food aid shipments and locally grown crops, leaving people to die.[4]

Assuring the nutritional health of the poor is equally difficult without respect for local cooking traditions. Peasant cultures throughout the world have developed nutritionally balanced diets of complementary vegetable proteins, for example, rice and soybeans in Asia, or maize and beans in the Americas, to replace expensive animal proteins. Industrial processed foods such as powdered milk can supplement these diets in important ways, but the devaluation of traditional cooking through transnational advertising and misplaced ideals of modernity has primarily increased the consumption of junk foods based on fats and sugars. The gravest risks lie in the transition between traditional and industrial diets, as poor Mexicans substitute *alimentos pacotilla* (snack foods) for vegetable proteins, but cannot afford the meats that supply protein to the diets of the rich.[5]

The rising domination of the Maseca corporation over Mexican corn production illustrates an equally important point for cultural studies: the homogenizing effects of national food processing companies may pose as great a threat to local cultures as the more visible cultural imperialism represented by Ronald McDonald. With government assistance, Maseca executives are well on the way to achieving their dream of processing all of the maize in Mexico, removing the "imperfections" that many people believe give *tortillas* their character. Global corporations have meanwhile learned that to compete successfully in national markets they need to modify their products to suit native consumers. A Big Mac with fries may taste exactly the same in Mexico City, Beijing, or Oak Brook, but even McDonald's has adapted to local markets, either by serving salsa with the fries or by posing the eponymous clown as Buddha. No doubt the world will continue to grow more like the United States, as the Cassandras of cultural imperialism have warned, but the converse is equally true, as ever more people in the United States eat Maseca *tortillas*. The rise of a uniquely Mexican *tortilla* industry therefore merits careful analysis.

From the *Metate* to Maseca

The modernization of food production in Mexico has been one of the primary tools for incorporating subsistence peasants into the market economy. The first step in this process came at the beginning of the twentieth century with the development of corn mills to replace laborious hand grinding of corn dough on the *metate*. By midcentury, a cottage industry of *tortilla* factories had automated the skills of patting out and cooking *tortillas*. Fifty years later, corn processing had been centralized in the hands of industrial conglomerates producing dehydrated *tortilla* flour. Each change entailed a loss of taste and texture, to the point that the modern *tortilla* would be virtually unrecognizable to peasant women of a century before. Moreover, agricultural modernization and government policies favoring urban industry depressed rural incomes, ultimately forcing the peasants of Chiapas into rebellion under the name of the agrarian martyr Emiliano Zapata.

Native Americans often referred to themselves as the people of corn, and the basically vegetarian diet eaten by all but a small nobility in pre-Hispanic Mesoamerica clearly justified such identification. Even though maize provided as much as 80 percent of the daily intake, when combined with beans, chiles, and squash, it formed the basis for a nutritionally balanced diet. The complementarity between corn and beans, each of which supplied amino acids missing in the other, assured a regular supply of high-quality proteins in the absence of European domesticated animals such as cattle, pigs, or chickens. The Aztec empire, with a population that has been estimated at as high as 25 million people, comprised diverse regional cuisines comparable with those of China and India. For example, a wide variety of chile peppers imparted subtle flavors to the *moles* (chile pepper stews) of the Mixtecs and Zapotecs in what is now the southern state of Oaxaca, while along the Gulf Coast in the Huasteca (the land of plenty), Totonac Indians specialized in creating *tamales*, dumplings wrapped in cornhusks.[6]

The labor-intensive cooking techniques developed by pre-Hispanic *campesinas* continued to dominate Mexican kitchens at the start of the twentieth century. The basic utensil was the *metate*, a tablet of black volcanic rock, sloping forward on three stubby legs, used to grind corn for *tortillas* and *tamales*, chiles and seeds for sauces, and fruits and chocolate to drink. Women spent up to five hours each day preparing *tortillas* to feed their families. Work began the night before, when the woman simmered the corn in a solution of mineral lime to make *nixtamal*. She arose before dawn to grind the corn into a moist dough called *masa*, and immediately before each meal, she deftly patted the dough into flat, round *tortillas* and cooked them briefly over the *comal*, an earthenware griddle. Elite stereotypes of Native Americans as long-suffering wretches owed much to the image of women kneeling at the *metate*. *Tortillas* could not be saved for the following day, or even the next meal, because they became hard and inedible in a few hours. The dough likewise would not keep more than a day before it began to ferment.[7]

Hard labor at the *metate* at least gave women status and identity within the family and the community. Historian Wendy Waters has examined these social implications using the field notes of anthropological studies conducted from the 1920s to the 1940s in Tepoztlán, Morelos. *Tortilla* making was so essential to domestic life that no woman in the village became eligible for marriage until she had demonstrated this skill. Men complimented women by praising their *tortillas*, and some even claimed to be able to identify the unique taste and texture of corn ground on their wives' *metate*. Women expressed affection through their role of feeding the family, offering favorite children extra helpings of beans or reserving for them the best *tortillas*. As a result, children were sensitive to the size of their portions and to the order in which they were fed. Food served to communicate anger as well as love; a wife could burn her husband's *tortillas* if she suspected him of infidelity.[8] The symbolic connections between cook and food, already present in the daily preparation of *tortillas*, beans, and chile peppers, grew exponentially during festive meals, when women spent whole days and nights bent over their *metates* preparing *moles* and *tamales*. They undertook such arduous work to help assure the stability of the entire community – indeed, memories of *mole* continue to draw modern migrant workers home each year to participate – and women gained respect and authority as a result.[9]

Thus, although water-powered grain mills had come into use in Europe before the birth of Christ, most *campesinas* still prepared corn by hand in the early twentieth century, leading one Mexican politician to exclaim that "we still live in the Stone Age!"[10] Technologically, the need to precook the corn with mineral lime and grind the dough while still wet made stone mills impractical for producing *nixtamal*. The late-nineteenth-century development of portable steel mills powered by electricity made it possible to grind *masa* sufficiently fine to make an acceptable *tortilla*, although it was still coarser and less tasty than corn prepared on a *metate*. By 1900, more than fifty of these mills operated in Mexico City alone, and they gained rapid acceptance among urban women. Women still cooked their own corn each evening, then carried it to the neighborhood mill in the morning to be ground for a few centavos. The adoption of machinery also made it culturally acceptable for men to take over the management of *tortillerías*, once an exclusively female occupation.[11]

Commercial *nixtamal* mills took decades to spread through the countryside because of both the relatively high monetary cost in a largely subsistence economy and the challenge they posed to women's established domestic roles. Technical flaws in the early mills allowed women to demonstrate their superiority over machines and assert their place within the family. Because villages lacked electricity, early models operated on gas engines, which caused the *tortillas* to come out tasting of high-octane fuel. Even when gas generators were separated from electric motors, the corn acquired a metallic taste and rough texture. Women could avoid these unpleasant side effects by briefly regrinding the *masa* on the *metate*, yet many refused to patronize the mills, indicating deeper social concerns about grinding corn. Gossip in the village of Tepoztlán questioned the femininity of anyone who carried her corn to a commercial mill. Many women feared that neglecting the *metate* would lead to a dangerous swelling of the joints called "laziness of the knees."[12]

While the arrival of a *nixtamal* mill often worried village women, it absolutely infuriated men. Many forbade their wives and daughters from patronizing the new establishments, fearing a direct challenge to their patriarchal authority. Without the discipline of the *metate*, some believed women would become lazy and promiscuous. As one old-timer from the Yucatán explained, the mill "starts early and so women go out before dawn to grind their own corn the way they used to at home. They meet boys in the dark and that's why illegitimacy is caused by the *nixtamal*." To prevent such danger, the men of one agricultural cooperative that received a mill locked it away from their wives. In another case, a group of women who attempted to organize for their right to a mill were physically assaulted by disgruntled men.[13]

Some of the first rural women to patronize the new mills were those who had fled the countryside during the decade of revolutionary fighting (1910–20) and discovered the convenience of machine-ground corn in cities or towns. Financial considerations also helped determine who took their corn to the mill. Relatively poor women whose families held little land, contrary perhaps to expectations, often had the greatest incentive to pay for machine-ground corn. Although this service required a few centavos, it freed women from several hours of daily work. They could use that time to engage in artisanal crafts or to become petty merchants, traveling to nearby towns to buy cheaper products, and thus earn enough money to offset the cost of milling. The acceptance of the mill as a natural tool therefore helped draw subsistence farmers into the money economy. Wealthier families who could easily afford the added expense of milling were often the last ones to give up the *metate*. Some considered home-ground corn a status marker, a way of asserting that they lived better than their neighbors because they ate better *tortillas*. Of course, they could also pay poorer women to do the actual grinding.[14]

Political as well as economic issues influenced the reception of mechanical mills in rural Mexico. Established *caciques* (political bosses) often enriched themselves by asserting monopolistic control over *nixtamal* mills, while aspiring populist leaders used them as a form of patronage to organize supporters. President Lázaro Cárdenas (1934–40) used grants of *nixtamal* mills to encourage membership in the official party and to discourage rival church organizations. Women learned to phrase their requests for cooperative mills within the dominant developmentalist discourse; for example, the women of Rancho Las Canoas, on the shores of Lake Pátzcuaro, Michoacán, formed a Women's Anticlerical and Anti-Alcohol League to petition the president for a corn mill and in this way to liberate them from the "bitter, black stone with three feet called the *metate*."[15]

Tortilla production was mechanized further in the postwar era with the development of an integrated factory comprising a *nixtamal* mill that ground the corn, a rotating press to form it into the proper shape, and an "endless *comal*" conveyer belt to cook it. Mexican inventors had first attempted to duplicate the subtle skills of the *tortillera* in the late nineteenth century, but it was not until the 1950s that they resolved all the technical problems to mass-produce an adequate *tortilla*. By the 1970s, these small-scale factories, capable of producing a few thousand *tortillas* per hour, operated conveniently in urban barrios and rural communities throughout the republic. *Tortilla* aficionados clearly recognized the difference between hand-patted and factory-pressed *tortillas*. Relatively wealthy peasant women, who could afford to devote themselves exclusively to domestic work, rejected machine-made *tortillas* as "raw" because they stuck together. While ordinary *campesinas* began to purchase tortillas for everyday consumption and used the time saved to earn outside income, the *metate* and *comal* came out for festive occasions, when only a philistine would eat *tortillas* that "tasted like electricity" because they had not been cooked over a wood-burning fire.[16]

The arrival of *nixtamal* mills in the countryside transformed the lives of Mexican women, freeing them from hard labor at the *metate* while drawing them into the money economy and often into political organization as well. The male activity of growing maize underwent equally dramatic changes as the government shifted its goals from an agrarian revolution to the Green Revolution, emphasizing large-scale commercial agriculture to support urban industrialization. Land reform had culminated under President Cárdenas, who distributed nearly fifty million acres to *campesinos* in the form of communally owned *ejidos*. Nevertheless, the very magnitude of the reforms, together with financial crises and a fierce conservative reaction, prevented Cárdenas from providing the infrastructure of machinery, irrigation, and credit necessary to make even the most favorable of *ejido* grants into viable commercial operations, and this neglect only grew worse under subsequent administrations. In 1943, a team of agronomists sponsored by the Rockefeller Foundation arrived to supplement Mexican programs aimed at increasing farm productivity, which had been ongoing since the 1920s. Within two decades, the use of hybrid seeds, fertilizers, and pesticides had doubled the production of Mexican corn and quadrupled that of wheat, but the profits accrued primarily to affluent commercial farmers who had the resources to benefit from the technological improvements.[17]

Historian Enrique Ochoa has shown how the Mexican State Food Agency, founded in 1937 by Cárdenas to help small farmers compete in the marketplace, was diverted to support the goal of industrialization. Political crises, particularly urban inflation and food shortages, invariably disrupted rural development plans, as bureaucrats purchased staple crops from a few commercial growers in the Pacific Northwest and imports from the United States rather than from large numbers of small *ejidos* in central and southern Mexico. The construction of grain storage facilities around urban centers and in ports on the Gulf of Mexico perpetuated this bias in the 1950s. The agency provided cheap food to the cities in order to win populist political support while at the same time containing union demands for higher wages, thereby indirectly subsidizing private industry. For example, the agency supplied low-cost corn to the politically powerful *nixtamal* millers in Mexico City, who then sold *tortillas* to the public at fixed prices, gaining substantial profits for themselves in the process. By the 1960s, decades of official neglect led impoverished farmers to begin taking up arms and demanding a return to agrarian reform. The government responded by repressing the rebels and then extending the welfare programs to supply industrial processed food to the countryside as well. This expansion into food processing to provision the new rural stores prompted cries of socialist intervention by business leaders, who nevertheless continued to profit from agency supplies of subsidized raw materials for their own factories.[18]

The creation of a dehydrated *tortilla* flour industry illustrates this mutually beneficial relationship between state-owned and private enterprises. In 1949, the federal government established the first *masa harina* or *nixtamal* flour mill, called Maiz Industrializado, SA (Minsa) in Tlalnepantla, Mexico, the site of giant corn silos for the Mexico City market. That same year, Roberto González opened a rival facility in Cerralvo, Nuevo León, under the trade name Molinos Azteca, SA (Maseca). The two firms collaborated on research and development for more than a decade before arriving at a suitable formulation that could be turned into *tortilla masa* with just the addition of water. By the mid-1970s, *tortilla* flour production surpassed 500,000 tons, 5 percent of all the corn consumed in Mexico, with the majority of the market going to the private firm, Maseca, in part because the powerful corn millers used political channels to slow the growth of the state corporation, Minsa.[19]

Government officials justified support for the industry by pointing to economies of scale, since cornmeal could be produced, transported, and stored more cheaply than whole corn. Centralized production also limited the risk of irregularities within neighborhood *tortilla* factories in addition to offering nutritional benefits. For the nominal cost of $10 a ton, Maseca could enrich its *masa harina* with enough protein and vitamins to satisfy minimum daily requirements, but the company has nevertheless resisted implementing the strategy. Although vitamin and protein enrichment would make little difference in taste beyond the already significant change from freshly ground to dehydrated corn, the politically powerful company feared that any additives would undermine its market share.[20]

By the end of the millennium, the dismantling of the State Food Agency by neoliberal governments left the *masa harina* industry poised to dominate Mexican corn markets. President Carlos Salinas de Gortari (1988–94) first cut the subsidy to corn millers in an attempt to target welfare assistance. In its place he established a program giving poor people *tortilla* vouchers called *tortivales*, which were quickly dubbed *tortivotos* by political opponents who accused the government of using food to buy votes. The president also privatized the state firm, Minsa, selling it to a rival consortium of Maseca. Finally, in January 1999, his successor, Ernesto Zedillo (1994–2000), eliminated the *tortilla* subsidy completely along with price controls. The nutritional consequences of this policy remain to be seen, although standards of living for poor Mexicans have already slipped dramatically in the past two decades.[21] Nevertheless, the demise of family-owned *tortilla* factories has already become clear. Alma Guillermoprieto graphically explained that "when the privatization program of Mexico's notorious former President Carlos Salinas delivered the future of the *tortilla* into their hands...[the *tortilla* magnates] served up to the Mexican people the rounds of grilled cardboard that at present constitute the nation's basic foodstuff."[22] Many would apply that same description to the processed foods offered by multinational corporations, and while the reception of those foods has followed a unique trajectory, the effects on Mexican nutrition have been equally grim.

The Other Pepsi Generation

The Tzotzil Indians of San Juan Chamula may never appear on television commercials in the United States, but they nevertheless form part of the Pepsi Generation. While Mexicans usually celebrate religious festivals with beer or tequila, in this highland Chiapas community toasts are invariably made with Pepsi-Cola. The Tzotzil devotion to soft drinks illustrates the ubiquitous presence of industrial processed food in even the most remote indigenous regions – and the fact that the *cacique* controls the Pepsi distributorship. The arrival of Pepsi and other junk foods has brought tremendous changes in food consumption, with serious nutritional consequences for the lower classes, yet cultural imperialism has not overwhelmed traditional Mexican cooking. At worst, a form of hybridization has taken place as Mexicans have incorporated foreign foods into established eating patterns. Balanced against this have been the efforts of middle-class cooks to create a unified cuisine as part of a self-conscious nationalist program.

The vision of a billion Chinese just waiting to buy Big Macs, Coca-Cola, and other consumer goods formed a crucial element of Western propaganda during the Cold War. This image was as simplistic as it was ethnocentric, and yet it provides a useful corrective to the likewise oversimplified view of neocolonial agribusiness producing luxury goods in the former colonies for sale in the affluent markets of the old colonial powers.[23] The capitalist dream that the fall of Communism would make all the world into a giant McDonaldland overlooked the global ecosystem's inability to sustain the livestock needed to serve billions of hamburgers daily. Moreover, rural incomes in China, as elsewhere in the developing world, were insufficient to purchase even fries and a shake. Nevertheless, multinational food corporations developed long-range plans to transform those rural masses into loyal customers as incomes gradually rose. Businesses built their rural marketing infrastructure from the ground up, starting with low-cost, easily transportable items such as bulk vegetable oils and dehydrated baby formula, in order to reach the eventual goal of a McDonald's drive-through window.

Meanwhile, the urban middle classes in these developing countries provided an immediate market for the whole range of industrial foods, from breakfast cereals to fast-food chains. One of the images used most frequently to prove the West had won the Cold War was the opening of McDonald's restaurants in Moscow and Beijing. It seemed irrelevant that Chinese customers did not particularly like the hamburgers and were more interested in the restaurants as a medium for experiencing life in the United States.[24] Fast foods and soft drinks likewise became fashionable among India's urban elite as economic "liberalization" in the 1990s led the country to abandon its gastronomic nonalignment.[25] Food-processing businesses producing refrigerated meats, canned vegetables, and bottled drinks emerged in Mexico during the industrial boom of the 1890s, yet their expansion was also limited to small urban markets. By the 1940s, the first Mexican supermarket chains, SUMESA and Aurrera, had opened in upper-middle-class neighborhoods, selling Aunt Jemima pancake mix and the Mexican version of Wonder Bread, known by the brand name Bimbo. Housewives not only began replacing crusty *bolillos* (rolls) fresh from neighborhood bakeries with chewy, plastic-wrapped *pan de caja* (bread from a box), they also conducted bizarre experiments using mass-produced ingredients to create such hybrid dishes as shrimp and cornflakes, calf brains with crackers, macaroni and milk soup, and pork loin in Pepsi-Cola.[26]

These examples may well illustrate a dark side of mass production, but they do not portend the annihilation of Mexican gastronomy. Cultural differences make it risky to generalize between the Mexican middle classes and their counterparts in the United States. Simple household appliances demonstrate subtle but important distinctions. For example, Mexicans used their newly purchased refrigerators to store soft drinks and beer instead of a week's worth of groceries. And while the most valuable appliances north of the border may have been electric toasters and cake mixers, Mexicans preferred the electric blender, the juice press, and the pressure cooker. The blender's facility in grinding chile sauces relegated the *metate* to the status of a kitchen curiosity, and the juicer turned Mexico's ubiquitous oranges into daily glasses of fresh juice. The pressure cooker solved the age-old problem of boiling water at high altitudes in central

Mexico. Beans can now be prepared in less than an hour, saving on fuel costs as well as time, and the toughest beef can be made edible in minutes.

Perhaps the limitations of culinary technology could be used to demonstrate the relative "underdevelopment" of Mexican kitchens: housewives continued to shop for groceries every day and spurned such conveniences as canned beans and frozen orange juice concentrate. Yet the Mexican woman's skepticism of the doctrine that time is money may reflect a more realistic view of the limitations of household technology. Ruth Schwartz Cowan observed that mechanizing housework in the United States had the ironic effect of creating "more work for mother." Time saved by laundry machines, for example, was spent in the automobile working as the family chauffeur. Mexican women at least had the satisfaction of feeding their families fresh food.[27]

Moreover, many foreign manufacturers won customers in the 1940s and 1950s by demonstrating the utility of their products for making national dishes. Glasbake Cookware ran a series of newspaper advertisements featuring recipes for Mexican regional dishes such as *mole michoacano*. Appliance makers depicted giant *cazuelas* simmering on top of their modern stoves, and an advertisement for pressure cookers made the justifiable claim that "Mexican cooking enters a new epoch with the *Olla presto*." Even Coca-Cola appealed to Mexican customers with nostalgic scenes of picnics at Chapultepec Park.[28]

Mexicans also appropriated elements of foreign culture to their own purposes. Domestic soft-drink manufacturers such as Mundet competed with Coke and Pepsi by introducing lines of soda flavors adapted to Mexican tastes for orange, mango, and apple cider. Local chip makers such as Sabritas and Bali contracted with the North American food technologists who had manufactured MSG in the 1950s to transform wheat pellets into artificial *chicharrones* (fried pork skins).[29] The habit of eating eggs for breakfast, when transferred from the United States to Mexico, stimulated creative experimentation rather than slavish imitation. In searching for national counterparts to eggs benedict, Mexican chefs served *huevos rancheros* (ranch-style eggs) fried with tomato-and-chile sauce, *huevos albañiles* (bricklayers' eggs) scrambled with a similar sauce, and *huevos motuleños* (from Motul, Yucatán) fried with beans, ham, and peas. Soon, no hotel with pretensions to luxury could neglect having its own "traditional" egg dish on the breakfast menu.

The modern desire to preserve traditional Mexican cooking, or to create new traditions when appropriate ones could not be found, also inspired a flurry of folkloric studies in the countryside. Josefina Velázquez de León brought together the country's diverse regional cuisines for the first time in a single work, *Platillos regionales de la República mexicana* (*Regional Dishes of the Mexican Republic*, Mexico City: Ediciones J. Veláquez de León, 1946; Mexico City: Editorial Pro-mama, 1965). Virginia Rodríguez Rivera published another classic volume, *La cocina en el México antiguo y moderno* (*Cooking in Ancient and Modern Mexico*, Mexico City: Editorial Aomamma, 1965), featuring nineteenth-century dishes with recipes drawn from oral history interviews. Mexican women thus displayed a mania for preserving their culinary past even as it began to slip away. When electric blenders finally began to replace the grinding stone, a society columnist warned women to save their *metates*, "because this Mexican cooking utensil has still not been supplanted by any modern appliance."[30]

Nevertheless, they had mixed success in preserving traditional cooking. Attempts to construct a national cuisine reduced complex regional cooking styles to a few stereotyped dishes, which often misrepresented the foods eaten in those areas. Even an author as sensitive as Josefina Velázquez de León adapted traditional village recipes to the needs of urban cooks. For the *zacahuil*, the giant Huastecan pit-barbecued corn cake, wrapped in banana leaves and capable of feeding an entire community, she instructed readers to use a scanty three kilograms of maize and to bake it in the oven. Arjun Appadurai has described a similar process of imagining culinary communities in postcolonial India, as middle-class cookbook authors presented their regional foods to readers across the subcontinent, but he noted also that "one of the results of the exchange of culinary images is the elimination of the most exotic, peculiar, distinctive, or domestic nuances in a particular specialized cuisine."[31]

Just as middle-class cooks struggled to adapt traditional Mexican foods to new urban lifestyles, multinational corporations attempted to transform eating habits in the countryside. Creating an infrastructure of rural marketing networks for processed foods required significant investments. Pre-Hispanic merchants had carried on an extensive trade in nonperishable, relatively high-value goods such as cacao and dried chiles, supplemented in the colonial period by coffee, sugar, and spices, but it was more difficult to transport Pepsi by mule. Fortunately for businessmen, revolutionary governments of the 1920s and 1930s placed a high priority on road-building to unify the country and its markets. Soft-drink and beer distributors were among the first entrepreneurs to take advantage of these highways to send glass bottles from regional plants to consumers and then to return the empties safely for refilling – an essential step to keep prices affordable. Both Coke and beer arrived in the village of Tepoztlán within six years after the opening of a road from the state capital in 1936. The appearance of Pepsi in the 1940s and the growth of national breweries helped foster competition in local markets.[32]

Food distributorships therefore developed in a hybrid fashion, combining modern and traditional marketing methods. Even today, supermarket chains remain concentrated in upper-middle-class neighborhoods, while manufactured foods reach the rest of the population through small-scale grocers, often in municipal markets, and ambulant vendors. These merchants depended on corporate distributors for credit as well as business supplies such as display cases and refrigerators.[33] One shopkeeper considered the Coke deliveryman so important to his livelihood that he invited the driver to his daughter's fifteenth birthday party. The costs of establishing and maintaining these delivery routes encouraged the centralization of Mexican food processing within large industrial groups. The largest Coke franchise in the world, for example, Fomento Económico Mexicano SA, also included Cervecería Cuauhtémoc within the Monterrey-based Garza Sada conglomerate. Pepsico, meanwhile, diversified into the complementary snack-food industry, merging with Frito-Lay in the United States, then acquiring Mexican chip makers Sabritas and Bali.[34] As in the case of *tortilla* flour, the government encouraged the growth of these companies through ostensibly competitive state food corporations. Rural stores established in the 1960s and 1970s by the State Food Agency stocked products such as animal crackers and soft drinks, either produced by state factories or purchased from private groups, thereby helping to incorporate rural consumers into larger national markets.[35]

Mexican politicians have meanwhile foregone many potential health benefits that their economic ventures might have achieved. They conceded to food manufacturers the educational power of the mass media, allowing massive advertising campaigns for soft drinks and snack candies, with "small print" advice to eat fresh fruits and vegetables included as the only concession to public health.[36] Programs to supplement processed foods, including *tortilla* flour, have been initiated periodically but never carried through. Perhaps the most nutritionally irresponsible example of state assistance to private enterprise lay in the subsidies on flour and sugar given to snack-food producers, which made this business, in the words of one health official, a "*negociazo*" (scam).[37]

Even with government assistance, transnational advertising campaigns had a difficult time instilling North American and western European values in the Mexican countryside. The example of Pepsi in San Juan Chamula illustrates the ways that modernizing societies adapt consumer products to fit their cultures. Rather than drinking Pepsi as a daily snack in imitation of the middle classes in either Mexico or the United States, the Chamulans incorporated the soft drink into the community's ritual life, for example, giving cases of Pepsi as dowries for brides. Religious leaders celebrated church services with Pepsi instead of wine, telling parishioners that carbonation drives off evil spirits and cleanses the soul. The natives even hung Pepsi posters in their homes beside the family crucifix, for as one person explained to an anthropologist: "When men burp, their hearts open."[38]

The resilience of local customs has not offset the nutritional damage of the transition from traditional to industrial diets. Studies by the National Nutrition Institute and by numerous anthropologists from the 1960s to the 1990s have documented a fundamental trend toward the replacement of corn and beans by sugar and fats. Well-to-do Yucatecan peasants and working-class Mexico City residents both derive an average of 20 percent of their calories from processed foods, including soft drinks, beer, chips, and candy. The rural poor, unable to afford such snacks except on special occasions, dump heaped spoonfuls of sugar into weak coffee. So pervasive has sucrose become that one study recommended vitamin-enriched sugar as the most efficient means of improving rural nutrition.[39] The convenience of processed foods often came at the expense of nutrition, as when cooks used dried consommé instead of tomatoes and onions, in effect replacing vegetables with salt. Poverty further distorted the diets of *campesinos* subsisting on the fringes of the market economy. The rising price of beans forced many poor families to buy cheaper wheat pasta, with grave dietary consequences. While corn and beans together provide high-quality protein, corn and spaghetti do not.[40]

The food processing industry has waged a century-long campaign to remove consumers from the source of their nourishment, to make packaged foods seem natural and living plants and animals unwholesome. For example, transnational executives hoping to establish modern chicken packing plants in Mexico expressed the long-term goal of persuading consumers that poultry tastes best when purchased from a plastic bag in the refrigerated section.[41] The combination of manufactured foods and traditional cooking styles has had mixed results, introducing valuable new sources of protein to poor consumers, but also destabilizing their nutritional intake. It remains to be seen how successful the chicken packers will be in convincing Mexicans that "parts are parts."

Conclusion

This essay has attempted to untangle the complex negotiations of identity and markets among traditional peasant cooks, progressive urban gourmets, food-processing corporations, and an unfortunately far from impartial state. Connections between food consumption and elite identity can be seen in the current fad for the so-called *nueva cocina mexicana*. Chefs have turned to Native American plants and animals in order to claim an equal standing with the great cuisines of Europe and Asia, while preparing these ingredients with the difficult techniques of European *haute cuisine* to maintain their cultural distinction from the popular masses. Thus Arnulfo Luengas, chef of the Banco Nacional de México's executive dining room, created avocado mousse with shrimp, Beef Wellington with chiles, and chicken supremes with *cuitlacoche*.[42] Some might question the *mexicanidad* of such dishes, but the prominent cookbook author Alicia Gironella De'Angeli insisted that this was "the same food we serve at home. It is one of two tendencies in Mexican cooking. The other is the popular Mexican food, the kind with the grease and cheese and everything fried. It is the traditional food that we are reinterpreting." She asserted that the new dishes actually are derived from pre-Hispanic origins. "We did not have the lard and the grease that most people think of as Mexican in our roots. The Spaniards brought the pigs."[43] In this way, she appropriated Aztec authenticity for elite cuisine and associated lower-class foods with the villainous conquistadors.

The popular sectors would not allow her to have such international sophistication and eat it too with a nationalist flourish. They formulated their own diverse ideas of what constituted authentic Mexican food. Maize of course constituted the quintessential cuisine of rural Mexico. During a drought in the Huasteca, when corn shipments arrived from the United States to relieve local shortages, *campesinos* claimed that even the pigs turned up their snouts at the imported grain.[44] Meanwhile, authenticity meant something entirely different to cooks patting out *tortillas* by hand in restaurants on scenic Janitzio Island, Lake Pátzcuaro, where they started with Maseca brand *masa harina* then reground it on the *metate* for the tourists' benefit.

The government has likewise had its say in defining Mexican cuisine through an often-contradictory set of food policies. The National Nutrition Institute developed programs to improve the health of rural and urban poor through educational campaigns about the best ways to use both traditional staples and vitamin and protein supplements. The state food agencies also provided infrastructure to assist small farmers in selling corn to lucrative urban markets, thus preserving their livelihoods. Far more of the government's resources went to promoting domestic manufacturers, even to the point of subsidizing the junk-food industry. These businesses have in turn adopted the mantle of authenticity, even when they represented foreign owners. Advertising billboards informed Mexicans that "*tortillas* taste good, and better with Maseca." Transnational corporations meanwhile adapted their products to Mexican tastes in order to face off local competitors. Bags of Sabritas *chicharrones* (pork rinds) shared counter space with Fritos potato chips, while Mundet *cidral* (carbonated apple cider) sat in the refrigerator with Pepsi-Cola. This goes to show that Macario, the Tzotzil Faust, does not need a North American Mephistopheles to sell his soul.

The nutritional consequences of this partial transition from peasant to industrial diets were profound regardless of their source. Adolfo Chávez, director of the Community Nutrition Division of the National Nutrition Institute, has described an epidemiological trap in which Mexicans have fallen victim to the dietary diseases of the rich world without escaping the nutritional deficiencies of the poor world. Serum cholesterol levels among residents of the wealthy, meat-consuming areas of northern Mexico average higher than those in the United States. Heart disease has become a serious problem throughout Mexico, and ranks as the leading cause of death even among indigenous peasants in Yucatán and other southern states. Excessive sugar consumption has meanwhile created an epidemic of diabetes, the fourth leading cause of death nationwide. Hypoglycemia, hypertension, arteriosclerosis, and various forms of cancer have likewise grown more common. These diseases seemed all the more tragic given the continuing prevalence of serious malnutrition in Mexico. Adults often suffered from both obesity and anemia at the same time, and the nutritional consequences for infants were even worse. The economic downturn of the 1980s led to a rise in mortality from nutritional deficiencies from 1 percent to 5.2 percent among infants and from 1.5 percent to 9.1 percent among preschool-age children.[45]

The hunger of Mexico's poor also portends an ominous future for the national cuisine, which has always derived inspiration from *campesino* kitchens, regardless of the pretensions of European-trained chefs. The heart of this cuisine, *tortillas* made of freshly ground corn, has become particularly vulnerable to industrialization. Economist Felipe Torres Torres explained that "the business of the *tortilla* has expanded under the articulation of an economic model, and not of the historic preferences of consumers, who deep down maintain a vigilant rejection of the new product, although ... [neoliberal political economy has] not permitted them any alternative; in such a case, it is possible that future generations will definitively abandon the consumption of maize before the low quality of a food that is especially sensitive to the criteria of modernity."[46] Of course, gourmet boutiques will always exist, recreating a folkloric past through the performances of women, perhaps with indigenous features or costumes, making *tortillas* of organically grown and freshly ground corn for affluent consumers. Indeed, one of the modern world's great ironies is that only the wealthy can afford to eat like peasants.

NOTES

1   Enrique Ochoa, *Feeding Mexico: The Political Uses of Food Since 1910* (Wilmington, DE: SR Books, 2000), p. 219; Alma Guillermoprieto, "In Search of the Real Tortilla," *The New Yorker* (November 29, 1999): pp. 46–8.
2   Nestor García Canclini, *Hybrid Cultures: Strategies for Entering and Leaving Modernity* (Minneapolis: University of Minnesota Press, 1996).
3   Cynthia Hewitt de Alcántara, *Modernizing Mexican Agriculture: Socioeconomic Implications of Technological Change, 1940–1970* (Geneva: United Nations Research Institute for Social Development, 1976); Ochoa, *Feeding Mexico*, pp. 7–9, 225–32.
4   Jean Drèze and Amartya Sen, *Hunger and Public Action* (Oxford: Clarendon Press, 1989), pp. 9–10, 68, 91, 122.

5   Alberto Ysunza Ogazón, et al., *Dietas de transición y riesgo nutricional en población migratoria* (Mexico City: Instituto Nacional de Nutrición, 1985); Lucia Batrouni, et al., *Situación de barrios marginados de Teziutlán* (Mexico City: Instituto Nacional de Nutrición, 1983); Adolfo Chávez, et al., *La nutrición en México y la transición epidemiologica* (Mexico City: Instituto Nacional de Nutrición, 1993).

6   On the nutritional value of the pre-Hispanic maize complex, see William T. Sanders, Jeffrey R. Parsons, and Robert S. Santley, *The Basin of Mexico: Ecological Processes in the Evolution of a Civilization* (New York: Academic Press, 1979), p. 376; Hector Arraya, Marina Flores, and Guillermo Arroyave, "Nutritive Value of Basic Foods and Common Dishes of the Guatemalan Rural Populations: A Theoretical Approach," *Ecology of Food and Nutrition* 11 (1981): 171–6. The population estimate comes from Woodrow Borah and Sherburne F. Cook, *The Aboriginal Population of Central Mexico on the Eve of the Spanish Conquest* (Berkeley: University of California Press, 1963).

7   Margaret Park Redfield, "Notes on the Cookery of Tepoztlan, Morelos," *American Journal of Folklore* 42, no. 164 (April–June 1929): 167–96; Nathanial Whetten, *Rural Mexico* (Chicago: University of Chicago Press, 1948), p. 305; Oscar Lewis, *Life in a Mexican Village: Tepoztlán Revisited* (Urbana: University of Illinois Press, 1951), p. 72.

8   "Roads, the Carnivalesque, and the Mexican Revolution: Transforming Modernity in Tepoztlán, 1928–1943," MA thesis, Texas Christian University, 1994, pp. 165–70.

9   Lynn Stephen, *Zapotec Women* (Austin: University of Texas Press, 1991), 186.

10 *El Universal* (November 11, 1933).

11 Dawn Keremitsis, "Del metate al molino: La mujer mexicana de 1910 a 1940," *Historia Mexicana* 33 (October–December 1983): 297; John Mraz, "'En calidad de esclavas': obreras en los molinos de nixtamal, México, diciembre, 1919," *Historia obrera* 6:24 (March 1982): 2–14.

12 Quote in Redfield, "Notes on Cookery of Tepoztlan," 182; *El maíz, fundamento de la cultura popular mexicana* (Mexico: Museo Nacional de Culturas Populares, 1982), p. 82.

13 Archivo General de la Nación, Mexico City (hereafter cited as AGN), Ramo Presidentes, Lázaro Cárdenas, 604.11/21, 149, 155; quote from Arnold J. Bauer, "Millers and Grinders: Technology and Household Economy in Meso-America," *Agricultural History* 64, no. 1 (Winter 1990): 16.

14 Waters, "Roads and the Mexican Revolution," 167, 173.

15 AGN, Cárdenas, exp. 604.11/67, 91, 92, 121; Keremitsis, "Del metate al molino," 297.

16 Robert V. Kemper, *Migration and Adaptation: Tzintzuntzan Peasants in Mexico City* (Beverly Hills: Sage Publications, 1977), pp. 29, 152; Maria da Glória Marroni de Velázquez, "Changes in Rural Society and Domestic Labor in Atlixco, Puebla, 1940–1990," in *Creating Spaces, Shaping Transitions: Women of the Mexican Countryside, 1850–1990*, ed. Heather Fowler-Salamini and Mary Kay Vaughan (Tucson: University of Arizona Press, 1994), p. 223; Jaime Aboites A., *Breve historia de un invento olvidado: Las máquinas tortilladoras en México* (Mexico City: Universidad Autónoma Metropolitana, 1989), pp. 39, 47; *El maíz*, p. 82.

17 Joseph Cotter, "The Origins of the Green Revolution in Mexico: Continuity or Change?" in *Latin America in the 1940s: War and Postwar Transitions*, ed. David Rock (Berkeley: University of California Press, 1993); Deborah Fitzgerald, "Exporting American Agriculture: The Rockefeller Foundation in Mexico, 1943–1953," in *Missionaries of Science: The Rockefeller Foundation in Latin America*, ed. Marcos Cueto (Bloomington: Indiana University Press, 1994); Hewitt de Alcántara, *Modernizing Mexican Agriculture*, pp. 118–20, 173–80.

18 Ochoa, *Feeding Mexico*, chaps. 3, 5, 8.

19 Nacional Financiera, *La industría de la harina de maíz* (Mexico City: NAFINSA, 1982), pp. 13–14; *La industria de maíz* (Mexico City: Primsa Editorial, 1989), pp. 108–14;

Adrian Cópil, "La guerra de las tortillas," *Contenido* (July 1992): 42–7; Ochoa, *Feeding Mexico*, p. 121; Aboites, *Breve historia de un invento*, pp. 50–1.

20   Nacional Financiero, *La industria de la harina de maíz* (Mexico City: NAFINSA, 1982), p. 51; Ana Naranjo B., *Informe de programas y proyectos de doce años, 1976–1987* (Mexico City: Instituto Nacional de Nutrición, 1987), pp. 225–6.

21   Ochoa, *Feeding Mexico*, pp. 210–12, 219.

22   Guillermoprieto, "In Search of the Real Tortilla," p. 46.

23   See, for example, Richard W. Franke, "The Effects of Colonialism and Neocolonialism on the Gastronomic Patterns of the Third World," in *Food and Evolution*, ed. Marvin Harris and Eric B. Ross (Philadelphia: Temple University Press, 1987), p. 455.

24   See the fascinating studies in James L. Watson, ed., *Golden Arches East: McDonald's in East Asia* (Stanford: Stanford University Press, 1997).

25   Uma Narayan, "Eating Cultures: Incorporation, Identity and Indian Food," *Social Identities* 1:1 (1995): 69.

26   Jeffrey M. Pilcher, *¡Que vivan los tamales! Food and the Making of Mexican Identity* (Albuquerque: University of New Mexico Press, 1998), p. 127.

27   Ruth Schwartz Cowan, *More Work for Mother: The Ironies of Household Technology from the Open Hearth to the Microwave* (New York: Basic Books, 1983).

28   *Excelsior*, April 15, July 14, September 1, December 16, 1945; June 2, 1947.

29   Robert Sietsema, "My Father the Formulator," *Gourmet* (February 2000), p. 91.

30   *Excelsior*, August 13, 1947. See, for comparison, Eric Hobsbawm and Terence Ranger, eds., *The Invention of Tradition* (Cambridge: Cambridge University Press, 1983).

31   Arjun Appadurai, "How to Make a National Cuisine: Cookbooks in Contemporary India," *Comparative Studies in Society and History* 30, no. 1 (January 1988): 17.

32   Waters, "Roads and the Mexican Revolution," p. 78; J. C. Louis and Harvey Z. Yazijian, *The Cola Wars* (New York: Everest House, 1980), pp. 46, 60.

33   Fernando Rello and Demetrio Sodi, *Abasto y distribución de alimentos en las grandes metropolis* (Mexico City: Nueva Imagen, 1989), pp. 68–80.

34   José Antonio Roldán Amaro, *Hambre y riqueza en la historia contemporanea de México*, anexo 1 of *Historia del hambre en México*, ed. Pablo González Casanova (Mexico City: Instituto Nacional de Nutrición, 1986), p. 40; Carol Meyers de Ortiz, *Pequeño comercio de alimentos en colonias populares de Ciudad Nezahuacóyotl: Análisis de su papel en la estructura socioe-conómica urbana* (Guadalajara: Editorial Universidad de Guadalajara, 1990), p. 33; Matt Moffett, "A Mexican War Heats Up for Cola Giants," *Wall Street Journal* (April 26, 1993): B1, 6; Young and Yazijian, *The Cola Wars*, p. 133.

35   Ochoa, *Feeding Mexico*, p. 165.

36   David Márquez Ayala, "Las empresas transnacionales y sus efectos en el consumo alimentario," in *Transnacionales, agricultura, y alimentación*, ed. Rodolfo Echeverría Zuno (Mexico City: Editorial Nueva Imagen, 1982), p. 218; Naranjo, *Informe de programas*, pp. 228–34.

37   Quote from "La entrevista: Dr. Adolfo Chávez Villasana," *Cuadernos de Nutrición* 6, no. 9 (July–September 1983): 12–16.

38   Matt Moffett, "Mexicans Convert as a Matter of Politics," *Wall Street Journal* (June 1, 1988).

39   Gilberto Balam, "La alimentación de los campesinos mayas del estado de Yucatán (Primera parte)," *Cuadernos de Nutrición* 16, no. 6 (November–December 1993): 41; Chávez, *La nutrición en México*, pp. 33, 78; Jesús Ruvalcaba Mercado, *Vida cotidiana y consumo de maíz en la huasteca veracruzana* (Mexico City: Centro de Investigaciones y Estudios Superiores en Antropología Social, 1987), pp. 31, 39. The Mexican case thus confirms the hypotheses put forward by Sydney Mintz, *Sweetness and Power: The Place of Sugar in Modern History* (New York: Viking, 1985).

40   K. M. DeWalt, P. B. Kelly, and G. H. Pelto, "Nutritional Correlates of Economic Microdifferentiation in a Highland Mexican Community," in *Nutritional Anthropology: Contemporary Approaches to Diet and Culture*, ed. Norge W. Jerome, Randy F. Kandel, Gretel H. Pelto (Pleasantville, NY: Redgrave Publishing, 1980), p. 213; Serrano Andrade, "El consumo de alimentos industrializados," p. 29; Chávez, *La nutrición en México*, p. 28; Balam, "Alimentación de los campesinos mayas," p. 43.

41   Personal communication from John Hart, Mexico City, July 16, 1997.

42   *El universo de la cocina mexicana: Recetario* (Mexico City: Fomento Cultural Banamex, 1988), pp. 18, 40, 48.

43   Quoted in Florence Fabricant, "Mexican Chefs Embrace a Lighter Cuisine of Old," *New York Times* (May 3, 1995): B3.

44   Ruvalcaba Mercado, *Maíz en la huasteca*, p. 85.

45   Chávez, et al., *La nutrición en México*, pp. 47–78; Ochoa, *Feeding Mexico*, p. 208.

46   "Antecedentes del debate actual sobre el maíz en México," in *La industria de la masa y la tortilla: Desarrollo y tecnología*, ed. Felipe Torres, et al. (Mexico: UNAM, 1996), p. 26.

15

Food, Hunger, and the State

Susan Brownell

Against a Background of Hunger

Until recently, perhaps the main reason parents wanted their children to attend sports schools was because they received extra food subsidies (*huoshi buzhu*). Food subsidies have been an important part of China's sports effort since the implementation of the sports school system in 1955. Food is not something that Chinese people take for granted; it occupies an important part in their calculations about social relations, future survival, and success. When asked about the benefits of their chosen career, sportspeople are likely to answer that their work is "bitter," their salaries and prestige are average, "but we eat a little better" than people in other occupations. Despite eating better than nonathletes, Chinese athletes at all levels express constant concern that they will not be able to eat enough food to support hard training, that their "nutrition can't keep up" (*yingyang genbushang*). This constant sense of scarcity was puzzling to me since I knew that athletes' diets were far richer than the average Chinese diet. Could the hunger that athletes felt in fact be due to inadequate nutrition?

Certainly there is evidence that malnutrition was still widespread in the 1980s. A national survey of nearly one million Chinese between seven and twenty-two years old from all parts of China concluded that, according to the height-weight ratio established by the World Health Organization, 28.98 percent of male students and 36.60 percent of female students in China suffered from malnutrition. They were, however, taller and heavier than ever before, and rural students were growing faster than urban ones (Wu Jingshu 1988). Iron deficiency was common and was related to the low consumption of meat (*China Daily* 1987, 1988).

Moreover, in the not so distant past there were periods of real deprivation. Cao Xiangjun, member of the Beijing City handball team, recalled that after they won the championship in the 1959 National Games, they returned to the dorms for dinner. Tears welled up in her eyes when she saw the pitiful portions they had. One of the courses was the left-over leaf droppings from cabbages, boiled in salt. The kitchen staff felt very badly. They were still hungry when the "victory banquet" was over. Even in 1979, there was a story that the women's national racewalking team all became anemic during a training camp. Their meal allowance was then 1.5 yuan (40 cents) per day. Their coach gathered orange peels and sold them to raise money to buy ginseng and a clay pot with which he boiled the women a medicinal soup (Li Jian 1987). A State Sports Commission document issued in 1981 stated that "some athletes have acquired anemia and other diseases of malnourishment" and tried to rectify the situation by revising nutritional standards (Guojia tiwei zhengce yanjiushi 1982: 872). Anemia is perceived as the most immediate danger of inadequate nutrition. The word for anemia (*pinxue*) literally means "poor blood." That concern about malnourishment focuses on the blood is another example of the way in which complex social situations are condensed into the symbolism of body fluids.

Children must be put into sports schools at a young age in order to receive food subsidies during their most important growth years. Events in which training usually starts at older ages may be affected by early malnutrition. For example, a track and field coach who liked to recruit peasants for their endurance and toughness said that he was careful to examine the family's economic situation before he accepted the child for training. If the family was poor, the child might not have had adequate nutrition when young and might not be able to stand hard training.

In sum, many Chinese, even urban Chinese, actually do experience hunger. And even if they are not experiencing it now, many people have recent and vivid memories of hunger. It has been my experience that people who have known hunger can never forget the importance of food. This is the background for the obsession with food among contemporary Chinese.

However, when one examines the situations of specific individual athletes, it is hard to believe that they are suffering from malnourishment. Since they are obviously in good health, I am inclined to believe that their perception of hunger is not due to outright malnourishment, but rather to the social and cultural frames within which food is distributed. Food is very much a part of an entire hierarchical system, with the state at the top of the food chain and the athletes very close to the bottom.

Food and the State

There are a multitude of phrases in Chinese that portray the relationship between the individual and the state in terms of food. The ubiquitous phrase "eating out of the big pot" is a metaphor for dependence on the state for subsistence and security. To have an "iron rice bowl" is to have the lifelong job security promised by socialism. Sun Lung-kee argues that food is the central problem of any Chinese state: "If only they 'have a bite of food to eat,' the common Chinese people will not revolt" (Sun Lung-kee 1983: 39). In other words, the central problem for the Chinese state is to control its "person-mouths" (*renkou*) – its population.

One of the benefits of being a high official in China is access to more and better food. A high official is often literally a "big man." I was told that the same bureau that supplies food to the national sports team in Beijing also supplies the nation's top leaders. When the Party has attacked governmental corruption, official banquets have been a prime target (Anderson 1988: 245). Banquets are one of the techniques for establishing and maintaining the *guanxi* ("connections") that is perceived as the root of bureaucratic corruption.

In Mayfair Yang's analysis (1989), food is so important in the establishment of *guanxi* because of the symbolism of incorporating another's substance into oneself. Those who are lower in social status tend to give the banquet and those who are higher in status receive it. To incorporate another's substance is to be possessed by the other and therefore to be beholden to and dependent on the donor (pp. 43–4). Thus, those of lower status use the gift of food as a means of extracting favors from those of higher status. Food is used to transform an outsider into an insider. A familiar person is a *shuren*, which literally means a "cooked or ripe person"; a stranger is a *shengren*, literally a "raw or unripe person." The transformation of the "raw" into the "cooked" makes the establishment of *guanxi* possible (p. 40).

It goes without saying that food is also extremely important within the family. Traditionally in rural China, a family was primarily defined as the group of people who ate food cooked on one stove (see Wolf 1968: 28). A family member was called a "one-mouth-person" (*yikou ren*).

Food is clearly an important expression of social relationships. How then are we to view the effects of state rationing on perceptions of the relationship between the individual and the state?

In the late 1980s, athletes, like coaches and physical education teachers, received a food subsidy from their work unit, with the amount determined both by state policy and by the local cost of food. The subsidy was in addition to the grain rations that all urban Chinese received; athletes received the higher level of grain ration that was reserved for people engaged in hard manual labor (25 kg per month). According to policy guidelines, the subsidy could not be given directly to the athletes in cash but was calculated into the preparation of food in the communal cafeteria. Eating in the team cafeteria was a prerequisite to receiving the subsidy.

Many athletes left home at a young age to board at sports schools. For them, the locus of food-sharing shifted from the family to the communal cafeteria that dished out food based on athletic performance. Since the food subsidies were set by state policy, athletes were very conscious of the fact that the state provided them with their food. Eating in a communal cafeteria meant that the times of meals and the dishes offered were highly regimented and allowed little room for individual prefer-ence. In a pointed critique of the communal cafeterias in sports teams, Yin Weixing referred to the phrase "eating out of the big pot" as a metaphor for dependence on the state and observed, "The true 'big pot' cannot be any more fully embodied than it is inside the sports team cafeteria" (Yin Weixing 1988: 113). Oversize shotputters and undersize gymnasts all received the same subsidy. So did women and men. Unlike in many other realms of life, with respect to food subsidies the uniform state policy was perceived as discriminating against men since they actually needed more food than women.

The national team athletes received the highest subsidies. One physical education institute student commented that being on the national team was like having an "iron rice bowl" – not like in the United States where you have to pay for your recreation. The national team athletes each received 15 yuan per day, and they also received special foods which could not be bought on the open market. At 600 yuan

($162) per month, this level of nutrition was far beyond the reach of the average monthly wage of 100 yuan; as one professor noted, at this rate even the premier of China could not afford to raise a top athlete. Professional athletes ate more food and higher-quality food than the average person. By a "high-quality" diet, my informants meant primarily two things: more meat or fish and more dairy products (primarily milk and yogurt). Dairy products are not a typical part of the Chinese diet. The emphasis on them for athletes is a result of an awareness that they form a large part of the Western diet, the assumption being that they explain the greater size and musculature of Western athletes.

Provincial and municipal team athletes also ate well, with an allowance of 12 to 15 yuan per day. The amount varies according to the cost of living in the area, which is usually lower than in Beijing, so that provincial athletes claim they eat better than Beijing athletes. Zhejiang Province athletes, for example, got three dishes for lunch and dinner, two of which contained meat. These numbers were fixed by policy. They also received many supplements, such as oranges, apples, and other fruit, and "royal jelly" (a substance made by honey bees which is often used as a dietary supplement). Even with all of these extras, young women on the team laughed about the fact that when they weren't eating they were snacking, so that they actually ate all day long.

The situation of physical education institute students shows the importance of food subsidies. In order to encourage students to become teachers in a country that had frequently denounced teachers (and worse) in the previous decades, the Education Commission gave students in teacher training programs a food subsidy. In 1988 at the Beijing Physical Education Institute, this subsidy was one yuan per day, which at 30 yuan per month was still almost one-third of a lecturer's salary. This subsidy was distributed in the form of vegetable tickets (*caipiao*) to be used in the school cafeteria and was combined with grain ration tickets (*mianpiao*) of 45 *jin* (25 kg) per month.

Everyone I talked to maintained that this allowance was not enough to maintain hard physical training, and most students required up to 40 yuan extra from their parents. They repeatedly told me they were afraid to train hard because their nutrition "can't keep up." This was despite the fact that many acknowledged they had more grain tickets than they could possibly use. Grain tickets were exchanged for rice and flour products, primarily steamed buns (*mantou*). Students explained that they could only eat so many steamed buns. What they really needed was meat and vegetables.

Nutrition was given as the reason that provincial and national team athletes who came to the physical education institute often saw their performances decline. One athlete had been accustomed to eating 15 yuan per day of food on the Guizhou team and was now eating only four yuan; it was easy to see why she felt deprived, even though she still received more than the one yuan given to most physical education institute students. Her four-yuan subsidy was due to her former status as an athlete and a "model worker." She often fondly recalled the meals on the provincial team. When I asked her if she ate better before coming to Beijing, she replied, "Of course I ate better then. Now I'm paying for my own food." On another occasion, she made a statement that shows how food and emotions are wrapped together. She noted that she felt she could adapt to the inferior nutrition at the physical education institute, she could adapt to living with five other roommates, but the hardest thing was getting used to not being pampered. "I couldn't adapt to that."

One shotput and discus coach at the Beijing Institute of Physical Education complained that food was a particular problem for male throwers. They simply could not eat enough to become big enough to throw well. He complained that in the past, the institute had given a subsidy in addition to the Education Commission subsidy, but now it claimed "economic difficulties." Sweeping his arm toward the new gymnasium being erected for the Asian Games, he asked, "Tell me, what economic difficulties are there?"

If the physical education institute students could not eat their fill, then the regular college student, who received no subsidy at all from the Education Commission, was even worse off. However, members of college teams were given a special subsidy that steadily increased as efforts were made to raise the level of college sports. In 1985, Beijing city gave 0.30 yuan (8 cents) to college athletes for each day of training, based on daily roll taken at team practice. I consistently received more money than the other women because I did not miss practice during my menstrual period (I tried to refuse the money, but my coach explained, "This is the state's money. If you don't take it, it just goes to waste.") This was increased to one yuan per day early in 1986 in preparation for the Second National College Games, but only those selected to participate in the Games received the subsidy. In preparation for the third Games in 1988, the amount was raised to four yuan per day. Food prices had also risen considerably in that time. However, four yuan made a difference, in contrast to the 0.30 yuan in 1985 which, as one athlete complained, "Won't even buy one bottle of yogurt!"

When I participated in the training camp for the 1986 National College Games, a topic of utmost concern was whether or not the cafeteria staff was skimping on our daily six yuan ($2) worth of food. Heated debates at team meetings and repeated complaints resulted in a guarantee that we would get at least one meat or fish dish at lunch and supper and that each supper would include two bottles of yogurt per person. The conflict had caused relationships with the cafeteria staff to deteriorate to the point that the service was very surly. A strategy for rectifying this by giving some "face" to the staff was suggested during a team meeting by one of the Party members on the team. He sneaked into the cafeteria one night to hang a large "commendatory poster" (biaoyangshu) on the wall praising the staff for their service to the cause of the Beijing City College Team. When the staff entered the next morning, they were pleasantly surprised and friendly relations were restored.

Twice a day we received cucumbers, tomatoes, green peppers, bamboo shoots, eggplant, or mushrooms stir-fried with eggs, shrimp, beef, pork, or fish. The elements stayed the same, but the combinations changed. Because there was a heat wave, we also received a weekly "nutritional supplement" of twenty-four bottles of lemon-lime or orange soda pop and three watermelons. My teammates were very conscious of the fact that they were not allowed to receive their six yuan directly, but that it was given to the cafeteria, while the coaches and leaders received theirs in cash and then saved some of it by eating at home. Over two months, this would come to 360 yuan, no small sum. A younger coach asked rhetorically,

Is it fair that they get as much as the athletes, who train hard, put out lots of sweat, experience fatigue? I'm a coach, and I don't think it's fair. And why do you have to have so many coaches? When we go to Dalian [for the National Collegiate Games] at the very least there will be one official for every athlete, if you include all the workers. And *they* will all get a subsidy, too. That's China. It's just the way it is.

In this hierarchical system, the hunger for food was intimately linked with the hunger for athletic success and ultimately for the security that success brings. Most people would be unable to completely fulfill their personal aspirations. Thus, hunger could refer to "the lack of fulfillment of personal aspirations and desires" as much as to real malnourishment (Kahn 1986: 122).

That the food subsidy was based on performance was peculiar to the lives of athletes. However, it was part of a wider pattern that applied to Chinese society as a whole. Food was an important marker of hierarchy and insiderhood long before the current ration system was put into place. This use of food persists, but it has been taken over by the state in both formal and informal ways. In this way the state can partly dictate the hierarchical structure of Chinese society. According to the traditional symbolism of food, by providing food to people the state is reinforcing its superior social position and making its recipients beholden to and dependent on it. Mayfair Yang even suggests it is "possessing" the recipient (1989: 44). Top state leaders can ensure themselves access to better food. Lower-level officials can expect to be treated to banquets. Even coaches on a municipal college team can set themselves apart from their athletes by taking their meals at home and saving the subsidy while requiring that the athletes eat in the cafeteria. These practices stimulate much resentment. Food and power are intimately linked. Food is one of the main ways in which the Chinese state is symbolically constructed as provider, superior, and incorporated part of the self.

Thus, it is not surprising that food played an important symbolic role in the student demonstrations of 1989. The mass hunger strikes in Tiananmen Square were begun as a way to break away from an authoritarian family that was perceived as acting in complicity with state power. Refusing food was an act of rebellion against the family because in the Confucian scheme of things, to damage the body inherited from one's parents was unfilial (Chiu 1991: 342). At the same time, the students were very conscious that food also symbolized Chinese people's relation to the state. Chiu, a graduate student from Hong Kong, wrote that he had a late night conversation with a group of students in the square in which the question of "who fed whom?" arose. He pointed out to the students that they received monthly subsidies from the state; didn't they owe the state something in return? The students replied, "No! We were taught to think so ever since we were born. And some may still be accustomed to thinking so. But not any more." "To take the Party as our mother and give thanks for its breast-feeding? Not a chance, not any more!" "We finally learned that They don't ever feed anybody. On the contrary, They themselves were fed, and far over-fed all those years" (1991: 341).

Thus, the student hunger strike was an attempt to break away from the family and the state by constructing new boundaries around individual bodies, outlining a new and different conception of self in the process.

Conclusions: The Body Caught in the Middle

Because of the nature of their occupation, athletes rely on their bodies as vehicles to improve their lot in life. However, the aspects of their bodies that most preoccupy them are not so much things like bigger muscles or better endurance, but aspects related to reproduction and nutrition. These physiological processes are central to the two most important dependencies in a Chinese person's social life: dependence on family and state. Because a person has little control over these dependencies, the processes attached to them are a subject of much anxiety and calculation.

While reproduction and food have always been central in Chinese culture, many things have changed. Previously, they were embedded in an entire hierarchical cosmology that saw humans and nature as engaging in a never-ending exchange of essences. Human social life was one manifestation of these cosmic exchanges. Today, reproduction and digestion are no longer embedded in an entire "cosmic hierarchical biology," though fragments remain. For example, the 6:30 morning exercises required of physical education institute students, in which inhalation is emphasized, probably stem from the ancient belief that these *yin* hours are best for augmenting one's *qi* (Ware 1966: 139). However, what remains of the classical conceptions of body and cosmos are partial fragments. By contrast, the socialist state and its communist ideology are ever-present in the birth control policy and the food rationing system. Family and class allegiances are sometimes in conflict with the state. The bodies of athletes are caught in the midst of pressures to produce better sports performances for the state and oneself but at the same time to avoid damaging one's ability to marry (and marry well) and to produce children.

One similarity between contemporary and historical China is that the web of dependencies is nearly inescapable because it is so complete. As a result, the boundaries between the body, the family, and the state are more fluid than in the West. The body is not a sealed vessel situated at the center of these social axes, and the person who possesses that body does not do so completely. The "disorganization of the self" described by Sun reflects the social pressures that continuously pull the individual's identity in different directions, while the somatization of Chinese culture reflects the individual's attempt to pull together the fragments of the body that are particularly subject to these centrifugal forces. Because of the importance of food in this process, the student hunger strike in 1989 stands as a powerful symbolic effort to stake out a space for a new and more autonomous self.

REFERENCES

Anderson, E. N.
1988   *The Food of China*. New Haven: Yale University Press.
China Daily
1988   *"Iron Deficiency Affecting Babies," 5 January.
1987   "Children's Diet Improved – Report," 3 November.

Chiu, Fred Y. L.
1991 "The Specificity of the Political on Tiananmen Square, or A Poetics of the Popular Resistance in Beijing." *Dialectical Anthropology* 16 (3–4): 333–47.
Guojia tiwei zhengce yanjiushi [State Sports Commission Policy Research Division]
1982 *Tiyu yundong wenjian xuanbian 1949–1981 [Selected Physical Culture and Sport Documents, 1949–1981].* Beijing: Renmin tiyu chubanshe.
Kahn, Miriam
1986 *Always Hungry, Never Greedy: Food and the Expression of Gender in a Melanesian Society.* Cambridge: Cambridge University Press.
Li Jian
1987 "Xia yige mubiao: sanlianguan!" [Set a Goal – Three Championships in a Row!]. *Nanzihan [Real Man]*, May.
Sun Lung-kee
1983 *Zhongguo wenhuade "shenceng jiegou" [The "Deep Structure" of Chinese Culture].* Hong Kong: Jixianshe.
Ware, James R., trans.
1966 *Alchemy, Medicine, and Religion in the China of* A.D. *320: The Nei P'ien of Ko Hung.* New York: Dover.
Wolf, Margery
1968 *The House of Lim: A Study of a Chinese Farm Family.* Englewood Cliffs, NJ: Prentice-Hall.
Wu Jingshu
1988 "Youngsters Taller but Still Facing Nutrition Problems." *China Daily*, 9 May.
Yang, Mayfair Mei-hui
1989 "The Gift Economy and State Power in China." *Comparative Studies in Society and History* 31 (1): 25–54.
Yin Weixing
1988 "Zhongguo tiyujie" [The Chinese Sportsworld], part 2. *Huacheng [Flower City]* 1: 104–41.

16

The Bakers of Bernburg and the Logics of Communism and Capitalism

Hans Buechler and Judith-Maria Buechler

Baked goods are a hallmark of German culture. Ready access to freshly baked goods is deemed essential to German well-being and to identity.[1] In both Germanies, the skills necessary to ensure the quality of the product were acquired by a long period of apprenticeship combined with formal training at vocational schools. In the GDR, certification as a master artisan was a precondition for obtaining a license to open a private enterprise. State training centers including local enterprise academies (*Berufsschulen*) provided free formal schooling, while private firms took charge of the practical component (Pickel 1992:134–5).

In spite of their recognized status as craftsmen both in the past and in recent history, bakers have occupied a beleaguered position in the German economy and in German society. Particularly since the 16th century, the control that the urban guilds had once held over production of many kinds of goods was gradually undermined by merchant capitalists who managed to bypass the guilds' hold over labor in such craft occupations as weaving by hiring cheap rural workers who worked at home under putting-out contracts (Kriedte 1981). This process continued during the industrial revolution and eliminated many crafts trades altogether. In Germany, however, the development of home work controlled by merchant capitalists did not reach the importance it attained in England. Rather, the impact of industrialization was more abrupt, leading to serious dislocations and pronounced anti-modernism at the end of the 19th century (Volkov 1978:52–3). Concomitantly, unlike England, where crafts guilds gradually lost their importance, the remaining crafts guilds in Germany continued to have considerable political clout throughout the 19th century and to some extent to the present day. Regarding themselves as the upholders of "family values" and other values of "responsible" citizens, artisans sometimes acted independently and sometimes in consort with property owners to uphold or re-establish regulations such as a circumscribed lengthy apprenticeship and a master examination as a precondition to manage a workshop in order to limit competition. Indeed, in 1932, their disillusionment with the liberal policies of the Weimar regime led many of them to support the National Socialists, who promised but then partly reneged on their pledge to enact favorable legislation.[2]

Bakers (as well as butchers) held a relatively favorable position within the crafts trades. They did not face significant competition from industrial production until the second half of the twentieth century. Small operations continued to dominate food processing. Thus, in 1920, 97.5 percent of the enterprises engaged in food processing worked with three or fewer trained workers. This did not mean that the baking trade retained an archaic form. By the mid-1920s, 40 percent of the bakeries were already partly mechanized (Lenger 1988:174). At the same time, they were able to offset the inroads of industrial bakeries by engaging in secondary activities such as the sale of flour and other staples, the production of pastries, or, in the case of rural bakeries, involvement in agriculture (Lenger 1988:175).[3] Industrial bakeries began to increase their share of production significantly only after the mid-1950s. In Western Germany, between 1955 and 1964, output of the bread industries increased by 69.7 percent, from 596 million Deutschmark to 1,011 million Deutschmark, while output from artisanal bakeries grew by only 35.5 percent, from 3,197 million Deutschmark to 4,332 million Deutschmark (Beckermann 1965:60). Since then, the number of artisanal bakeries appears to have fallen dramatically, ceding to large-scale ones with multiple outlets. A western owner of a large-scale bakery in the western German city of Dortmund figured that the number of bakers had dropped from 55 in 1960 to four or five in 1994, while his enterprise alone had eight branch stores in Dortmund. Nevertheless, according to one of our eastern German informants, who heads the Bernburg bakers' guild, artisanal bakeries continue to produce 70 percent of the bread in western Germany.[4]

In the GDR, small bakeries also continued to maintain an important position and, according to the informant quoted above, the proportions produced by artisanal and industrial firms were similar. The GDR was unable to provide for such culturally determined needs as provisioning consumers with freshly baked bread by means of the hegemonic public sector, which by 1972 had incorporated almost all industrial production. By then, agriculture had been fully collectivized, and many artisan trades had been partially collectivized. As Baylis has observed, "'socialism in the colors of the GDR' (to use a slogan from the waning days of the regime) came to be an odd mixture of one-party rule, Marxist–Leninist rhetoric, and a panoply of concessions to western consumerism and cultural values" (1995:136). Hence, although bread was also produced in large state factories, the state was forced to abstain from collectivizing bakers and to allow the continued existence and limited reproduction of small-scale private baking enterprises and pastry shops. In 1986, private bakeries accounted for 43 percent of all baked goods (Pickel 1992:89). Bakeries as well as artisanal enterprises engaged in the repair and service trades (other than construction) were allowed to remain preponderantly in private hands (84 percent in 1986 [Pickel 1992:89]).[5]

The state's relationship to private enterprise in these circumscribed sectors went beyond mere tolerance. The East German state formally legitimized these private activities, establishing a well-defined legal framework (see Pickel 1992). In the case of private bakeries, the basic raw materials – flour, margarine, and sugar – were assured, and competition was nonexistent. As one baker explained, if the state allowed a person to establish a firm, it also had to guarantee its survival by providing the essential means of production: credit to establish or reestablish the workshop and the basic inputs. A license, then, entailed an obligation on the part of the state as well as the licensed artisan. The state was caught in a bind. On the one hand, it wished to promote the dominant path to socialist production – which, ironically, parallelled the Fordist model, except that the capitalists were replaced by the state. At the same time, once it had officially allowed the continuation of certain unortho-dox individualistic practices, it was formally obligated to enable them to work. This incorporation of private business into the state plan was different from other communist countries, where the sector was relegated to a shadow economy, as occurred in Bulgaria (see, e.g., Creed 1998) and, to a lesser extent, Hungary (see, e.g., Burawoy and Lukács 1992; Szelényi 1988).

At the same time, the East German state remained ambivalent about allowing free enterprise. In the 1960s, the state attempted to move private and cooperative enterprises out of the more lucrative production and into repair activities, since private production was perceived as a serious competitive threat to state enterprises. In order to prevent this competition, the state resorted to economic levers and taxation. When the firms did not respond as expected, the state took more drastic measures. It bought out private and cooperative firms engaged in production. In addition, only artisans could become members of artisan cooperatives, and (with a few exceptions) the latter could no longer hire nonmembers (Roesler 1990:111–26). Although by 1976 the state had completed its drive to nationalize industry and collectivize agriculture, it continued to define its relationship with the remaining private entrepreneurs in oppositional terms. In particular, at the local and regional levels, officials used state policies to curtail private enterprises altogether by refusing to concede new licenses or by channeling apprentices away from private artisans into state firms (Roesler 1990:125). Thus the state, once permissive of private enterprise, became increasingly intolerant and hostile.

The private entrepreneurs regarded themselves simultaneously as a cog in the national economy, with certain obligations and expectations, and as outcasts left to their own devices. Although many of the ways in which they coped were shared by the average consumer and, to a degree, the managers of public firms as well, they, unlike the latter, had to hide any success they had achieved. These artisans could always be accused of attempting to reinstate capitalism rather than merely providing services that the state could not fully provide; their continued visible and officially authorized existence was a constant reminder of the inadequacy of a centrally plan-ned production and distribution system. Artisan trades were predicated on the individual and family rather than on collectivities that grew progressively larger with the development of communism; they centered on entrepreneurship as opposed to the redistributive role of the state; they entailed little specialization within the productive unit as opposed to the increasingly narrow definition of roles in state and collective enterprises; and they focused on local needs rather than those of wider geographical areas. The policies regarding artisan trades were not only highly contradictory but also unpredictable. In an economy where all inputs and resources are controlled and allocated by the state, a policy that tolerates private firms but then partially reneges on a truce that runs counter to communist ideology might not be unexpected. This certainly took place (see, for example, Roesler 1990:120–5), but the contradictions between stated policies and ideology and hence the ambiva-lence with which the state regarded its own policies ran much deeper. On the surface, it appeared as though artisans were completely incorporated into the system, as their rights and obligations were well defined. Thus the state did more than renege on a truce when it placed obstacles in the path of the private artisans, obstacles that went much further than those dictated by the chronic scarcity of inputs that affected all enterprises as well as all consumers. The state, in fact, contradicted its own stated policy of incorporation.

Historically then, the position of the bakers changed from a situation in which they were considered necessary but increasingly anachronistic, to a situation in which they were reluctantly tolerated and incongruously incorporated in a formal manner into a system with an alien logic. Their example shows that hegemonizing articulation may entail more than finding common ground among compatible elements, as Laclau and Mouffe (1985) seem to propose. It may also include attempts to incorporate antagonistic elements that cannot be eliminated altogether by a combination of coercion and the provision of a circumscribed niche.

Working Conditions and Coping Mechanisms

The ambiguity with which the state regarded private enterprises is clearly apparent in the manner in which it controlled producers and provided inputs. The mandate to provide bread for the population did not lie lightly on the shoulders of the bakers. The emphasis was on high volume. As one young baker couple described it:

> Imagine, in our small bakery we baked 800 three-pound loaves of bread [a day]! One hundred fit into the oven at one time. They would be gone even before we were able to put the next loaves into the oven. Then some time during the day we would say, "Well, now we will stop." Bread cost only a fifth of what it does now, and we sometimes had a higher turnover than at present. And at that time we had a single store and now we have five outlets and a mobile sales vehicle!

In order to produce such large quantities of bread, a long workday was required. As one informant explained, "It was very hard. We would get up at 3:00 A.M. and work 12 hours every day." The state made sure that the bakers fulfilled their designated role by instituting an elaborate regulatory system:

> They were glad that we took care of providing the population with bread. That was important. It was the alpha and omega. We could not, for heaven's sake, slip up and run out of bread. To make sure that we still had bread in the evening at five or even shortly before six, they undertook spot checks. If we had run out of bread, our subsidies would have been taken away. They said, "You receive the support, but you must provide the public with bread." So they sent employees from the large state industries who volun-teered to act as controllers. They also controlled the prices and weights. They would place the bread on the scale. Did it really weigh three pounds? Then they would place the rolls on the scale, 20 at a time. Had the baker made them too small? Woe be the baker when that proved to be the case. That was considered an act of cheating the

people. Again the subsidies would be cut. It happened to me once, too. They cut the subsidies I received from the state for three months. It amounted to 5,000 marks. That hurt. It was a lot of money. I will show you the price list so that you can see what that entailed in terms of capital formation. I still hang the old list up, for people to see. Those were our prices: *Bienenstich* [a honey cake] 35 Pfennig, poppy seed cake 25 [i.e., a quarter or less of the present price]. There was no great wealth in that.

Neither was there any incentive to make anything but the standard fare even with those ingredients that were available.

Whatever was available was strictly rationed according to the number of workers an artisan employed. The rations in turn depended on the judgment of the authorities. The *Kreis* (country) council had a unit in charge of "Commerce and Provisioning." They distributed whatever was allotted to them for the craftsmen. As one informant said:

It went so far that we had to plan at the end of the year how much flour, sugar, and so forth we would require for the coming year. Of course that was insane. One could not plan one's needs like that.... There was always an adequate supply of flour, but sugar was often scarce. During the Cuban crisis it was really bad. Almost no sugar reached us. Like today, those were the times when you had to elbow your way in and use your connections. One had to know a lot of people, acquaintances and friends, who could help you. We begged and wrangled our materials from everywhere, even other Kreise. Can *you* help me? Can *you* help me? I was constantly on the road looking for things.... Often I would be able to obtain a keg of cottage cheese [*Quark*]. Then I would find a colleague who had poppy seed. So I would say, "You can have half a keg of cottage cheese if you give me half a bag of poppy seed." We had an enormous circle of acquaintances and friends that we created out of necessity. It was like that in all artisan occupations: the struggle for material, to be able to work.

Such stories of struggling to secure inputs are not confined to private GDR enterprises. The former head of a baking and chewing gum factory who now heads a western-owned, large-scale bakery had similar stories to tell about the battle for inputs for the state-owned enterprise which he managed.

We were just as accountable for the unit we managed as we are today, but the state intervened much more in internal matters. We were always severely reprimanded when there was a shortfall of basic foodstuff such as bread and rolls. So we were forced to improvise much more in GDR times. For example, in summer we would hire 15 school kids and rent an entire cherry orchard from someone. The kids would harvest the cherries and we would freeze them and have enough sour cherries to last us for the whole year. Or we might buy up an entire strawberry crop [from a collective] without anyone's knowledge. One just had to refrain from telling anybody what one was up to.... Yes, as a state enterprise we did have an advantage over the cooperatives, where the manager would make decisions for his own benefit. The artisans were even worse off. They received practically nothing. We still had the best conditions, but we also knew how to go about doing things.

Some of our informants conceded that the quality of baked goods was lower then than it is today, which they attributed to inferior technology. Not that the baking industry was not heavily mechanized. The emphasis on high volume would not have been possible without machinery. But the equipment was often old if not antiquated. For example, one baker made do with 50-to 60-year-old machines. Artisans were low on the client priority list of the manufacturers. Producers of bakery equipment were capable of making state of the art equipment, but the best equipment was exported and was available only to state industries if at all.

[. . .]

One of the most negative aspects of working as a private businessman in the GDR was the near impossibility of going beyond the narrow state-defined parameters. For example, our youngest baker informant wished to offer baked goods for diabetics; however, he was refused the right. "I sometimes asked myself why I bothered [to fight the authorities]. But as a young person, I had the urge to undertake something new."

The ambivalence with which the state viewed artisans is very evident in the restrictions imposed on the number of workers they could employ and the kind of training they could provide. Bakers were allowed to train apprentices in production, but not in sales, which was a prerogative of state-owned retail stores. They could only hire unskilled salespersons. They could theoretically employ up to the equivalent of ten full-time workers, but the actual number depended on the authorities, who could allocate as few as they chose. Thus our young informant only received permission to employ three full-time equivalents. . . .

There was not much incentive to work as a journeyman in the private baking business. One informant said, "Wages did not amount to much. [In 1990] the people who worked for me earned only 600 marks a month [half of what someone could earn in the industry for $8\frac{3}{4}$ hours of work per day]. We couldn't pay them more, given the low prices we had to charge. Also, wages were fixed by decree. And we were allowed to pay for only 15 hours of overtime per month."

On the positive side, artisans had the advantage of cheap rent. One baker paid 550 marks to the city for production facilities in two buildings. Another figured that he is now paying ten times as much. Artisans also had no great expenses associated with sales or advertising. No particular salesmanship skills were required either. Consumers came to the bakery, and there was no need to deliver even to the many large-scale public customers who fed their workers.

In combination with the need to share scarce resources, the lack of competition for a share of the market also led to the strengthening of social networks. "We shared everything we had. If a colleague came and wanted a recipe, we gave it to him because there was no competition. We sold what we baked and that was that. Today that wouldn't work. I am more reticent now. That's what may have suffered most. But it's normal. I believe that it is like that over there [in the west] too."

Access to resources, then, was indicative of the ambiguous position of private bakers in GDR society. While they never appeared to have lacked the basic ingredients for making bread, they suffered more than their public counterparts – the large-scale state-owned bread factories – in obtaining anything beyond these basic ingredients. They struggled to produce with woefully inadequate equipment. In addition, they were subjected to constant official scrutiny to ensure that they used the allocated resources only in state-approved ways for prescribed markets.

[. . .]

The Wende

When asked why customers didn't mind purchasing day-old bread in large western-owned supermarkets, one of our baker informants exploded with sarcasm:

> No, in the [new western] supermarkets it can't be old enough to be considered fresh. [But if they come here] then even warm bread is not good enough for them. It has to be still hot. If you are forced to let it drop because it is so hot, then only is it fresh. Warm bread is not fresh enough, "No, we will come again. When will the next batch be ready? In an hour? Well, then we will come back again in an hour." It isn't just one or two customers who make such demands. Many do. And if four or five make a fuss each day, one has had it.

As many observers of eastern Germany at the time of the Wende have noted (e.g., Borneman 1991), the promise of an instant consumer paradise was certainly among the major incentives for rapid reunification. Western goods were considered intrinsically superior to eastern goods, and the seemingly unlimited supply led many consumers to believe that the market could fulfill even their most outlandish desires. For the bakers, this insatiable demand for western products and the seemingly limitless possibilities to raise expected standards for locally produced ones, even when the currency was still the *Ostmark*, meant a scramble to adapt rapidly or to be overwhelmed by the offerings from the west. Some with western experience were psychologically prepared for the transition. As one of our most reflective informants put it, "Because of my brother [who owns a bakery in the west], I had some insight into the market economy and therefore into what was going to happen to us. I did not see the situation with rose-colored glasses. I reflected and asked myself, 'What will befall me? What must I do about it?' I had no false illusions."

Others espoused the consumer mentality uncritically. They purchased the latest equipment, purchased or rented new sales facilities pushed by western salesmen, and remodeled these in the hottest and most expensive western fashions. They accepted the notion that capitalism meant expansion and that the means of achieving the amortization of this expansion would come automatically through increased turnover. As the baker couple whose story opens our article explained it, "The sales representatives for store installations would always try to convince us that the appearance of a store was the be all and end all. They said that image was everything. In GDR times there was none of that. Everything was simple. So we had this urge to make everything beautiful." The response of the bakers to the hegemonic ideas introduced by the Wende thus ranged from exasperated sarcasm or conservative pragmatism to an undaunted espousal of what appeared to be the fundamental principals of modern capitalism.

Interestingly, some of the initial reactions of our bakers were predicated upon the confusion of capitalist notions with past economic concepts. Accepting the notion of increasing production as a primary goal of an enterprise was easy for our young informant quoted above since production targets were the cornerstone of GDR economic development rhetoric. Production costs came second, if they could be calculated at all. Similarly, as in other communist economies (see, e.g., Verdery

1996: ch. 1), demand could be taken for granted, and the limiting factor was the supply of inputs. Not surprisingly, the first reaction of many producers to the Wende was to take advantage of the new opportunities to increase production. When the border was opened, the bakers gained ready access to formerly scarce inputs such as fruit – especially raisins, bananas, and citrus fruit – and other ingredients for pies and cakes, and thus were able to expand their offerings of sweet baked goods. New kinds of flour and other ingredients became available to make hitherto unknown specialty breads as well. According to one informant, "When we had the possibility of importing materials from the west, the demand was very, very great. I have to add, however, that the prices we charged for special breads were low. We were happy that we were able to produce them at all. After all, we still had a lot to learn in this respect."

Consumer behavior changed again, at least temporarily, with monetary union. As the same informant explained, "The demand stopped immediately when the Deutschmark was introduced. People closed their wallets right away. These were, of course, costly items. Now there was no demand, nothing. Later, we slowly began to sell special breads again, but not at the rate of the old *Bundesländer* [i.e., western Germany]."

Past notions of the value of commodities in an economy where you could not go wrong if you acquired and hoarded goods underlay the panicky behavior of the consumers on the eve of monetary union. Another baker described it most vividly:

> Monetary union took place on a weekend. On Friday, all hell broke loose. It was a madhouse. It was the worst day in my life. The large stores ceased to exist as a result of monetary union. They had to take inventory and many of them already closed at noon that day. They had no bread because they were closed. At that time we already had Tschibo coffee[6] that we sold for DDR-marks. One pound cost between 28 and 32 marks. I still have the price tags. But everybody wanted to buy coffee anyway. Workers' collectives that had small accounts for coffee or whatever wanted to convert their money into something tangible. What could they do? Well, they could buy coffee. One wanted 130 pounds! Others wanted coffee for 600 marks. And so it went.... In all this turmoil, a few reporters from *Stern* magazine appeared on the scene and asked me how I felt. I said that I felt like I did in 1945. "What do you mean by that?" they asked. I answered, "In '45 the Russians came and said: Turn left! Now you are coming and saying: Turn right!"

Competing in a Changing Market

The confusion in the aftermath of events of 1989–90 notwithstanding, the basic cultural underpinnings of consumer demand for freshly baked goods did not change in spite of the immediate invasion of industrially produced bread sold by western supermarket chains in the east, thus continuing to provide a potential niche for small-scale bakeries; however, the nature of the competition changed. While in GDR times competition was not regarded as an issue among bakers, today, both in the east and in the west, small-scale bakers must increasingly compete with large-scale bakeries that emulate artisanal bakeries while enjoying economies of scale in those aspects of production that are amenable to such devices. Thus in Bernburg the local bakers operate under the shadow of a powerful, worldly wise 72-year-old western entrepreneur who began his career as a traditional small-scale baker himself and expanded his enterprise into a large-scale operation. After reunification, he extended his production of a wide assortment of artisanal quality breads to Bernburg, which also became the center of 52 stores, including the prized supermarket outlets, served by a fleet of 35 specially heated trucks. Ironically, the success of this expansion was predicated, in part, upon the fact that he was able to take over the local state-owned industrial bakery. The long-term manager of this operation – who presently runs the plant – had already streamlined its operation after the Wende in preparation for privatization. A large-scale program instituted by the Treuhand (the agency in charge of privatization) had enabled him to appropriate the most profitable part of the former complex and secure a number of well-located outlets that had been part of a state-operated chain. The success was also based on the western entrepreneur's extensive know-how and personal business ties with supermarket chain managers.

In the aftermath of reunification, a considerable number of bakers went out of business and, indeed, according to the master of the bakers' guild, the proportion of the bread produced by artisanal bakers and by industrial bakers has been reversed since the Wende, with the artisans now only producing 30 percent of the total output.[7] Western observers of the economic transformation in eastern Germany after the Wende often comment about the irony that many private businesses that had weathered the adverse conditions in the GDR did not survive the advent of capitalism. They have come to the conclusion that GDR private enterprises survived only because they enjoyed the protection of the state. Our baker informants consider this view as based on too superficial an analysis of the actual facts. They argue that the opportunity for early retirement and difficulties with finding a successor rather than economic failure were the major causes for the closure of bakeries after reunification. Working individuals 55 and over had the one-time opportunity to retire with generous benefits, an option that few individuals in any occupation could afford to forfeit. Others blamed the supermarkets and other new competitors from the west. In addition, the bakers who closed shop had no family members willing to succeed them.

Those who continued faced major changes. Suddenly there were no limits imposed on annual earnings. A spouse (in this case, invariably a wife) could be paid a salary and receive social security benefits. From an emphasis on producing large quantities of goods,[8] bakers had to shift to improving quality and searching for new outlets. All this had to be accomplished with a much lower profit margin than in the west; for, as one informant explained, the fact that some bakers had been able to acquire their bakeries before the Wende or still paid low rents enabled them to offer their wares at low prices, forcing the bakers who were less fortunate to content themselves with profit margins well under western norms.

In order to compete with the newcomer from the west and with other small bakeries, all bakers were forced to invest considerable sums to modernize their operations and, in most cases, to open new outlets. Those who did not already own a bakery and a house sought to purchase them. Not only could they thereby reduce their long-term overhead by beating the rapidly increasing rents, but they could use them as collateral for bank loans as well. Our youngest informant tried to purchase his bakery from the city even before the Wende, but he was unsuccessful and had to pay over 250,000 Deutschmark after the Wende. Worse yet, an older informant has been unable to purchase his bakery for a reasonable price. The owner, a westerner who claimed ownership after the Wende, wants to charge him a sum that is far above what our informant thinks the building is worth. Building from scratch is also beyond his means, so he is postponing the decision through legal maneuvers. In the long run, he is thinking about transforming some unused space in one of several buildings where he has rented space for his outlets.

All bakers survived the economic transformation after reunification only as a result of very considerable self-exploitation and postponement of consumption. But the transition was more of a shock for some bakers than it was for others. The "expert advice" of western German sales representatives of baking products and equipment, financial advisors, and tax consultants, who descended in droves on Bernburg, was of very uneven value. One baker was duped by a salesman into buying a machine rejected in the west because of its design flaws. But the young baker who was lured by the slick salesman was ultimately saved from bankruptcy by a competent western German consultant who had saved bakeries in the west before.

Others weathered the initial turmoil and adapted to the new order with fewer ups and downs. One politically aware baker, with a brother in the west, had already prepared himself for the possibility of a change by investing in real estate for his children before the Wende. Others addressed consumer demand for high quality by paying more attention to quality and offering a wider assortment of products even at a considerable sacrifice. The fascination with new things is evident in the comments of one baker:

> Over the years, one comes up with new ideas. I ask around. That's what is fun in the profession, that one doesn't just put things together any old way... but one isn't just born with the knowledge.... One acquires that over many years.... For example, the last time when I went on vacation, I brought a roll back for my daughter. I have to figure out how it's made. That is the interesting part of the profession. That one doesn't just bake. One has to have fun with it.

Another baker immediately discarded his antiquated kneading machine and began kneading the dough by hand again, like his grandfather (from whom he had inherited the business) had done, until he was able to afford a western machine that could ensure the same results. Consequently, his firm did not suffer the same decrease in turnover as most other bakeries. As we have shown at the beginning of this article, this was precisely the strategy suggested by the elderly western entrepreneur who said that one had to start out modestly – although this advice was not what one might expect given the stress that western advisors often place on rapid increase in scale and the recent history of this entrepreneur's own firm. Had he not initially distributed bread by bicycle?

Indeed, a wholesale redirection of economic strategies toward ever-increasing economies of scale was but one of several possible routes followed by our informants, and our young baker who made the most radical moves in this direction also placed himself into the most precarious economic position. Rather, the same survival strategies that had proven adaptive before World War II and later during communism (reliance on family resources combined with mechanization to the degree possible but without incurring excessive indebtedness) continued to be valuable under the new conditions. Our informants felt that shrewd maneuvering, a basic commitment to their trade as a vocation and to their clientele, and a willing successor continued to be the best guarantee for success.

It would also be incorrect to argue, however, that the baking trade was based on the survival of pre-communist artisan traditions and an acceptance of market principles alone, for traditions developed during communism also had an impact on the survival of the trade in post-Wende eastern Germany.

The Reassertion of GDR Identities

After an initial experimentation with the trendy, some bakers began to cater to the nostalgia for "*unsere Zeit*" (literally "our time," i.e., the old days). This nostalgia, which has been noted by many observers, may be regarded as the reassertion of a separate GDR identity, "defensively and obstinately documenting the present limits of westernization" (Kocka, quoted in Baylis 1995:136). The baker who had almost lost his shirt modernizing stores discovered that his most successful store was the old-fashioned (but also centrally located) one where older and poorer clients felt comfortable and where he reintroduced small, hard-crusted *ossi* (a derogatory term for easterner) rolls. Our young informant explained:

> The main part of our operation is here. I have modernized it completely. After the Wende, people saw how the rolls were in the west. They thought that everything should be just like in the west. So we changed the technology. But then they found out that they didn't like the taste after all. Well, now we had a problem. But, by happenstance, I was able to rent an outlet in midtown, which came with an old bakery equipped with an old oven of the kind we had used before. So now we produce the other type of rolls very successfully. The old method doesn't correspond with what one is taught in school at all.[9] But the people want them like that. You can produce perfect buns of the highest quality, but if people don't like them that way, it is to no avail. . . . It doesn't matter what the store looks like. All our other stores are modern. We invested a lot of money in them. But in that store we decided not to invest anything. You will laugh your head off, if you go there. But that store sells.[10] I sometimes have the impression that, especially in these rural areas or small cities where customers know the master baker, they say, "He has bought all of this [fancy stuff] with our money. We are paying part of this." And, in the last analysis, they are right. They are jealous. There was a period when I noticed that people just refused to buy from me out of protest. In the beginning, when I let myself be influenced by what the westerners told me to do, I advertised my business with identical advertisements on all my vehicles and a corresponding campaign in print. All nonsense.

Reliance on word-of-mouth advertising rather than expensive campaigns appears to be a widespread strategy. Another baker explained the rationale:

> One can find particular niches and produce things that are out of the ordinary. I make certain fruit and cream cakes that can't be found everywhere: hazelnut-gooseberry cakes and kirsch cakes. The word spreads. That happens very slowly. One does not need to advertise. No, it's better not to when one isn't quite sure about something and it doesn't come out too well yet. That has negative consequences. I do it the other way

around. I say that the goods have to advertise themselves. Also, I have kept those things that were already good here. I still make the bread without additives. I employ a three-stage process to make the dough rise. First, the ingredients are cheaper, even though there is more work involved. I have to get back to the bakery and make sour dough in the evening. But there is nothing quite like it. It's the sourdough bread like it was invented 2,000 years ago, but more developed.

He then went into a long discussion about the scientific development of the method and its use during the war when rationalization was essential. "But then, after the Wende, the firms came and said, 'Here, take these additives. You just have to mix them in and success is assured.' In the beginning, everybody was delighted. Now people are going back to the old methods. Now we let nature do it again." The bakers and clients, then, are defining the limits of the new order in controlling taste.

Even bakers who are at the forefront of innovation, for example a baker who in addition to making traditional German breads also makes French baguettes, do not necessarily believe that they could be more creative at present than they had been in the past. When asked whether she could be more creative now with access to a greater variety of ingredients, one informant said that, on the contrary, it was more creative to do something with whatever was at hand. "Now that everything is available, it's no longer any fun. Then, one had to figure out what one could do with what one had. My master always told me, 'The art of cooking is to make something out of nothing.' And so it is. It is indeed possible." Another informant echoed this nostalgia for "our time" when one had to improvise. He said, "Somehow, thinking back on it, it also was fun. There was something nostalgic about it."

After the experimentation during the initial euphoria of the opening of the border, many eastern Germans resisted the hegemony of western tastes by reasserting their own regional predilections, some of which, like the ossi rolls, were borne out of the perseverance, during GDR times, of technologies long obsolete in the west. More generally, the easterners reacted against capitalism, with its increasing economic differentiation, by rejecting some of the outward symbols of wealth. A number of observers of the post-communist transition have commented on the yearning for a more egalitarian society. For example, Holy (1992:240–1) comments on the Czechs' criticism of the entrepreneurs because of their fear that they will enrich themselves at the cost of others (see also Holy 1996). While Holy sees the roots of Czech egalitarianism as predating communism, roots that he regards as having predisposed Czechs to the acceptance of this aspect of socialist ideology, such a claim could certainly not be made for eastern German society, which was highly stratified before Russian occupation. We encountered it even among highly successful business managers who were reluctant to display their wealth for fear of social opprobrium and tried their utmost to conserve jobs, or to create or find jobs elsewhere for the workers they were forced to let go in order to rationalize their operations (see Buechler and Buechler 1997). [. . .]

The Nature of the New Eastern German Capitalism

The particular brand of capitalism introduced into eastern Germany after the Wende and – inseparable from its nature – the manner in which it was introduced and its representations by the actors involved was as fraught with contradictions as the communist economic system that had preceded it. Indeed, the precipitous nature of the transformation fostered even greater inconsistencies between actions and results and among the different policies. On the one hand, the German state seemed friendly to small family businesses reflecting the various constituencies, including small-scale farming in Bavaria and elsewhere. On the other, the large, well-endowed western firms had an advantage in taking over the state bakeries. Although in Bernburg the latter had essentially rationalized production and adapted to a market economy, the former managers lacked the capital to continue on their own. In contrast, the westerners had no difficulties obtaining bank loans and hence could also take advantage of the high investment subsidies (32 percent for the initial investment in the case of the western baker) and the fact that initial losses could be written off against profit made on western operations. ... Thus, unlike agriculture, where local cooperative managers were able to maintain control over a large proportion of the land (see Buechler and Buechler 1995, 2000), and the construction industry, where capital requirements were not quite as daunting, privatization of manufacturing largely favored the westerners. At best, the latter took over the more promising factories and continued production, and at worst the factories were closed either because they could not be rehabilitated to function economically or simply because they competed with western enterprises. Similarly, large-scale merchandising is also predominantly in the hands of western chain stores that came over almost immediately after the Wende and first operated out of makeshift quarters and then built more permanent facilities of their own. The state-run outlets were never given a chance to restructure themselves as private chains. Thus, even though the westerners (and some of the eastern consultants whom they had trained) professed adherence to liberal economic principles to a much greater degree than they did in western Germany where market socialism was only beginning to come under attack in the early 1990s, political clout, patronage and established social networks played a much greater role than the westerners were willing to concede.[11] The principles of pure capitalism often professed by westerners in the east neither correspond to the situation in the west nor to the massively subsidized economy in the east. They do come in handy to convince those with less power to accede to the demands of those with more power.

Conclusion

[...]

The case of the bakers in communist and post-communist eastern Germany presents the opportunity for observing the operation of divergent hegemonic processes. Analyses of the incongruous positions of social practices highlighted by the nature of continuity and change after the Wende not only demonstrates that unorthodox practices were not entirely subsumed by hegemonic structures under communism, but also give us a better understanding of the mechanisms of (attempted) articulation. In GDR times, the bakers of Bernburg regarded themselves as embattled independent artisans who often had difficulties establishing themselves, but also as a "protected species" crucial to the functioning of the economy and with a relatively well-defined niche in the economic structure (see Pickel 1992). They were both outside (and opposed to) and within the logic of the communist economy. The effect of the process of confrontation-cum-partial articulation was that in spite of the emphasis on Taylorism in the GDR, there were *more* artisanal bakeries before than after the Wende. The limited space allocated to them constrained them but also ensured their survival. They became, beyond a point, impervious to the competition from mass production but also from competition in general. As far as we know, there were no moonlighting bakers. But even when officially recognized artisans did face competition from moonlighting factory workers, their privileged access to inputs distributed by the state assured their survival. The bakers survived because they adopted mass production techniques and because industrial bakers also suffered from inadequate technology, although to a lesser degree.

As Pickel has shown, attempts at incorporation in the GDR were not immediately reflected in the official ideology. Thus the SED (communist party) first incorporated a mixed economy into its own special variety of communist ideology only in the 1960s (Pickel 1992:10). Subsequently, that incorporation was, in practice, again largely repudiated during several waves of nationalization, but what remained of the private sector continued to be legitimized ideologically by stressing the concept of an alliance between workers and craftsmen against capital (Pickel 1992:20).[12] While there were no further attempts to nationalize or even to cooperativize craftsmen since 1976, the position of crafts enterprises continued to be contested particularly in highly industrial regions such as the Bezirk of Halle. Ideological inconsistency, then, became an integral part of the hegemony.[13] Ironically, through the very limitations it imposed upon artisanal firms, including those on succession, communism ensured the continued location of a public function in the family sphere and lent it official symbolic recognition, thereby presenting to the public a possible alternative, one that had to be constantly neutralized by means of what Verdery (1996) calls the "spoiler" role of communism.

[...]

Today the position of the bakers in the economy is almost as ambiguous as it was before the Wende. On the one hand, locally owned and controlled businesses are regarded by the German government as one of the clearest signs of a successful transition to capitalism – a kind of *Urform* of capitalism – and are granted considerable government subsidies. On the other hand, bakers now not only face the competition of industrial producers – a factor that did not bother our informants too much, as they had faced such competition from state enterprises before the Wende – they now also face the competition of a large-scale, high-quality producer with stores in both residential areas as well as in shopping malls. The artisans and more generally the family firm, including family farmers, are faced with the strange situation where such firms are regarded as the hallmark of entrepreneurship at the same time that most of the material and organizational support of the state and financial institutions goes to the large-scale enterprises mostly originating in the west.

The bakers did not expect special protection, but they did expect fair rules of competition within the new hegemonic large-scale capitalism. Given their own background as private artisans, some viewed the western entrepreneur's cornering of supermarket outlets as an example of the failure to uphold capitalist principles.

We are reminded of Scott's observation that, as their needs change, capitalists continuously subvert the hegemonic precepts they have themselves helped to create and maintain and it is the subaltern classes that are often the upholders of orthodox understandings (1985:345–7).[14]

[...]

NOTES

1   Bread is consumed at every meal, and fresh bread represents the least common denominator of a good meal. Fresh bread can archetypically serve to underlie the enjoyment of commensality and caring of those who provided and prepared the meal.

2   It should be noted that in the November 1932 elections, the support for the National Socialists among the artisans had weakened again. By then, however, it was too late to stop the party's momentum (Wulf 1969:141–8; see also Lenger 1988:190–2 and Volkov 1978).

3   Artisanal bakeries appear to have enjoyed a significant cost advantage in retailing compared to industrial producers. In 1953, costs of retailing bread in western Germany constituted 22.5 percent of the total costs for industrial bakeries and only 13.5 percent for artisanal bakeries (Beckermann 1959:64). It is interesting to note that bakers have used innovative ways to expand their activities in earlier times as well. For example, in the early 19th century, bakers in Bavaria began brewing beer to supplement their income (Frey 1998).

4   It is not clear whether this figure includes semi-industrial bakeries who produce at a relatively large scale but who continue to employ many artisanal features like the baker in our opening paragraph.

5   This model of private production was extended to small-scale primary household production as well. Households were paid subsidized prices for privately produced pork, veal, eggs, and produce.

6   Tschibo is a western German, cooperatively owned supplier to small stores.

7   According to the same informant, there were 101 private bakers in Bernburg in 1966; around 45 in 1975; and still some 25 just before the Wende. At present, only 12 small-scale bakeries remain.

8   One informant figured that he was transforming only half of the amount of flour he had used before the Wende.

9   The ingredients for the two kinds of breads are the same. The difference lies entirely in the type of oven. The new ovens are convection ovens with circulating hot air. The old ovens used hot water lines to warm the air, which did not circulate. Interestingly, a short visit in November and December 1999 revealed that our informant had had to scrap the old oven, but had painstakingly succeeded in having the system replicated in his new facilities.

10   By 1999, following the example of most, if not all commercial establishments in Bernberg, even this store had been renovated.

11   To his credit, the western entrepreneur was quite open about the importance of his personal connections among western supermarket chain managers, to which he ascribed his success in monopolizing this segment of the market.

12   Historically, such an alliance was actually highly problematic. Owners of craft enterprises were always pitted against their own workers, while the industrial workers could not identify with the craft masters' antimodernism (see Volkov 1978).

13   Other scholars of socialist systems have also questioned the "omnipotence of the dominant class and the reproduction of class domination" and have argued instead that this
class has been forced into making "lasting and strategically important concessions"
(Szelényi 1988). But the implications for destabilizing the very logic of hegemonies
have not been considered by these authors.

14   Similar observations have been made for situations under communism. Thus Burawoy
and Lukács (1992:134) posit that workers in state socialist economies such as Hungary
were constantly faced with the discrepancy between the ideal world of productive
relations "painted" (as they put it) by the authorities and the actual relations they
experienced in the workplace.

References

Baylis, Thomas
    1995 Eastern Germany. *In* The Legacies of Communism in Eastern Europe. Zoltan Barany
    and Ivan Volgyes, eds. Pp. 111–37. Baltimore, MD: John Hopkins University Press.
Beckermann, Theo
    1959 Das Handwerk – gestern und heute. Essen: Rheinisch-Westfälisches Institut für
    Wirtschaftsforschung, No. 15.
    1965 Das Handwerk. Essen: Rheinisch-Westfälisches Institut für Wirtschaftsforschung.
Borneman, John
    1991 After the Wall: East Meets West in the New Berlin. New York: Basic Books.
Buechler, Hans, and Judith-Maria Buechler
    1995 The Many Faces of Agricultural Privatization in Eastern Germany. *Anthropology of
    Work Review* 16(3–4):32–9.
    1997 "Incorporated Ambiguities" in Pre- and Post-*Wende* Economic Systems in Eastern
    Germany. Paper presented at the 23rd New Hampshire Symposium "Beyond the East?
    Heading West? East German Perspectives and Prospects in the United Germany," June
    20–27.
    2000 Farmers, Conflict and Identity in Eastern Germany. *Identities: Global Studies in
    Culture and Power* 7(1):39–83.
Burawoy, Michael, and János Lukács
    1992 The Radiant Past: Ideology and Reality in Hungary's Road to Capitalism. Chicago:
    University of Chicago Press.
Creed, Gerald
    1998 Domesticating Revolution: From Socialist Reform to Ambivalent Transition in a
    Bulgarian Village. University Park: Pennsylvania State University Press.
Frey, Dennis
    1998 Wealth Management and the *Handwerker* Household in Göppingen 1735–1865.
    Ph.D. dissertation, Department of History, Syracuse University.
Holy, Ladislav
    1992 Culture, Market Ideology and Economic Reform in Czechoslovakia. In Contesting
    Markets: Analyses of Ideology, Discourse and Practice. Roy Dilley, ed. Pp. 231–43. Edin-
    burgh: Edinburgh University Press.
    1996 The Little Czech and the Great Czech Nation: National Identity and the Post-
    Communist Social Transformation. Cambridge: Cambridge University Press.
Kriedte, Peter
    1981 The Origins, the Agrarian Context, and the Conditions in the World Market. *In*
    Industrialization before Industrialization. Studies in Modern Capitalism. Peter Kriedte,

Hans Medick, and Jürgen Schlumborn, eds. Pp. 12–37. Cambridge: Cambridge University Press.

Laclau, Ernesto, and Chantal Mouffe
  1985 Hegemony and Socialist Strategy: Towards a Radical Democratic Politics. London: Verso.

Lenger, Friederich
  1988 Sozialgeschichte der deutschen Handwerker seit 1800. Frankfurt: Suhrkamp.

Pickel, Andreas
  1992 Radical Transitions: The Survival of Entrepreneurship in the GDR. Boulder, CO: Westview Press.

Roesler, Jörg
  1990 Zwischen Plan und Markt: Die Wirtschaftsreform 1963–1970 in der DDR. Berlin: Haufe.

Scott, James C.
  1985 Weapons of the Weak: Everyday Forms of Peasant Resistance. New Haven, CT: Yale University Press.

Szelényi, Iván
  1988 Socialist Entrepreneurs: Embourgeoisement in Rural Hungary. Madison: University of Wisconsin Press.

Verdery, Katherine
  1996 What Was Socialism, and What Comes Next? Princeton, NJ: Princeton University Press.

Volkov, Sulami
  1978 The Rise of Popular Antimodernism in Germany: The Urban Master Artisans, 1873–1896. Princeton, NJ: Princeton University Press.

Wulf, Peter
  1969 Die politische Haltung des schleswig-holsteinsichen Handwerks 1928–1932. Kölns & Opladen: Westdeutscher Verlag.

17

The Global Food Fight

Robert Paarlberg

Food for Thought

Powerful new technologies often provoke strong resistance. When the internal combustion engine gave us automobiles, advocates of horse-drawn buggies scorned the fad. When nuclear fission was first mastered, much sentiment turned against its use – even for peaceful purposes. Thus today's backlash against the commercial use of recombinant DNA technology for food production should not be surprising. Consumer and environmental groups, mostly in Europe, depict genetically modified (GM) food crops, produced mostly in the United States, as dangerous to human health and the environment. These critics want tight labeling for GM foods, limits on international trade in GM crops, and perhaps even a moratorium on any further commercial development of this new technology – all to prevent risks that are still mostly hypothetical.

The international debate over GM crops pits a cautious, consumer-driven Europe against aggressive American industry. Yet the real stakeholders in this debate are poor farmers and poorly fed consumers in Asia, Africa, and Latin America. These are the regions most in need of new transgenic crop technologies, given their difficult farming conditions and rapidly growing populations. Yet poor farmers in tropical countries are neither participating in nor profiting from the GM crop revolution.

Gene Genie

The genetic modification of plants and animals through domestication and controlled breeding has gone on with little debate for roughly 10,000 years. But since 1973, genetic modification has also been possible through the transfer of isolated genes into the DNA of another organism. This type of genetic engineering – also known as genetic transformation, transgenesis, or simply GM – is a more powerful and more precise method of modifying life. Genes carrying specific traits can be transferred using a "gene gun" between species that would not normally be able to exchange genetic material. A trait for cold resistance, for example, can be transferred from a fish to a plant.

As powerful as GM technology is, the large corporate investments needed to develop commercial applications for transgenic crops did not begin until 1980, when the US Supreme Court extended patent protection to new types of plants and plant parts, including seeds, tissue cultures, and genes. Only after the Court guaranteed the protection of intellectual property rights did private corporations make the substantial investments necessary to develop commercially attractive transgenic crops.

The first GM crops that emerged were designed to solve important farm problems: pest control, weed control, and soil protection. The Monsanto Company, for example, developed soybeans with a built-in immunity to glyphosate, the active ingredient in the Monsanto herbicide Roundup. Having planted these GM soybeans, farmers could control weeds with a single spray of glyphosate, which had previously been lethal to the soybean plant. This reduced the need to employ more toxic and long-lasting weed killers or soil-damaging tillage. Several companies also developed GM varieties of cotton and corn engineered to contain a naturally occurring toxin – *Bacillus thuringiensis* (also known as Bt) – that minimizes insect damage to plants while dramatically reducing the need for chemical sprays.

These new GM field crops were finally released for large-scale commercial use by US farmers in 1996. This followed years of laboratory testing and controlled field trials to screen for risks to other crops and animals, to the larger environment, and to human health. Once the Environmental Protection Agency, the Food and Drug Administration (FDA), and the US Department of Agriculture approved the new GM seeds, American farmers gave them a try and instantly liked the results. By 1999, roughly half the US soybean crop and one-third of the corn crop were genetically modified. While the seed companies made money, American farmers were the biggest winners, capturing roughly half of the total economic benefit from the new technology. (Patent-holders and seed companies gained only about a third of the added profits, while consumers got less than that.)

Enthusiasm for GM crops among American farmers is not hard to understand, given the decreased need for chemical sprays and tillage. Most US farmers growing "Roundup Ready" soybeans need to spray only once, cutting chemical costs by 10–40 percent. Transgenic cotton often requires no spraying at all (compared to the 4–6 sprayings previously needed), reducing production costs by $60–$120 per acre.

Surprisingly, however, the GM seed boom has only been effectively realized in three countries. In 1999, 72 percent of all land planted with transgenics worldwide was in the United States, while Argentina had 17 percent and Canada 10 percent. The nine other countries that were (openly, at least) growing some transgenic crops – China, Australia, South Africa, Mexico, Spain, France, Portugal, Romania, and Ukraine – split the remaining one percent.

The weak participation of tropical countries can be partly explained by the industry's initial focus on temperate-zone crops such as soybeans and corn. But how can we explain the lack of enthusiasm among farmers in western Europe? There should have been nothing to prevent these farmers from making the switch to GM seeds. American companies have tried to market transgenic seeds in Europe, and some attractive GM crops have also been developed and patented by European-based companies. Yet within the European Union the new technology has not taken hold. As of 1999, only a few farms in Spain, France, and Portugal were planting transgenic crops.

Allergic Reaction

European farmers have stayed away from transgenic crops largely because European consumers have become frightened of eating them. Consumers in Europe are now leading a backlash against GM crops – even though no safety risks linked to any GM crops on the market have ever been documented in Europe or anywhere else. After conducting its own 18-month study of this question, the UK-based Nuffield Council on Bioethics published the following conclusion in May 1999:

> We have not been able to find any evidence of harm. We are satisfied that all products currently on the market have been rigorously screened by the regulatory authorities, that they continue to be monitored, and that no evidence of harm has been detected. We have concluded that all the GM food so far on the market in this country is safe for consumption.

Yet such expert reassurances are discounted by European consumers, distrustful since the 1996 "mad cow disease" scare. That crisis undermined consumer trust in expert opinion after UK public health officials gave consumers what proved to be a false assurance that there was no danger in eating beef from diseased animals. Although mad cow disease had nothing to do with the genetic modification of food, it generated new consumer anxieties about food safety at precisely the moment in 1996 when US-grown GM soybeans were first being cleared for import into the EU.

Exploiting such anxieties, a number of third parties, including nongovernmental organizations (NGOs), quickly stepped into the fray. Greenpeace and other European activist groups that had previously struggled against nuclear power and the use of various man-made chemicals (especially chlorine, which Greenpeace had tried to label "the Devil's chemical") inflamed consumer phobias of GM foods. In Britain, Prince Charles (a self-described organic farmer) and Paul McCartney joined the chorus. In France – where food is never just food – a broad coalition of farmers, labor unions, environmentalists, and communists launched attacks against not only GM food but also McDonald's, imported beef grown with (non-GM) hormones, Coca-Cola, and various other threats to what they called French "culinary sovereignty." In Germany, GM opponents drew dark parallels between the genetic manipulation of food and their country's earlier lapse into human eugenics.

These well-publicized campaigns forced significant corporate and government concessions in Europe. In April 1998, without scientific evidence of any harm from GM foods, Brussels stopped approving new GM crops for use in or import into the EU. This has meant a de facto ban on all corn imports from the United States (worth roughly $200 million annually), since bulk shipments might contain some

GM varieties not yet approved. The EU also enacted a GM food labeling provision in 1998, requiring its 15 member states to begin marking all packaged foods that contain GM corn and soy. The United Kingdom went even further, requiring that restaurants, caterers, and bakers either list all GM ingredients or face fines of up to $8,400. To avoid consumer boycotts and lawsuits brought by activist groups, a growing number of food companies, retail stores, and fast-food chains (including both Burger King and McDonald's) in Europe pledged in 1999 not to use GM ingredients – at least where it could be avoided.

This backlash began to spread in 1999 to food-importing nations outside of Europe. Japan, South Korea, Australia, and New Zealand made plans to begin mandatory labeling for some transgenic foods, including heavily imported products such as GM soybeans and GM corn if intended for human consumption (as opposed to animal feed). Japan and South Korea together represent an $11.3 billion annual market for US agriculture, and US officials have worried that protectionist farm interests lie behind these labeling moves. But consumer anxiety is once again the more powerful factor at play. Responding to such fears, Japan's Kirin Brewery Company recently announced that starting in 2001 it would use only non-GM cornstarch for its beer; Kirin's competitor, Sapporo Breweries, made a similar announcement the next day.

Over Here

Europe's consumer-led backlash against GM crops put US officials in an awkward spot. Usually the United States urges Europe and Japan to be more market-oriented in their food and agricultural policies; now, consumer-led market forces obliged the United States to adjust. US officials have opposed the mandatory labeling of GM products. But the US farm sector is so heavily export-oriented (US farmers export more than 25 percent of the corn, soybean, and cotton they produce, and more than 50 percent of wheat and rice) that foreign pressure is prompting an informal movement in the other direction. The Archer Daniels Midland Company, a prominent US-based soy-processing and export firm, announced in 1999 that it would henceforth ask US farmers to deliver their GM and non-GM soybeans in separate batches so ADM could offer "GM free" products to consumers in Europe and Japan. Two large US-based baby-food companies, Gerber and H. J. Heinz, announced in 1999 that they would soon switch to non-GM ingredients – not because of any new evidence that transgenic ingredients were unsafe, but out of fear of a Greenpeace-led boycott. Frito-Lay, the nation's major snack-food provider, followed suit, announcing that it would no longer use GM corn. In November 1999, several members of Congress introduced a "Genetically Engineered Food Right to Know" bill that would require labels on any food containing at least 0.10 percent GM ingredients. The Grocery Manufacturers of America opposed this measure but supported stronger consultation requirements between food companies and the FDA, hoping to boost consumer confidence.

Credible labeling of all food produced from GM commodities would be an expensive proposition for US farms, agribusinesses, and consumers. It would require complete physical segregation of GM and non-GM food along every step of production, from the farm gate to the grocery shelf. US officials estimate that this could increase costs by 10–30 percent.

In the meantime, the European and Asian backlash against US-grown GM crops could generate sharp conflicts in several international settings, including the World Trade Organization (WTO) and the Convention on Biological Diversity (CBD). Within the WTO, the Sanitary and Phytosanitary (SPS) Agreement permits nations to restrict imports in the name of health or environmental protection. But an unresolved question is whether governments can restrict imports under conditions of scientific uncertainty, on a precautionary basis. The SPS agreement allows import restrictions only on a provisional basis while governments seek additional information.

The EU is trying to weaken this WTO requirement. In January 2000, it managed to insert language supporting its precautionary principle into the text of the new Protocol on Biosafety in the CBD. Hammered out by environmental rather than trade ministers, this protocol was drafted specifically to govern international trade in transgenic organisms, and it now states in several places that a "lack of scientific certainty due to insufficient relevant scientific information and knowledge" should not prevent states from taking precautionary import actions. The protocol then goes on to oblige exporters of living modified organisms meant for environmental release (such as plants or seeds) to provide prior notification of relevant biosafety information and to solicit an informed consent agreement from importers.

The United States fought to include language in the protocol that would place it under the authority of WTO rules, but was blocked from doing so by the EU and most developing countries. State Department officials reluctantly accepted the final terms of the protocol, partly with the hope that it might calm consumer and importer fears if the United States and the EU were seen to agree on the issue. By accepting the protocol, the United States also avoided further isolation within the CBD (to which Washington is not yet a formal party, since the Senate has failed to ratify it). But this acquiescence may have weakened America's hand on future GM trade issues within the WTO.

Such conflicts between the United States and Europe over GM crops may continue to escalate in the months and years ahead. Yet the most important stakeholders in the fight over GM foods have not been heard. It is among poor farmers and poor consumers in developing countries that the potential gains from this new technology are most significant. In the tropics, many consumers are not yet well fed and most farmers are not yet wealthy. Larger investments in the genetic modification of some crops could open a new avenue of escape from poverty and malnutrition for hundreds of millions of citizens in Asia, Africa, and Latin America. Yet far too little is being done to make that happen.

Serious Stakes

If properly exploited, the GM crop revolution will have life-changing – and even life-saving – implications in developing countries. Food-production requirements are increasing rapidly in the tropics due to population growth. Yet agriculture there is lagging, in part because of poor soil; extremes of moisture, heat, and drought; and a plenitude of pests and diseases that attack animals and crops. Poor farmers in tropical Asia and Africa currently lose much of their crop production every year (often more than 30 percent) to insects and plant disease.

Here is where modern transgenic technology carries special promise for the tropics: it can engineer plants and animals with highly specific pest and disease resistances. For example, poor farmers in Kenya today lose 15–45 percent of their maize to stem borers and other insects. If they could plant maize seeds engineered to contain Bt, a pest-killing toxin, they could reduce their losses without reliance on chemical sprays. Similarly, transgenic virus-resistant potatoes could help small-scale farmers in Mexico who currently suffer substantial crop damage. And a World Bank panel has estimated that transgenic technologies could increase rice production in Asia by 10–25 percent within the next decade. Without such gains, increasing demand from a growing population could push the price of rice beyond the reach of the poor.

Genetic technology could also improve nutrition. If the 250 million malnourished Asians who currently subsist on rice were able to grow and consume rice genetically modified to contain Vitamin A and iron, cases of Vitamin A deficiency (which currently kills 2 million a year and blinds hundreds of thousands of children) would fall, as would the incidence of anemia (one of the main killers of women of childbearing age).

The UN's Food and Agriculture Organization has recently estimated that one out of every five citizens of the developing world – 828 million people in all – still suffers from chronic undernourishment. The reason for this is lagging agricultural production in some poor regions despite the earlier innovations of the so-called green revolution. The disadvantaged (and mostly female) farmers of Africa were bypassed by the dramatic gains brought on by the conventional (non-GM) plant-breeding breakthroughs of the 1960s and 1970s. Between 1970 and 1983, new high-yielding rice varieties spread to about 50 percent of Asia's vast rice lands but to only about 15 percent in sub-Saharan Africa. Similarly, improved wheat varieties spread to more than 90 percent of Asia and Latin America but to only 59 percent of sub-Saharan Africa. This helps explain why agricultural production has increased ahead of population growth in both East and South Asia while falling behind population growth in sub-Saharan Africa – leaving an estimated 39 percent of Africans undernourished.

African farmers fell behind because they had greater difficulty than Asians in getting access to the full package of green revolution technology. Earlier cross-bred crops still required farmers to buy supplementary products, such as chemical sprays. But with new transgenic crops, all the potential for enhanced productivity exists in the seed itself. Pests and diseases are managed not with chemicals but through genetic engineering.

Critics of the GM revolution fear that the environment might be hurt if engineered crops are released into rural tropical settings where wild relatives of food plants can often be found. If an engineered herbicide-resistance trait breeds into a weedy wild relative, the result might be a hard-to-manage "superweed." Or widespread planting of Bt crops might trigger an evolving population of "superbugs" resistant to the toxin. Legitimate biosafety concerns such as these have so far been addressed in rich countries on a case-by-case basis, through field testing under closely monitored conditions; the means for such testing and monitoring are still largely missing in the developing world. Even so, the hypothetical threat to biosafety posed by GM crops remains demonstrably smaller than the actual threat posed by invasions of exotic but non-GM plant and animal species. By some estimates, exotic species movements (having nothing to do with genetic engineering) currently generate tens of billions of dollars in losses to agriculture annually in the developing world. If these countries are truly concerned with biosafety, GM crops should hardly be their first focus.

Transgenic products not only reduce chemical sprays, they can also aid in land conservation and species protection. For small farmers in the tropics, if GM crops or animal vaccines make farm and grazing lands more productive, there will be less need to plow up or graze more fragile lands in the future. In sub-Saharan Africa, roughly 5 million hectares of forest are lost every year, primarily to new clearance for low-yield agriculture. The real threat to biodiversity in poor countries today comes from such cutting of natural habitats. Thus the ultimate environmental payoff from transgenic crop technologies could include fewer watersheds destroyed, fewer hillsides plowed, fewer trees cut, and more species saved.

Pound Foolish

Although the GM crop revolution could greatly benefit poor farmers in poor countries, this potential is not being realized. As noted above, their relatively prosperous colleagues in North America and Argentina grow 99 percent of all GM crops. Why have poor farmers in developing countries not participated in the boom?

First, consider the market-driven motives of the private GM seed companies that have been making the largest investments in this new technology. These multinationals have been criticized for their alleged efforts to make poor farmers in the developing world dependent on GM seeds. In fact, the GM seeds these companies are bringing to market have mostly been designed for sale to farmers in rich (mostly temperate-zone) countries. The danger is not that poor farmers in the tropics will become dependent on these companies; the danger is that corporate investments will mostly ignore the tropics because farmers there do not have the purchasing power to buy expensive GM seeds.

Some GM crop technologies originally developed for the temperate zone (Bt maize and cotton, for example) might readily be adapted for use in the tropics by transferring the desirable GM traits into locally grown crops through conventional plant breeding. Private companies, however, have little incentive to invest in such local adaptations where farmers are poor. Worse, they may seek to block local adaptations if poor countries are not willing to protect corporate intellectual property rights (IPRS). Seed companies had once hoped to solve piracy problems by engineering a natural sterility (called gene-use restriction technology, or GURT) into the seeds of GM plants. But such thoughts were set aside in 1999 when Monsanto agreed, under intense pressure from critics, not to commercialize its "terminator" GURT technology.

Protection of intellectual property is less of a problem in rich countries such as the United States. If anything, the US Patent and Trademark Office has given corporations more protection than is good for them. Companies can now patent not just the inventive use of plant traits and genes, but also some of the smallest fragments of genetic material. Since the commercialization of a single transgenic insect-tolerant plant can now require the combination of many separately patented subtechnologies, problems with legal gridlock arise.

In most developing countries, however, IPR protection for GM crops tends to be too weak rather than too strong. A WTO agreement on trade-related aspects of intellectual property rights (TRIPS), reached during the Uruguay Round of negotiations, requires that all WTO members – including even the poorest countries after 2006 – provide IPR protection for plant varieties. Yet many developing countries will try to satisfy TRIPS without giving up the traditional privileges of farmers to replicate and replant protected seeds on their farms.

This being the case, corporations will remain wary. As long as both purchasing power and IPR protection remain missing, private firms will probably not invest in the innovations most needed by poor farmers in tropical countries. For these farmers, the marketplace by itself is unlikely to produce much GM magic. Market forces have not prompted international drug companies to do adequate research in tropical diseases such as malaria. Similarly, market forces alone will not trigger the GM crop investments most needed by poor farmers in Asia and Africa.

A historical comparison drives the point home. Hundreds of millions of poor farmers in the developing world (at least those on good land) benefited from the earlier green revolution because in that case private multinationals were not in the lead. Instead, the leaders were governments, international financial institutions, and private philanthropies (especially the Ford and Rockefeller foundations). Market-oriented corporations did not build the laboratories or support the plant-breeding efforts in Mexico and in the Philippines that led to new, high-yielding varieties of wheat and rice in the 1950s and 1960s. These strains were developed and later adapted for local use by plant breeders working within the public sector, paid for in large part by Cold War-era foreign aid. The adapted local varieties were then replicated by national seed companies and given away to farmers. Intellectual property rights were not an issue, since government agencies wanted the seeds to spread as fast as possible. During this original green revolution, the public sector often went so far as to extend subsidies to farmers for cheap irrigation and fertilizers along with the seeds themselves.

Today's public-sector institutions are showing much less leadership in promoting the gene revolution. Reasons for this include a mistaken impression that all regions shared in the green revolution's success; the much larger and riskier investments in science that are needed to develop and commercialize new GM crop varieties; the dramatic shrinkage in budget leeway in most developing countries since the 1980s debt crisis; the model of market-led development pushed onto borrowing countries by the World Bank and the International Monetary Fund after that crisis; the disrepute of public sector-led development following the collapse of the Soviet Union; and finally, the diminished rationale for generous foreign aid to poor countries following the end of the Cold War.

Unfortunately, public development institutions also shy away from investment in GM technology out of fear: fear of media criticism, of litigation, or of physical attack by anti-GM activists. These are not imagined risks. The headquarters of the US Agency for International Development's principal developing-country biotechnology support project, located at Michigan State University, was set on fire just before midnight on December 31, 1999, by an underground group calling itself the Earth Liberation Front.

More than just GM research is being left undone. Public-sector support for agricultural development has collapsed across the board. Annual foreign aid to agriculture in poor countries fell by 57 percent between 1988 and 1996 (from $9.24 billion down to just $4.0 billion, measured in constant 1990 dollars), and annual World Bank lending for agriculture and rural development fell by 47 percent between 1986 and 1998 (from $6 billion to just $3.2 billion, measured in constant 1996 dollars). As donors have pulled back, governments in the developing world have not filled the gap. Poor countries remain notoriously unmindful of the need to invest in agriculture, despite the documented high payoffs. These governments are distracted by demands from more powerful urban constituencies, often led by the army, state-owned industries, or the state bureaucracy. On average, developing countries devote only 7.5 percent of total government spending to agriculture, and little of this goes for research. Sub-Saharan Africa has only 42 agricultural researchers per million economically active persons in agriculture, compared with an average of 2,458 researchers per million in developed countries.

Even taking these private-sector limitations and public-sector lapses into account, the near total exclusion of poor-country farmers from today's GM crop revolution remains surprising. Even where useful GM technologies are commercially available, officials in poor countries have been curiously slow to allow their use. One reason has been the export to the developing world of the highly cautious attitude of European consumers and environmental groups toward GM crops. European fears have been exported both through market channels and through activist campaigns launched or supported by European-based NGOs.

In Thailand, for example, where exports of agricultural products such as rice, shrimp, tapioca, and poultry provide 23 percent of total export earnings and where local scientists have already engineered some improved GM crop varieties under greenhouse conditions, the actual planting of GM seeds is now blocked by the government. Warnings from customers in Europe and Australia that Thai exports might be shunned if they include any GM ingredients prompted Bangkok to announce, in mid-1999, that henceforth GM seeds would not be brought into the country until proven safe for human consumption. Some GM soybean and cotton seeds (grown safely and profitably by farmers in the United States since 1996) are rumored to be reaching Thai farmers through black-market channels, but the Thai government – which until recently had supported GM crops – now views such imports as criminal.

In Brazil, farmers who had hoped to plant herbicide-resistant soybeans in 1999 were blocked at the last moment when a federal judge granted an injunction filed by Greenpeace and a Brazilian consumer institute on grounds of a possible threat to the Brazilian environment. Higher courts are now reviewing the case, but a ban on planting remains in place. Farmers eager to get GM soybean seeds have been smuggling them in from Argentina, but the state government of Rio Grande do Sul, partly in hopes of being able to offer GM-free products to customers in Europe and Japan, has threatened to burn their fields and jail any farmers found to be growing GM soybeans. Greenpeace has thrown its weight behind efforts to keep Rio Grande do Sul a "GM-free zone."

In India, devastating bollworm infestations in cotton plants have brought despair – and reportedly hundreds of suicides – to poor cotton farmers. Insects have developed resistance to the heavy volume of pesticides sprayed on Indian fields. (Cotton accounts for 50 percent of all pesticide sprayed in India, even though the crop takes up only 5 percent of total farmland.) In recent Indian field tests, a GM cotton variety genetically modified to control bollworm increased crop yields by 40 percent while permitting seven fewer sprayings. But commercial release has been delayed because NGOs have filed a public-interest lawsuit against the government agency that authorized the trials, and activists have destroyed some of the test fields. Many of the same activist groups that oppose GM seeds in India today also opposed the introduction of improved non-GM seeds during the earlier green revolution.

Tragically, the leading players in this global GM food fight – US-based industry advocates on the one hand and European consumers and environmentalists on the other – simply do not reliably represent the interests of farmers or consumers in poor countries. With government leadership and investment missing, the public interest has been poorly served. When national governments, foreign donors, and international institutions pull back from making investments of their own in shaping a potentially valuable new technology, the subsequent public debate naturally deteriorates into a grudge match between aggressive corporations and their most confrontational NGO adversaries. This confrontation then frightens the public sector, deepening the paralysis.

Breaking that paralysis will require courageous leadership, especially from policymakers in developing countries. These leaders need to carve out a greater measure of independence from the GM food debate in Europe and the United States. Much larger public-sector investments of their own in basic and applied agricultural research will be necessary to achieve this autonomy. New investments in locally generated technology represent not just a path to sustainable food security for the rural poor in these countries; in today's knowledge-driven world, such investments are increasingly the key to independence itself.

18

Half-lives and Healthy Bodies: Discourses on "Contaminated" Food and Healing in Post-Chernobyl Ukraine

Sarah Drue Phillips

"We'll never know what real damage Chernobyl has wrought," said Ludmila, a doctor at Kyiv's Clinic of the Radiation Register, where the bodies of Chernobyl victims are examined, scanned, and evaluated on a yearly basis. "Chernobyl is like a big experiment, and all of us are reluctant lab rats." On April 26, 1986, an accident at the V. I. Lenin Nuclear Power Plant at Chernobyl, Ukraine, resulted in the release of millions of curies of radionuclides such as iodine-131, cesium-137, and strontium-90 (Chernousenko 1991:viii). In Ukraine, over 90 million acres of land – 14 percent of the country's total area – were contaminated with radioactive cesium-137, with contamination levels ranging from over one curie per square kilometer to more than 15 curies per square kilometer (Page et al. 1995:143; Marples 1993:3).

Residents of Kyiv, the capital city located a mere 72 miles from the damaged reactor, were not told of the accident until April 29, three days after the event. The first health warning concerning the dangers of radioactive fallout was issued only on May 5 (Marples 1988:114–15). By that time, Kyiv's children had been forced to march in the annual May Day parade in the Soviet regime's efforts to maintain an air of normalcy. The parade took place during a time when radiation levels in Kyiv were highest. Lydia, a physicist, told me: "That was when we really began to question the Soviet system. We realized that the regime was not working for *us*. The interests of the people were not important." Indeed, scholars such as Catherine Wanner (1998:33) and Roman Solchanyk (1992:xiii) cite the Chernobyl catastrophe as one of the major catalysts that ignited the struggle for national independence in Ukraine, which began to gain momentum in the late 1980s.

[...]

In my research on the legacy of Chernobyl in Ukraine, I have been especially interested to examine how debates and practices concerning Chernobyl and its effects reflect state–citizen relationships that are fraught with tension. In this article I will consider post-Chernobyl food consumption as a lens through which to explore a variety of discourses produced and reproduced by Ukrainians. The article will focus primarily on food discourses as reflecting critiques of the Soviet and Ukrainian states for failing to adequately care for citizens, and also as indexing ambivalent attitudes toward the role science should play in everyday life. Other topics explored include the invention of post-socialist/post-Chernobyl selves through food discourses and practices that speak to class identities and inequalities in food consumption, particularly the consumption of "clean" and "radioprotective" foodstuffs.

Chernobyl, Food, and Public Health

Following the Chernobyl accident in 1986, the territory around ground zero was divided into three zones that were delineated according to levels of radioactive contamination. The most contaminated zone is the so-called "exclusion zone" or "dead zone," which surrounds the Chernobyl nuclear plant and covers a total area of 4,300 square kilometers. This zone is also called the "30-kilometer zone," since it includes the territory within 30 kilometers of ground zero in all directions. The exclusion zone of "obligatory evacuation" is considered too contaminated to be fit for human life. Nevertheless, as of 1995, approximately 1,000 so-called "partisans" had returned to the 30-kilometer zone and had taken up residence in their former homes (Sayenko 1996:147).[1]

The second zone is also theoretically a zone of obligatory evacuation, despite the fact that hundreds of thousands still live in the second zone today. The third zone, the zone of "voluntary" or "free-will" evacuation, exhibits contamination levels of between 5 and 15 curies per square kilometer. This zone is also home to hundreds of thousands of residents. Officially, residents of the second and third zones are entitled to state-provided housing in a "clean" area should they choose to relocate. In practice, the government is financially unable or unwilling to provide this compensation. Although according to the Chernobyl "liquidation" program (the official strategy to rid Ukraine of the ill effects of the nuclear disaster) 250,000 persons should have been relocated from contaminated zones, only half this number were actually evacuated. This means that at least 125,000 persons in Ukraine still live in areas significantly contaminated by radionuclides (Sayenko and Prylypko 1996:123).

Millions of others in Ukraine, including the residents of Kyiv, live in conditions of long-term exposure to low-dose radiation (Greenpeace 1994:31; Institute for Experimental Radiology 1998:1). Because of the nature of the radionuclides released during the accident, the ill effects of the disaster will be long-lived (cesium-137 has a half-life of 30.1 years; strontium-90 has a half-life of 28.6 years) (Mould 1988:118). Fourteen years after the nuclear accident, intake of radionuclides is almost exclusively a result of drinking contaminated water and milk and eating foods grown in contaminated soil.[2] According to the Soviet-era data of the radiological section of the sanitary epidemiological department (Rus. *sanepidstantsiia*),[3] during the last two-thirds of 1986 (that is, after Chernobyl), in the Ukrainian SSR levels of stron-tium-90 in foodstuffs rose significantly from 1985 levels. Levels rose significantly in staples of the Ukrainian diet: nine times in milk and nearly four times in wheat bread and potatoes (Knizhnikov et al. 1988:69).[4] It was concluded that the average citizen's daily intake of cesium-137 and cesium-134 after Chernobyl increased seventy times over (Knizhnikov et al. 1988:70).

While measures were taken by the Soviet regime to monitor food contamination immediately after the disaster and continuing until around 1995, such efforts have been largely abandoned, in part because of a lack of economic resources. Until 1995, food vendors at Kyiv's food markets were required to have their products measured for radiation contamination, and to receive a certificate showing the level or radio-nuclides present. Buyers could then ask vendors to see their certificates and feel somewhat confident that they were buying "clean" foods.[5] No such measures are in force today, and residents of Kyiv have no assurance that the fruits, vegetables, meat, milk products, and the like that they purchase from vendors at the city's large bazaars have not been grown in contaminated regions. Many food manufacturers place labels on their products reading "radiation control guaranteed," or "ecologic-ally clean." I found, however, that many consumers doubt the truth of these claims.

People refer to food suspected to have been grown in radiation-laden soil as "dirty" (Ukr. *brudnyi;* Rus. *griaznoe*), but radionuclides are not, of course, "ordinary" dirt. Radiation is invisible, odorless, and tasteless. It is at once everywhere yet nowhere, and its consumption in food products – especially for those living near Chernobyl – is practically unavoidable. While many city-dwellers made efforts immediately after the accident to acquire and consume foods deemed "clean," such evaluations have given way to other, more pressing concerns. Amidst the various postindependence economic and social crises, most Ukrainians are compelled to worry more about putting food on the table than about the "ecological state" (*ekolohichnyi stan*) of that food. Radiation surveillance of foodstuffs is a rare luxury, as is calorie counting in a country where the average monthly salary is around \$250–300. Viktor, a young professional in Kyiv in his mid-20s, related the anxiety and uncertainty that accompany food shopping in post-Chernobyl Ukraine:

> ...A huge percentage of foodstuffs are bought now from a free market called a "bazaar" because it is cheaper [than buying food in stores]. And it is practically impossible to check if food is from the Chernobyl zone. Of course, people think about the fact that they might be eating "not-clean" food grown at a "dirty" place, but what can they do about it? Nothing.

Another consultant, a young biologist in Kyiv named Oleg, commented:

> As to the products with labels saying they are ecologically clean – you can find such products often, and they are really varied. At the dentist's office they even showed me a certificate confirming that their fillings are ecologically clean! Many firms of course put such labels on ordinary products so they will sell better, but our people don't really look at those labels, they look at the price. A lot of foodstuffs from contaminated zones are sold at the market, especially berries, potatoes, and mushrooms.[6]

In Ukraine, long-term low-dose radiation exposure is blamed for a great number of illnesses and deleterious health conditions. Cancer is the most obvious of these, especially thyroid cancer, whose incidence has increased at least tenfold since the Chernobyl accident (Shcherbak 1996:47–8). Intake of radionuclides is said to leach the bones of calcium, making the exposed person more susceptible to fractures and breaks.[7] Accelerated aging is also blamed on the nuclear accident (Akhaladze et al. 1997; Akhaladze 1998),[8] as are a large number of digestive, circulatory, and respiratory problems. Studies have associated long-term low-dose radiation exposure among children living in contaminated territories with chronic respiratory infections; illnesses of the tonsils and adenoids; diseases of the oral cavity, liver, and pancreas; and pathologies of the blood and blood forming organs, especially iron-deficiency anemia (Nahorna et al. 1998). Many in Ukraine complain of a general weakening of the organism and its capacity to fight disease, an anomalous condition referred to as "radiation AIDS." A similar condition among children in particular is called "Chernobyl syndrome."

Ukrainian researchers claim that the effects of ingesting radionuclides are made worse due to the high-stress environment in which many Ukrainians live today. Such stress is largely a result of the country's continuous socioeconomic crises and the pervasive mood of uncertainty about the future. The joint effects of radiation and intense stress, some medical experts assert, compromise the organism's immune, nervous, and endocrine systems, making post-Chernobyl bodies ready conduits for chronic illness and disease (Institute for Experimental Radiology 1998:4).

Since it is extremely difficult to link a specific illness directly to Chernobyl, the disaster's role as an etiological factor in all of these health problems is, of course, contested. People in positions of power have used references to "radiophobia" to discredit citizens' claims that their health problems are Chernobyl-related. Such accusations emphasize the "psychological" effects of the disaster while minimizing the perception of health effects. The fact remains, however, that post-Chernobyl eating can pose risks to health. In the following case study, I trace one family's Chernobyl-related food experiences since 1986. Many people in Ukraine, I found, have resigned themselves to the radiation exposure inherent in consuming post-Chernobyl foodstuffs. On the other hand, some persons, even in contexts of near destitution, may take up specific food strategies to decrease the dangers of post-Chernobyl eating.

Post-Chernobyl Foodways in One Ukrainian Household

Lydia, now divorced and in her mid-40s, lives with her 19-year-old son, Myron, in a one-room apartment in Kyiv. Lydia, like most Ukrainian women, is the exclusive food-acquirer and preparer for her family. As in many countries of the former Soviet bloc (and in many countries worldwide), in Ukraine "cooking contributes to the social and moral evaluation of full female personhood" (West 2000:117). Under state socialism, women in Ukraine were expected to work full-time outside the home and simultaneously perform their "womanly duties" in the domestic sphere – cooking, cleaning, laundering, and childcare. Today paternalist/nationalist narratives in Ukraine also encourage women to "fulfil their primary maternal obligations"

(Pavylchko 1992:93) by protecting the family hearth and inscribing Ukrainian national ideals and traditions in the hearts and minds of their children. Women's roles are largely "ideologically circumscribed by the household" (West 2000:122), and food preparation is a duty ascribed almost exclusively to women.

Therefore, like most women in Ukraine, Lydia has been obliged to cultivate an especially deep concern for the subtleties of food consumption since the Chernobyl accident. Worldwide, women are responsible for feeding their families in ways that take into account the preferences of "tastes" of other family members, adhere to budgetary constraints, and are considered "healthy" (Caplan 1997:9). Women like Lydia in Ukraine, however, also must take into account the ill effects of Chernobyl when making food-related decisions for their families. Ukrainian women's food-related decisions, in other words, affect the health and well-being of their family members in an especially conspicuous fashion (Counihan and Kaplan 1998).

Lydia told me that the moment she learned of the nuclear accident, her relation-ship to food changed. As a physicist, she understood the potentially devastating consequences of the disaster for her health and that of her husband and son. Lydia and her husband immediately arranged for their then five-year-old child to spend the summer with relatives in Poltava oblast' (province), located east of Kyiv oblast' and well out of Chernobyl's reach. Staying behind in Kyiv, Lydia and her husband restricted their intake of milk products, meat, vegetables and berries – foods that were especially susceptible to radiation contamination. During the period directly following the accident, they consumed cereal grains (*kashy*) and canned foods that had been bought or prepared predisaster, as did many other people. In Kyiv imme-diately after the Chernobyl accident, the consumption of milk and milk products decreased by 27 percent, fruits and berries by 24 percent and vegetables by 22 percent (Page et al. 1995:145).

Each summer, Lydia and her son traveled to clean Poltava oblast', where she hoped he could drink his fill of non-contaminated milk. She did her canning in Poltava as well, using food products grown in that clean area. Like Lydia's son, during the first three summers following the Chernobyl accident, the majority of Kyiv's children spent their summers vacationing in clean regions. For three years after the disaster, Lydia restricted her family's diet almost exclusively to foodstuffs that her parents sent them via railway from noncontaminated Poltava. The practice of importing foods from clean regions after Chernobyl was common among those Kyivans who had relatives in clean areas and could afford the expense. For Lydia, the impracticalities and high cost of such food-importing practices eventually proved too much. This became increasingly true during the difficult years of *perestroika* (restructuring), especially in 1989, 1990, and 1991, when citizens all over the Soviet Union were faced with near-economic destitution.

"Now we never eat clean foods," Lydia told me in 1998. Like most in Kyiv, today Lydia does not follow strict Chernobyl-related dietary restrictions. It would be impossible, she says, to calculate the levels of radiation present in the foods she buys at local markets. When the state-enforced system of "radiation control" of foods sold in state-run stores and open-air bazaars was in place, Lydia was careful about the products she purchased. She always insisted on seeing the vendors' certificate proving that the foodstuffs had been monitored for radionuclides. Now, she lamented, no such assurances are available for consumers.

The state's contemporary hands-off approach to the radiation monitoring of food is disturbing to Lydia and other informants, who feel powerless to make informed decisions about which food products are clean and thus pose least risk to health. To complicate matters, Lydia's pitiful salary of $120 per month does not allow her to be choosy about what to purchase and consume.[9] Like many of my consultants in Kyiv, Lydia does not go to the market to buy specific food items, but rather to buy those products that are being offered at the cheapest prices. Her family's daily menu is usually based not on what she and her son would like to eat, but rather on what they can afford to eat. Lydia does not have the resources to buy imported foods (like milk and milk products, for example) that might be radiologically cleaner than local products.

At times Lydia does, however, purchase low-cost foods that she conceptualizes to be "radioprotectors." These foods act as "sorbents," said Lydia, latching onto radionuclides in the organism and removing them from the body. She makes salads from vitamin-rich canned seaweed, for example, increases the pectins in her family's diet by using apples in a variety of recipes, and tries to consume a good deal of beta-carotene rich foods such as carrots and other orange vegetables. The overflowing bookshelves in her tiny apartment include books and pamphlets on healthy eating in the post-Chernobyl context. As a scientist, Lydia has read widely about the health effects of Chernobyl and about consumption strategies to minimize one's exposure to radiation through food and water.

[...]

In Chernobyl's wake the notion that certain "substances" (Ukr. *rechovyny*; Rus. *veshchestva*) could serve the body as radioprotectors emerged. While several Ukrainian research institutes were involved in developing and testing radioprotective products before Chernobyl, since the disaster such efforts have been pursued more intensely.[10] Simply put, radioprotectors are foods and foodstuffs that have been shown to decrease the effects of ionizing radiation on the human organism. One scientist at Kyiv's Institute for Experimental Radiology (where potential radioprotectors are tested on irradiated rats before being approved for production) described radioprotector to me as "substances that increase the defensive properties of the cells and of the organism in general. They bind up radionuclides and hard metals in the stomach and intestines and flush (*vyvedut*) them from the organism."

Vitamins C, A, and E, beta-carotene, pectins, iodine, and folic acid are considered radioprotectors. They are all vitamins, provitamins, and micro-elements that are naturally present in many fruits and vegetables. Their radioprotective qualities are derived from their ability to act as antioxidants, or scavengers of free radicals in the body. In order to maximize the radio-protective potential of antioxidants, Ukrainian scientists have included them in concentrated form in balsams, juices, powders, tablets, and effervescent wafers. Some examples include dissolvable tablets called *Iablopekt* that contains pectins; the non-alcoholic balsam *Il'ia Murometz* (made from concentrated apple and grape juices, sugar-based sweeteners, and an infusion of herbs); the non-alcoholic drink *Barbi-Kola* (a combination of concentrated apple juice, pumpkin puree, honey, and purified water); *Kosmol* (a "food additive" made from dried skim milk, protein concentrate from whole milk, malted barley extract, vegetable oil, calcium lactate, and ascorbic acid); and *Spirulina Platensys* (a "food additive" derived from vitamin-rich seaweed). There is also a widespread belief that red wine and vodka are radioprotectors, but scientists refute such claims, countering that alcohol robs the organism of essential vitamins and therefore does more harm than good.

[...]

Post-Chernobyl Food, the State, and the Market

[T]he phenomena of radioprotectors – and narratives surrounding post-Chernobyl eating, science, and health that are connected to them – index a profound critique of the Ukrainian state by citizens. Struggles over eating after Chernobyl involve debates about which foods are healthy and clean, and whose responsibility it is to ensure healthy eating options for Ukraine's citizenry. My consultants interpreted the dearth of manufactured radioprotectors as evidence of the state's unwillingness to take responsibility for the Chernobyl disaster and its ill effects on health. They criticized the state for failing to take adequate measures to ensure post-Chernobyl food safety, especially since the technology and know-how was in place. Scientists at the Institute of Biocolloidal Chemistry, for example, have developed low-cost methods of "deactivating" (decontaminating) irradiated milk. The Ukrainian state, however, shows no interest in implementing (and paying for) these procedures, which are designed to cleanse milk produced by cows in second- and third-zone villages.[11] The Institute's research is sponsored by a Spanish scientific establishment, an arrangement the Ukrainian scientists find ironic.

On the whole, specially manufactured radioprotectors are neither mass produced nor widely available to consumers. In February 1998, I joined acquaintances from the Institute for Experimental Radiology at an exposition in Kyiv devoted to health and health care. The scientists arranged an impressive booth and displayed a wide variety of radioprotective products behind glass windows. All of these balsams, jams, sauces, purees, and food additives had been studied and certified by the Institute's scientists as effective radioprotectors. Of the approximately 15–20 different items on display at the exposition, however, only three were available for purchase by expo-goers. This deceivingly well-stocked booth was testimony that while many radioprotective products have been developed and proven to be effective, very few of them are actually produced for consumption by Ukrainians in conditions of post-Chernobyl low dose radiation. In a small household health survey that I conducted during 1998 among 68 persons in Kyiv,[12] 63 percent (43 respondents) reported that they did not use radioprotectors regularly, while 37 percent (25 respondents) said they did use food substances they believed to be radioprotectors. Because of the cost and lack of availability, most who use radioprotectors do so by consuming foods known to be high in certain radioprotective elements, rather than partaking of specially manufactured food and food additives.

The lack of readily available radioprotectors, I found, represented for many the state's neglect of citizens' "needs." Consumption in the Soviet bloc – where production and redistribution were state-controlled – was always political, since the limited availability of many consumer goods meant that citizens had to devise their own strategies to obtain scarce goods (Verdery 1996:27–8). They did so by participating in the "second" or "informal" economy (the black market). Today, the introduction of a free market system in the former Soviet Union and privatization of enterprises complicates the issue of needs – how are citizens' needs to be defined, and which institutions or agents are responsible for meeting these needs?

In post-socialist countries such as Ukraine, the role of the state vis-à-vis citizens is being furiously debated. With limited resources, the Ukrainian state is renegotiating its responsibilities toward citizens, and international lending agencies such as the International Monetary Fund (IMF) push Ukraine toward "structural adjustment," which involves the dismantling of socialist-era social safety nets.[13] Struggles over the role of the state revolve around the question of whether the state should focus on protecting citizens, or whether it should act primarily as guarantor of market and private property per neoliberal economic policy. These opposing duties of the state epitomize the difference between the commitments of the state socialist system of government and the country's newly adopted capitalist market system. Citizens, who are used to being cared for by the "socialist nanny state," feel that the state has failed them, in part because the state has let market concerns take priority over the welfare of citizens. Many in Ukraine mourn the demise of the Soviet state, and feel that the state has abandoned them.

[...]

In my interviews with respondents, I found that they frequently indexed their use of various healing practices – including food therapies involving radioprotectors – in narratives through which they constructed specific class identities. In the Soviet Union, real differences in income between more- and less-educated workers were small, yet a distinction between the intelligentsia and the working class was central to perceptions of difference, often labelled as one's level of culture (kul'turnist'). Therefore, social differentiation was based not on monetary capital, but rather on cultural capital, which was assessed by calculating education and qualifications, social ties, and access to information and resources. This system of social differentiation continues in Ukraine, even in conditions of an increasingly stratified society in terms of socioeconomics. Post-socialism has seen the rise of Ukrainian *nouveaux riches* ("New Ukrainians"), many of whom are very wealthy businessmen (*biznesmeny*). The New Ukrainians are perceived much like the New Russians, who are represented in popular discourse as wealthy yet dim-witted men who lack culture and education, have poor taste, and exhibit bad manners.

[...]

In consultants' food-related narratives, knowledge and use of radioprotectors and other health-maintenance practices to counter the ill effects of Chernobyl were associated with high levels of education, intelligence, and awareness. Lydia told me, for example, that "people who didn't know – those people began to forget [about Chernobyl] three years after [the accident]." Another consultant compared the class distinctions embedded in radioprotector use with those that inform language politics in post-Soviet Ukraine. The phenomenon of radioprotector use, he said, reminded him of intelligentsia families he knew in Kyiv who made it family policy to speak only Ukrainian after independence. Ukrainian-language use, like knowledge and use of radioprotectors, he said, has become a sign of prestige and culture in contemporary Kyiv.

Indeed, my surveys in Kyiv showed that higher levels of income were not predictors of radioprotector use in general. One consultant, a young woman who was an unemployed accountant, reported that she used radioprotector, even though her monthly income was only around $3.00. Obviously unable to afford manufactured radioprotectors, this young woman instead tried to consume foods known to be high in radioprotective elements. In fact, the same was true for nearly all of the survey respondents who said they used radioprotectors. This is further evidence that high socioeconomic status and radioprotector use are not necessarily correlates, since a variety of foods with radioprotective qualities are widely available. One can thus strive to consume radioprotective foods without purchasing manufactured radio-protectors. ...

Interestingly, but not unexpectedly, my findings showed that people in medical and/or scientific professions were more likely to have knowledge about both natural and manufactured radioprotectors and were more likely to use them. The majority of consultants who used both types of radioprotectors were doctors, nurses, and scientific researchers. These people were part of social networks in which discus-sions about health, the body, and Chernobyl were frequent. As well, their consump-tion practices were influenced by those around them, especially by their work colleagues, with whom they shared health and nutrition-related advice. Most con-sultants narrated their use of radioprotective foodstuffs as part of a larger strategy to maintain a healthy way of life. They used talk about radioprotectors to shore up their senses of self as knowledgeable, resourceful, and body and health-conscious persons.

Galina Lindquist's (2001) analysis of healing systems in contemporary Russia is relevant to a discussion of how people in post-Chernobyl Ukraine construct their senses of personhood in dialogue with various events, persons, and material objects (Bakhtin 1981; Bruner 1986; Rosaldo 1984). Lindquist (2001:18) writes:

> ...In Russia, individual health-seeking strategies may be pragmatic last resorts; but they may also be political and ideological statements of identity and of belonging to different social groups, of cultural and ideological strands and flows, as well as attitudes to past and present.

Using and talking about radioprotectors was precisely one way my consultants were able to position themselves as members of a group of citizens who were concerned about their health, and actively took up strategies to ensure good health and clean eating after Chernobyl. Though impoverished and often unable to buy specially prepared radioprotectors, these people are able to assert their social worth in other ways. Namely, they index their high levels of education (almost all had higher educations) and underline their self-respect by taking up certain food strat-egies. Those who prefer to use imported radioprotectors from Germany thus assert their place in a globalizing world and take up critiques of the Ukrainian state and its pharmaceutical industry. Discourses on radioprotectors interrogate the role of sci-ence and raise questions regarding the Ukrainian state's responsibilities towards citizens. By utilizing radioprotectors, people commit themselves to a particular post-Chernobyl "body culture" and also take up a variety of narratives concerning science, the state, and the market. Such debates and practices – and the "ideological strands and flows" they index – are crucial to the invention of post-Chernobyl, post-Soviet selves in Ukraine.

Conclusion

Chernobyl fundamentally changed how persons in Ukraine think about and consume food. Indeed, post-Chernobyl food practices reflect ways in which Ukrainians are rethinking health, illness, and the body when faced with what Petryna (1995:197) has called "the blinding and incomprehensible light delivered by Chernobyl." Discourses surrounding post-Chernobyl consumption reveal how class is conceptualized in Ukraine, and how even persons with limited incomes can empower themselves through their decisions to engage in healthy eating by including radioprotective foods in their diets. At the same time, manufactured radioprotectors are still cost-prohibitive for many, and such products are not widely available. This means that citizens must develop their own strategies to counter the ill effects of contaminated food. In so doing they take up a range of narratives to position themselves vis-à-vis various post-socialist institutions. Food strategies such as the utilization of radioprotectors thus reflect ways in which post-socialist, post-Chernobyl selves are being refashioned through discourses and bodily practices that manifest ambivalent attitudes toward science, the state and the market.

NOTES

1   A sociological survey conducted by Yury Sayenko of the Institute of Sociology in Kyiv showed that 94 percent of the "partisans" were 51 years of age and older; 81 percent lived with a spouse in two-person households. In 1999, to much fanfare, residents of the "exclusion" zone welcomed the first baby to be born there since the 1986 disaster. The baby, who by all reports was born healthy, was named Maria, a name that evoked for Ukrainians associations with the Virgin Mary. Her birth therefore was interpreted symbolically in the popular media as a sign of rejuvenation and post-Chernobyl resilience.

2   The contamination of Kyiv's drinking water by radionuclides has been a source of concern since the accident. The Chernobyl plant is located on the upper reaches of the Dnipro River, which is used extensively as a source of drinking water in Kyiv. The Kyiv Reservoir is located partially within the 30-kilometer "exclusion zone" around the Chernobyl nuclear power plant. While contamination levels of surface water have dropped since the accident, experts warn that "there is still a danger from pulses of radioactivity from the runoff following spring thaw or high-precipitation events" (Page et al. 1995:143). It was not until 10 years after the Chernobyl accident that deep artesian wells were dug in the city of Kyiv as sources of safe drinking water for residents. Today, many families draw drinking water exclusively from these wells, which are located throughout the city.

3   Both Ukrainian and Russian are used in Ukraine. Russian words in the text are demarcated by the abbreviation "Rus." and Ukrainian words are indicated by "Ukr." No abbreviation indicates that the word is Ukrainian.

4   Statistics reported during the Soviet era regarding the effects of Chernobyl where notoriously conservative. It is possible that contamination levels were higher than those reported in scholarly reports such as the one cited here.

5   It should be considered, however, that the Soviet regime actually went to extreme lengths to cover up the ecological and health consequences of the Chernobyl accident. Radiological data was frequently falsified, and dosimeters given to clean-up workers (called

"liquidators") were even programmed to show deceivingly low readings of radiation. It is not surprising, then, that many doubted the veracity of claims of "effective radiation control" at Kyiv's markets and were skeptical about the authenticity and reliability of the certificates issued to vendors.

6   Though most of the fallout from Chernobyl was confined to the territories of Ukraine, Belarus, and Russia, residents of these countries are not the only Europeans who might worry about consuming foods grown in contaminated areas. During research trips to villages in Rivne oblast', in western Ukraine, I found that persons living in the third zone had been hired to pick local wild mushrooms and berries which were then illegally shipped to France and Italy for processing and marketing.

7   I met one man living in the third zone who had suffered 15 broken bones since Chernobyl. When I asked his family members the reason for his weak bones, they replied without hesitation: "Chernobyl."

8   Ludmila (the doctor at Kyiv's Clinic of the Radiation Register cited earlier) takes part in a project to monitor the health of *Chernobyltsi*, or "Chernobyl victims," a group comprised of liquidators (the men and women who took part in the disaster clean-up) and persons evacuated from contaminated areas after the disaster. Ludmila told me, "I am continually amazed by how old *Chernobyltsi* look. The radiation has aged them prematurely. Just the other day a middle-aged woman came in with all kinds of health problems. But the thing is I just thought she was middle-aged. I couldn't believe it when she told me she was only seventeen!"

9   In 1999, the average per capita GDP in Ukraine was $3,458. The estimated earned income for men was $4,576, and for women $2,488 (United Nations Development Programme Human Development Report 2001).

10 Institutes and research centers that have worked on developing and testing radioprotectors include the Institute for Experimental Radiology, the Institute of Toxicology, the Ukrainian Center for Scientific Hygiene, and the Scientific Research Institute for Food Hygiene, among others.

11 Some state employees – specifically those working in research institutions where they faced elevated radiation exposure – did receive food subsidies from the government in the form of milk and cheese.

12 This survey was conducted in the Ukrainian cities of Kyiv, Kharkiv, and Ivano-Frankivsk. The total number of respondents was 139; for this analysis I am focusing only on the data gathered from the 68 respondents in Kyiv. I utilized snowball sampling, and therefore do not assert that the survey data are representative of Kyiv's population as a whole.

13 See Field et al. (2000) for an analysis of the negative impact of Russia's new neoliberal economic policy for citizens, especially in terms of health outcomes.

REFERENCES

Akhaladze, M. G. 1998. "Biological age assessment and Chernobyl disaster: Cross-sectional and longitudinal studies." *Proceedings of the Second International Conference Long-Term Health Consequences of the Chernobyl Disaster*, eds. A. Nyagu et al., p. 175. Kyiv: Chernobylinterinform.

Akhaladze, M. G., L. M. Ena, and P. P. Chayalo. 1997. "Tempy starinnia i chynnyky, shcho ioho formujut', u likvidatoriv avarii na ChAES: Rezul'taty poperechnykh i lonhitudynal'-nykhdoslidzhen'" ("Aging Rate and Factors Determining it in Liquidators of the Chernobyl NPP Accident: The Results of a Cross-sectional and Longitudinal Study"). *Diahnostika to profilakytka nehatyvnyukh naslidkiv radiatsii* (*Diagnostics and Prophylactics of Negative Effects of Radiation*), pp. 15–18. Kyiv: Institute for Experimental Radiology, National Center for Radiation Medicine, Academy of Medical Sciences of Ukraine; International Organization "Zhinocha Hromada."

Bakhtin, Mikhail M. 1981. *The Dialogic Imagination: Four Essays*, ed. Michael Holquist. Translated by Caryl Emerson and Michael Holquist. Austin: University of Texas Press.

Bruner, Jerome. 1986. *Actual Minds, Possible Worlds*. Cambridge: Harvard University Press.

Caplan, Pat, 1997. "Approaches to the Study of Food, Health and Identity." *Food, Health and Identity*, ed. Pat Caplan, pp. 1–31. London and New York: Routledge.

Chernousenko, Vladimir M. 1991. *Chernobyl: Insight from the Inside*. Berlin and Heidelberg: Springer-Verlag.

Counihan, Carole M. and Steven L. Kaplan, eds. 1998. *Food and Gender: Identity and Power*, Amsterdam: Harwood Academic Publishers.

Field, Mark, David Kotz, and Gene Bukhman. 2000. "Neoliberal Economic Policy, 'State Desertion,' and the Russian Health Crisis." *Dying for Growth: Global Inequality and the Health of the Poor*, eds. Jim Yong Kim, Joyce Millen, Alec Irwin, and John Gershman, pp. 155–73. Monroe, Maine: Common Courage Press.

Greenpeace International. 1994. *An Investigation of Contamination by Radionuclides, Toxic Metals, Organic Compounds and other Environmental Contaminants In Ukraine*. Amsterdam: Greenpeace International.

Institute for Experimental Radiology, National Center for Radiation Medicine, Academy of Medical Sciences of Ukraine. 1998. "Printsipy pitaniia v usloviiakh vozdeistviia malykh doz radiatsii" ("Principles of Nutrition under Conditions of the Effects of Low Doses of Radiation"). Monograph.

Knizhnikov, V. A., et al. 1988. "Postuplenie radionuklidov po pishchevym tsepiam kak factor oblucheniia naseleniia SSSR posle avarii na Chernobyl'skoi AES" ("The introduction of radionuclides into the food chain as a factor in the exposure of the population of the USSR after the accident at the Chernobyl nuclear station"). *Meditsinskie Aspekty Avarii na Chernobyl'skoi Atomnoi Elektrostantsii* (*Medical Aspects of the Accident at the Chernobyl Atomic Electrostation*), eds. A. E. Romanenko et al., pp. 66–76. Kyiv: "Zdorov'ia"

Lindquist, Galina. 2001. "Wizards, Gurus, and Energy-Information Fields: Wielding Legitimacy in Contemporary Russian Healing." *The Anthropology of East Europe Review* 19(1):16–28.

Marples, David. 1988. *The Social Impact of the Chernobyl disaster*. New York: St. Martin's Press.

——. 1993. Chernobyl's Lengthening Shadow. *The Bulletin of Atomic Scientist*, p. 3. (http://www.bullatomsci.org/issues/1993/s93s93

Mould, Richard F. 1998. *Chernobyl: The Real Story*. Oxford: Pergamon Press.

Nahorna, A. M., T. L. Proklina, and G. V. Osnach. 1998. "Dynamics of Children Health Indices at the Radioactively Contaminated Territories." *Proceedings of the Second International Conference Long-Term Health Consequences of the Chernobyl Disaster*, eds. A. I. Nyagu et al., p. 95. Kyiv: Chernobylinterinform.

Page, G. William, Olga Alexandrovna Bobyleva, Marina Vasilievna Naboka, and Viacheslav Mikhailovich Shestopalov, 1995. "Environmental Health Policy in Ukraine after the Chernobyl Accident." *Policy Studies Journal* 23(1):141–51.

Pavlychko, Solomea. 1992. "Between Feminism and Nationalism: New Women's Groups in the Ukraine." *Perestroika and Soviet Women*, ed. Mary Buckley, pp. 82–96. Cambridge: Cambridge University Press.

Petryna, Adriana. 1995. "Sarcophagus: Chernobyl in Historical Light." *Cultural Anthropology* 10(2):196–220.

Phillips, Sarah. 2000. "NGOs in Ukraine: The Makings of a Women's Space?" *The Anthropology of East Europe Review* 18(2):23–9.

Rosaldo, Michelle Z. 1984. "Toward an Anthropology of Self and Feeling." *Culture Theory: Essays on Mind, Self, and Emotion*, eds. Robert Levine and Richard Shweder, pp. 137–57.

Sayenko, Yury, 1996. "'Samoseli,' abo Zhiteli Mervoi Zony Chornobilia" ("'Samoseli', or Residents of the Dead Chornobyl'Zone"). *Sotsail' ni Naslidky Chornobyl's 'koi Katastrofy: Rezul'taty Sotsiolohichnykh Doslidzhen' 1986–1995 (Social Consequences of the Chernobyl' Catastrophe: Results of Sociological Research 1986–1995)*, eds. V. Vorona, E. Golovakha, and Y. Sayenko, pp. 147–52. Kharkiv: Folio.

Sayenko, Y. and V. Prylypko. 1996. "Ekspertni Otsinky Protsesu Pereselennia" ("Expert Analyses of the Evacuation Relocation Process"). *Sotsial'ni Naslidlky Chornobyl's 'koi Katastrofy: Rezul'taty Sotsiolohichnykh Doslidzhen' 1986–1995 (Social Consequences of the Chernobyl' Catastrophe: Results of Sociological Research 1986–1995)*, eds. V. Vorona, E. Golovakha and Y. Sayenko, pp. 123–60. Kharkiv: Folio

Shcherbak, Iurii. 1996. "Ten Years of the Chernobyl Era." *Scientific American* 274(4):47–8.

Solchanyk, Roman, 1992. "Introduction." *Ukraine: from Chernobyl' to Sovereignty*, ed. Roman Solchanyk, pp. xiii–xxvi. New York: St Martin's Press.

United Nations Development Programme. 2001. *Human Development Report 2001*. (http://www.undp.prg/ hdr2001/indicator/cty f UKR.html)

Verdery, Katherine. 1996. *What was Socialism, and What Comes Next?* Princeton, NJ: Princeton University Press.

Wanner, Catherine. 1998. *Burden of Dreams: History and Identity in Post-Soviet Ukraine*. University Park, PA: Pennsylvania State University Press.

West, Barbara. 2000. "Personhood on a Plate: Gender and Food in the Construction of Proper Hungarian Women." *The Anthropology of East Europe Review* 18(2): 117–23.

19

Mad Cow Mysteries

Harriet Ritvo

When mad cow disease arrived in the British headlines to stay, not everyone was shocked. Faithful listeners to *Farming Today*, which airs just after six o'clock every morning on BBC Radio 4, already understood that the spread of mad cow disease might lead to a variety of terrible consequences, human illness among them. Anyone seriously concerned with British cattle – or, indeed, anyone who had paid cumulative attention to the intermittent but increasingly troublesome reportage of the previous decade – would have developed a good deal of apprehension on the subject. As a cultural historian who is particularly interested in domesticated animals, spends a good deal of time in British libraries, and listens to *Farming Today*, I belong to both these audiences; so I was dismayed but not surprised when, in March 1996, the British government dramatically abandoned its previous reassuring line and admitted that whatever was making the cattle stagger and collapse might possibly be transmitted to humans – with similarly fatal effects.

Less bovine-oriented consumers of news had apparently not been so attentive. The immediate response to this reversal of official doctrine indicated that much of Britain's population and many of its trading partners had not been prepared for its most alarming implications. Many nations, including New Zealand, Egypt, South Korea, and South Africa, as well as Britain's fellow members of the European Union, suspended the importation of British beef. At home, consumers expressed their concern with their feet, leaving steaks and joints to languish on the shelves of supermarkets and butcher shops. McDonald's restaurants in the United Kingdom quickly announced that their burgers would henceforward be innocent of native beef.

The decisiveness of this reaction (as well as the complacence that had preceded it) could be interpreted as testimony to the influence and credibility of the British government. But a more modest and more complicated assessment would probably be nearer the mark. After all, the official announcement hardly signaled a novel source of concern. Even during the decade of public denial, mad cow disease (technically known as bovine spongiform encephalopathy, or BSE for short, because it afflicted cattle by causing their brains to become spongy) had lurked on the fringes of British consciousness. The possibility that it might pose a threat to the health of beef-eating people had been recognized, at least in theory, from the initial observation of its alarming symptoms, even if no one knew what was making the cattle sick or how they had been exposed to the unknown agent. This baseline anxiety was intermittently intensified by reports that the BSE agent seemed to be able to jump species. In 1990, for example, the disease was identified in kudu, oryx, eland, nyala, and gemsbok (all antelopes, which are closely related to cattle), as well as in the domestic cat (a carnivore, and therefore only remotely related to cattle). Further, mad cow disease was recognized as belonging to a group of lethal neurological diseases – spongiform encephalopathies – that included scrapie (a common affliction of sheep), kuru (common only among a small group of New Guinean people), and CJD or Creutzfeldt-Jakob disease (extremely rare but widely distributed among human populations). Speculation arose that the BSE agent might also cause a newly identified variant of CJD, which affected younger people and took longer to run its fatal course. In 1993 the *Lancet* suggested that the death of a farmer from CJD had been caused by an occupational hazard: contact with his BSE-infected herd.

Responses to these inconclusive but troublesome suggestions varied. Australia and the United States banned the importation of British beef and cattle in 1989. Several European countries followed suit in 1990 but quickly reversed their decision after reassurances from the British government. On the whole, however, such reassurances were not required. Even at home, where BSE-related items appeared most frequently in the news, and where consumption of British cattle products, and therefore exposure to anything harmful that they might contain, was highest, the disease was routinely trivialized. The flurries of alarm that greeted each new revelation tended to die down quickly, although they sometimes left added precautions in their wake, and they inevitably contributed to a latent sense of unease. Tory politicians (the Conservative party was in power throughout this period) tended to view mad cow disease through the eyes of the beef industry, as a potential economic catastrophe rather than as a threat to public health. They instituted regulations reluctantly and implemented them without conviction. They repeatedly downplayed the possibility of transmission to humans, most flamboyantly in 1990 when Minister of Agriculture John Gummer, for the edification of the public, confidently fed his four-year-old daughter a hamburger. (Because they included beef products of varied derivation, fast-food burgers attracted special suspicion.)

Gummer's lighthearted attitude was widely shared by both journalists and the larger public. The first cat to die of BSE was headlined as "Mad Moggy." One of the many websites devoted to mad cow disease featured a pasture full of loopy cartoon cattle, with revolving pinwheels for eyes. And, although the beef coolers at my local Sainsbury's were completely empty only a few days after the official bombshell of March 1996, the first explanation that occurred to me turned out to be completely wrong. I guessed that the unpurchased meat had spoiled and been returned whence it had come. But instead, in response to shoppers' initial shocked avoidance, Sainsbury's (along with the other large supermarket chains) had simply cut beef prices in half. Many customers eagerly stocked their freezers with meat that had seemed too dangerous at regular rates.

British beef consumption soon returned nearly to pre-scare levels, perhaps encouraged by official measures and explanations (including the removal of cattle more than thirty months old from the food chain, the exclusion of meat and bonemeal from feed destined for farm animals, and the assurance that the heads of slaughtered cattle would join their spinal cords and other organs suspected of concentrating the BSE agent as "specified bovine offal" that could not be unrecognizably reprocessed into other food products). The response, however, was varied – among non-vegetarians of my acquaintance, some totally avoided beef, some avoided ground beef, some were skeptical, and some were fatalistically indifferent. But, in any case, the sense of renewed security enjoyed by some British beefeaters ended at the beaches. The European Union imposed a ban on the export of British beef and beef products, not only to other member nations, but throughout the world. As I write in early 1998, this ban is still in place, although under the newly elected Labour government, as under the old Conservatives, the British Ministry of Agriculture, Fisheries, and Food has made repeated and energetic attempts to have it rescinded. Despite the defensive efforts of their governments, continental consumers have proved less easily mollified than their insular counterparts. Like British consumers, they conceived an instant aversion to beef after the announcement of March 1996, but unlike the British, they did not change their minds – despite the embargo on British beef, the very small number of cases of mad cow disease that had been reported in continental herds, and the fact that local beef was prominently labeled, with words and even with flags. They have resisted both official blandishments and those of their beef industries, and beef consumption has remained far below pre-1996 levels.

It is interesting that governments and citizens on either side of the English Channel reacted so differently. Of course, official responses were heavily influenced by economic self-interest: the British desire to preserve the international markets for their beef and beef products, and the somewhat incompatible desire of other European Union members to avoid having their own beef industries tarred with the brush of British BSE. But cattle farmers and meat processors, and the food industry more generally, were not the only groups with a potential stake in BSE policy, although they were by far the best organized ones. If mad cow disease was transmissible to other species, including humans, then the general public had an interest in its control and elimination that transcended the merely financial. Once the possibility of transmission was seriously acknowledged, governments were self-consciously setting policies with potentially enormous public health consequences, and individuals were making, on their own behalf and that of their children, what might literally prove to be life-and-death decisions. Not even the Conservative government, with its bottom-line and value-for-money orientation, conceived its mission so narrowly as to exclude this kind of unquantifiable moral responsibility. It would not have been able (or inclined) to defend a policy that demonstrably sacrificed the health of large numbers of citizens in an attempt to maintain the profits of an industry.

But it is not necessary to posit any such sinister calculation to account for British policy. One reason that so many inconsistent courses of action seemed possible in March 1996 was that decision making was relatively unconstrained by information. The answer to the most important question – whether mad cow disease posed a significant threat to human health – was, and remains, unclear, although the indications have become increasingly troubling, as the number of human cases slowly accumulates and the relationship between BSE and the new variant of Creutzfeldt-Jakob demonstrably strengthens. Even the basic facts of the mad cow epidemic were and are subject to wide interpretation. For example, between its first official recognition in 1986 and the spring of 1997, 168,382 diseased cattle were identified in the United Kingdom, a figure of impressive but possibly misleading precision. The equivalent figure for non-British BSE underlines the problems implicit in such quantifications. Approximately 400 cases have been reported in other European nations, mostly in Switzerland. This number is surprisingly small when it is considered that, before 1990, thousands of British cattle, along with large quantities of beef, bonemeal, and other cattle products, were regularly imported by those nations. It has been plausibly suggested, especially but not exclusively by politicians protesting the ban on British beef, that European incidence of the disease has been seriously underreported, as a consequence both of draconian sanctions, such as the destruction of any herd in which a single case appears, and of the inadequate compensation paid to the unfortunate farmer who owns it. This was the reverse of what was intended, but, given human nature, predictable enough.

Within the United Kingdom, the pattern of infection was equally puzzling, if better documented. Mad cow disease was more prevalent in dairy herds than among beef cattle, more common in England than in Scotland. Some herds, even in areas where it was prevalent, remained untouched. Epidemiological analysis of the first rash of cases identified commercial feed that incorporated meat and other material from sheep, and possibly also from cattle, as the only factor that linked all the outbreaks. It was theorized that the cattle had ingested the BSE agent as they munched the remains of their ruminant brothers and sisters – possibly transmogrified from scrapie-infected sheep, possibly simply transmitted from an already afflicted cow or bull. (As with the AIDS epidemic, which seemed at first to have come from nowhere, retrospective reflection revealed possible earlier cases, suggesting that the disease might previously have been endemic at a very low level.) The feed hypothesis was plausible, and it has provided the basis of the most effective disease-control measures. Indeed, the elimination of meat and meat by-products from livestock feed is largely responsible for the dramatic drop in BSE cases in recent years (a drop that had begun before the scare of March 1996); it is possible that within a few years, due to this measure alone, mad cow disease will have been eliminated from British herds. But if contaminated feed was the cause, why was its effect lethal in some cases and innocuous in others? Given the protracted incubation period of BSE, longer than the lifetime of many beef cattle, could absence of disease be reliably taken to indicate absence of infection? And what of other associations, less powerful but still suggestive, especially exposure to certain organo-phosphorus compounds used in agriculture?

Another set of questions clustered around the elusive agent. The language of epidemics and transmission in which mad cow disease was normally discussed suggested infection, rather than poisoning, although clearly this was no ordinary contagion. Gradually, a scientific consensus emerged that, in the case of BSE, as with the other spongiform encephalopathies, the agent was a distorted prion, a kind of protein molecule found in the brain. (The apparent strength of this consensus was enhanced last year when Stanley Prusiner, the controversial theorist on prions, won the Nobel Prize in biology.) But although this focus on prions clarified further directions for research, it did nothing to simplify the task of formulating practical responses. For example, it did not explain how animals became infected with mad cow disease. New cases kept appearing after the suspect feed was banned, and only some of these cases could be attributed to farmers thriftily ignoring public health regulations in order to use up feed that they had already paid for. Could it be transmitted from animal to animal within a herd? From mother to calf? (In the latter case, the ban on beef from animals more than thirty months old was beside the point.) Could the infective agent somehow linger in fields where sick animals had been pastured, as was the case with scrapie?

Indeed, because prions were not well understood, and because they turned out to be practically indestructible (in particular, enormously resistant to heat), their implication in the spread of the disease significantly complicated one facet of policy making. Although the elimination of BSE in cattle offered the obvious ultimate solution to the problem, in the interim it was necessary to protect members of other species, especially humans, from contact with potentially infective material. Removing all cattle from herds with any BSE cases from the food chain, and removing the brain, vertebral column, and other suspect organs from all butchered cattle were only the first steps. Assuming it was successfully accomplished (an assumption not always justified), this triage yielded an immense volume of rejected offal and carcasses. The unsavory material then had to be disposed of in a sterile or sanitary way, so that the distorted prions did not re-enter the food chain or, worse, were not somehow more widely disseminated. Burying was clearly out of the question, as was disposal in coastal waters, where marine mammals might be exposed and where neighboring countries might object. Cremation at unusually high temperatures seemed like the only practicable solution, but not all incinerators were properly equipped for such procedures. If infected material was inadequately burnt, prions might survive in the smoke and be scattered by the wind, ultimately to settle in soil or in water, ready for re-ingestion. Developing adequate capacity and procedures for this massive slaughtering and incineration has proved unexpectedly challenging. In the meantime, contaminated carcasses and offal have accumulated in storage.

The toughness of prions also complicated decisions about which beef products posed a risk of transmitting mad cow disease. Although dairy products were generally pronounced safe, opinions varied about gelatin, a substance present in a wide variety of prepared foods, including some, such as packaged cookies or biscuits, routinely eaten by unwary vegetarians. Gelatin is much more heavily processed than milk or cheese, but it includes boiled-down material from suspect cattle parts. In April 1996, a government regulation prohibited the use not only of meat but also of bonemeal as fertilizer on agricultural land, although use in private gardens and in greenhouses was still permitted. (Prudent gardeners, however, were advised to wear gloves and masks.) And the identification of prions as the BSE agent did nothing to allay concerns about their possible cross-species transmission during the previous decade, perhaps (again in analogy to AIDS) seeding a devastating human epidemic, the scale of which would not become obvious for years or decades. In the nightmare scenario delineated by Richard Rhodes in *Deadly Feasts: Tracking the Secrets of a Terrifying New Plague*, the rogue prions have already become so widely disseminated that stopping their further destructive spread will be nearly impossible.

The official announcement of March 1996 did not tilt the odds – or change the reality, whatever it turns out to be – in one direction or the other. But, by altering public awareness, it produced a need for governmental action, both in Britain and in other countries. And if information is not available (indeed, often, even if it is), policies must be formulated on other grounds. This is not to suggest that ignorance was foregrounded as the basis of official decision making. On the contrary, one of the most striking features of the Conservative government's attempt to defend the lighthearted negligence of its previous treatment of the BSE issue was the repeated invocation of "scientific advice" as the touchstone of its policy. Although the specific content of this advice was seldom alluded to, ministers and government spokesmen referred to it as definitive and authoritative – the quintessential black box – at a time when most scientists concerned with BSE were emphasizing the prevalence of uncertainty. (The relevant expert community in Britain was in any case smaller than it might have been, as a result of earlier official reluctance to fund research that might produce disturbing results.) And the government was aided in this misrepresentation by the fact that, with some notable exceptions such as the *New Scientist*, science journalism is underdeveloped in Britain, as is the popular audience for such reportage.

Although the government proclaimed its policy was based on "scientific advice," it was more transparently founded on patriotism, which had the advantage of immediate public appeal. From this perspective, the interests of the nation, its citizens, and its cattle industry were happily indistinguishable from each other and from those of the animals themselves. Editorial cartoons portrayed a blighted countryside, heavily shadowed by smoke from a holocaust of innocent cattle – a sad contrast with the beautiful placid herds to be seen throughout rural Britain, and one that ignored the similarity between BSE-induced culling and ordinary slaughtering from the bovine point of view. Those inclined to continue or to resume their previous dietary preferences could see eating British beef as a declaration of loyalty, even as an assertion of national courage and common sense against the scaremongering of experts and foreigners. Soon after the announcement of March 1996, I went to a Chinese restaurant in Cambridge with a group of people, some of whom, in this enthusiastic spirit, made a point of ordering beef dishes to be shared. They also made a point of noticing who declined to share them.

Simple jingoism, however, does not sufficiently explain the widespread willingness to ignore a risk that, although it might well not exist at all, might also lead to the most dreadful consequences. Food contamination alarms are not routinely viewed with indifference by the British public. For example, a 1988 uproar about salmonella in eggs was countered by the heavily publicized consumption of a runny omelette by the prime minister herself. Further, the British tend not to regulate their everyday behavior according to knee-jerk patriotism (certainly, they are less inclined to do so than are Americans); and the word of the superannuated Tory government had long ceased to inspire implicit confidence, as was confirmed by its decisive defeat at the polls [later].

Beef, and the cattle that produce it, holds a special place in British national myth-ology. Before John Bull was a canine he was a bovine. The wealthy eighteenth-century landowners who devoted themselves to agriculture took special pride in the creation of improved breeds of livestock, such as the shorthorn cattle that remained internationally preeminent for the succeeding century. In this enterprise, the breeders celebrated themselves. It was no accident that the entries in studbooks, herd books, and flock books closely resembled those in Burke's and Debrett's catalogues of the aristocracy and gentry. But the breeders also claimed to represent the entire nation at its best, a claim that many ordinary citizens accepted without demur. Many were eager to pay homage to the breeders' magnificent beasts when they were exhibited at national livestock shows by, as one agricultural journalist put it, "closely inspecting, admiring, and tormenting the bullocks sent by Dukes and Earls." The public appar-ently agreed with Julius Caesar, who had suggested that cattle constituted the true wealth of the Britons, and with an early president of the Royal Agricultural Society, who discerned "in the people of this country a peculiar disposition and talent for encouraging the finest animal forms."

The sustenance derived by such people from such cattle was inevitably profound and complex. The roast beef of Old England has for centuries been valued as much more than an efficient source of nourishment. To it was attributed, at least in part, the superiority of the British soldier to his European and imperial antagonists; more generally it has been viewed by observers within the British polity and outside it as an essential component of the national character. As Charles Dickens reflected more than a century ago in *Household Words*, "beef is a great connecting link and bond of better feeling between the great classes of the commonwealth," inspiring respect second only to "the Habeas Corpus and the Freedom of the Press." Further, British naturalists and agricultural experts, chefs and gourmets have tended to agree about their nation's preeminence with regard to the quality of the meat it produces, as well as the quantity it consumes. For example, a Victorian gastronomer celebrated native beef while disparaging native cuisine and foreign livestock: "If the poor, half-fed meats of France, were dressed as our cooks … dress our well-fed, excellent meats, they would be absolutely uneatable." As a result, a deeply ingrained tradition of metonymic identification has developed, affectionately acknowledged when the British call themselves "beefeaters," less affectionately when their nearest continen-tal neighbors call them "rosbifs."

In any country, the possible condemnation of the national cattle herd would be viewed as an impending disaster, both economic and epidemiological, even if it was not associated with a potentially serious threat to human health. But the time-honored identification of Britain with its beef has made the BSE crisis especially difficult. And the resonance of this patriotic symbolism has not been exclusively domestic. It seems likely that the intransigence with which Britain's trading partners in the European Union have defended their import bans, once imposed, as well as the obsessive avoidance of beef by many European consumers also reflect historic associations and aversions.

At present, the story of mad cow disease is far from over. Even as the number of bovine BSE cases continues to tumble, and the very small number of human CJD cases fails to rise, new prophylactic measures continue to be imposed. In response to scientific evidence that the BSE agent could be carried by nerve tissue near the spinal cord, the Labour government banned the sale of beef on the bone just before Christmas. The ban has been unduly flouted by both butchers and eaters; a Scottish hotelier who organized a ballyhooed "prohibition dinner" is scheduled for trial. And the quest for answers goes on, in the hearing room as well as in the laboratory. An official team has recently been appointed to inquire into the political, economic, and administrative causes of the decade-long catastrophe. Their report is due in December 1999.

Despite all this questioning, few answers have yet emerged. None of the projected scenarios, from the most reassuring to the most alarming, has been definitively eliminated, either in the laboratory or through epidemiological study. Sooner or later, however, the medical and veterinary cases will be closed, and it will be possible to determine who was prudent, who was alarmist, who was foolhardy. But for several reasons such a restricted accounting should not constitute the final word on BSE. Although mad cow disease happened to strike British herds, it does not seem to have resulted from idiosyncratically British attitudes or practices. Large-scale livestock farming is similar throughout the world, as are the relations between major industries and their national governments. At first glance the reactions of European governments seemed to compare favorably with that of their British colleagues, as they made the health of their citizens their first priority. But when the potential danger to health came from their domestic beef industries rather than from the foreign menace, their inclination was generally similar to that of the Tories. The same point could be made with regard to the United States, which has stalwartly maintained its early ban on British beef products. Officially, according to the Department of Agriculture, we have no BSE – but the Department also goes to the trouble of denying that downer cow syndrome, which afflicts thousands of American cattle each year, is related to mad cow disease. As Oprah Winfrey's recent legal troubles demonstrate, not everyone is persuaded by this denial.

The shared inadequacy of these responses points to a larger problem that is also shared: the difficulty of dealing with complex technical crises. Such crises by definition require the attention of experts – experts that strapped or stingy governments probably do not have on the payroll. Often such expertise exists only within the industries or institutions with the largest financial stake in the outcome; sometimes, as with mad cow disease, such expertise has not yet been sufficiently developed. In either case, before the public becomes alarmed, policy tends to be determined by these interest groups. Afterwards, at least in democracies, the technical crisis is inevitably compounded by a crisis of public relations. Politicians must be seen to act quickly and firmly, whether or not they have any basis for their actions.

Such can-do decision making, however impressive and reassuring in the heat of the moment, is unlikely to produce wise policy. On the contrary, it risks catastrophe. It was sobering to realize, during the spring of 1996, that it was impossible for politicians in power to acknowledge that they lacked sufficient information to decide how to protect people from the threat of mad cow disease. It was therefore impossible for them to act with appropriate circumspection – to concede that there are times when discretion is indeed the better part of valor. If the protracted scandal of mad cow disease were to lead to a recognition of this problem, that would constitute a faintly silver lining.

Index